# a special gift

**presented to:**

_____

**from:**

_____

**date:**

_____

*The Lord gives grace and glory;*
*No good thing does He withhold from those who walk uprightly.*

—Psalm 84:11, NASB

# grace
# notes

# The Women's Devotional Series

To order, call **1-800-765-6955.**
Visit us at **www.reviewandherald.com**
for more information on other Review and Herald® products.

# grace
# notes

*edited by*
*ardis dick stenbakken*

REVIEW AND HERALD® PUBLISHING ASSOCIATION
Since 1861 | www.reviewandherald.com

This book was
Edited by Jeannette R. Johnson
Copyedited by James Cavil
Cover designed by Patricia Wegh
Cover photos © 2008 iStockphoto
Interior designed by Heather Rogers
Typeset: Minion 11/13

PRINTED IN U.S.A.

12  11  10  09  08          5  4  3  2  1

**Library of Congress Cataloging-in-Publication Data**
Grace notes / edited by Ardis Dick Stenbakken.
     p. cm.
1. Seventh-day Adventist women—Prayers and devotions. 2. Devotional calendars—Seventh-day Adventists.  I. Stenbakken, Ardis Dick.
  BV4844.G69 2008
  242'.643—dc22

                          2008013914

ISBN 978-0-8280-2359-7

# There is an aspect of this book that is unique.

None of these contributors has been paid—they have shared freely
so that all profits go to scholarships for women. As this book goes to press,
1,456 scholarships have been given to women in 105 countries.
For more current information, or to contribute to these scholarships,
please go to http://wmgc.adventist.org/Pages/Wmscholarship—html#sos.
In this way, you too can add grace notes to the lives of others.

# And No One Was Denied

*Praise be to the God and Father of our Lord Jesus Christ! In his
great mercy he has given us new birth into a living hope through
the resurrection of Jesus Christ from the dead, and into an
inheritance that can never perish, spoil or fade—kept in heaven
for you. 1 Peter 1:3, 4, NIV.*

WHEN I WAS A CHILD, we were taught that only good children can
go to heaven; if I were disobedient in any way, I couldn't go to heaven.
That thought frightened me considerably, and I tried to be a good girl.
Parents, teachers, pastors, all seemed to say the same thing—good behavior would get us saved. How we dreamed of the heavenly mansions, only to
be discouraged when we disobeyed. It was all based on behaviorism.

Then while I was attending a Christian college, I was with a group of
girls who were visiting a faculty member in her home. We gathered around
the piano to sing as one girl played what was then a new song, "The Holy
City." For the first time I heard and sang these words, "The gates were open
wide, and all who would might enter, and no one was denied!" For the first
time it dawned on me that there was a chance for me—that it's not behavior that saves us, but the grace of our Lord Jesus Christ, by His blood, shed
on Calvary! I began to accept that grace and believe by faith in Christ's
righteousness. What hope!

Some years later I began to hear consistently a more hopeful message:
we are saved by faith in the righteousness of Christ. His grace saves us from
eternal death when we accept His forgiveness by confessing our sins. And
we find a daily relationship with Him. I wondered why it took so long for
that direction to change.

I memorized Romans 5:1-9 and found the hope I needed, hope like this:
"Since we have now been justified by his blood, how much more shall we be
saved from God's wrath through him!" (verse 9, NIV) and "For it is by grace
you have been saved, through faith—and this not from yourselves, it is the
gift of God—not by works, so that no one can boast" (Eph. 2:8, 9, NIV). How
I treasured those words! And I found many more such verses in my Bible.

Gone were the dreadful fears of eternal loss because of my wrong behavior, or failure in any detail of life. Gone was the pride in my good
works! As we begin this new year, won't you join me in making it our
goal to cling to our Savior's grace (which brings out our love for
Him), and give ourselves in His service? What joy!

**Bessie Siemens Lobsien**

# Prayer and Doubt

*Therefore I say unto you, What things soever ye desire, when ye pray, believe that ye receive them, and ye shall have them. Mark 11:24.*

**DEAR JESUS,** *why do I feel so tired today? I went to bed early last night!* I thought to myself as I worked in the emergency room. *And why are body fluids suddenly nauseating me? I can handle a little blood—I'm a nurse.*

Then the thought came to me that *my* body wasn't functioning normally. Could this really be happening? *But didn't I pray for this, God? I had this on my list, so why do I now doubt Your response to my prayer? Really, though, I wasn't expecting You to answer me so quickly—I've only been married a year. Surely You would want me to spend some quality time with my husband . . . Lord, I couldn't be pregnant, could I?*

I couldn't concentrate on work, so I asked my supervisor for permission to be excused for a few minutes. I really needed to know.

So much anxiety overwhelmed me that I bought myself a pregnancy kit. And to my surprise, the indicator registered blue. *Blue! Let me do this again.* So I purchased another kit, and this time—it was still blue. I didn't know how to respond, what to do, or whom to call. I was pregnant!

How many times have we asked God for something, yet lacked faith in Him, not believing that He would answer our prayers in His own time, not in ours. "O ye of little faith" (Matt. 6:30). Where is our faith? "Faith is the substance of things hoped for, the evidence of things not seen" (Heb. 11:1).

Today you may have received an answer to a prayer—a prayer that you prayed long ago. Trust and believe that this is the answer to your prayer. But if you have never prayed a prayer, pray and believe today, and God will respond.

*Lord, today help me to trust You with my life, knowing that You will do what is best for me. Thank You, God, for blessing me with this wonderful child. Thank You for answering my prayer.*

**Shelly-Ann Patricia Zabala**

# That Great Waking-up Morning

*Marvel not at this: for the hour is coming, in the which all that are in the graves shall hear his voice. John 5:28.*

IN 2003 A YOUNG MAN (whom I'll call Jerry) suddenly uttered the word "Mom" after being in a coma for 19 years! Comatose since an auto accident in 1984, he had at last "returned" to his astounded and delighted family by responding to things he heard them say. Though still a quadriplegic because of the accident, Jerry gained in speaking ability as the days went by. However, he still thought he was living in 1984, even though several presidents had come and gone, and elderly family members had passed away. Being none the wiser, Jerry was focused on the past.

Several months ago my 85-year-old mother slipped into a coma and died a day later. As Jerry did, she will soon hear a voice—but hers will be the joyful call of Jesus on that great resurrection morning. She too will wake up. Oh, she may briefly recall the last few days of her life prior to becoming comatose. She may entertain a fleeting memory of her last visit to the doctor's office in a stretcher borne by a medical transport vehicle. She may remember the frightful loss of her ability to swallow near the end. She may even remember family members holding her and telling her how much they loved her before she slipped into unconsciousness. Yet she won't stay focused on the past for very long—not with all the activity going on around her!

Imagine her squinting against the brilliance of the bright cloud, that vast cloud of numberless angels reaping a harvest of both the living and the resurrected (1 Thess. 4:16-18). Imagine her staring in amazement at her own youthful arms, wrapped around the neck of a powerful angel, bearing her upward toward the seated King! Imagine her unspeakable joy at being reunited with her husband, whom she outlived by only a year and a half, or at seeing her father, whom she lost to cancer when she was only 16. Mother won't have time to dwell on the past, because the eternally joyful present will have burst so suddenly and so definitively upon her.

Yes, we can imagine the joyful frenzy of the preceding scenes. We can do so because the Bible tells us to "marvel not," for on that day the dead who died in Him will hear God's voice and come forth from their graves to a "resurrection of life" (John 5:28, 29). I can hardly wait!

**Carolyn Rathbun Sutton**

# My Idol

*I have been crucified with Christ and I no longer live, but Christ lives in me. The life I live in the body, I live by faith in the Son of God, who loved me and gave himself for me. Gal. 2:20, NIV.*

IT WAS THE BEGINNING of a new year. The feeling of holidays, joy, and cordiality still existed in the stores. In a large supermarket I was taking advantage of the very good bargains. A song by a very popular artist, even considered an idol by some, was playing over the public address system. But I was so accustomed to songs that are played so often at the end of the year that I didn't even pay attention. After some time I realized that the songs being played were all by the same singer.

However, as I left the store, I discovered that the songs were being sung live, not by the original artist but by someone whose voice was very similar and who looked a lot like him—same clothing, same hair, same way of holding the microphone, same way he stood. And at that moment the performer said something so that I would associate him with the singer he was imitating.

This was hard to believe! Why would someone want to be so much like another person that he would, even for a few minutes, try to deceive someone regarding his own identity? During the entire walk back home I thought about this. If I concern myself so much with wanting to imitate another person, no matter how good she or he may be, I am still a sinner, filled with errors, vices, and bad intentions. So how can I not make an effort to imitate Jesus?

Jesus! Yes, I should imitate Him! God, who became man so as to serve as a model. He is an example without sin, filled with love and kindness, always helping the needy people around Him, a friend of children, youth, adults, and seniors. Jesus always had a prayer in His heart, was always doing the will of the Father, always preaching and teaching people how to choose the right path, the path that leads to heaven.

Jesus is the one who left His throne of glory and suffered humiliation to the point of dying on a cross to save me, to give me a chance to enjoy eternal life. Jesus! Yes, He should be my idol!

**Marinês Aparecida da Silva Oliveira**

# Unemployed

*"I say this because I know what I am planning for you," says the Lord.*
*"I have good plans for you, not plans to hurt you. I will give you hope*
*and a good future." Jer. 29:11, NCV.*

WHEN MY SON BEGAN SCHOOL and my daughter kindergarten, I
wanted to go back to work. Because of maternity leave I was no longer current in my profession. I had no choice but to go to the employment agency.
I received unemployment benefits and took a computer course. I soon
learned how to handle this new technology. After completing the course, I
continued to look for a job. In the meantime, I had a computer at home
and kept filling out one job application after the other.

I applied for a job in a grocery store that was still under construction. I
received a negative reply—I couldn't work in the afternoons and on
Saturdays. Three weeks later the boss called me again, inviting me to come
in for a job interview. I was happy! We both had a good first impression of
each other, and I started work in that grocery store. Because the store was
newly constructed, the shelves had to be stocked. It was a joy for me to
work every day. Before long I knew where everything was in the store, and I
got along well with the customers and my colleagues. And I had my own
department. My relationship with the boss and his wife seemed to be good.

However, shortly before my fortieth birthday, everything changed. I
was called into the office and received my dismissal. I couldn't believe it!
Why? When I had started working three years before, I had thanked God
that He had enabled me to get that job at the right time. All this made the
last days at work very difficult. I don't know why God allowed my job,
which I enjoyed, to be taken from me. But God knows me, and He certainly
knows why.

I was unemployed again—but this was exactly the time my son needed
me. Being home and having time for him in the afternoon was good for
both of us. It also did my daughter good that I was there to keep an eye on
her while she did her homework.

A year has passed, and I'm still unemployed. I don't know what God
has planned for me, but I trust Him. He knows me, and He knows my
sorrows. You too may be facing challenges as this year begins, but God
does have good plans for us. Let's believe—and cling to Him daily.

**Sandra Widulle**

# It Helped Me to Understand Better

*Are not two sparrows sold for a farthing? and one of them shall not fall on the ground without your Father. . . . Fear ye not therefore, ye are of more value than many sparrows. Matt. 10:29-31.*

IT WAS OUR FIRST WINTER to live in the desert in southern California, and it had been a wet, cold, and rainy one. Some days I was even a bit out of sorts because my husband was working on a project in Loma Linda, about an hour's drive away. When he was gone, I had no car to go anywhere myself. It wasn't my idea of how we should be spending time here as "snowbirds."

Now the work was completed, and it was nearly time to go back up north, but I was still feeling a little cheated. As I prayed for the Lord to give me a better attitude, my husband rushed into the house to inform me that we had a dove nest in the palm tree next to our deck, and another one in the bougainvillea vine over our carport. He set up a ladder, grabbed the camera, and rushed outside to take pictures.

A few days later, however, after an unusually strong windstorm, my husband shared with me that the babies had been blown from the nest in the night, and they were huddled on the ground with the mama and daddy bird sitting on either side of them, probably wondering what to do. In that moment I thought of how valuable those little birds are to our heavenly Father.

Yet as much as He loves and cares for these little birds, He loves us even more. I felt ashamed for my grumbling about what I thought had been such an awful winter. God showed me how much I had to be thankful for. He is my heavenly Father, and He cares about me. The rain we had endured had made the desert absolutely beautiful with greenery and flowers. I had been able to complete some projects in the quiet days I had to myself. The winter didn't seem so bad anymore. We had friends and family within walking distance, and the walking was good for me. It dawned on me once again that it is not so much our circumstances as it is our attitude that makes us content or unhappy.

*Lord, help me to remember that I'm of even more value than the little birds that fall from their nests. You care about how I feel, and I pray that I may always look to You for love and guidance.*

**Anna May Radke Waters**

# No Longer Proud

*May I never boast except in the cross of our Lord Jesus Christ,*
*through which the world has been crucified to me, and I to the world.*
*Gal. 6:14, NIV.*

EVERYTHING HAD BEEN GOING WELL in my life for the past year. I was working and going to college for the degree I had always dreamed of. I was content and proud of myself for the things that I had accomplished through my own efforts, my work, my money, my—my—

The holidays passed, and life fell back into its normal routine. The first several months of the new year, however, were marked by problems and deceptions. On one of the first days my new cell phone was stolen. Several days later I received the news that my mother had cancer in an advanced stage. One day as I was returning home from church, the bus on which I was riding came under assault. Several days later I was fired from one of my jobs.

Suddenly I saw all my dreams and expectations for the new year crumble. Everything I had been so proud of vanished into thin air. My self-esteem plummeted. I felt discouraged, sad, and without hope for better days. The future seemed very dim.

I then understood that all my pride in the things that I owned had blinded me and not allowed me to feel my dependence on God. In reality I needed to lose so that I could truly gain.

Little by little I began to recover my self-esteem and to regain what I had lost.

Every time that I obtained something, my first thought was gratitude to God for the blessing received. This created in me a spirit of gratitude and praise as I saw each act of God in my life. Seeing the sunrise of another day, being able to earn my own way, to sleep peacefully in Jesus' arms, are blessings that I'm thankful for each day. I'm proud of myself for being able to know Him, to love Him, to serve Him, and to witness to His love for me.

Today I praise God because in spite of all the difficulties, I feel He has been by my side. He prepared the way so that I could understand that all things on this earth are temporary, and that what truly counts are the blessings we receive and the time we spend in the presence of this wonderful God!

*Thank You, Lord, for remaining at my side even when I forget You.*
*Help me always to be grateful and conscious of Your presence. Amen!*

**Carmem Virgínia**

# Mister Dog

*Inasmuch as ye have done it unto one of the least of these my brethren, ye have done it unto me. Matt. 25:40.*

ONE DAY AS I WAS OUT WALKING, an old stray dog, one of many in this area, came up beside me. I reached down and patted his head and scratched him behind the ears, where it was all matted with ticks. He was pretty pitiful to look at, but so happy with this little bit of attention.

Of course he followed me home, where I gave him a drink of water. Then I told him, "You go on home now." Well, he wasn't about to walk away from a good thing. However, even though my husband loves dogs and cats, he said, "No! No dogs!"

It was getting chilly when the time came to close up the house for the night. I noticed Mister Dog was still out by the back door. He soon started whining and scratching. When that got him nowhere, he went around the house to the front door and repeated the whining and scratching. After a while, because we stayed very quiet inside, he decided to give up and leave.

After that, every time I went for a walk Mister Dog tagged along. Even if I were in the car, he'd run after me, barking. But after a few weeks of receiving no attention in return, he gave up.

There are so many people who remind me of Mister Dog. They need a kind word from someone, anyone. A little hug will do, or a hand placed gently on their shoulder. So often, though, we just pass them by—or perhaps even go the other way when we see them coming. We'd rather not speak to them because we know they will cling to us like Mister Dog clung to me, and we'll never get away from them. We hope that if we ignore them, they'll find someone else to follow. Shame on us! Perhaps we need to look for the underlying problem and help to solve it. Then these people will be less dependent and clingy. If we had found a home for Mister Dog, he would have left me alone, I'm sure.

What kind of Christian would do this to someone? Certainly not one who has Christ's character. As you have done (or not done) this to the least of them, you have done this to Me, says Jesus.

*Lord, help us to desire Your loving, kind spirit. We long for it, Lord.*

**Janet Thornton**

# Watch the Words You Say!

*Whoso offereth praise glorifieth me: and to him that ordereth his conversation aright will I shew the salvation of God. Ps. 50:23.*

THERE IS AN OLD SAYING I learned while growing up in rural Jamaica: "Sticks and stones will break my bones, but the words you say will not hurt me." We would use this phrase to those with whom we'd had a conflict, "assuring" them in a proud manner that whatever they said to us would have no impact on us whatsoever. Using this phrase would, in a strange way, give us comfort and confidence when we had occasions to confront our foes. But oddly enough, as I grew and matured and had time to reflect on those childhood experiences, I came to the conclusion that though sticks and stones can break my bones if the right force is applied, the words we speak can also have far-reaching effects.

James 3:5-10 says, "The tongue is a little member and boasts great things. See how great a forest a little fire kindles! . . . But no man can tame the tongue. It is an unruly evil, full of deadly poison. . . . Out of the same mouth proceed blessing and cursing" (NKJV). Wow! We know that broken bones can be mended, and the younger you are, the faster the healing takes place. But the words we speak can make, or break, a person.

A story is told of a horse that fell into a large hole and couldn't get out. So the owner of the horse decided to bury him there. He called his neighbors, and together they started throwing dirt into the hole to bury the horse. But after a few hours the horse leaped from the hole and was free. How did he get his freedom? Every time they threw dirt on him he shook it off and stood on it. Little by little he lifted himself out.

What must we do when hurtful situations arise? Shake them off! Remember, we can do all things through Christ who strengthens us (Phil. 4:13). Every time I've called on Jesus He has seen me through. I haven't always behaved myself as I should—sometimes I've taken matters into my own hands, which have ended in disaster. But even then, when I repented and called on Him, He rescued me. The God we serve is a never-failing God; He's always on time to rescue us from all our foes. So let's take Psalm 50:23 as our source of strength and offer praise to God. Let's order our conversation aright, and He will show us His salvation.

**Thamer Cassandra Smikle**

# A Slip of the Tongue— or Pen

*For out of the abundance of the heart the mouth speaketh.*
*Matt. 12:34.*

HAVE YOU EVER MADE a Freudian slip, suddenly blurting out something that had been long repressed? Have you said what was on your mind, and it was hurtful, or socially unacceptable? This happens to me occasionally. As I'm a writer, it usually occurs while I'm typing.

I did some clerical work in the financial aid department while in college. On one occasion I needed to write to the department of highways in an Ohio town. Someone there had requested some of our college brochures and catalogs. I was to package them and take them, with a cover letter, to the mailroom.

As I typed the label, I was thinking about how sleepy I felt. My schedule—with husband, children, schoolwork, housekeeping, taking care of two sick relatives, and fitting in my freelance writing—was a real juggling act. So it's hardly surprising that my tiredness came to the forefront, and I addressed the label to the Highway Napping Department, instead of the Highway Mapping Department. My supervisor and I had a good chuckle as I typed another label.

Another such typo could have been much more serious had the letter gone out the way I typed it. I was a church secretary at the time. There was a woman I knew and disliked because many of her words and actions made people feel that she thought she knew more and was better than everyone else. So I privately gave Mrs. Beasley a new name. One day the pastor asked me to type a letter of appreciation to her for her musical contribution to the previous week's church service. I dutifully wrote the letter and proofed it. Oops! My greeting read, "Dear Mrs. Beastly."

The unkind thoughts I'd been having about her had surfaced! I asked God to forgive me for harboring such ill will. The woman, after all, did have some good qualities. Since the paper was erasable bond, I easily fixed my mistake.

The truth of today's text really hit me. Do you too have similar problems at times? God has promised, "A new heart also will I give you, and a new spirit will I put within you: and I will take away the stony heart . . . and I will give you an heart of flesh" (Eze. 36:26). If we ask Him, He will give us more loving, compassionate hearts. I want a spiritual heart transplant, don't you?

**Bonnie Moyers**

# Keeping Our Priorities Right

*But seek first the kingdom of God and His righteousness,*
*and all these things shall be added to you. Matt. 6:33, NKJV.*

DO YOU SUPPOSE this text is a command from the Lord so that we, His daughters, may be in line, in harmony, with His perfect will? We may forget this many times as we go our own way, and troubles usually follow. What are our priorities in life? Are we sometimes caught in the middle of compromise, and then give up what is right? Do we say, "Only this once, and no more"?

My older daughter, her husband, and their four children were visiting us when my husband and I were still working in Hawaii. Our son and his family also came. So that Christmas holiday season we had a full house. We were very delighted to have them visit us for several days. What a treat!

One late afternoon, to keep our six grandchildren "busy," our daughter let them watch a nature video. It was interesting how a video could quiet a rowdy group of children. And I had my peaceful time too as I prepared supper for the 12 of us. Soon I announced, "Food is ready!" Well, all the children were engrossed in watching the video—all except Annelise, the next-to-the-youngest. No one seemed to pay attention until I heard her say, in her best commanding general voice, "Did you hear what Grandma said? Food is ready!" When nobody moved, General Annelise stood up, went straight to the TV, and turned it off amid loud protests of the four older grandchildren.

I was amused about the incident, but I took note of it. Annelise's priority was to pay attention to what Grandma was saying. And, from her perspective, not only was paying attention necessary, but obeying was also significant.

Are our priorities in line with the Master's—or are we majoring in minors? God gave us an injunction to seek first His kingdom and His righteousness. Perhaps we aren't putting priorities in proper perspective in our lives. We must not forget that if we put God first as our priority, everything will fall in the proper places. As this new year begins, we really do need to be sure our priorities are in line with God's.

**Ofelia Pangan**

# Thank God for Pain

*The Lord has done great things for us, and we are glad.*
*Ps. 126:3, NKJV.*

I KNEW THERE WAS SOMETHING WRONG when the doctor didn't come to see me right after my colonoscopy examination. I learned that he was waiting until my husband came to pick me up so that he could talk to us together when he broke the news: I had cancer.

I had been having some mild abdominal symptoms for some months, but it wasn't until a month before we were to move to a different house that I really had some intermittent cramping in my abdomen. When I did go to see my doctor, we had just moved, and I had had no pain for about a week. By then I felt that the visit wasn't really necessary, but my general practitioner said I should see the specialist anyway. By the time I saw him, the pain had returned. He thought there wasn't anything seriously wrong, but he would arrange a colonoscopy anyway. That's when he found it—a large cancerous tumor in the colon.

Within two weeks I had surgery to remove the cancer, as well as more than half of my colon. The surgeon told us that the tumor had spread right down through the muscle wall of the bowel, but hadn't broken through the outer layer of cells. There were some cancer cells in the lymph vessels nearby, but none of the 12 lymph nodes removed had any cancer in them. He told us how fortunate I was that it was discovered at that point. I thought about how wonderful God is to care for me in this way. If it hadn't been for the pain that I'd had intermittently during those three weeks before I called the doctor's office, I might not have had such a good outcome. I thank God for pain and for concerned physicians. Cancer is often not painful in the initial phase of the disease. Mine was painful because the cancer was causing intermittent partial blockage of the bowel. God was in control, though, and He saw to it that there was no pain for the week before, or the week after we moved to our house. I've had a course of chemotherapy, after which I was tested for cancer. It appears that I'm clear of it at present.

Yes, God is so good! I pray that He will bless you, as He has blessed me. When we stop to think about it, the Lord has already done great things for all of us. So let us be glad and give Him the glory!

**Ruth Lennox**

# The Missing Letter

*You have been weighed in the balances, and found wanting.*
*Dan. 5:27, NKJV.*

MY HUSBAND AGREED to present some devotions to the Tamil people during the 1998 camp meeting in Sri Lanka. I had heard much about the camp meetings where all the believers—English, Tamils, Sinhalese—gather, so I decided to join him to enjoy the fellowship as well as the beauty of the island, and to shop for the Japanese saris.

The first time he'd been invited to Sri Lanka was in the late 1980s. He went to the airport, but that evening he walked back into the house. His flight had been canceled because of a bomb blast at the Colombo airport in Sri Lanka.

On the day of this journey we drove seven hours to the Trichy airport, and went in. The gentleman at the counter looked at our tickets and then at us, quizzically. He flipped the sheets and looked at us again. I panicked. *God, let everything be all right*! Slowly and emphatically he said, "I'm sorry. Only Mr. Kore can travel. Mrs. Kore is not on the list."

"Why? We have two tickets. They were booked together by the same agent. My name should be there. Please check again," I pleaded.

Surprisingly, we found two *Mr.* Kores on the passenger list—the "s" in "Mrs." was missing. Imagine missing a long-awaited trip because of someone else's one-letter mistake! Finally the senior officer intervened and listened as I pleaded my case again, prayerfully. The kind officer then arranged for my boarding pass.

The camp meeting enriched me spiritually, and we prayed earnestly before going to the airport to go home. The gentleman at the counter looked at our passports and tickets, returned them, and told us to wait. We moved to the side and waited. For more than an hour. *We can't miss the flight! Lord, what are You trying to teach us? Are we harassed because we are Tamils from India? Please clear all the hindrances,"* I prayed silently. We went to the counter again, fearing the outcome. But without saying a word, the man gave us our boarding passes.

Just one missing letter . . . This trip taught me that if I lack in even one small thing I will not enter the Promised Land. Praise God that Jesus can supply all I need. So I pray, *Lord, let not any of us be found wanting on the day of judgment.*

**Hepzibah Kore**

# Wounding Words

*May the words of my mouth and the meditation of my heart be pleasing in your sight, O Lord, my Rock and my Redeemer. Ps. 19:14, NIV.*

MY PROBLEM WITH BEING SLOW to ask forgiveness is that I don't always see how things I do can affect God. I mean, I don't commit any obvious sins, such as lying, cheating, or stealing; and I certainly haven't killed anyone. Now, I realize there's more to being a Christian than just obeying the Ten Commandments. Sometimes I think that what I'm doing is only hurting myself, and I don't realize that my actions are really hurting others. Usually people apologize when they put other people down, but recently I found myself apologizing for putting myself down.

One of my failings as a Christian is my serious lack of self-esteem. In my heart I know I'm a child of the King, but when I look in the mirror I don't see a princess; I see a peasant. I compare myself to the people around me, and I end up feeling ugly and stupid. I've fallen into the habit of knocking myself verbally. I know I'm not the only woman who does this or feels she's less than a princess.

I made the mistake of talking to my best friend about how ugly I was. I wasn't prepared for her reaction. Instead of telling me to stop or ignoring my put-downs, she actually started crying.

"You don't know how beautiful you are," she said. "Why can't you see what I see?"

I ended up apologizing profusely. I thought I was only hurting myself when I talked that way, but it turns out I was also hurting the people who loved me.

Every evening I try to spend some time talking to God in a private place. During one of those prayers I was impressed with the idea that if my words wounded my friend to the point of tears, how much more must they hurt my Creator? If God loved me enough to offer His Son, how can I look down on myself?

Asking for forgiveness sincerely means not only admitting to wrongdoing but also trying to make sure you don't repeat the same offense. I'm sorry to say that a bad habit of years doesn't vanish overnight. But I know that both God and my friend have forgiven me, and I'm determined to cut out my wounding words.

**Gina Lee**

# Sleeping on Duty

*While the bridegroom tarried, they all slumbered and slept. Matt. 25:5.*

WHEN MY HUSBAND, Morris, and I travel long distances, he does the driving, and I give the directions. Recently we headed for Kentucky on our way to Hinsdale, Illinois, to visit our daughter Chioma and grandson Nikolas. The night before, I took care of last-minute details and didn't get much sleep. About two hours into the trip I was suddenly awakened from a deep sleep by my husband's agonizing cry, "Oh, no! The police are following me." I looked back to see what I dreaded most—blue and red flashing lights.

Morris pulled over, and the policeman approached my side of the car. "Sir, do you know you were speeding? Let me have your driver's license and registration," the policeman commanded.

Nervously my husband retrieved the documents. The officer took them to his car and, after a few minutes, returned with a speeding ticket. I wasn't happy and told the officer that he could have given my husband a warning instead of a ticket.

"Ma'am, he was going 85 miles an hour in a 70-mile-an-hour zone!" he replied sternly.

We had the option of appearing before a judge the following week or paying the $187.50 fine, the price for one airline ticket. Morris had declined our daughter's offer to purchase airline tickets for us. Guilt overwhelmed me as I looked at the speeding ticket. Had I been awake, I might have alerted my husband to the fact that he was speeding.

Sadly we continued our journey, but thoughts of Jesus' second coming and the 10 virgins kept surfacing in my mind. Every day signs of His imminent return are bombarding us. There is not much time left. Many of us are asleep, oblivious to what's happening around us. Soon the loud cry will resound: "Behold, the bridegroom cometh!" (Matt. 25:6). Will I be among those who will look up and say, "Lo, this is our God; we have waited for him, and he will save us" (Isa. 25:9), or will I again be found sleeping on duty?

My husband had two options—and so do we. We can either confess our sins now and make things right, or appear before the Judge, Jesus Christ, to answer for the wrongs we have committed. The choice is ours. I want to be ready to see Jesus when He comes. How about you?

**Shirley C. Iheanacho**

# To Have Friends

*A man who has friends must himself be friendly, But there is a friend who sticks closer than a brother. Prov. 18:24, NKJV.*

"MOM, I'M GOING TO THE CAR!" I said these words each Sabbath after the church service was over. Then I would disappear from the group.

It hadn't been easy becoming a Christian in my teen years. All the young people in my new place of worship had known each other for years. I was the "new kid on the block," and I felt that no one wanted to be friends with me. Whenever Mom voiced her concerns about what I did each Sabbath, I'd tell her, "Nobody wants to be friends with me."

Each morning, before Dad or I woke from sleep, my loving mother would be sitting on an outcropping of rock, enjoying a panoramic view of our farm. This was her favorite spot to talk to God and meditate. No doubt she had taken her petitions on my behalf to the Lord.

One day she said to me, "Lynn, dear, has it occurred to you that to have friends you must show yourself to be friendly?" Slowly it dawned on me: I needed to do my part; and with the Lord's help I endeavored to reach out to my new acquaintances and to stop disappearing into the car after the church service concluded each week.

I also read the book *How to Win Friends and Influence People,* and found the advice contained in its chapters to be very helpful. As each Sabbath dawned I was amazed by the way the Lord heard my heartfelt petitions to help me overcome my shyness and to let go and let God rule in my life.

The years passed quickly; my new acquaintances became friends for life, and eventually it was time to continue my tertiary education. With the Lord's continued help, that shy young schoolgirl eventually became a primary schoolteacher.

When I look back over the 38 years of my teaching ministry, I think of the many times the Lord has sustained me and given me the words to speak. Many people have inquired about the secret of my naturally friendly personality. I can answer that with the Lord's help all things are possible— after all, if He can change a shy country girl like me into a teacher, there is nothing too hard for Him!

**Lynn Howell**

# The Garment

*He hath clothed me with the garments of salvation, he hath covered me with the robe of righteousness, as a bridegroom decketh himself with ornaments, and as a bride adorneth herself with her jewels. Isa. 61:10.*

IF THERE WERE A PROMOTION at the mall and a famous jeans company were giving out free jeans—no strings attached, no questions, no limited supply, no need for pushing and shoving, guaranteed that everyone in the line would get a pair of totally free jeans in their size—would we not call all our friends and tell them to go get in line for their free jeans? And wouldn't we be there?

What we really need, however, is the garment that Jesus alone can give. First, He gave His blood for us; then He gave us His coat of righteousness to cover our filthy rags (see Zech. 3:1-5 and Matt. 22:1-13). But we have to accept the garment and put it on. We can accept it only by faith. It is our only hope now and in the judgment.

We must have enough faith to believe that Jesus wants to cover our sins, and we must accept that—but there is another part to this. When we realize how fortunate we are to have this offer of the free garment, we will become so grateful to Jesus for offering it that we will want to obey Him in everything He asks us to do. We will get so excited about receiving the free garment that we will want to tell our family, our friends, those with whom we work, and even strangers on the street!

Jesus is giving a free garment, and we need to get excited about His offer! Many of us believe that He will give us the garment for free, and perhaps we accept it (or think we have accepted it). But maybe we accept on our own terms, or with a little doubt. But on whatever terms we have accepted it, somehow we don't fully believe that it is totally free for everyone, or that there is an unending supply, so we don't get excited enough to tell our family, our friends, our neighbors, and everyone we pass on the street. We accept the gift, but we hoard it and don't share the good news about this free gift with others. Are we afraid that they won't like the style, or that the supply will run out, or that if we need a replacement there won't be any left? Sisters, these are free garments! This is so awesome! Go; tell your friends before the offer ends!

**Elizabeth Versteegh Odiyar**

# My Own Name

*I'll give the sacred manna to every conqueror; I'll also give a clear, smooth stone inscribed with your new name, your secret new name. Rev. 2:17, Message.*

MY MAIDEN NAME was Dick, which often led to a lot of confusion. For instance, I once got assigned to the men's dorm when I was in college; but to make things worse, my husband is Richard, usually called Dick. When we were dating, people used to ask if we knew that we both had the same name. Yes, we knew. What amazes me now is that people frequently ask me why I have my husband's name on my books, such as this devotional book. I tell them his name is not on the book, and that I had the name first.

Having our own name is so important. The first time I tried to rent a car I presented the credit card I had used all the time. But it was my husband's name on the card, not mine. And they would not rent a car to me. I hastily applied for a credit card in my own name.

There are so many customs for using one's name. Here in the United States a woman has to decide if she will take her husband's name, keep her maiden name, or hyphenate the two. And there are even variations of these options. Many countries have other customs: is the surname first or last? And Hispanic names are a total bewilderment to me, such as which name to use when listing the names in alphabetical order. Names—so important to each of us. And we want our own name listed and spelled correctly.

God's name is important too, but not as some people make it, insisting that the name must be spelled or pronounced a certain way. The Bible is full of references to God's name, so we need to understand that His name refers to His character—what He represents, what He is. When we pray the Lord's Prayer, we say, "Hallowed be thy name." And then there is Acts 4:12: "There is salvation in no one else, for there is no other name under heaven given among mortals by which we must be saved" (NRSV). We are baptized in His name, His character. Miracles are performed in this name, and martyrs have died for this name.

Revelation 3:5 is incredible. It promises, "I will not blot your name out of the book of life; I will confess your name before my Father and before his angels" (NRSV). Not only will we receive a new name, but our Father confesses our name. Praise His name!

**Ardis Dick Stenbakken**

# The Ugly Duckling

*For God so loved the world, that he gave his only begotten Son, that whosoever believeth in him should not perish, but have everlasting life. John 3:16.*

JOHN 3:16 IS MY FAVORITE TEXT; it is my passport into the heavenly kingdom. There is so much love and promise in the verse. We are God's created beings, and He loved us so much that He was willing that His Son should suffer and die for us. In return for this great sacrifice, and by our belief in the grace of Jesus, we can have a home in the eternal kingdom. Heaven is where we belong—this earth is only a temporary home in which to prepare for our home with our God.

This is a text that I always take with me. It was there as I served in the mission field, as I traveled throughout Russia, lived and taught in China, and as I worked with the children in the different schools. I need to re-member it each day as I interact with different people in various situations. It helps me to believe that each person I meet and deal with is a loved one of God—we are brothers and sisters. How dare I mistreat anyone, as we are all bound together by our being created in the image of God. He wants each one of us to have everlasting life.

It is important for me to keep this always in mind as I work with chil-dren in the school system—regardless of their ethnic background, behavior, or dress. I work with many ethnic groups of children. One day as I worked with a classroom of 20 children I read to them the story of the ugly duck-ling, in which the cygnet turns into a beautiful swan. I've seen cygnets, and they are not pretty (although I don't like to exactly call them ugly). I always read the books upside down so the children can see the pictures. And I often stop for questions and discussions. When I turned to the page of the ugly cygnet, Zach, a little African-American boy, raised his hand. "Yup, that's me; nobody likes me." John 3:16 helps me to give him assurance. It is always there, whether I quote it or use the meaning of it.

When I taught my students in China, I began with this verse to explain why I was there, and why and how I loved them and, more important, how God loves them! I stressed to them how God loves the crippled beggar down on the sidewalk as much as He loves them or me.

We all have the same promise of love and the same hope of an eter-nal life. I want to show God's love this day as I meet my brothers and sisters.

**Dessa Weisz Hardin**

# Pray for Me

*For he will command his angels concerning you to guard you in all your ways. Ps. 91:11, NIV.*

FORGET THE HOT SUMMER AFTERNOON of January 20, 1987? Hardly!

That day I found myself getting ready for surgery, and my dear husband was with me. Concern was normal, because the diagnosis was breast cancer; there would be general anesthesia, and treatment would follow the surgery. Soon I would be heading to the operating room, but I was feeling more and more tranquil. *Why am I so peaceful? so calm?* I wondered. Then I remembered that an entire church was praying for me. I felt as if I were in Jesus' arms, that He was caring for me as though I were His only daughter. What comfort! What assurance! What peace I felt! When people pray, something happens! God listens. God answers. God makes changes. God touches lives.

The surgery was successful. I've been very blessed and now lead a normal, healthy life. Gratitude still lingers in my heart for all those who prayed for me. I recognize that God is a Father of love who cares for each child as His only child. I can say with assurance, "God is our refuge and strength, an ever-present help in trouble" (Ps. 46:1, NIV). The God who created all things, who maintains them, who created you and me, who knows how many strands of hair are on our heads, is the same one who cares for each detail of our lives.

I love the following quote about God's love and trust: "Nature and revelation alike testify of God's love. Our Father in heaven is the source of life, of wisdom, and of joy. Look at the wonderful and beautiful things of nature. Think of their marvelous adaptation to the needs and happiness, not only of man, but of all living creatures. The sunshine and the rain, that gladden and refresh the earth, the hills and seas and plains, all speak to us of the Creator's love. It is God who supplies the daily needs of all His creatures" (*Steps to Christ*, p. 9).

"Let the soul be drawn out and upward, that God may grant us a breath of the heavenly atmosphere. We may keep so near to God that in every unexpected trial our thoughts will turn to Him as naturally as the flower turns to the sun" (*ibid.*, pp. 99, 100).

It is worthwhile to trust in Him.

**Elza C. dos Santos**

# Flash Burn

*Let us fix our eyes on Jesus, the author and perfecter of our faith, who for the joy set before him endured the cross, scorning its shame, and sat down at the right hand of the throne of God. Heb. 12:2, NIV.*

I USED TO BE EMPLOYED by a company that specialized in making service bodies for trucks. These service bodies would equip the trucks with compartments of various sizes, and doors that were ideal for utility companies, plumbers, and other industries.

As a member of the safety committee, I would walk through the manufacturing plant, keeping an eye out for violations. Safety was our number one concern. Everyone who entered the plant was required to wear safety glasses as a precaution, even the office personnel and visitors. But even safety glasses couldn't prevent the number one injury that occurred—flash burn.

Flash burn is just that—a burn to the cornea of the eye that happens in a flash. When the welding arc is hot, its ultraviolet light is like the sun. You can't look at it with the naked eye without causing damage. The welders protect themselves with specialized safety glasses and welding hoods. But if anyone casts a glance at the flaming torch and lingers there too long, they will wake up the next morning in severe pain and unable to see clearly. You see, the cornea protects deeper structures of the eye, acting like a windshield to the eye. The flash burn condition is usually short-term and can be treated with medication. There is no mistaking the symptoms, though—a feeling like there is sandpaper in the eye. It's painful and uncomfortable.

What if we were inflicted with flash burn every time our eyes lingered where they didn't belong? Or worse, what if we were turned into a pillar of salt, as was Lot's wife when she looked back on Sodom after God instructed her not to do so? She didn't have the faith to keep her eyes away from the danger.

Our deeper spiritual structure inside of us needs protection too. God has given us this protection in His Word. Bible study and prayer act not only as protection, but also as the solution when we do get in trouble. Without the medication of God's Word, we can lose our spiritual vision. Let's pray each day that we can keep our eyes fixed on Him, the author and perfecter of our faith.

**Karen Phillips**

# The Gift of Gratitude

*We give thanks to you, O God, we give thanks, for your Name is near; men tell of your wonderful deeds. Ps. 75:1, NIV.*

MY MOTHER HAD THE GIFT OF GRATITUDE, and that impressed me, even when I was small. In all situations, even the most difficult, she found reasons to thank the Lord. Today, at 78 years of age, she still dedicates a good part of her time to prayer and gratitude.

I've known many grateful people, and also many whose main intention was to convince those who would listen that everything that happened to them was horrible and without solution. Never did they take into account the numerous blessings received. Unfortunately, ungrateful people appreciate their blessings only when they lose them. But then they usually put blame on others for their own irresponsibility and are never happy.

In self-help recovery groups for addictions, it is recommended that you begin the day listing reasons for gratitude: life, sight, health, peace, liberty, daily bread, work, family, and friends. It has been proven that the grateful person can adjust herself better to the frustration that privation and addiction may cause. Additionally, grateful people develop stronger family ties, are more productive, suffer fewer illnesses, have less depression, and overcome losses more quickly.

On the other hand, counting our blessings also makes us consider the unfavorable situation of less-fortunate fellow human beings and stimulates our solidarity and compassion.

There are various forms of gratitude, but the most important is the heart that is grateful to the Lord. As today's verse states, His works speak of His wonderful deeds.

If you cultivate a spirit of gratitude, you will note an immediate improvement in all areas of your life, especially the spiritual area. You will realize that you have much more than you thought, more joy and creativity. A well-known Christian writer recommends making a written record of these blessings. Then, when things don't go well, you will have accumulated experiences that will help you overcome adversity. A friend of mine, a Holocaust survivor, says, "One must accept life as it is and be grateful for the good things one has."

Tonight, go over your day and once again be thankful for what you have received. In this manner you will also declare how wonderful His name is.

**María Susana Mistretta de Golubizky**

# Oh, No! It's Raining!

*I set My rainbow in the cloud, and it shall be for the sign of the covenant between Me and the earth. . . . And I will remember My covenant which is between Me and you and every living creature of all flesh; the waters shall never again become a flood to destroy all flesh. Gen. 9:13-15, NKJV.*

IT HAD BEEN A QUIET WINTER DAY, but in midafternoon I heard rain begin to fall. I thought, *Oh, no!* That may seem like a strange reaction for someone who lives in western Washington and hears rain often; however, the twin cities near our home had just experienced severe flooding earlier in the week. Two days before, it had finally stopped raining, and people were deciding what to do with their soggy, muddy homes. Now it was raining again! What if it doesn't stop?

Then God reminded me of Genesis 6-9, the story of the first flood. The very first time it rained it didn't stop until the water covered the highest hills. God had warned them that this would happen, and had provided a way for them to be safe. It had never rained before, and the people weren't used to believing God, whether there was evidence for what He was saying or not. They stayed with their homes and lost their lives. When Noah and his family came out of the ark, they began to replenish the earth, as God had originally told Adam and Eve to do.

Probably, each time it rained they told their children the story of the Flood. When the rainbow appeared, they told them of God's promise. But some people still chose not to trust God. When it rained, they remembered only the Flood and, afraid it might happen again, decided to do something, just in case.

I thought of those who started building the Tower of Babel in order to save themselves. I wasn't so critical of them now. I could feel the strength of their temptation. I also thought of those who believed God and didn't join in the tower building. I admire them for their faith. They definitely belong among the heroes listed in Hebrews 11

Though it was wrong not to trust God now that it seemed to keep raining here in our town, I could see what God had known all along—the next time it began to rain they would panic. God knew how frightening it would be, so He put the rainbow in the clouds as a promise that there would never be another flood to cover the whole earth. I can depend on that promise too.

**Lana Fletcher**

# Our Choice

*Cast your cares on the Lord and he will sustain you;*
*he will never let the righteous fall. Ps. 55:22, NIV.*

I WAS IN THE LONG BEACH AIRPORT with my mother-in-law, waiting for our flight to Dulles International in Washington, D.C. We had almost two hours to wait before our flight, and, as usual, I needed to do something before boredom attacked me.

I took my computer out of my bag and turned it on, but then started watching the passers-by. A woman rushed to the gate with what seemed to be a heavily loaded bag. She carried it with one hand, making her shoulder sag, forgetting that the bag had wheels—it would have been easier and faster to wheel it. A man passed by with two carry-on bags, plus a plastic bag, probably with food for the flight. I smiled; he seemed to be struggling with the load and didn't notice his shirt was all twisted.

Another woman, dressed-up in high heels and with just a small purse, passed by. That's what I call traveling in style. I don't know, but it seems that each time I travel I always have two carry-on bags, both loaded to the maximum. I long for the day when I can travel lightly, like that high-heeled woman.

I watched a family of six. The little girls were full of life, all giggling, jumping, and lying on the floor. The parents struggled to get them cleaned up in time for their flight.

We are all travelers to our heavenly home. What is amazing is that we travel to our heavenly home just as we travel here on earth. Some of us travel with loads of fear, worries, and discouragement that weigh us down. We forget that we can easily hand our load to the Lord, and He can wheel it for us. Others travel with baggage of hatred, envy, and anger—baggage that we don't need as we travel. Others of us get all dirty with sin and need to be cleaned up.

Praise God, though, for those who travel in style. They travel light, trusting everything to the Lord, and the Lord carries it all for them.

The choice is ours today. My prayer is that we travel in style, giving all our burdens to the Lord. Let's make our travel fun by heeding His commands and letting Him lead the way. "Cast your cares on the Lord and he will sustain you."

**Jemima D. Orillosa**

# Of Waves and Toothaches

*[He] said to the sea, "Peace, be still!" . . . And there was a great calm.*
*Mark 4:39, NKJV.*

IT WAS THE SEASON OF CARNIVAL, and, as was their custom, my parents attended a spiritual retreat at a Christian campsite. I, however, looked forward to "babysitting" their house for those four days and getting some much-needed alone time with God. I arrived late Saturday night and simply crashed on the sofa, since the living room is a central area where one can hear any unusual noise around the house.

Early the next morning I was awakened by our neighbor's rooster's energetic crows; the noise left me with only one option—getting up. But it was worth it; I had a spirit-filled devotional illuminated by the soft orange-pink rays of dawn.

With a song in my heart I went straight to the kitchen to prepare one of my favorite breakfast dishes: patacones (fried green plantain) and eggs. Breakfast made, I went to the den to view the movie *The Sound of Music,* while I enjoyed my meal. But just as I bit into one of the patacones, I felt a shock of pain from my upper left molar that was so severe I couldn't finish chewing. Somehow I had managed to break a tooth filling, exposing the nerve. At least that's how it felt.

That was the end of my breakfast and movie. I spent the rest of the day in agony. I could bear only to drink water with my painkiller, but no relief came. I sadly concluded that I would have to return to the city on Monday to see my dentist and hope that she would be open during this long festive weekend.

As I lay on the sofa, crying myself to sleep, I thought of how Jesus had calmed the threatening waves with a simple "Peace, be still." It then dawned on me that Jesus also wanted to spend those four days alone with me, and that He also felt my pain. Right then and there I thanked Him for those thoughts of comfort and begged Him to relieve my pain.

As I awoke Monday morning, I felt no pain! Jesus had calmed the waves of pain that had threatened my peace, and now He and I had all the alone time we had planned.

When something like that happens to you, do you just want to praise God, from whom all blessings flow? I did, and I'm glad.

**Evelia R. Cargill**

# Parable of the Lost Glove

*Ask and it will be given to you; seek and you will find.*
*Matt. 7:7, NIV.*

ONE COLD NIGHT IN JANUARY we traveled for nearly two hours to attend a charity concert in the church of which a friend is the pastor. As we walked to the church in the bitter cold, I regretted forgetting my gloves in the car. They had been a present from a friend at Christmas, the best driving gloves I had ever owned. They fit my small hands perfectly, so I treasured them.

Returning to the car after the concert, I discovered that my gloves weren't there. David, my husband, joined me as I searched under the seat and all around the car. When our friends arrived, they too joined in the search. Then David remembered that he had let me out of the car before he parked it, so we walked to the place he had stopped. Imagine my delight when I saw a glove lying on the ground—but there was only one! All of us searched again, but found nothing. The pastor promised that he'd return the next morning, when it was light, and have another look.

My first thought the next morning was of my missing glove, so I was glad when my friend phoned. Unfortunately, he hadn't found the glove. "If this were an Uncle Arthur's bedtime story [referring to stories we used to read to our children], we'd pray, and you would find the glove," I said jokingly.

When I put the phone down, I sent up a rather self-conscious prayer to God, asking that my friend would find my precious glove. Not five minutes later the phone rang again. "I've found it!" John said excitedly. "It was in the hedge behind the electrical box." You can imagine our jubilation—and the prayer of thanks that went up to God. It was, in fact, just like an Uncle Arthur bedtime story answer.

Later, contemplating God's interest in our mundane lives, John likened our experience to the three parables Jesus told in Luke 15 about a woman who found her lost coin, a shepherd who found his lost sheep, and a father who found his lost son. Their delight wasn't anything, Jesus told His listeners, compared to the rejoicing in heaven over a sinner who repents. The parables, and my experience, made me ponder how highly I value God's gift of grace. It made me determine to stay closer to Him so that I will not be lost.

**Audrey Balderstone**

# Human Wisdom

*For the wisdom of this world is foolishness in God's sight. 1 Cor. 3:19, NIV.*

I WAS FINISHING my master's degree, and my professor for the module on infectious-contagious diseases was a physician with 60 years of experience. One day he was asked about the cure for endemic pemphigus foliaceus (fogo selvagem). He responded emphatically that there was no cure. I was surprised, because some time before I had read the book that told the story of the first woman cured of fogo selvagem.

What should I do? Should I say something in a class of 42 students, students who were physicians, nurses, lawyers, and nutritionists? Would it be correct to challenge an epidemiologist with 60 years of experience? At that moment I didn't have any scientific resources to contest what the professor had said. Not knowing what else to do, I prayed, asking for wisdom.

Then I raised my hand and mentioned to the professor a hospital in Campo Grande, Mato Grosso do Sul, Brazil, that successfully offers treatment to many patients with this disease. Offended by the comments, my professor pointed his finger at me and said, "Look, young lady, in 60 years of practicing medicine I've never heard that a cure exists for this disease. I want you to prove what you are affirming." I didn't count on this challenge, and was embarrassed by the looks I received from my classmates. Once again I prayed for help to bring a successful end to this situation.

The following day I called a professor at Brazil College. He assured me I would have the material in a short time. A letter was sent to the hospital in Campo Grande, requesting that they send specific documents. Fifteen days later I received the scientific material necessary, and even stories of many people who had been cured. I spent an entire evening studying the material and thanking God for the answer. I made the necessary copies and gave them to my professor.

Three months later that professor and I met in the hallway. He shook my hand, thanked me for the material, and stated, "I thought I knew everything, but I was wrong. That material you gave me has been distributed to more than 50 public health institutions in São Paulo."

Praise God for His wonders and for providing heaven-sent wisdom when needed!

**Maria Chèvre**

# What's in a Name?

*And thou shalt be called by a new name,*
*which the mouth of the Lord shall name. Isa. 62:2.*

DO YOU LIKE YOUR NAME?

I was born the eldest of 12 children. For the first 10 years or so, I paid no attention to my name. But as I grew into my teens I began to dislike being called Vidella. After I was born and 11 more kids came along, I think my mom got tired of thinking up unusual names, because my siblings all had simple names, such as Shirley, Beverly, Marvin, and Karen. I cringed when I was called Vi-del-la, because I knew I was in trouble for something. How I longed to be called Mary, Elsie, or Hazel, just a common, ordinary name.

One day I decided to call myself just plain Vi. Short and simple. There were other Vi's, and I didn't feel so odd. Later, I added an *e* ; now most people call me Vie.

A few years ago at our women's retreat I unburdened my heart to Joyce about how I felt about my name. She, like others before, said how pretty my name was, but I never thought so. Joyce and I had quite a lengthy talk, and she encouraged me to look at it in a more positive way.

As the firstborn I was very special, so Mom wanted a special name for me. After all, she waited nine months to have this special child. Her name is Ella Viola, so my name is part of hers, just as I'm part of her. I'm a unique person with a unique name. I can picture my mother cradling me in her arms, looking into my tiny face, and putting her heart and soul into what to call me. No doubt many names crossed her mind.

Nowadays there are hundreds of different and seemingly made-up names, but all have significance, meaning, some reason in someone's heart as to why they named their child what they did.

I have a whole new outlook about my name now. There is no other name like mine; it is one of a kind, just as I am one of a kind.

There is coming a day when again I will have a new name. I don't know what it will be, but I know it will have a special meaning, and it will be very beautiful. It is so exciting to have that to look forward to! I can hardly wait.

**Vidella McClellan**

# Heavenly Company

*Never will I leave you; never will I forsake you. Heb. 13:5, NIV.*

CATS ARE VERY INDEPENDENT CREATURES. They move so quietly that they seem to slink around—in sight one minute, out of sight the next. My long-haired calico, Tibby, can be ever so loving, curling up beside me. But at other times, when I'm feeling blue and wanting her love, she's apt to turn up her nose or even disappear. She seems to "forsake" me.

I live alone and use a walker, but I still drive. I don't like to cook for one, so I usually eat my main meal of the day out at lunch. One Sunday I was at the local Shoney's, enjoying my lunch. They were quite busy, especially when the after-church crowd arrived. I began "people watching" and noticed something—there were couples, there were families, and there were groups of friends; but I seemed to be the only person alone. Of course, I couldn't see everyone from my small booth, but I began to feel lonely. It helped some that I knew most of the servers, and they spoke to me: "Hello, Miss Patsy!" "Do you need anything, sweetie?" But I still felt lonely. Forsaken.

I once talked to Dick, a friend at church, about how I felt. He told me that when he feels that way he remembers his "heavenly" company—God, Jesus, the Holy Spirit, and the angels. That thought helps me.

But what about the times you want to be with people you can see, talk to, and hug? That's harder.

Sometimes, when I know my neighbors are going to be home (both women work), I ask one of them if they'd be willing to meet me at Shoney's, because I'd like to treat them to lunch and to visit awhile. Or when Kathy, my once-a-week helper, comes, some cleaning and laundry is done, and then we have lunch somewhere. After we do errands, we head to Wal-Mart for groceries.

*Thank You, Jesus, for Your promise, "And surely I am with you always [, Patsy], to the very end of the age"* (Matt. 28:20, NIV).

I'm sure many readers appreciate the heavenly company the way I do. There must be many lonely people out there, too, who also appreciate real people with whom to spend time.

**Patsy Murdoch Meeker**

# Heritage Gift

*For God so loved the world, that he gave his only begotten Son, that whosoever believeth in him should not perish, but have everlasting life. John 3:16.*

A CHILDHOOD FRIEND and I kept in touch even after we parted ways to further our education. When Doris died suddenly at age 27, she left behind many memories of our growing-up years. We had been inseparable playmates in an old country school. We did everything together, even to visiting the two-seater outhouse in a clump of trees behind the schoolhouse.

I often wondered what became of her 6-year-old daughter, bereaved of a mother. Had she grown to womanhood as sweet as her mother had been? I had never met Doris's husband or her daughter, and didn't have pictures of either.

Forty years later, when I needed to downsize to move into a condominium, I spent time deciding what to keep, throw away, give away, or sell. Finally I came to a dozen photo albums. Few pictures were labeled, so I began the process of adding names for those who might browse through them someday. Then I thought, *Why not return old photos and snapshots to family members?*

When I came across a photo of Doris in her nurse's uniform, I thought of her little girl, who probably didn't have many memories of her mother. I made an effort to get her address, and then wrote a long letter, telling her how special her mother had been to me. I enclosed the photo and some snapshots, hoping to hear from her. I told her of one simple gift I still treasured from her mother and offered to mail it to her if she would like it.

How disappointed I was not to hear from her! Nothing in my imagination could justify her rejection. Whatever her reasons, I decided not to impose myself on her again. The gift, a clear glass Santa boot, has served as a toothpick holder in my kitchen cupboard ever since the tiny bottle of perfume that once nestled in the boot was depleted. Memories live forever.

You and I have received a letter from a Friend. He has offered a gift far more precious than I had to offer Doris's daughter. Do we keep in touch with Him? Have we accepted His gift of eternal life? Are we extending the invitation to others? He is waiting.

**Edith Fitch**

# The Dove of Peace

*Who are these that fly as a cloud, and as the doves to their windows?*
*Isa. 60:8.*

DURING MY 40-YEAR CAREER as a nurse, I've worked in many areas of the hospital and have held several positions. My favorite is working on the postsurgical floor; I'm never happier than when I'm doing bedside nursing. I feel like this is where the Lord uses me best and where I receive my best job satisfaction. My least-favorite assignment is being the charge nurse on our busy 40-bed medical/surgical floor.

One winter morning I arrived at work to find that I'd been assigned to be the charge nurse for the day. One of my duties was to listen to the full prerecorded report on all 40 patients. I grabbed my clipboard, obtained an accurate patient list, and proceeded to the room where we receive the report. I sat down facing the four large windows that overlook the beautiful mountains, hoping to get a glimpse of the sunrise to cheer me as I took my lengthy report. A fresh snow had fallen during the night, and I occasionally glanced out the windows. The view was indeed lovely. I led the other nurses in a short devotion, asking for divine help. Some of the nurses had already taken the report, and two others took two recorders elsewhere to finish their report, leaving me alone. I pushed the play button on the one remaining recorder, sighed, and began to take notes as the report proceeded. As I listened to the information being given on each patient, I felt the heavy weight of my responsibilities. Some patients were not expected to improve; others were not doing well. The longer I listened, the heavier the weight became. I bowed my head in despair and prayed, "O Lord, how am I ever going to make a difference in all this or handle all the demands made on me today?" As I lifted my eyes they were immediately drawn to something on the windowsill. Directly in front of me was a beautiful white dove. She sat there in the light snow; her bright eyes fastened on me as she turned her head from side to side. At that very moment I felt a wonderful peace settle on me, as if the dear Lord was sending me a message: "Don't be afraid; you asked Me for help, and I will help you today." I finished my report with renewed strength and courage.

I had never seen a dove there before, so I know the dear Lord sent me a message of hope straight from heaven. And He will do the same for you!

**Rose Neff Sikora**

# My Heavenly Husband

*For your Maker is your husband—the Lord Almighty is his name.
Isa. 54:5, NIV.*

WHEN MY HUSBAND LEFT ME after 23 years of marriage, I experienced an overwhelming sense of panic. I had never lived on my own and had no idea how I would take care of myself. My husband was a handyman who had always repaired our cars and household items, and I knew that I couldn't physically or financially take care of the house, the car, and the yard by myself.

While I was struggling with grief and anxiety, a friend at work shared a wonderful Bible text with me: "For your maker is your husband— the Lord almighty is his name" (Isa. 54:5, NIV). I immediately began claiming that text as a promise. Everything I had previously relied on my husband for, I began to rely on God to take care of. And He took care of me in so many marvelous ways that I can hardly count them! For example, when my car battery died, it died in my garage instead of leaving me stranded away from home. At times He gave me courage I didn't know I had so that I could do things for myself, such as working on a ladder despite my fear of heights.

My loving Lord even took away my lifelong fear of being alone at night—without my asking. About three months after my husband left, I realized that I no longer lay in bed at night listening anxiously to strange noises in the house. Instead, I slept soundly all night. I knew immediately that this sense of peace was a gift from God.

In answer to prayer God impressed my employers to give me a promotion that provided just enough more money to take care of all my living expenses. Until then I had been living with a credit card debt to cover some living expenses.

I once complained to the Lord that as a single person I couldn't afford to take vacations, and that I missed being able to travel to new places. Amazingly, a few years later He blessed me with a job that included frequent travel.

It has been many years since my divorce, and I can honestly say that my heavenly Husband has been faithful to supply all my needs and many of my "wants." The Lord Almighty is truly his name! Perhaps more important, He has satisfied the longings of my soul beyond all I could have imagined.

**Carla Baker**

# Vacation

*I go to prepare a place for you. . . . I will came again, and receive you unto myself. John 14:2, 3.*

OUR FAMILY PLANNED to go on vacation to one of the islands. We didn't all live in the same city, so a lot of communication took place. We had to decide on where we would stay and for how long. Then we had to find out what the hotel had to offer.

We had to decide what clothes and how much cash to take, and of course we had to take our cameras to capture the memories. I packed and unpacked to make sure I took everything I thought I would need. We were very excited, and we couldn't wait.

When we arrived, everyone was so happy to see each other! There were hugs and kisses all around. After checking in, we looked around and acquainted ourselves with the place. We spent a lot of time by the pool and had lots of fun going down the slides. On top of that, the food was good, and we had lots of choices.

We met new people, went on tours, bought souvenirs, and took pictures. It was a wonderful vacation, but finally it came to an end. Of course, we were happy to get back home, but we were sad that the vacation was over.

As I thought about it, my mind went back to a poem I heard several years ago about going on vacation to heaven. I can't remember the words, but a beautiful picture was described, making one eager to be there. As the Bible says: "Eye hath not seen, nor ear heard, . . . the things which God hath prepared for them that love him" (1 Cor. 2:9).

The wonderful thing about the heavenly vacation is that it costs us nothing because Jesus has paid the price. We simply need to accept it. He has made all the preparation, and He is coming to escort us there. Further, that vacation will have no end—it will be our permanent home forever. Of course, we will not be idle there. We will be working and building houses, and children will not need to go to day care.

I like going on vacations and am always excited, but I'm more excited about my never-ending vacation in heaven. Friends, let us endeavor to spend our vacation in heaven. With God's help, I hope to be there. How about you?

**Ena Thorpe**

# A New Person

*Therefore, if anyone is in Christ, he is a new creation;*
*old things have passed away; behold all things have become new.*
*2 Cor. 5:17, NKJV.*

THE SPASMS IN MY NECK racked my whole body. I dared not turn my head for fear my muscles would explode into a new frenzy of pain. Nothing I did seemed to help for very long. Someone who noticed my pain recommended a deep-tissue massage at a particular wellness spa. I quickly booked an appointment and anxiously awaited the time. Would it help, or just make it worse?

When I arrived at the spa, I was instantly put at ease by the professional yet empathetic manner of the massage therapist. After one hour under her skillful ministrations I felt like a new person! I could move my head and neck without fear. That evening, and for the next few days, I found myself repeatedly telling people about my experience. "That therapist was just great!" I said. "If you need a massage, go to her." A few terrible days of pain had been alleviated by the skill of her hands.

I'm no stranger to transformation. Once, my entire life was filled with pain and despair. The threat of eternal destruction was very real. Then the Therapist, Jesus, put His skillful hands on my life and made me into a new creation. I no longer need to fear the consequences of sin and guilt, because Jesus has paid the price.

As I ponder this wonderful reality I realize that I'm not always ready to recommend Jesus the way I did the massage therapist. Fear of rejection and what others may think often keeps me silent. The benefits, however, far outweigh the risks, real or perceived. The alternative to eternal life is eternal damnation, but Jesus has already made provision for everyone in the world to choose life instead of death. The more I think of what God has done for me, the more I feel like shouting it from the mountaintops!

*Dear Father, please keep me ever mindful of the change that You have wrought in my life. Forgive me for the times I've kept silent about You. Give me the zeal and boldness to share the Source of eternal life with others around me. As I look forward to the glories of heaven, may I bring others along with me. Amen.*

**Abigail Blake Parchment**

# Two and Two Make Four, Not Seven

*Who may live on your holy hill? . . . He . . . who . . . casts no slur on his fellowman. Ps. 15:1-3, NIV.*

IT WAS LATE, and the traffic had been horrible. In addition, the weather was cold, and I was tired. There was just time to fill the tank, drop the rental car off at the airport, get through security, and get to my gate. Pulling into the station, I jumped out of the car, swiped my credit card, and shoved the nozzle into the gas tank. Glancing around me, I nearly gasped. Not 15 feet away, at the next pump, a woman was performing a similar task and smoking at the same time! I could see a portion of the cigarette dangling from her lips, little puffs of smoke curling into the air.

*Doesn't she know about the dangers of smoking while refueling?* I muttered under my breath. *One spark, and we could all be blown to smithereens!*

I stood there fuming and glowering in her direction as the gasoline poured into the tank. Thoughts raced around in my head. Did I dare say something to her? I did. I wouldn't let this pass! Taking a deep breath, I opened my mouth to give her a piece of my mind. But just then she turned toward me. Lights from the service station shone directly on her face, and I swallowed my words—all of them!

No cigarette after all. A piece of white stick candy dangled from her lips. No cigarette smoke, either. Just her breath as it condensed in little puffs in the frigid air. The woman smiled and nodded as she replaced the nozzle, slipped into her car, and drove away.

My face was very red, and it wasn't from the cold. *I thought I'd learned that lesson*, I muttered to myself, *but I just did it again. Jumped to conclusions! And I knew better—I really did.*

At my gate I pondered the experience. Thankfully, it hadn't impacted the other woman negatively, but my body had pumped a pile of adrenaline as I put two and two together and came up with seven instead of four. Plus, I'd put a completely inaccurate spin on the seven! I breathed a prayer: *Please let this be the last time I jump to conclusions; may I learn this lesson once and for all!*

**Arlene Taylor**

# The Difference He Makes

*A new command I give you: Love one another. As I have loved you, so you must love one another. John 13:34, NIV.*

PHILIP YANCEY, in *The Jesus I Never Knew,* tells of waiting impatiently at O'Hare Airport for a flight that was delayed five hours. He struck up a conversation with a woman bound for the same conference. The two shared disappointments with the church and certain questions of faith. Philip was writing *Disappointment With God* and felt burdened by other people's pain, sorrow, and unanswered prayers. His travel companion listened in silence, and then out of nowhere asked a pointed question: "Philip, do you ever just let God love you?" Yancey states that the question brought him face to face with a gaping hole in his spiritual life.

Sometimes I have wondered about my own life. I'm presently five days from departing for a three-week trip to the Ukraine, where I will work with a pastor in evangelistic meetings. I will host a party for 250 women at a church in Kiev, visit an orphanage and a Chernobyl hospital, teach a relationship seminar at a seminary, and host a party for 50 students. My mind whirls with the donations of money, clothing, and felts that I'm responsible for distributing.

In addition to preparing for the trip, my regular life continues—counseling, teaching a weekend family seminar, a Mexican fiesta at my home to raise funds for this trip, writing devotionals, plus an all-day seminar the day before I leave.

It's time to turn the question my direction: "Nancy, do you ever just let God love you?" Am I so busy doing for everybody else, so dedicated to fixing everyone else's problems, that I don't have time to let God love me? I question what I believe. Salvation by works?

In the midst of my hectic schedule I must slow the pace and allow God to love me, to soothe and comfort me. For all my absorption in being a Christian and doing good as a Christian should, I dare not miss the most important message of all—His love for *me.* Unless I recognize this, all the good that I attempt to do will remain "only a resounding gong or a clanging cymbal. . . . If I give all I possess to the poor and surrender my body to the flames, but have not love, I gain nothing" (1 Cor. 13:1-3, NIV).

*Slow me down, Lord, and fill me with Your love so that I've something to give to others.*

**Nancy Van Pelt**

# Breathe Now

*And when he had said this, he breathed on them, and saith unto them, Receive ye the Holy Ghost. John 20:22.*

DURING A CONSULTATION with my doctor he ordered a CT scan on my head, chest, and abdomen. This sounded scary to me, a simple Fiji Islander from the South Pacific who had only seen a CT scan on TV. I had mixed feelings. But my desire for full recovery made me brave.

Anne Korup, senior nurse at the university, organized a booking for me the very next day. She took me in and was with me throughout the whole day. Two doctors and a nursing sister attended to me. After the necessary procedure and medication, they laid me on the little narrow bed, strapped me to it, and padded my head. The doctor instructed me to lie still throughout the examination. He explained that he would scan my head first, then my chest, then my abdomen. He would ask that I stop breathing at times and that he would speak to me from the control room through a built-in speaker. He reassured me that all would be well. I breathed a prayer of thanks to my heavenly Father for such wonderful doctors.

The doctors left for the control room, leaving me alone. The scan procedure started. After what seemed like ages, I then heard the doctor say, "Stop breathing." I stopped breathing instantly; there was movement and noise, and then he announced, "Breathe now." This happened several times. I was indeed glad when this ended. My great relief was short-lived, however. The nurse injected some medication into my left arm, and the procedure began again.

When I heard the familiar voice announce, "Stop breathing," I stopped breathing and shut my eyes. Then again I heard a faint voice from a distance saying, "Stop Breathing." I hadn't been breathing since the last time, and I was absolutely desperate for air. I couldn't hold my breath any longer—I felt on the verge of suffocation. What should I do? Just then I heard the sweetest announcement loud and clear: "Breathe now." I took the deepest breath I'd ever taken. It was life, refreshing life, for me!

I'm reminded that Jesus breathed the breath of life on His disciples, and He does the same to us. The breath of life is the Holy Spirit. Let's remember that even in our most desperate moment of need, the sweet Spirit comes and refreshes us and strengthens us.

**Fulori Bola**

# My Alarm Clock

*And seek not ye what ye shall eat, or what ye shall drink, neither be ye of doubtful mind. For all these things do the nations of the world seek after: and your Father knoweth that ye have need of these things. Luke 12:29, 30.*

ALARM CLOCKS are not for me! When I try to use them, either they don't work or they get broken, or I break them or don't hear them ringing. So every time I need to wake up early I ask God to wake me up, and He always wakes me up 15 to 20 minutes before the time I need to get up—extra time for my devotionals! You can be certain that God provides for it each day.

When I began to go to school in the mornings, my prayers included the request that I not sleep too much. God was waking me up each day. Months went by like this, until one day something different happened. That day two thirds of my grade in Portuguese would be decided. This was a day that I certainly couldn't miss class.

When I awoke, I couldn't believe the clock. I remember closing my eyes hard and opening them again to see if I had really seen correctly. In exactly 20 minutes class would start. And 20 minutes is exactly the time I needed for my devotional. God didn't wake me early that day!

I would like to say that I didn't get upset, although the two or three minutes of devotional that day demonstrated something to the contrary. In spite of this I decided not to say anything to God about my feelings—after all, who am I to be upset with God? But I was. Not even the 45 minutes that it took me to get to school was enough time for me to cheer up—although it usually takes an hour and a half.

When I reached the hallway near the classroom, I heard some classmates comment that this was the first time during the whole year that our professor was absent.

Well, imagine how ashamed I felt! We are more accustomed to a God who does great miracles, not a God who is sweet enough just to let us rest a little more!

I invite you to read Matthew's version of today's text (6:27-31). Jesus wants us to place complete trust in Him. God doesn't have to save us from disease for us to see that He is taking care of each of us. Sometimes it is very simple to notice, as simple as an alarm clock in the morning.

**Eline dos Reis Souza**

# Lilica's Jealousy

*Love is patient, love is kind. It does not envy, it does not boast,*
*it is not proud. 1 Cor. 13:4, NIV.*

ENVY IS SOMETHING impossible to explain, a bad feeling that hurts someone on the inside and leaves enormous scars. Unfortunately, every human being is tempted to fall into the valley of jealousy. When we give in to this evil, we feel emptiness within; our self-esteem becomes weak, and worthlessness sets in.

I was planting flowers when Brinda, a little poodle that likes to play, came up to me. She jumped and put her paws on me, showing that she was very happy that I had given her a little attention. Then my dog, Lilica, showed up and wasn't a bit happy that I was petting another animal. Not being able to control her jealousy, Lilica jumped to bite Brinda with all of her anger. Brinda had no alternative but to quickly escape.

I instantly learned a great lesson. At times I may be reacting like Lilica, letting my uncontrollable feelings speak much louder than reason. Unfortunately, humankind is like that—we are possessive of the things we have. We are jealous of our children, our husband, our grandparents, our friends. As incredible as it may seem, we don't want to share what we have with others because of the jealousy that governs us.

The only solution is the Word of God. If we pay attention to God's teaching, we will become stronger people in the moment of crisis.

I imagine our heavenly Father saying to me, "Dear daughter, why live like this? Have I not told you that My love is sufficient, that I care for you each day? Living your life filled with negative feelings is going to make you suffer."

The unfortunate fact is that in this sinful world we are surrounded by this emotion; even little animals are affected by jealousy.

We need to stop and think about what it means to have a holy, powerful Being willing to forgive the sins we commit. Having a God who identifies with us to the point of calling us His children is too wonderful for words!

*Lord, help me today to place my thoughts and emotions in Your hands so that they may be correct, according to Your will.*

**Célia de Paulo da Silva**

# Whose Face Is on Your Passport?

*They'll look on his face, their foreheads mirroring God.*
*Rev. 22:4, Message.*

THE LINE SNAKED toward the American Airlines counter as I patiently waited my turn. A friend and I were visiting another island and had arrived at the airport with plenty of time to spare. For once we didn't have to rush, and I felt really pleased with myself.

When I reached the counter, I greeted the attendant and handed her my passport. Her first question shocked me: "Whose picture is this?" When I leaned over to look at the passport, there was the face of my youngest son staring at me. My whole world seemed to turn upside down.

My friend had flown from the United States so that we could make this trip together. She would be disappointed if it were postponed. With all the illegal immigrants entering the country, here was I trying to travel with a passport belonging to a child. The attendant was gracious, however, and asked if I had any other identification.

By this time I was so embarrassed and nervous that I simply couldn't find anything in my wallet. Anxiously I searched through my bag with clumsy fingers until eventually I found my senior citizen ID. It must have been only a few minutes, but it seemed like an eternity, for several persons behind me were wating to check in. Finally the transactions were completed, and I was handed my boarding pass. I heaved a sigh of relief, but still couldn't relax. I had to be inspected by the immigration officer. Would he allow me to travel?

My friend and I spent the night at our destination, but I couldn't enjoy the trip. I kept wondering if I would be able to pass inspection on the way back home. Fortunately, everything went smoothly, and I could finally relax when I was seated on the plane to make the return trip home.

I had felt so confident when I had begun the trip. I was early. I had my travel documents (or so I thought). Everything was great until it was time to pass inspection. Many Christians are on the road to heaven. Some can even boast of having cast out devils and doing wondrous works in God's name. In spite of all the appearances and confidence, Jesus will be the one to inspect the documents. He will accept no other form of identification. It behooves us all to make our calling and election sure, for His stamp of approval must validate our passport for the trip to heaven.

**Candace Sprauve**

# Hallowed Field Trip

*For where two or three are gathered together in my name,*
*there am I in the midst of them. Matt. 18:20.*

FOR WEEKS MY HUSBAND and I had pondered plans for a church bulletin board—we'd take pictures of area churches, along with our thoughts on Matthew 18:20. Each time we planned to make the trip, though, something else took precedence. Finally flu recuperation gave reprieve for our hallowed rendezvous on a Thursday afternoon. Circling through our valley, we captured pictures of 19 respites nestled in the valley.

The churches stood quiet and serene, still hallowed by the Lord's presence lingering over the week. We listened to the silence, the birds, the streams, and an occasional human voice. Many different places to worship the same awesome God—brick ones, old ones, new ones, some made with old clapboards, some with stained-glass windows, some with little outhouses. Some had bell towers and steeples; one had a birdbath. One seemed to top the world, keeping watch over the valley. Some had marquee displays announcing events; some had flowering wreaths decorating the doors. Some had large air-conditioners awaiting the hostile summer heat; others had large windows that would waft the breezes. Some were in town; others stood solemn and graceful among the trees; and some marked manicured plots carved from pastures. One had cows fenced so close that a bellowing cow might be heard above the notes of a hymn. One had praying hands on the steeple; another had a dove; some had crosses of paint, stone, or wood. Some had picnic tables nestled close. One had scaffolding towering high; and a man in coveralls painted the frame of another. Most had gravestones pointing heavenward, pressed safely within God's hallowed ground, remembrances marking heroes of the faith.

Religious author Frederick Buechner penned some thoughts on churches that goes something like this: "Beneath these roofs we offer up the most precious moments of our lives, believing there is a God who will hallow those moments. . . . Here our wedding vows are spoken and sealed, our children are blessed, and we come here to bury our cherished dead. Somewhere in the midst of the silence and prayers and music, we listen for the voice of God and trust He will speak to us and bless us." This blessing is awaiting all of us each and every day.

**Judy Good Silver**

# Passing the First Time

*Commit to the Lord whatever you do, and your plans will succeed. Prov. 16:3, NIV.*

IT WAS ALMOST MY TURN to take the driving test at the transportation department, and I was very nervous. The necessary classes had been taken, but the general commentary of those waiting to take the test was that "passing the first time" was very difficult. The examination officer arrived, read the names of the individuals who would take the test with him, and then called the first name on the list. The remaining individuals stayed to observe. To add to our unease, some people were taking the test the second and third time.

We verified that the first individual who took the test hadn't passed. She hadn't even gone out to take the driving portion of the test. The second candidate also failed on the requirement regarding the ramp, which is one of the first items. Her test had ended right there. Finally my turn came, and I began my test. I got in the car and smiled at the examining officer. I completed the ramp portion, immediately followed by the parallel parking. However, I forgot the turn signal and lost three points. If I had four points deducted I would automatically fail. We went out for the second stage of this test. On the route outside of the transportation department all the traffic lights were green, which made the second portion very easy. God assured that this should happen, I'm convinced, because during the classes in the driving school this had never happened. Think about it—if just one light were red, considering my nervousness about being evaluated, I could have easily made an error, and then I would have failed.

At the end of the test the officer said, "Cristiane, in spite of the three points, you are able to drive. You have passed the first time."

During the entire time that I was waiting—and during the driving test—my husband was in his car praying that I would be successful.

When we ask God to bless our plans, they will work out. "To man belong the plans of the heart, but from the Lord comes the reply of the tongue" (Prov. 16:1, NIV). Believe it. Those who trust in the Lord and place their plans in His hands will find success and happiness.

**Cristiane Morais dos Santos**

50

# Take the Name of Jesus With You

*Let us therefore come boldly to the throne of grace, that we may obtain mercy and find grace to help in time of need. Heb. 4:16, NKJV.*

SIX COUPLES AND I GATHERED at Skip and Joni's home on Sunday evening to celebrate Valentine's Day. We had fun with games and delicious red-and-white heart-shaped desserts. But by 9:20 we were ready to go home. It had snowed lightly during the past four hours, and there were two inches on the ground. If I were at home looking out at the clean white snow reflecting the brightness of the full moon, a vision of heaven would have soothed my soul. But now it was a completely different matter—I was driving, and the roads were slick.

Driving home slowly, I was suddenly blinded by the glaring lights of a sheriff's car behind me. Realizing that I was the only one on the road, I pulled over and waited. *Dear God*, I prayed, *after such sweet spiritual fellowship, please don't curse me with a ticket*. My thoughts raced to Proverbs 3:5: "Trust in the Lord with all thine heart; and lean not unto thine own understanding." *This verse is enough for me now*, I told myself as I waited.

Approaching my car window, the officer asked for my driver's license and registration. Then it was time to beg. "Sir," I pleaded humbly, "could you please open the back door of my car and pass me my handbag?" When I looked in my wallet, the spot where I keep the cards was blank. Thoughts of an $80 ticket blinded my focus. I exuded confusion. The sheriff's roaming flashlight highlighted the picture of Jesus I've carried for years over my driver's license, and I felt the peace that only the face of Jesus can bring me.

The officer watched my fruitless search, then said gently, "My reason for stopping you is simply to advise you to drive slowly. Our purpose is prevention and not recovery under these conditions. Go 25 miles an hour or less." Politely I thanked him and drove home, knowing that it was the picture of Jesus that had made the difference.

Being stopped by that sheriff turned out to be a blessing. Two days later I flew to Maryland. Without the sheriff's intervention, I would have gone to the airport a half hour away from home lacking the identification I needed for security clearance. But God in His grace had taken care of me days before.

**Marian Holder**

# Prayer Is the Answer

*Ask, and it shall be given you; seek, and ye shall find;*
*knock, and it shall be opened unto you. Matt. 7:7.*

YEARNING TO TAKE A TRIP to see my godchild (the son of my lifelong girlfriend), who had just been diagnosed with prostate cancer, I realized that I was financially strapped. My credit cards were maxed out, and I had no disposable cash. I couldn't afford the trip. With tears streaming down my cheeks, I knelt to ask my God to help me. *O dear Lord,* I pleaded, *You know how sick Ricardo is. I really need to see him. I would hate for him to think I'm ignoring him. Please, Lord, I beg You, make a way for me to visit him.*

And then I suddenly remembered something: I had flown to our church's worldwide conference in St. Louis, Missouri, the year before. It had been a wonderful though expensive experience, and I had been inspired. But coming back from the conference was a completely different story.

Making my last connection in Atlanta, I discovered that there were too many passengers trying to get to the place I needed to be. I chose to give up my seat. The grateful airline representatives gave me a voucher, which, they explained, I could use on a later flight. This happened two times more. Finally, exhausted but happy, I got home. The airline had given me enough money for a round-trip ticket to anywhere I wanted to go in the United States.

But I hadn't remembered that incident until my God reminded me on my knees that day. I asked, and God had answered my prayer months before I had even known what to ask for.

With a light heart I hurried to the airport to consult with the representatives. "Yes," they told me, "you have enough funds to purchase a ticket." I couldn't stop praising the Lord. Now I could fly to see my godchild.

When I saw my godson recovering from the treatment, I couldn't help saying, "What a mighty God we serve!" I thanked God for Ricardo's health, and for reminding me that all we have to do is trust Him.

*Thank You, Father, for the power of prayer, for helping me to understand that You know the end from the beginning, and for strengthening my faith and blessing me and those I love.*

**G. G. (Geneva Gwendolyn) Taylor**

# Taking Advantage of the 80 Percent

*Beloved, let us love one another, for love is of God; and everyone who loves is born of God and knows God. 1 John 4:7, NKJV.*

ONE HUSBAND HAS SOME excellent advice to give to lovers, young and old alike. He believes that if couples are open-minded and generous in spirit they will likely see their partners live up to about 80 percent of their expectations. But what about the other 20 percent, you ask? Well, we can make it our business to chip away at it throughout life without seeing much change in behavior. Or we may choose to thoroughly embrace the 80 percent, and both will be happy.

As the years have come and gone I see so much truth in this principle. There are rich rewards in being willing to accept differences while being thankful for what one receives. A good rule of thumb is to attempt to give more that you expect to receive; you're likely to be happy the majority of the time. And from someone who celebrated 50 years of Valentine's Days this year, I can tell you that the more you give, the more you get, in terms of a loving relationship.

My husband began giving me roses on Valentine's Day when I was 15 years old. We were high school students, and he managed to hitchhike to the nearest small town to get a haircut and a yellow rose corsage for me. I was speechless when he came to the dorm lobby to present his sweet offering. But I must have made him feel appreciated, because he's given me roses on every Valentine's Day since.

One year I was sure I wouldn't see a rose. I felt a bit sorry for him because he had such a good record going. But that year we were involved in ministry in the former Soviet Union, and it was snowing and bitterly cold. I doubted that there was a rose to be found in all of Moscow, but he spread the word to some of the younger members of the team, and they came through! While enjoying our evening meal in the seminary cafeteria, a young red-faced man came bursting into the room with a bouquet of deep-red roses. Mission accomplished! So let's live our lives with a grateful heart. Let's make thanksgiving a habit every day and take advantage of the 80 percent!

**Rose Otis**

# Passing On God's Comfort

*Who comforts us in all our troubles, so that we can comfort those in any trouble with the comfort we ourselves have received from God. 2 Cor. 1:4, NIV.*

MY PASTOR WAS VISITING ME in the hospital. "Are you ready to die?" she asked me. Even though I knew I was very sick I hadn't thought about dying. I was concentrating only on living and what the next step would be in that process. But I knew that I could say, "Yes, I know I've a Savior. I know that I've asked Him to take control of my life, and I know I've accepted His gift of salvation. I'm ready to meet my Jesus in heaven." She prayed with me, and I felt calm and comforted.

I had previously asked the pastor to have an anointing service for me. After some songs, Bible verses, and the prayers, I felt such comfort and peace. I was able to prepare for my stay in the hospital and the treatment I would be receiving for the cancer I had.

About this time two friends, who had gone to school with me, were also battling cancer. Both of them were as much prayed for as I was, but they both died. My treatment was successful. Each day I was getting better. I marveled at modern medicine. I marveled at how "fearfully and wonder-fully" we are made (Ps. 139:14). I wondered, "Why am I getting better? Why am I healing and others haven't been healed? What does God have in mind for my purpose on earth?"

One day I was encouraging a friend who was facing some difficult times. As we were talking I mentioned my questions about why the prayers for me had been answered. Her reply will go with me the rest of my life: "Carol, what you are doing for me right now is what God wants you to do—and there is even a verse in the Bible to remind you. God has com-forted you. It is your responsibility to pass on that hope and peace." That was it—sharing the comfort God had given me.

As I look back now, I realize how very sick I had been. I had been living from one blood transfusion to the next. But I wasn't worried. I had a peace that I couldn't explain.

I pray that we all will have that "peace of God, which transcends all under-standing" (Phil. 4:7, NIV), and that we will be able to pass it on to others.

**Carol Nicks**

# My Gift From Grandma

*I will bless the Lord at all times: his praise shall continually*
*be in my mouth. Ps. 34:1.*

MY GREAT-GRANDPARENTS lived on a plantation as slaves; therefore, my grandmother wasn't privileged to attend school, so she couldn't read. As soon as I learned to read, Grandma would ask me to read to her. She was thrilled as she listened to me read Bible stories, and I was fascinated at the way she explained Bible truths to me. At that early age she taught me of the love of God and His Son, Jesus.

One day Grandma asked, "Ollie, could you teach me some verses from Psalm 34?"

"Oh, sure, Grandma," I answered. "Let's begin right now."

I read the words to her, and she repeated them again and again until she knew them from memory. We were both happy and proud. When I was 7, Grandma taught me that God loves and cares for us. This incredible gift Grandma gave me has been my bulwark throughout my adult life.

A few days ago this wonderful legacy shone brilliantly through an interesting experience. About five minutes after returning home from the bank at which I had made some transactions, the telephone rang.

"May I speak with Mrs. Lindo?" the caller inquired.

"This is Mrs. Lindo speaking," I answered.

The unfamiliar voice continued, "Mrs. Lindo, we have your wallet with your documents here at the bank. Could you come by to pick them up?"

I was totally confused. How could someone have my documents that I thought were safe in my purse? Nervously I lost no time in returning to the bank. When I entered the bank office, the manager handed me my wallet. "Someone turned it in to the secretary," he explained.

I graciously thanked the manager and lifted a silent prayer of gratitude to my heavenly Father for His love to me in taking care of my wallet containing all my identifications papers, credit cards, and insurance and health cards. If these had fallen into dishonest hands or become lost, it would have caused me severe difficulties.

Remember, my sister, wherever you are, whoever you are, whatever your situation, God's love reaches, enfolds, and includes you.

**Olga Corbin de Lindo**

# Rest Awhile

*Come ye yourselves apart into a desert place, and rest a while. Mark 6:31.*

I WAS SICK—really sick. And I asked, *Why, Lord? Don't I try to obey all the health rules and try to be an example to others of what the health rules can do for one when obeyed?*

We had been to Florida for a week, and the weather was very unpredictable. It was cold and windy, then sunny and warm. When I began to feel ill, we drove back to Calhoun, Georgia, where my daughter practices medicine. She diagnosed my condition as bronchitis and gave me the proper medications and ordered bed rest. We went to our home in Tennessee, where a friend brought in meals for us because I was too sick to get out of bed. I felt terribly guilty—aren't we admonished to work in God's vineyard? And so I grumbled and whined, much to my husband's dismay, until I remembered the admonition by Jesus to His disciples in today's text.

Now I must rest. I've time to study my Bible study guides leisurely instead of spending a few minutes before bolting out the door to the office. Now I've time to gaze upon the picture of Christ on the cross on the front of my lesson and try to internalize the greatness of His sacrifice, the depth of His love for me—an undeserving servant but beloved child nevertheless.

Now I can pray—on my knees, while sitting, while lying in the bed—for my children and grandchildren, my siblings, and all their loved ones, all the people on our women's prayer circle list, for the school where we live on campus, for the staff and students, and for all the people of the world who need Jesus.

Also, I've time to listen to some beautiful tapes of poems and songs made by our now-deceased friend, Rowena Rogers. She prepared these tapes, "Thoughts of Comfort," for the residents of the nursing home that she and her husband operated, that emphasize faith, trust, meditation, hope, and peace. Rowena provided these beautiful sources of comfort to anyone who requested them, without cost. And now I'm enjoying them again myself.

I'm eagerly looking forward to returning to my work, but I've been blessed by my period of rest. Do you, too, need to "rest a while"?

**Rubye Sue**

# Packing Dilemma

*Blessed are those who trust in the Lord, whose trust is the Lord.*
*Jer. 17:7, NRSV.*

IT HAD BEEN A MAJOR DECISION for me to put my house on the market, sell it, and buy a condo. My husband had died four years before, and it was time to downsize and move on with my life.

My house sold more quickly than I thought it would; of course, there were the usual inspections to go through, and it would be about six weeks before the closing. My real estate broker thought I should wait to pack, just to make sure the contract wouldn't be rejected because of the inspections or the bank. But just in case, I decided to begin packing anyway—and was I ever glad I did!

Before I knew how quickly my house would sell, I had committed myself to stay with my grandson, Christopher, while his parents were away for about a week. Fortunately, I could fly from Florida to Michigan instead of driving, so that would allow me a couple more days at home to pack.

When I returned home 10 days later, I was a bit overwhelmed with all I had to do. I had a women's Bible study meeting at my home each week, and I asked them to pray about my dilemma. Immediately one of the women offered her assistance. My friend Norma said she would come to help me after school and on Sundays. I needed boxes, and Norma scoured the school and local stores for more and more boxes. Each time she came her van was full of boxes. I had sold many items, but I still had more to dispose of in some way. About that time Norma's church was having a yard sale for the Hurricane Katrina victims. So after we unloaded boxes, we reloaded her van with many items for the sale.

The Lord was so good. The boxes were packed in time, and people were helped from the items sold, items I didn't need anymore.

When we finished packing the last boxes just before the movers came, we had just enough boxes. No extra, and no shortage. The Lord is so gracious and benevolent!

"I sought the Lord, and he answered me, and delivered me from all my fears" (Ps. 34:4, NRSV). He will do the same for you today.

**Patricia Mulraney Kovalski**

# Serendipity

*But he said to me, "My grace is sufficient for you."*
*2 Cor. 12:9, NIV.*

I RECENTLY MOVED across the nation from a pleasant retirement complex in Loma Linda, California, to a small townhouse in Cleveland, Tennessee. I had thought I would never move again, but after the death of my first husband, and then my second, I wanted to spend my remaining years close to my three daughters, who now live just minutes away from me. More than I could have ever dreamed, they have lovingly anticipated my needs, helped me through each challenge, included me in every family get-together, and continually blessed me with little surprises.

One day my eldest daughter and I went to the local shopping mall. My watch had stopped, and I needed to replace the battery. As my daughter shopped in a department store, I found a jewelry store only a few feet away in the mall. "My battery is dead," I said, smiling at the amiable clerk. He examined my watch, raised his eyebrows, and announced, "That will be $12.95."

I gave him the nod, and he left to replace the battery. I had my debit card ready to give him when he returned. "There won't be any charge for you today," he smiled broadly. My mouth dropped open. I wasn't prepared for such unexpected kindness and protested, pushing my card closer to him. But his warmth was genuine, and all I could say was "Thank you. Thank you so very much!"

I've pondered that act of serendipity by that kind store clerk. It has reminded me of the many times my children have showered me with their deeds of affection and the numerous ways my heavenly Father surprises me with His own special unexpected gifts of love. I want more than anything else to tell Him, "Thank You. Thank You so very much!"

The only way I know to do that is to live each day of my life as He would have me live; to give my heart to Him, my best friend and Savior. It is all He has ever asked of me. God's unconditional love—serendipity in its purest form! Isn't that just another name for His overwhelming grace? Undeserved, unmerited, unlimited—it is truly sufficient for our every need.

**Lorraine Hudgins-Hirsch**

# Lavished With His Love

*How great is the love the Father has lavished on us. 1 John 3:1, NIV.*

AS I UNFOLDED THE INVITATION I gasped with surprise. We had been invited to a special marriage retreat for church leaders. It was to be a gift for us. That would have been special enough, but the retreat was at one of the most luxurious hotels in England. As a little girl I would drive past the Welcombe Hotel with my family, see the beautiful gardens, and wonder what it was like inside. My parents would talk about the hotel with a sense of awe, and I dreamed of being able to go there one day when I was all grown up.

And now we were being invited to the hotel as a gift, with nothing to pay! Many of the other couples would have no idea about the quality of the hotel. To them it was just a name on a piece of paper. But I knew how special the gift was, and that added to my sense of excitement—and also to my curiosity. Why such a venue? We would have felt pampered in a Comfort Inn!

The hotel was everything I had imagined. The rooms were gorgeous, the menus were sumptuous and creative, and the food was exquisitely presented. Nothing was too much trouble for the staff. We could have anything we wished.

We savored every moment and felt so special. During one of the seminars the speaker said, "You may have wondered why we have brought all of you church leaders to this hotel. Well, we know that many of you put your needs at the bottom of the pile. So often you make do with less than second best. You buy your clothes in thrift shops and hardly ever have the chance to eat out together. So we wanted to show you how much God thinks of you, and how much He loves you. Even all of this doesn't begin to express how much He appreciates what you do, and the value He places on you and your relationships and your ministry."

Tears came to my eyes as I realized that these two days of sheer luxury were a gift to show us God's love and grace. In that moment all the struggles, pain, and sadness we had ever encountered in our ministry were soothed and comforted; and even to this day, when the demands of ministry seem overwhelming, I remember the Welcombe Hotel and the way God welcomes me into a place of grace and luxury with Him, to show me how special I am to Him.

**Karen Holford**

# The Need to Pray

*The hour has come for you to wake up from your slumber,
because our salvation is nearer now than when we first believed.
Rom. 13:11, NIV.*

IT WAS TIME ONCE MORE for the women of the university to go
on a retreat. We had decided this time to do what we greatly needed:
have a prayer retreat.

The theme "If My People Pray" was chosen to remind us of God's
promise that if we humble ourselves and pray, confess our sins, and seek
His face, He will hear us and heal our land (2 Cor. 7:14). But the devil was
at work. Some members of the retreat planning committee couldn't continue because of illness. The rest of us on the committee disagreed on the
intensity of prayer in the program, and I, as acting women's ministries
leader, felt overwhelmed by this confusion. I needed much time in prayer
for guidance and strength.

Then I remembered that Jesus Himself took time to pray for refresh-
ment and empowerment every day. If Jesus, the God of this universe, felt
His need for God, how much more would I, a frail human, need God? This
was a testing moment for me. While reading Randy Maxwell's book in
preparation for this retreat, I had been encouraged by the experiences
shared. I needed to be humble and spend time in prayer and seek God's
presence continuously. I started praying for unity and humility. God has
been so real and kind to me. I've gained much since joining women's ministries, and I praise God that He has used other women on this campus to
help me see my gift and how to use it to God's glory.

The day for the retreat eventually came. The center was full. Prayer was
the focus, and the speaker helped us with spiritual formation, beginning
with Scripture journaling and meditation. To help us with meditation, a
university artist blessed us with fine artwork.

Yes, the devil knows that he has little time. He wanted to spoil this retreat, but I praise God that He is victorious and He gives us victory. We
were all united, and we all witnessed God at work in our lives.

I learned that the work I need to do most is to pray. God has rightfully
said that the time has come for us to wake from our slumber because our
salvation is nearer now than when we first believed. Let us continue to
spend time with our Lord in prayer.

**Loretta Botong**

# Heaven Is My Goal

*Pay close attention now: I'm creating new heavens and a new earth. All the earlier troubles, chaos, and pain are things of the past, to be forgotten. Isa. 65:17, Message.*

DURING A TRIP TO PERU our tour group visited the famous Inca ruins, Machu Picchu, in the heart of the beautiful Andes Mountains. Upon arriving by train in Aqua Caliente from Cusco, we took a bus up the mountain to the ruins. After several hours of sightseeing, we enjoyed a tasty meal and again boarded a bus for our trip down the mountain.

This road, the same one on which we traveled up the mountain, was no ordinary road. It zigzagged its way down the mountain with switchback after switchback. Near the top of the mountain a young sandal-footed Inca lad stood at the side of the road, waving to us and greeting us in his native tongue. As we proceeded down the mountain and rounded a switchback, lo and behold, there he was again. Then we saw him take off on a dead run down the mountain only to have him greet us again when we got directly below the place we had seen him the last time. After about the fourth encounter, the bus driver stopped the bus and invited him in to ride the short distance left to reach our destination.

His tenaciousness, agility, and speed amazed us. Beads of perspiration stood out on his face and neck, and he breathed rapidly. He strode through the bus collecting coins and goodies until his pouch was overflowing from the generosity of the tourists. His courteous *gracias* could be heard after receiving each gift.

Many of the Inca Indian families are poor, and their children share in providing their livelihood. Evidently this young man's need served to set the goal for his intentional actions.

Goals are important. Without them we often allow unimportant issues, events, and activities to distract us.

Heaven is my goal, and I must pursue it as earnestly as the Inca boy pursued his. Allowing Christ to live out his life within me needs to be my daily pursuit. The results will be a much greater reward than coins and goodies, which are consumable and last for only a short time.

The gift of heaven is eternal. Oh, how I want to be there! Don't you?

**Marian M. Hart**

# "Blessons" From my Rosebush

*See how the lilies of the field grow. They do not labor or spin. Yet I tell you that not even Solomon in all his splendor was dressed like one of these. Matt. 6:28, 29, NIV.*

"BLESSON" is a word that surfaced in contemporary religious circles recently, particularly in women's circles. It hasn't yet graced our dictionaries, but its meaning is clear. It's a blend of both a blessing and a lesson. I got a series of "blessons" from a rosebush experience recently.

A beautiful person blessed me with a rosebush as a birthday gift. I'm usually very good at nurturing plants, but in less than a month this one was almost on its last leg. Discouraged, I took it from the office to care for it at my house. I repotted it, gave it new earth, watered it, put it in the sun. Even though I talked to it lovingly, I could see no improvement. Finally I gave up and put the pot in the yard among other plants and left it alone.

Blesson number one: Let go, and let God work.

One year later I was literally stopped in my tracks as I walked past the plant. There on the bush were several beautiful red buds. I couldn't restrain myself. I jumped for joy in the summer sunshine! Then I became even more conscientious: I weeded around it some more, making sure that I gave it as much water as it needed.

Blesson number two: God's got it; worry not.

Our Father tells us that He cares about us more than He does the lilies of the field and the birds of the air. They worry not (Matt. 6:25-34) why should we? Why do I?

I habitually worry about a great many things. Where will I live? How should I travel? What should I do about work, school, friends, family, and finances? Where should I go? I ask these, and other, questions time and time again, and God always answers.

I've often thought about the two "blessons" behind that rosebush experience, but there's a bigger third: God cares about every aspect of my being. When I cast worry aside, my trust in Christ increases, and then, like the patriarch Moses, I realize that I must take off my shoes, because the place where I'm standing is holy ground. God is there.

*Lord, please help me let go and let You take complete control of all my life. Help me to learn from each "blesson" You send me.*

Nivischi Ngozi Edwards

# Lessons From a Kitten

*Cast all your anxiety on him because he cares for you. 1 Peter 5:7, NIV.*

I REALLY LIKED MICHE; she was a faithful cat companion and friend during my childhood. Unfortunately, just before she turned 14, she died. I realize that I learned many things with this little cat that I had the privilege of living with for many years.

Miche, an excellent and dedicated mother, cared for her kittens very well. Once, while she cared for her seven kittens, one went away to play near some clay roof tile. Noise was all that we heard, but when we reached the location we found that a roof tile had fallen on the head of her little kitten, injuring it seriously. Promptly we returned it to the basket where the other kittens were sleeping on the terrace in the back of the house.

My sister and I were children and didn't know what first aid to offer. Miche didn't go far from the kitten and walked from one side to the other, meowing frequently. She stopped beside the injured little kitten and licked it, as though she were saying, "It's OK; Mommy is here!"

My father arrived from work to eat lunch, and Miche stayed close to him, meowing the entire time. Since my father didn't pay any attention, she went to the terrace, got the kitten by the neck, and put it at my father's feet. She was asking for help!

Touched by her action, he interrupted his lunch, picked up the little kitten, and cared for its injuries. As the days passed, the kitten's injuries healed.

Many times we go through doubtful paths in our life without realizing the danger that surrounds us. Then we are hit by roof tiles from the enemy, which come at unexpected times. Wounds and weakness afflict us, and we have no strength to get up.

But the Lord is near. We need only to let Him take us by the hand and lead us to a safe place. He treats our wounds, our spiritual bruises, and our emotional fractures, and gathers the pieces of our broken heart. It's as though He were telling us, "It's OK; I'm here!"

Then we can stand up and continue our journey, trusting in the certainty that He is by our side. We just need to be close to Him; we just need to give our life to Him; we just need to walk in the paths that He has shown us.

It is marvelous to know that we have a God who is so attentive!

**Juliane P. de Oliveira Caetano**

# The Blizzard

*For I the Lord thy God will hold thy right hand,*
*saying unto thee, Fear not; I will help thee. Isa. 41:13.*

I AWOKE AT 4:00 A.M. and peeked out the window, hoping the forecast of the evening before was wrong. But no, it was right. There was a blizzard in progress, and the ground was covered in about 10 inches of snow!

Since I'm petrified of falling in the snow, I prefer to deal with it on the first day, before it turns icy. So I decided to find a way to work by public transportation. That would mean leaving home early, no later than 5:30. Devotions and a check with mass transit were top priorities. Sure enough, the transit company reported that no buses were running. I would have to take the subway for three stops and walk 10 blocks.

I committed my fear of falling to God and made a request for help in getting to work. Then I walked cautiously one block to the subway. Just as I was about to enter the subway, a bus appeared, seemingly out of nowhere! But because of the deep snow—and my fear—I couldn't make it across the street fast enough. I missed the bus that wasn't supposed to be running. Turning back to the subway entrance, I was surprised to see another bus coming. This time I made it across the street and thanked the driver.

My travel would be six blocks on this bus; then a change to another bus would take me within one block of my destination. As we arrived at the first stop, there was the other bus. The bus driver stopped in the middle of the street and allowed me to cross to the other bus. Hallelujah! I was on my way. On reaching my destination, I said a prayer of thanksgiving and walked gingerly the one block to my workplace.

A coworker asked how I had gotten to work. I told him of my two-bus trip. "No," he said, "no bus is running on that route. One bus came and traveled on the snow route four blocks."

"But I came on the regular route," I replied. He seemed baffled, and continued to insist that he had traveled on the bus and had had to walk four blocks. I knew that I had come on the regular route, and thanked God for providing transportation at the right time and place. God had said, "Fear not; I'm with you." He had been—and He does.

**Maureen O. Burke**

# The Lost Letter

*She calls together her friends and neighbors, saying, "Rejoice with me, for I have found . . . which I had lost." Luke 15:8, 9, RSV.*

IT IS NOT A PLEASANT EXPERIENCE to lose something. My dear friend and I grew up in the same church together and attended the same school. Our families camped together. We played together and always enjoyed each other's company. As we grew up and married, our ways parted as we went in different directions. We lost contact with each other for a number of years; then finally I met her again.

Her husband had passed away after a short illness. She was lonely and needed support and comfort. To choose the right words to express sympathy is not always easy in situations such as these. Nevertheless, I tried to cheer her by sending her letters, poems, cards, and articles of encouragement on a regular basis. I also invited her to join our women's group functions.

When she attended a prayer breakfast one Sunday morning, I handed her a letter. She left as I was busy in the hall.

Monday evening the phone rang. She sounded upset. She had looked all over for her letter, but it was nowhere to be found. She appealed to me to please check the women's room at the hall where she had changed her shoes. The letter must have fallen out of her handbag without her noticing it.

I knew there was a very slim chance of finding it, as there had been so many women present. Whoever picked up the letter could have seen the name and handed it over to someone else who had the same name and initial in our church. This letter was personal, and I worried it would get into the wrong hands. On Tuesday evening I was back at the hall, looking, and asking everyone if they had picked up a letter. My concern knew no bounds; it was all I could speak about. Wednesday evening the phone rang. The letter had been found and was in safe hands. I was overjoyed! I told all my friends and neighbors that the lost letter was found.

It makes me think of what happens in heaven when a lost daughter of God is found. Oh, what rejoicing! We are each so personal and so valuable to God!

**Priscilla E. Adonis**

# On Stepping Back

*Now I will rescue you and make you both a symbol and a source of blessing. Zech. 8:13, NLT.*

IT HAD BECOME an unspoken tradition. Each time I traveled to the neighboring state during daylight hours, I would stop at a quaint little Italian bakery where they made the most delicious focaccia bread—the kind laden with fresh red and green peppers, green olives, and Vidalia onions, the kind that needed no advertising when the bakers took it out of the oven.

I had managed to shorten my last appointment. Now I had the time to stop by the bakery for the mouthwatering treat. When I got there, the bread hadn't yet come out of the oven, and the waiting queue was growing.

*I will wait,* I promised myself, knowing that my girlfriends were secretly hoping for the bread. Then the door flew open, and a windswept woman rushed in. "I'm late, but I have to buy the bread. I have to jump the line." She moved to stand right in front of me.

Without thinking, I stepped back, allowing her to take my place. I could hear the horrified whispers of the other patrons. One woman even murmured loud enough for everyone to hear, "There is a line, you know."

Then a charming silver-haired woman asked (more statement than query), "You're a Christian, aren't you?" Her statement made my unthinking action seem worthwhile, even if I were to get no bread.

It's not often that I get to see the immediate, positive rewards of my actions, but I'm grateful when they do come into view. I think Ellen G. White penned a powerful line when she wrote, "No one can give place in his own heart and life for the stream of God's blessing to flow to others, without receiving in himself a rich reward" (*Thoughts From the Mount of Blessing*, p. 81).

Sharing the focaccia bread with my friends later that day, I regaled them with the story of its purchase. They too reminded me of the blessings that acts of kindness reap both in this world and the one to come. I felt rewarded, and all I did was step back!

*Thank You, Lord, for using Your grace to develop in me traits of character that will refine and enrich my life.*

**Glenda-mae Greene**

# Hohenzollern Castle

*Know ye not that ye are the temple of God,*
*and that the Spirit of God dwelleth in you? 1 Cor. 3:16.*

PERCHED HIGH UP on a cone-shaped mountain is the Hohenzollern Castle, just outside the little town of Hechingen, Germany, where I live. With its high walls, towers, and drawbridges in medieval style, it is a beautiful and imposing sight. It houses three chapels, an armory, state rooms, and the private apartments of the Hohenzollern family.

Tourists from all over the world come to visit and admire the castle as well as the 360-degree view over the surrounding hills, towns, and villages of the Swuabian Alps. Each summer a drama group presents a Shakespeare play in the castle courtyard. In December a medieval Christmas market attracts people from all over.

On weekend nights the castle is illuminated. It is a beautiful sight, sometimes half hidden in mist. In the dark, under a full moon, it is a special sight. The silhouette in the early-morning light is impressive too. At sundown the windows reflect the golden light of the setting sun. Because it is a landmark that can be seen from far away, we are on the lookout for "our" castle. When we see it, we know that we are nearing home.

When the head of the Hohenzollern family is in residence, a huge flag with the family emblem flies high up on one of the towers. Nobody lives in the castle permanently—it is just too cold and humid up there. Sometimes the top of the mountain is hidden in misty clouds for days on end. Prince George Friedrich, great-grandson of the last German kaiser, sometimes comes up for a weekend. He would be the kaiser now if it hadn't been abolished in 1918.

I was on my way to church one morning when I looked up to the castle, as I always do, and saw the flag flying. A thought struck me: Everybody can see the flag showing that the prince is in residence. How can people see that the Holy Spirit is living within me? Do I invite the Spirit each morning to dwell in me? It is nice to see the castle any day. But it is a special feeling when you see that the family flag is up. We might be quite agreeable people by ourselves, but what a difference it makes when God's Spirit is in residence in us!

Let us invite the Holy Spirit to dwell in us today. He is waiting for our invitation.

**Hannele Ottschofski**

# Patience and Impatience

*Knowing this, that the trying of your faith worketh patience.*
*But let patience have her perfect work, that ye may be perfect*
*and entire, wanting nothing. James 1:3, 4.*

BEING A MINISTER'S WIFE can be a lonely path to walk at times. Frequent moves away from family and friends, transferring to different churches or countries, trying to find new friends, often being home alone, struggling to learn a new language if the move is to another country, or just trying to find a job can be difficult and frustrating. This has exactly been my situation—as well as the experience of many other ministers' wives to whom I've talked.

Why would God allow me to feel lonely when I'm trying to do His work? I should be bubbling over with joy—isn't this supposed to be an exciting experience? At least that is what I had been led to believe. Now I'm once again faced with a new experience and new challenges. I again have an opportunity to meet new people, to learn a new language, and to get used to a different culture. But who really likes change? They say change is good, but I say *not so often!* All of us have felt lonely at some time, so I'm not alone—I'm just lonely. There is a difference.

Abraham is set forth as an example for us to imitate. He patiently endured. He eventually obtained the promise in the birth of Isaac (Heb. 6:15). Because this Christian race is a lifelong experience, it calls for patience and perseverance—perseverance in the face of successive difficulties and disappointments, and patience to await the reward that is promised at the end of the course.

My friend, if you are experiencing a change in your life today, don't dread loneliness anymore, because God is your sustainer and companion. Claim the promise of Isaiah 41:10: "Fear thou not; for I am with thee: be not dismayed; for I am thy God: I will strengthen thee; yea, I will help thee; yea, I will uphold thee with the right hand of my righteousness." I'm sure that you, as well as I, have claimed this promise many times. I know I shall continue to do so.

*Help me, Lord, to be patient, knowing that You will supply all my needs.*
*Help me to look to You for strength to overcome every difficulty and to endure*
*to the end. It is so good to know that when I move You are still always there.*

**Shelly-Ann Patricia Zabala**

# Awaiting His Coming

*Behold, I come quickly: blessed is he that keepeth the sayings of the prophecy of this book. Rev. 22:7.*

MY HEART WAS BEATING RAPIDLY. My cheeks couldn't hide the glow. My husband was on his way home. After a week of being separated, I was filled with anticipation. I hurried to get my chores and errands done. He was coming home! I was going to see him again. My mind couldn't focus. I was too excited. I couldn't stop the happiness in my heart.

In anticipation of his return, I made his favorite meal, all with the hopes of his knowing how much I had missed him. Candles burned, lending a welcoming and comfortable atmosphere as I stood by the door waiting to see the car come into the garage. I checked the clock again and again, making sure that I would not miss his entrance. Even through the obstacles and chores I faced that day, my heart was overjoyed.

In a similar manner I'm preparing myself for the second coming of my Savior, Jesus Christ. I don't know when or at what time He will be here, but His coming should be really soon. I love Him and want to be with Him. To show Him how much I love Him, I want Him to find me prepared and waiting. In preparing for His return, I can also help prepare others. By sharing all that He has done for me and by telling how He sacrificed Himself so that I could be free, I hope to attract others to Him. I owe Him my life, and He continues to give me liberty. He left His book, the Bible, that I use as my reference on how to be prepared. If I'm not careful to accept the leading of His Spirit, I can miss His entrance. In the meantime, He has left His Spirit to counsel me and comfort me so that I'm never alone. He loves me, and He is returning soon. I've a glow on my cheeks that I cannot hide. He is coming back to take me home.

To someone who really does not know my Jesus, the wait might seem to be too long to bear. They may wonder why He is taking so long. However, He has never broken a promise to me, so I trust Him completely. Everything He has said, He has done. He has promised that He is coming back for me, and I've no doubt in my mind that He will do just that.

Are you preparing for His arrival as well? The waiting isn't always easy—there are many things to do, and life can be hectic. But I trust Him. Won't you?

**Diantha Hall-Smith**

# Fight the Good Fight

*Be sober, be vigilant; because your adversary the devil walks about like a roaring lion, seeking whom he may devour.*
*1 Peter 5:8, NKJV.*

**WHAT IS THAT?** I wondered. I felt my skin quiver and my flesh tingle as I gazed at the creature. My first thought was that it was a snake. But as I calmed down somewhat I realized it was a very large lizard, a very healthy-looking lizard about a foot long. And I didn't want it in my master bedroom!

I knew there was no need for me to call out for help, because I was the only help I had. So I thought quickly and decided to close all the doors to the area and then get my flashlight so I could see if it ran beneath or behind the furniture. Also, I would get my broom to hold it down—and oh, yes, a container of some kind to put over it. I didn't want to kill it—I just wanted it out of my house *now!*

The lizard turned out to be a feisty fellow despite the fact that it really was small, at least compared to me. Nevertheless, it opened its jaws wide and snapped at the approaching broom. I really needed everything I had gathered in preparation for the battle. It scurried from place to place in a desperate attempt to get away from me.

Fortunately, I finally trapped it under the straw end of my broom; then carefully but firmly I dragged it to an open area on the floor, where I was able to trap it under a wastepaper basket. By easing a dustpan beneath the wastepaper basket, I was able to move lizard, basket, and dustpan to the closest outside door, where I released it.

I watched the lizard for a few moments, but it didn't move. So I poked at it with the broom handle. It turned toward the broomstick, and its mouth snapped wide open in defiance. Yes, it was alive and apparently unhurt. Soon it seemed to realize it was outside and safe, and it hurried away.

After the ordeal ended, I asked myself, *Do I work as hard and diligently to rid my spiritual house of sin?* Yes, Satan loves to snap and roar at all of us. And yes, he is still very much alive. But, thank God, in dealing with Satan I can call on heaven for help. This will be one struggle in which I'm not alone.

**Mildred C. Williams**

# Sunrise of Hope

*While we wait for the blessed hope—the glorious appearing of our great God and Savior, Jesus Christ. Titus 2:13, NIV.*

AS THE SUN MEETS THE HORIZON golden rays cast a shimmering pathway across the calm sea. Fluffy clouds, touched with tinges of soft pink and mauve, hang beneath the blue sky, and in the distance a white lighthouse high up on the rocks reflects the first glow of daybreak.

Let your imagination rest on this peaceful scene as I explain that this picture hangs on the wall facing my bed, and is the first thing I see when I awake. To add a final touch and give a most powerful and meaningful message, the words "There is hope" are written beneath.

When my daughter gave me the picture some time ago, she didn't know how much encouragement I would draw from those words. When discouragement and disappointment hurt us, hope can quickly turn to despair.

Often we experience events in our daily lives that can appear hopeless to us. We think our cry for help goes unheard. At least that's the way I felt when I tried to lose weight. Everything had become an effort. My health suffered, and I was sick of hearing that I was overweight. While I knew there was a need to make an effort myself, I desired some encouragement and support. So last year I took up the challenge, and with God's help my 229 pounds (104 kilograms) have been reduced to 160 (73), and my dilemma has turned into victory.

Challenges in life, such as my weight, become insignificant when we compare them with the hopelessness suffered by many of our brothers and sisters in many parts of the world. Sin and sadness are wrought of Satan, and he plans to destroy and discourage wherever he can.

Working with the bereaved brings me close to people whose hopes have been crushed by death. When a husband struggles without his wife, or a mother becomes entombed in darkness by the side of an empty crib, sadness can be overwhelming, for, alas, many don't believe in the blessed hope that Jesus gives and are left without comfort or strength to draw from.

This morning I paused to look at my new Bible study lesson. Pictured on the cover are three empty crosses on the hill of Golgotha, silhouetted against a glorious sunrise. Praise the Lord for such an affirmation: "There is hope."

**Lyn Welk-Sandy**

# Perfect Praise

*Let everything that has breath praise the Lord. Praise the Lord. Ps. 150:6, NIV.*

ONE NIGHT I received an invitation to attend a symphonic orchestra presentation. That day the sixth symphony of Ludwig van Beethoven was presented. I was enchanted with the perfection of the harmony reproducing the sounds of birds, a storm, the wind, the dawning of the day—something that captivated me and made me remember the beautiful promise, "However, as it is written: 'No eye has seen, no ear has heard, no mind has conceived what God has prepared for those who love him' " (1 Cor. 2:9, NIV).

I began to imagine how it will be for us to sit and hear the angels singing the most perfect melodies of glory and honor to our God with harp accompaniment and other instruments that make up the harmony of the heavenly orchestra. I can imagine we also will be a part of the choir that will sing hosannas to Christ, the Lamb of God, who took away the sins of the world, the one who overcame Satan. Because of His supreme sacrifice on the cross in our place, He will give us the right to be in heaven, face to face with Him, participating in the heavenly choir.

The music stopped, and I returned to reality. If the earthly music could bring me such sweet thoughts, what will it be like when we, together with the millions and millions of those who were saved by Him, participate in the perfect praise to our Lord!

"Eye has not seen nor ear heard," but the promise is certain that things that have never entered into our heart, that we have never imagined, the Lord has already prepared for us. When we will be there, we will praise Him with the most perfect praise of which only He is worthy.

While we are on this earth our life, our acts, should motivate us to praise God and be part of our praise. When we are sad and tired of this world, we praise the Lord with purity of heart and with sincerity. When we are happy, we praise the Lord with all of the strength in our heart!

"Let everything that has breath praise the Lord." And as we express our praise to Him we are, in some way, experiencing here on earth what it will be like to be with angels in heaven, participating in perfect praise to our King and Savior.

**Carmem Virgínia**

# She Called Me Friend

*Behold, how good and how pleasant it is for brethren to dwell together in unity. Ps. 133:1.*

MY HUSBAND, our two children, and I moved to another city. We had been living in our former city for 18 years, and to leave old friends and support wasn't without tears and sadness. When we arrived in the new city, we had planned to spend a long time searching for just the right church. Then we visited one for a Wednesday night prayer meeting, and the people were so warm that we decided to postpone our search and stay awhile.

Over the next few weeks the people were kind, inviting, and open. We felt that we had found a home. However, my son was still unhappy and didn't even sit with us in church. Few people knew that he was ours. That placed a burden in my heart, and at times I felt lonely and friendless among these new church members.

About this time I went to church camp with my daughter and joined the prayer band. Still, my heart ached for the familiar, the comfortable friends I knew in the old home and former church. I longed for it for my children as well.

One day we were at a large church gathering that was held outside. Two women who had befriended me were seated under a tent. As my son walked past, one of the women mentioned to the other one that this was my son. That dear sister called my son over to her, shook his hand, and told him how it was nice to meet him. She told him her name and said, "I'm your mom's friend."

Did she say "friend"? She called me friend! Nothing else was said, and my new friend didn't know that she had just lifted a load of sadness from my heart. Jesus had given me a new friend—and many others—over the weeks and months as we worshipped and fellowshipped together.

Do I still miss my old friends? Of course I do. But my soul rejoices over my new ones. Their prayers and acceptance have helped my son to feel at home. And when my children are happy, I'm much happier. These precious Christians allowed the Lord to use them to love me and to love others.

*Lord, help me today to cheer someone else's heart with my words and actions.*

**Rose Joseph Thomas**

# The Burned Coat

*Whosoever therefore shall humble himself as this little child,
the same is greatest in the kingdom of heaven. Matt. 18:4.*

"MOMMY, can I go to Patti's to play?" asked my 5-year-old one busy Friday.

"Yes, you may go, but come home in one hour, OK?"

And off she went happily to play with a little neighbor girl.

The hour passed quickly for me, and just as I was checking the time the door opened, and Sherlyn came in. One look at her, and I knew something was wrong.

"Oh, Mommy," she sobbed, "something terrible happened!" When she turned around, I saw that the back of her coat had a big hole in it. There had been a little electric heater in Patti's room, and Sherlyn, not knowing what it was, had laid her coat across it. There were no clothing stores in our small town, and there was no money in our monthly budget for a coat. It was late Friday afternoon, and Sherlyn didn't have a coat to wear to church the next day. "Don't worry, Mommy," Sherlyn said. "Jesus will send me a coat. Let's kneel down and ask Him. I won't miss Sabbath school tomorrow." *Oh, the faith of a little child*, I thought as we knelt. I was afraid her faith would be tested this time.

Then Mrs. Clark, the neighbor across the street, called and asked me to come over for a few minutes. She worked out of town for a very wealthy family and sometimes brought clothes home for Sherlyn, very nice, hardly worn clothes—some still had the price tags on them. It had been quite a while since she had brought clothes, and I though she just wanted to chat for a few minutes. When I asked Sherlyn if she wanted to go too, she said, "Oh, it's a coat! I just know it!"

When Mrs. Clark opened the door, she smiled and said she had brought some things she hoped Sherlyn might want to wear. She held up a coat, and what a pretty coat it was! It was navy blue with a little white fur collar and a matching muff and hat. "Oh-oh-oh! I told you Jesus would answer my prayer and send me a coat! And it is the nicest one I could ever hope for!" Together we told Mrs. Clark the story about the burned coat and our prayers.

Sherlyn is grown now, with three daughters of her own. She often tells this story about the faith of a little child and how God does answer prayers—even for 5-year-olds.

**Nelda Bigelow**

# Me? Like Jonah?

*Where can I go from your Spirit? Where can I flee from your presence?*
*Ps. 139:7, NIV.*

I WAS INVITED to preach on Wednesday night at my church. After accepting the invitation, I immediately let my nerves take over. Guidance from the Lord would be necessary to prepare a sermon, and I asked Him to help me to at least meet the needs of someone that night.

I woke up on Wednesday with a tremendous headache. I took medication, but no relief came. In my condition I realized that I wouldn't have the strength—or the spirit—to preach that night.

Without consulting God's will, I grabbed my cell phone to ask the church elder to find someone to take my place for that evening. I attempted in vain to undo what God had asked of me. When I located the elder's name in my cell phone memory, I couldn't see the number, because the command wasn't working correctly. After three attempts I decided to begin with the letter A and go down, name by name, to E for Elias, the church elder's name. But when I reached his name, once again the cell phone malfunctioned.

I now tried to outsmart God. This time I began with the letter N. The same malfunction occurred. Then I understood that God wanted to use me through my sermon that night. The only thing left was to accept His will. I placed myself in His hands.

Even with a headache, I presented the sermon. When the worship service ended, a friend came to tell me that God had answered him through my words. I praised God for that blessing and for using me even though I wasn't worthy.

Dear friends, we are God's instruments, and even if we attempt to flee from His plans, He will always bring us back. My prayer is that we will not be like Jonah, resisting the Holy Spirit. Jonah tried to run away, but God brought him back. Let us be like Isaiah when he was called. Although initially reluctant, he was ultimately willing, saying to the Lord, "Here am I; send me" (Isa. 6:8).

Today God wants to use you to reach a soul who is thirsting for His love. Don't resist; just give yourself to be a living witness. May God bless you this day, and may other people be blessed through you.

**Nathaly Rose Garcez Rodrigues**

# His Wonderful Gaze

*The Lord turned and looked straight at Peter. Luke 22:61, NIV.*

WHEN DIFFICULT SITUATIONS ARISE, time seems to stop around us, and we feel the world crumbling in on top of us. We can see no further than our problems and difficulties. When we are most in need of someone to help, support, and listen, we can never seem to find them. Or are we the ones who distance ourselves from people and bury ourselves in the sadness that afflicts us?

It was on a day like this that I found myself immersed in pessimism and anguish. My husband and children were at home, but I felt as though I were alone. Lying on the sofa in the living room, I could think only about my sadness, my problems, my defects, feeling as if I were the worst of all creatures.

Then I raised my head for a moment, and my eyes found the face of Jesus in a picture hanging on the wall. It seemed that Jesus was looking right at me. Incredible! I could feel a peace overtake my being. How wonderful it is to feel the wonderful gaze of Jesus!

I remembered when Peter, after denying Jesus three times, found His wonderful gaze. He felt an immense sadness, but he also felt the great love of Jesus most intensely. Forgiveness was being offered to him even though he didn't deserve it—it was free. I think this is why Peter cried so bitterly.

For several minutes I insisted on imagining Jesus' countenance, His sweet smile looking at me. Certainly He saw my affliction! Yes! When I thought that no one cared for me, He was there, very close, looking for the opportunity to touch my heart. My fragility became hope. Through His countenance I felt how much He loves me, and I realized that I cannot be lost if I am under His eyes. My tears were now those of joy and gratitude because of His great love.

We are not alone. Even though life surprises and saddens us, even if we are without friends or relatives He is looking at us and searching for us.

*Thank You, Lord, for the comfort that comes even from Your wonderful gaze! Help me each day to be aware of Your presence in my life!*

**Marinês Aparecida da Silva Oliveira**

# Our Children, a Blessing

*"Do you hear what these children are saying?" they asked him. "Yes," replied Jesus, "have you never read, 'From the lips of children and infants you have ordained praise'?" Matt. 21:16, NIV.*

AFTER A RECENT MOVE to a different city, my 7-year-old son didn't feel well because of respiratory problems that left him very weak. One Friday afternoon at work I received a message that my son had been taken to the emergency room because his condition had worsened. I finished my class and went immediately to the hospital.

After receiving medicine, my son began to feel better. We stayed in the emergency room until 11:00 p.m., so that he could take the prescribed medication.

The next day we held a worship of thanksgiving at home. I began by telling my son a short story; then we sang and expressed our gratitude in prayer. I asked him to play a song of gratitude on his violin.

Seated on the bed, he began to play. His posture was incorrect, so I asked him to stand. He asked, "Why correct posture, Mommy? We are alone, just you and I."

I looked straight in his eyes and said, "Son, Jesus is here with us!" I passed my hand over the bed where we were. "Can you feel His presence?" He gazed directly at me as I continued, "We are not just two people—there are five of us here."

Looking more fixedly at me, he asked, "What do you mean, five?"

"Yes, five: my angel and me, your angel and you, and Jesus. I'm even going to fix my hair." And I put a clip in it.

Convinced, he quickly put his hand through his hair and asked, "And me, Mommy, how do I look?"

That day I learned a very meaningful lesson. I understood that there is innocence, frankness, trust, and humility in children, and that as followers of Jesus we need to have these same attributes. We should not be surprised when the Bible tells us, "And he said: 'I tell you the truth, unless you change and become like little children, you will never enter the kingdom of heaven'" (Matt. 18:3, NIV). I know I want to become a trusting child of God, and I'm sure you do, too.

**Rosinha Gomes Dias de Oliveira**

# A Song of Discord and Deliverance

*The man from whom the demons had gone out begged to go with him, but Jesus sent him away, saying, "Return home and tell how much God has done for you." So the man went away and told all over town how much Jesus had done for him. Luke 8:38, 39, NIV.*

I'M A MUSICIAN on Sabbaths at my own church, and I work part-time at West Augusta Methodist Church, providing music for the worshippers there. Several years ago I also did music at a second Methodist church, St. James. The pastor mentioned that he was speaking about how Christ exorcised the demon-possessed and how that kind of healing can still take place today. He requested that the hymn "Silence, Unclean, Frenzied Spirit" be used as a part of the service.

When I looked the song up, I learned that it had been composed in 1984, that Thomas Troeger had written the words and Carol Doran the music. When I started to play it, I groaned. The chords in the first two lines are so unharmonious that even when all the accidental sharps and flats are hit correctly, the hymn sounds discordant!

My first impulse was to strongly recommend something else as a substitute for this hymn. I searched through the hymnal in vain. Nothing else had words that fit in as well with Pastor Grow's sermon topic. So we would be using this song.

After practicing on both the organ and piano, I discovered that the last half of the song was less dissonant—more pleasing to the ear. I began to understand what the composers were attempting to portray. The jarring, introductory chords aptly convey that life for demon-possessed people is an ugly, chaotic mess. Their misery abates only when Christ frees them from the devil's power. Once that's done, the song becomes brighter and happier.

I too have found that there is no harmony or peace of mind if Christ isn't part of my life. Only He can take the jumbled notes that make up various parts of my life and sort them out and transform them into a melody that blesses everyone with whom I come in contact.

*Lord, we are all oppressed by sin and the devil. Be with us as we fight temptation and evil. Also be with those who are oppressed or possessed, who haven't yet found a hiding place or refuge in You. May their anguished cries for help be replaced with songs of deliverance and praise!*

**Bonnie Moyers**

# In the Garden

*Jesus said to her, "Mary!" She turned and said to him in Hebrew, "Rabbouni!" John 20:16, NRSV.*

I WOKE UP TIRED and concerned after a long, sleepless night. I said a prayer of praise and thanksgiving for the new day and the opportunity to serve God. Having a positive attitude and singing praises to God while doing chores helped. But my heart ached, burdened with unanswered questions, longing for assurance that the Lord was in control of my family. My husband's words were no comfort. When my family left for the day, I sought refuge in my Friend. Alone with Him at last, I didn't need to be strong anymore. I knelt, wept, and poured out my soul before Him.

Mary was anguished. Tears streamed down her cheeks, her heart broken by the death of her Master. Now His body wasn't in the grave! Immersed in her sorrow, she didn't recognize the voice she heard. *It must be the gardener,* she thought. Mary was in the very presence of Jesus without perceiving it! But Christ, who notices every teardrop and understands the longings of our hearts, saw her anguish and suffering. He spoke and called her name. When Mary recognized she was in the presence of her Master, everything changed. Tears turned to joy.

Like Mary, we often cry, but for different reasons. Although in the presence of our Master, our soul groans in pain and suffering. But the moment we hear His voice and listen to His words, He fills our heart with peace, assurance, and joy! That morning wonderful promises from God's Word filled my mind, bringing the much-needed assurance of His guidance. I placed all my burdens in His hands and felt great comfort and peace.

If amid sorrow we learn to listen to His voice, everything will change. Our loving Savior weeps with us, but also offers us His grace, His strength, and His peace. Even when we don't perceive Him, He's always by our side. Every day He calls our name, longing to comfort us. No matter the reason for our sorrow and anguish, when we seek Him in the garden He wipes our tears. What a wonderful Savior!

*Lord, You are my comfort. May I seek You in the garden each dawn so that we may walk, hand in hand, along life's narrow way. Amen.*

**Rhodi Alers de Lopez**

# Papa and the Bear

*I am the Lord, the God of all mankind. Is anything too hard for me? Jer. 32:27, NIV.*

PICTURE IT: a small man, five feet four inches, maybe 130 pounds after a good meal. He walks with a cane, has limited use of one arm, and is nearsighted. That's Papa. Now picture the bear: big, hungry, and armed with teeth and claws that can rip a man apart.

Papa had gone on a backpacking trip with my sister and her college roommate. While Papa had never let his disability get in the way of things he enjoyed doing, such as backpacking, he was a cautious, methodical man. One of his favorite lectures, delivered before camping trips, was on the subject of bears.

"Never confront a bear," Papa would say. "If he wants your backpack, let him have it. There's nothing in the pack that's worth risking your life for."

Apparently Papa wasn't paying attention to his own lectures, because one night when a big black bear grabbed a backpack from the ground and took off with it, Papa got out of his sleeping bag, grabbed his cane, and took off after the bear. The bear had one of the shoulder straps in his mouth while the other was dragging on the ground. Papa caught up with the bear and grabbed the dangling strap.

Then the tug-of-war started. The bear pulled and growled. Papa pulled and shouted. Back and forth the pack went between the two while the girls yelled for Papa to let go.

It was the bear that let go in the end. Perhaps the sight of an angry little man wearing long johns was too much for him. He went back into the woods without his prize. Papa had won. Not only was he alive, but he still had his backpack!

Whenever I hear the story of David and Goliath, I think about the story of Papa and the bear. In both cases there was a vast difference in size between the adversaries. The great thing about this story is that whether you step out in faith, as David did, or simply step out, as Papa did, we have someone standing right beside us. Whatever enemies we face—giants or bears, disease or poverty—God is bigger. With Him at our side we can fight the good fight. It doesn't matter how small we are, how fearful or inadequate, God is bigger. He will not fail us.

**Gina Lee**

# Distance Didn't Count

*Neither height nor depth, nor anything else in all creation, will be able to separate us from the love of God that is in Christ Jesus our Lord. Rom. 8:39, NIV.*

I ANSWERED THE PHONE and was surprised to hear the voice of Admire, the acting women's ministries director, and my assistant in The Gambia.

I had been in England for four months with ill health. The women had prayed, sent me cards, money, and greetings, hoping that I would be with them in no time, but I couldn't. I was still under medical care, which I couldn't get in The Gambia. They couldn't wait any longer, and couldn't travel to visit me in England because of distance and cost, so they decided to call.

The women all went to the mission house to have a special Wednesday evening prayer with my husband and to pray for me. After the prayer meeting they called me from my house in The Gambia, and all of them spoke to me on the phone, one after the other. Their short prayers, words of encouragement, and their familiar voices gave me hope and a new strength. I was so moved I shed tears of joy. Their action lifted my spirits up.

Is it not sweet to belong to such a family of God, a family closely knit together with sincere love of God? It's the kind of love that can overcome height, depth, and distance. Yes, the love of my friends shortened the thousands of miles between us and diminished the cost of the telephone call, just as the love of Christ for us reduced the distance between heaven and earth when He came down and died to redeem us. All the women showed their love. I know that it cost them a lot to talk to me, but they were ready to spend no matter what the cost.

Their aim to comfort me was achieved. As it says in 2 Corinthians 1:4: "We can comfort those in any trouble with the comfort we ourselves have received from God"(NIV).

I love my sisters in The Gambia because they were not discouraged by the distance between us. Their determination discounted distance and cost. They also made me realize that "where there is a will there is a way," and there is true love of God. "For nothing is impossible with God" (Luke 1:37, NIV).

Sometimes we let distance separate us from friends, and that is sad. But how much worse to let distance come between us and Jesus, or us and the comfort of the Holy Spirit.

**Mabel Kwei**

# Are We a Spectacle Unto the World?

*For we are made a spectacle unto the world,*
*and to angels, and to men. 1 Cor. 4:9.*

IN 1970 IN SHILLONG, INDIA, I was returning home in a bus to Jaintia when a fellow traveler, a native of Jaintia (called a *Pnar*), asked me, "Are you from Jaintia?"

"Yes, I am," I said.

"Your accent sounds like a Khasi," she snapped.

I chuckled to myself. I defended myself by saying, "I may not be a Pnar, but I work in Jaintia Hills. So I consider myself as such."

She raised her eyebrow because we Khasi class ourselves as superior to Pnar people, yet I identified myself as a Pnar. Are we a spectacle unto the world? Do they notice and wonder about who we are?

When my husband and I landed at a Chicago airport in 2000, we hopped on a bus for the last lap of our journey to reach our home in Michigan. At the halfway point we had to take another bus. While waiting for it, I got into a conversation with a woman. After some chitchat, she asked me, "Are you a Christian?" and she mentioned my denomination.

I said, "Yes, I am." Then I asked, "What makes you think so?"

"The way you talk made me think so," she said, smiling.

In that same year my daughter's neighbor became my friend. One day, with a twinkle in her eye, she asked, "By the way, do you have a congregation?" For a moment I was puzzled, then understood what she meant when she added, "You seem to know the Bible better than my pastor."

One morning while cleaning the footpath in front of my daughter's house, an old woman passed by. When I greeted her, she stopped to talk. She remarked, "You seem to know the Bible through and through." I took the opportunity to offer her a Bible study, and she gladly accepted. On a later visit to Michigan I spent more time with her to study the Bible and lead her to fully accept Jesus Christ as her Savior.

May God help us to be a spectacle unto the world. Can people see that we are Christ's followers? If we are, we shall see the result when we get to heaven.

**Annie M. Kujur**

# If God Guides, He Provides

*The Lord will guide you always; he will satisfy your needs in a sun-scorched land and will strengthen your frame. You will be like a well-watered garden, like a spring whose waters never fail. Isa. 58:11, NIV.*

WHEN I WAS IN HIGH SCHOOL, I really dreamed of studying at Mountain View College in Mindanao, Philippines. However, after my graduation I received a scholarship from one of the private schools in my hometown. I was confused as to which school to attend, and earnestly prayed that God would show me a sign. I was committed to follow wherever He would lead me, but deep in my heart I longed to go to MVC because I wanted to obtain a Christian education. I wanted to participate actively in missionary work.

In April God answered my prayers. Our church offered to sponsor my fare to Mountain View College. I was really happy to know about the help of the church, and decided not to accept the scholarship from that private school. I wasted no time; that night I packed up my things, ready to leave for MVC the next day. When I reached the college grounds, I could hardly believe my eyes—I had finally set foot on the school of my dream. It was beautiful, and it was the beginning of the fulfillment of those dreams.

I applied for work and was accepted in the sugarcane department. Although I worked in the heat of the sun and the cold of the rain for two semesters, I benefited much in experience and money. The next semester I transferred to Ruby Hall, one of the girls' dormitories, where I worked as an assistant dean for a year. The following year I applied to the physical education department, where I have worked for five years.

I'm now a senior, and I've worked both full-time and on a part-time basis to pay my way through college. However, I haven't had any worry, because God has been providing for my needs. I enjoy my life even if there are problems that I encounter along the way. Even though it is quite hard to both study and work, I'm thankful to God because it molds me to be an independent and strong person.

God provided a scholarship that has been a great blessing for me. I've really proven that if God guides, He provides.

**Annabel Petalcorin Aparece**

# Saint Patrick's Day Blizzard

*Though your sins be as scarlet, they shall be as white as snow.*
*Isa. 1:18.*

THE WIND HOWLED RELENTLESSLY around the corners of the house as swirling mounds of snow grew higher and higher. Now the windows were becoming snow-covered. Soon we wouldn't be able to see out at all—and that worried me. My husband worked 10 miles away at a hospital and couldn't get home. Other staff members couldn't get to the hospital.

My sister, Lorna, and I were alone in the house with our three girls. Of course, the little ones thought this was a big adventure. They eagerly watched as the snow covered the entire height of the windows.

There is something inviting about a cozy house in a Minnesota blizzard. It's a special time when we can forget about daily errands or chores. Instead, we work on picture puzzles, or read a good book, and make popcorn. This blizzard wasn't that relaxing, though, because it soon was apparent that both the front and back doors were buried in snow top to bottom. I tried to force them open, but they wouldn't budge. We read stories and played games with the girls until they were sleepy. They felt safe, but I wasn't so confident. I began to picture snow covering our chimney and was fearful of being asphyxiated. I knew the power and phones could go out, leaving us without heat or help.

After we got the children into bed, my sister and I began to pray. It was obvious we'd never be able to get out of the house in an emergency.

The blizzard raged on all the next day and night, finally stopping the morning of the third day. By afternoon snowplows had cleared the main highways, and my husband got someone to push snow from the front door. We dressed warmly and couldn't wait to get outside.

What a sight to behold! The snow was as high as the eaves of the house, and the sun shone on the drifts, creating thousands of tiny, glistening diamonds as far as the eye could see. Because the wind had pounded the drifts so fiercely, they were rock-hard, enabling us to walk on top of them onto our roof.

I've thought of that blizzard many times and am thankful that God has promised to cover our sin with a glorious white so that we might shine in the Son.

**Darlene Ytredal Burgeson**

# Butterflies

*God has made everything beautiful for its own time. Eccl. 3:11, NLT.*

ONE OF MY FAVORITE RELAXATIONS is to walk out into our backyard. With a view that overlooks the Ozarks and gardens that are just beginning to grow, it's a sight for my eyes. I look around the wildflower garden, out over the rolling hills, and let the wear and the tear of the day roll away.

Late last fall, as I strolled through our yard, I found two bright-green caterpillars on some cilantro-like foliage. Being the nature girl that I am, I scooped them up, along with plenty of foliage, and deposited them in a jar for closer observation. Knowing it was too late for them to survive outside, I did them the favor of a chance for survival.

Only one hatched into a pretty butterfly, but not one that I recognized. I looked online for some identification, but could find none. There was some defect in my butterfly. It couldn't fly well. It would take off all right, but soon ended up on the floor. Time after time I gently scooped it up, put it back up where it could find some food, only to find it later, again on the floor. Affectionately, and with great concern, I watched over that simple little butterfly. I watched it with great interest, willing it to thrive and survive. As I watched and prayed and repeatedly lifted it up, I realized in a small way just how God must feel about me as His little girl.

He knew me when He formed me in the womb. He knew the day I was born. He was with me as I grew and was nurtured by my earthly parents. As I grew older He longed after me, speaking to me at every opportunity. When I fell and got hurt, He lifted me up and healed my wounds.

In my adulthood He has never ceased to yearn after me. When I'm burdened with care, He gives me the words of a song to encourage me. When I fail and fall into sin, He patiently picks me up and forgives me and sends me on my way. God not only cares for us—He makes us beautiful as well. He not only wants us to survive—He wants us to thrive.

*I praise You, Father, for these wee creatures that speak to me of You and remind me of how deeply You care about me.*

**Becki Knobloch**

# Pets Validate Scripture

*Behold, I have given you every plant yielding seed that is on the face of all the earth, and every tree with seed in its fruit. Gen. 1:29, ESV.*

IT SEEMS BUT YESTERDAY when my first-grade son begged for another pet. "Just like my classmates have. There's one more left, Mommy. Can we get it now?" He promised to take good care of it. Curious, I consented to check it out. The phone call was positive. Furthermore, Allen had been kind and gentle to his cross-eyed Siamese kitten, Stubbie (named for her short tail), who had been given to us by our next-door neighbor. The runt had grown into a beautiful, fawn-colored, long-legged, dark-eared, well-behaved pet.

The woman met us and led us to a corner underneath the stairs. "The runt of a litter of five," she said, uncovering a black-and-white-striped bundle. Picking it up, she laid it in Allen's arms. He giggled as a tiny snout tried to hide under his shirt. "Get it de-scented," she advised, mentioning where the others had gone for the procedure. On the way home we came up with a name: Skinkie. Soon the veterinarian performed the minor surgery, a glandectomy. "He'll make a good, sweet pet," the doctor said.

Stubbie welcomed Skinkie with an all-over, tongue-licking scrub, and soon the two snuggled against each other. Skinkie liked fully ripe bananas and other kinds of fruit from the table, including avocado, peach, papaya, and watermelon. He shared Stubbie's water dish but hardly touched the cat food. Skinkie grew fast. He had a fat, round body and black, glossy fur with white stripes at the back. The two animals romped around, with short-legged Skinkie waddling after Stubbie.

Once we took the pets along for a drive. For a break, we stopped at a rest area. Soon vacationers came around, snapping pictures of Skinkie on a leash, his bushy tail held high, with Stubbie following.

Another day we took Skinkie to visit his littermates. We found two were pitifully tiny and crippled; two others had died. They'd been fed milk, eggs, and scraps of meat. Although Skinkie and Stubbie are long gone, and Allen now has his own little boy, we still believe that the original diet from the Garden of Eden made the difference for Skinkie—and maybe for people, too.

**Consuelo Roda Jackson**

# Bloom Where You're Planted

*And the remnant that is escaped of the house of Judah shall again take root downward, and bear fruit upward. Isa. 37:31.*

WHEN YOU THINK OF SPRING, I'm sure daffodils and magnolias may come to mind. Perhaps gardenias, impatiens, or tiger lilies spread their fragrance around your entryway. Whatever your thoughts about spring, life must be involved. It is a time of renewal, a renaissance at its best! Spring is my favorite season of the year, for it bursts with new energies, newly recognized opportunities, and a renewed hope.

I've discovered that sometimes the seeds of life that have been planted in the fall, in a dark, cold period of your life, begin to bear fruit in the spring.

Sometime ago I had an encounter at work that left me embittered by injustices. Though they were spiritual in nature, I didn't fully see these attacks as such during my private corporate storm. So I was totally unprepared for the words that exited the mouth of my supervisor, and they haunted my thoughts for months to follow: "Bloom where you're planted." I wondered how I could bloom in an environment that didn't foster growth. The soil was chemically imbalanced, the sunlight was selectively shining, and the water that gives life—the spigot yielded only an intermittent trickle. My answer to this unhealthy environment was the desire to seek fertile ground elsewhere. I wanted to run for the hills.

The Master Creator, the God of my universe, had other plans. He later allowed me to see that if you can't bloom as He intended, you can spread your roots. These roots should be shoots for joy, love, patience, longsuffering, kindness, and meekness. Now, we all know roots go deep and wide. They can even be tortuous to uproot. When these seedlings of the Spirit take root—watch out! The blessings of God are tenfold.

God did just that in my life. He allowed His seedlings to spread in my life to touch others in a more magnificent way, for His glory. In turn I've been strengthened and blessed to be a blessing.

Remember, if you can't bloom where you're planted, spread your roots. Network for the Lord. Be a fresh incense of praise!

**Lady Dana Austin**

# God's Flower Gardens

*This is what the Lord Almighty says: "In a little while I will once more shake the heavens and the earth, the sea and the dry land. I will shake all nations, and the desired of all nations will come, and I will fill this house with glory," says the Lord Almighty. Haggai 2:6, 7, NIV.*

MY HUSBAND AND I live in the boonies—way out in the boonies. And although we may not have ready access to arts and culture and other refinements of life, we do have our own unique beauty. I've dubbed it God's Garden.

Each year, as spring approaches, I wait with bated breath for the first wildflowers. The early golden arrays of dandelions and marsh marigolds promise greater things to come. By late June delicate wild roses, in varying shades of pink, decorate the roadsides. Soon after come the buttercups, the purple vetch, little orange flowers, and white daisies, all carpeting the meadows and fields, competing with one another in their glory. Five years have failed to dim the deep feeling of delight and awe that comes over me as I drink in this beauty each time we drive to town.

The first summer after we moved into our new home, it was the white daisies that put on the grand prize display. Around our house, masses of them covered the two acres that had recently been cleared of forest. I was thrilled to think I could anticipate this show each summer. But the next year they were sparse. I was so disappointed. Then when we burned some brush piles, the following summer these areas again produced hundreds of daisies, and the year after that. I began to notice that most of the daisies flanked the roadsides. They also bordered our driveway. Finally I came up with my own theory. These seeds must need some agitation in order to germinate. The constant snow removed from the roads and shoved to the sides provided that. So did the snowblower along the driveway, as had the original clearing of the land and later the burning of brush. Of course there are many daisies everywhere this time of year, but they are most prolific in the places where there was disturbance of the ground, where things were agitated or shaken up.

Is it any wonder that God needs to shake us up sometimes in order to bring our beauty to abundance?

**Dawna Beausoleil**

# High Time!

*Don't be afraid. . . . What I whisper in your ears, shout from the housetops for all to hear! Matt. 10:26, 27, NLT.*

IN THE SPRING OF 2003 I applied for Canadian citizenship because I wanted to make travel between Canada (which I love) and the United States (my homeland) as simple as possible. I became a landed immigrant when I married my Canadian husband more than 32 years ago. To have dual citizenship is a great privilege!

I was told that the process for citizenship would probably take a year or longer, and to use this time of waiting to study the citizenship booklet that I received in May. To my surprise, a letter came in November from the citizenship court advising me that I was to write the test on December 4 and take the oath of citizenship on December 5—"if you pass the test." Pushing panic aside, I decided to continue working on my Christmas card project—all 500—until it was finished. I took my booklet to work with me to study during my breaks.

I called a friend to double-check her address before mailing her card. Barb had recently become a Canadian citizen and told me that I should enroll in the free citizenship classes. She gave me the phone number of the instructor. Thank You, Jesus! Heaven knew that I needed help! My friend, Lyla, who is a schoolteacher and, like me, is the parent of a special-needs child, was my personal tutor. I always smile when people refer to us as comrades.

I passed the test! It was simple because I had studied. Lyla gave me a perfect commemorative gift: a large stuffed toy beaver, an official emblem of Canada's history.

On December 5, in Grande Prairie, Alberta, 41 people from 20 different countries publicly became new Canadian citizens. For me the ceremony will be a memory highlight set in gold forever. Some conditions to qualify for Canadian citizenship: you must have lived in Canada for at least four years, and you must be able to read and write in either French or English. Most of my citizenship classmates worked hard to learn English. I'm so proud of them!

Dual citizenship can be a benefit here on this earth, but there is no such thing for heaven. Jesus has granted citizenship to me, and I want to shout it from the housetop! Through Jesus, I've passed the test that really counts.

**Deborah Sanders**

# Awakened by an Angel

*The angel of the Lord encampeth round about them that fear him, and delivereth them Ps. 34:7.*

SUDDENLY THE ROOM WENT BLACK, which meant we once again had no electricity. It happened so often, maybe two or three times a day. Our outside chores had been accomplished, and everyone had gathered for family worship when the lights went out. My mother maintained family worship until she died. She said talking to God early in the morning and in the evening is a good way to start and end the day.

We had sung many songs, read the Bible, and then prayed, and then suddenly the electricity was gone. My two nieces lit a candle so that they could finish their homework assignment. They cautiously crept to their room and set the candle on the chair close to their bed. I went to my room and fell asleep immediately, overwhelmed by the day's chores.

In my deep sleep I heard someone call my name. Frightened, I opened my eyes and saw a bright light coming from my nieces' room. As I dozed off again, I said, "Betty, turn off the light," forgetting that when we went to bed there was no electricity. I fell asleep again, but soon felt someone shake me, not vigorously but gently. This time I was alert. I still saw the bright light in my nieces' room and called them again to turn off the light. When they didn't respond, I got up and went to their room. Black smoke poured from the room. The candle was burnt to the chair. The middle of the chair was all gone, and the bed my nieces were sleeping in had started to burn. My nieces were in such a deep, peaceful sleep that I had to pull them off the bed and get them out of the room. My nephew came to help me put out the fire.

The angels of the Lord protected my nieces from the fire and awakened me. What a mighty God we serve!

This experience constantly reminds me that the Lord sends His angels to watch over us. They protect us from an unknown number of dangers. They encamp around us and deliver us when we put our trust and our confidence in God. If we fear the Lord and are obedient to His words, there is nothing He will withhold from us. He will supply all our needs—either now or in the new earth. He is faithful.

**Patricia Hines**

# I Need Glasses!

*Your ears will hear a voice behind you, saying, "This is the way;
walk in it." Isa. 30:21, NIV.*

SINCE CHILDHOOD I've had a problem with my eyes. No one notices the
deviation in the right eye because the problem is internal, but it makes
things seem as if they are not in the right place.

Because of this I can't draw or write in a straight line on unlined paper.
I can't place a ruler correctly and worse, I don't drive straight. However,
these things happen only when I'm not wearing my glasses. With them I
can do tasks normally.

On the first day of driving classes I didn't have my glasses. To my eyes,
the car was going straight, but the instructor kept saying, "The car is going
to the right. . . . Go to the left. . . . Be careful. . . . Try to keep the car in line
with the road."

And I would answer, "But I'm going in a straight line." To me,
everything was just fine!

Now, I'm aware that without glasses I run a huge risk. In my spiritual
life the same thing can happen. There are paths that I plan with my defec-
tive eyes, thinking that everything is fine and that I'm doing the best that I
can do by myself. However, when I put on the glasses of faith I realize that
I'm off the path, and that I'm far from going the right direction. Then my
Instructor tells me, "This is the way; walk in it!"

With the glasses of faith, the hand of His Holy Spirit takes over and
steers my life and allows me see how far I've strayed from the correct way,
the way that He has indicated for me.

I realize how the glasses of faith permit me to see the road clearly. With
them I can continue on without falling to the left or the right. They help
me to go straight along the road of life. With them certainly I can see the
way that the Lord Jesus has prepared for me so that I can reach heaven. His
Holy Spirit shows me the way, and the glasses of faith make me see this
way, which has already been leveled—the path that Jesus has already
walked on. He has taken away the barriers and the stones that make me
trip and fall.

I need glasses, but most of all I need glasses of faith. And then when
He comes, these glasses will no longer be necessary, because I—and
you—can enjoy the perfect reality of eternal life with Christ!

**Juliane P. de Oliveira Caetano**

# Knight in Shining Armor

*I saw heaven standing open and there before me was a white horse, whose rider is called Faithful and True. With justice he judges and makes war. His eyes are like blazing fire, and on his head are many crowns. He has a name written on him that no one knows but he himself. . . .The armies of heaven were following him, riding on white horses and dressed in fine linen, white and clean. Rev. 19:11-14, NIV.*

HOW MANY TALES have been told of knights in shining armor coming to rescue the damsel in distress? How many young damsels wish it were true? The number would probably make mathematicians excited. Read again Revelation 19:11-16, and you may see why I believe that there really is a Knight in shining armor, and that He will come and rescue us.

I realize that many biblical scholars have studied prophetic language and probably have a different explanation for these verses, but just think—isn't it possible that Jesus is our knight? After all, He is the King of kings and Lord of lords. He comes to earth and rescues fallen humanity from spiritual distress. By dying on the cross, He paid the price for all people and defeated evil once and for all. Sounds like slaying the dragon to me.

However, He doesn't force this freedom from spiritual distress on anyone. John 3:16-18 makes clear that not only was this done out of love, but that we must choose to accept this gift.

Before Jesus returned to heaven after slaying this dragon, He gave us great hope and a purpose. The hope was that He would not leave us here to suffer physical distress forever but would come back to claim us. The purpose was to let others know of what He had done so that we could all be rescued both now and when He comes to claim us. So at the appointed time Jesus will come back in the clouds of glory with a blast of trumpets and a host of angels to rescue His damsel, or bride, from her distress. Talk about pageantry! Not only that, but Jesus takes His bride and carries her off—not just anywhere, but to a city that is filled with mansions. A city called heaven, in which we all really do live happily ever after.

He doesn't force anyone to go with Him. He claims only those who are His, those who have a relationship with Him, as any bride by choice would. It is because of His great love for us that Jesus is willing to take on this role of knight.

**Juli Blood**

# Hair We Go, Again!

*But God said unto him, Thou fool, this night thy soul shall be required of thee: then whose shall those things be, which thou hast provided? So is he that layeth up treasure for himself, and is not rich toward God. Luke 12:20, 21.*

MY HAIR HAS ALWAYS been an issue for me. I tell people that I come from a line of fine-haired, flat-chested people. A few years ago I found Judy, this really great hairstylist. She informed me that good hair doesn't depend only on a good haircut; it also depends on the products I use. Taking her advice, I began to develop an arsenal to attack all my hair issues.

I used to depend on perms so that I wouldn't have to curl my hair. When I first got a perm done, I would complain about the smell and about how I looked like a groomed poodle. As the perm loosened it would look a little better. Unfortunately, it didn't seem to last long, as the perm began to disappear. I used only mousse or a gel then. Now I have a multitude of choices.

When I get ready for my day, I lay all my hair tools on the countertop, which amazes my husband. This doesn't include the stash I have under the bathroom sink. I have at least four different brushes, not including the blow dryer hairbrush. The brushes are either small, large, round, or just plain pretty. I have several cans of mousse (for a curlier effect, to straighten, or to add body), several bottles of root lifter, two blow dryers (one for everyday and one for traveling—I prefer my ionic bionic one), and two curling irons (a medium barrel and a larger barrel). For the finishing touch, there are several choices of hairspray, depending on my mood. The interesting part is the contortions I do to get my hair dry and styled. One would think that with all these products my hair would be perfect. Just because I have these tools doesn't necessarily mean my hair gains an advantage (nor does it mean that I'm using them correctly).

In our Christian experience we may have several Bibles but read little, attend many church events yet leave empty, or go it alone without Jesus as our guide. My goal is to rely on His guidance continually. It doesn't depend on the amount of Christian "products" I have, but on how I use God's direct source that's available to me through prayer and study.

*Lord, thank You so much for Your love and guidance despite the clutter I think useful to increase my relationship with You.*

**Mary M. J. Wagoner-Angelin**

# Falling at the Feet of Jesus

*Cast all your anxiety on him because he cares for you.*
*1 Peter 5:7, NIV.*

TWO-YEAR-OLD EDUARDO was always healthy, glowing, filled with joy, a true present from God. During a trip from Paraná to São Paulo, Brazil, he came down with fever. We administered normal treatment for fever, thinking he had a cold. Three days later the fever still persisted. He was weak and anemic and had lost two pounds. We took him to a doctor, and medication was given. However, the fever persisted.

Another physician was visited. Now it wasn't just anemia but suspicion of an infection in his heart. Antibiotics and anti-inflammatory medication were prescribed. His situation, in spite of the medication, continued the same for 15 days. Then another specialist was consulted. Now leukemia was suspected. We went to a larger city where the hospitals were better equipped, and our son was entrusted to the care of a blood specialist. After admission to a hospital and examinations, the cause was still not discovered. "An unknown," stated the physician.

After nine more days in the hospital with a persistent fever, Eduardo was much thinner and more anemic, taking IVs and penicillin intravenously. On the ninth night we no longer knew what to do, where to go, whom to turn to. Our friends and relatives were already praying for God to comfort us, such was their certainty that the physicians could no longer do anything.

We fell on our knees, understanding we had done everything within our reach. In that prayer we pleaded with God to perform a miracle for our son. His guidance in all things was our request, because we wanted to serve Him; however, we wanted to have our son with us, too. Then, for the first time in almost 40 days, we finally said, "Lord, Your will be done, not ours."

That night and the following morning Eduardo no longer had fever. The doctors released him from the hospital. At home, though, the intense fever returned. A friend suggested a physician who was experienced in infectious diseases. That day he heard the case and concluded that Eduardo had a virus in his liver. This drained his strength, and all medications taken to this point had only strengthened the virus. A different medication was prescribed, and three days later our son was running around, bringing joy and the certainty that we always need to give God all of our desires, because He cares for us.

**Eva Maria Rossi Mello**

# Grandma, Are You Coming?

*Behold, I am coming soon! My reward is with me, and I will give to everyone according to what he has done. Rev. 22:12, NIV.*

AS THE WEATHER HAS ITS SEASONS—spring, summer, autumn, and winter—our life too passes through its seasons. Spring means new birth, growing, until everything is filled with flowers. In the summer responsibilities come—the choice of a profession, building a family, and children. In the autumn, with children raised, the little birds fly away, and there are empty nests and retirement. Then beautiful fruit begins to appear—grandchildren. I'm in this season, enjoying the delicacies of this fruit, the arrival of grandchildren.

God has given me six wonderful grandchildren, five boys and a girl. She is 15 and the oldest. What joy for grandparents when we hear the grandchildren on the telephone, or we can personally give them a big warm hug! How enchanting to see a little toddler place Grandfather's big straw hat on his head and go into the yard calling, "Ganpa, Ganpa!"

With our granddaughter I had the privilege of living nearby for seven years. But now we are 1,240 miles (2,000 kilometers) away, and we greatly miss her, as well as all our grandchildren.

One night the telephone rang. I answered, and on the other end I heard, "Hello, Grandma; are you coming? Oh, Grandma, why are you taking so long? I can't wait to be with you."

"My dear!" I answered. "I can't wait to be with you, either."

The anxiousness in that little voice was indescribable as it exclaimed and questioned at the same time, "Grandma, are you coming?"

What a wonder, joy, and reward that day will be when we will no longer need to use telephones or other means of communication to speak to or to see our dear ones. One day, not too far in the future, we will be all together—running, playing, enjoying ourselves—in that beautiful home! We will be with Jesus, and the seasons of life will no longer be registered.

May I say each day, "Jesus, O Lord, are You coming?" And may we live our lives so that this day will soon come. Jesus says, "I'm coming soon! My reward is with Me, especially for you."

**Jaci da Silva Vôos**

# The Eclipse

*But unto you that fear my name shall the Sun of righteousness arise with healing in his wings. Mal. 4:2.*

ON MARCH 29, 2006, there was a full eclipse of the sun by the moon, an event which would not recur for another 83 years. Here in biblical Berea we expected to enjoy an 82 percent view, though not the complete one, which would be visible in Greece only from the tiny island of Kastelorizo.

The great day dawned with seemingly nothing to set it apart from any other day. However, very gradually an eerie half-light began to creep over the town, the atmosphere grew decidedly cooler as the day wore on, and the moon cast its dark shadow between us and the sun. By midday there was a strange, misty darkness; a cold, unreal atmosphere; and excitement bordered on fear as people gathered outside in small groups to witness the phenomenon. And then it was over. The steadily increasing light slowly wiped out the darkness, the atmosphere cleared, and once again the sun blazed down from a cloudless sky.

Most of us cannot hope to watch another full eclipse of the sun by the moon, but how often do we experience our own small personal "eclipses" in everyday life? One day, when our Sun of righteousness is shining brightly in our lives and we are basking happily in the warmth of His love, it happens. Gradually the light lessens, and a cold, creeping darkness comes into our hearts. We look upward to our "Sun," but a shadow comes between Him and us, a dark, threatening shadow, and we feel cut off, cold, and discouraged, though we don't understand why.

At such times it helps to remember some eternal truths. First, these experiences are unavoidable and come to all of us at times. They are not permanent. They come and go. Most important, though, let us remember that even when Satan imposes his hideous shadow between us and our Son of righteousness, blotting out His warmth and light and chilling our hearts with his evil presence, the Son is still there and is still shedding the warmth of His love on us, even if, for a time, we can't feel it. Finally, let us not forget that others will be influenced by our mood and behavior, so when these days come, let us wait patiently and cheerfully until the evil shadow is removed and we once again bask in the sunshine of His love.

**Revel Papaioannou**

# God Never Gives Up

*Then you will call upon me and come and pray to me, and I will listen to you. You will seek me and find me when you seek for me with all your heart. Jer. 29:12, 13, NIV.*

ONE OF THE MOST REWARDING THINGS about teaching a Bible class for either children or adults is that the study in preparation for teaching often blesses us in ways beyond our expectations. One Sabbath morning I made a last-minute search for a text I wanted to use in my class. I remembered that one of the prophets had recorded that God says that if we seek for Him with all our hearts we will find Him. But I couldn't remember where to find it in the Bible! I took out my Bible concordance and began scanning the entries under "seek."

My first discovery was a passage in Deuteronomy in which Moses warned the Israelites, just before they entered the Promised Land, that when times got easy in their newly conquered land, and if they forgot God and turned to worship heathen idols, God would scatter them among the nations. But, Moses added, even in the places to which you have been banished, "if from there you seek the Lord your God, you will find him if you look for him with all your heart and with all your soul" (Deut. 4:29, NIV).

This sounded *almost* right—but not quite like the verse I remembered. Besides, I was sure that the verse I knew came later in the Old Testament. So I turned back to my concordance and located the entry from Jeremiah that's quoted at the beginning of this devotional.

What made these two passages so meaningful to me that Sabbath morning was seeing God's mercy played out before my eyes, right there in inspired history. In Deuteronomy Moses warned the people of what would happen if they forsook God. In Jeremiah's day, many years later, the people had not heeded God's warning and were now scattered among the nations, just as God had predicted they would be if they worshipped idols. Even then Jeremiah told the people that God is still listening. He is never far away. He is committed to us.

My heart swelled with love for a God like that! I could go to my class that morning with a fresh realization of God's love and compassion. I could tell the people that God never gives up on us. No matter how far we have strayed or how lost we are, God will show us the way home. If we seek Him, He will be found.

**Carrol Johnson Shewmake**

# Eighteen Inches Short of Heaven

*Jesus replied, "You are in error because you do not know the Scriptures or the power of God." Matt. 22:29, NIV.*

WHERE I WORK AND MINISTER, we have a slogan, a goal: "Tell the World." From pulpits all over the world pastors are stressing the importance of studying the Word of God. "Read the Bible" sounds almost trite, as you would think that all Christians would do that, because the Word of God is our sustenance.

In reality, many Christians don't study their Bibles every day, and the goal is to encourage them to do just that. I guess asking people to read their Bibles is pretty much the same as asking people to exercise. We all know that Bible reading is beneficial, just as we all know for a fact that exercise will keep us healthy. But somehow the discipline is lacking. We make resolutions that we will do it—tomorrow—but most don't get around to getting it done.

A pastor-friend once said that many will fall just 18 inches short of heaven. He explained that the distance between the brain and the heart is about 18 inches. Many Christians have only a "head-knowledge" religion. They know what they should do and ought to do, but fail to apply it. The head does not connect with the heart. Reading the Bible was what the Jewish leaders had done all their lives. They had committed it to memory, but it failed to touch their lives, to transform them. In John 5:39 Jesus rebuked them: "You diligently study the Scriptures because you think that by them you possess eternal life. These are the Scriptures that testify about me."

They thought the Scriptures alone could save them, and it is so sad that when the Christ that the Scriptures focused on appeared in their midst, they not only didn't recognize Him but condemned Him to a criminal's death.

Simply reading or studying the Bible alone is insufficient. The Bible has to become a part of our lives. It has to affect the way we talk, the way we behave, our attitudes, our innermost thoughts, and our relationships. When we read the Bible just for reading's sake, too often we fall 18 inches short of the mark.

Living a vibrant Christian life is not possible without studying God's Word, because it is the only way of connecting to Jesus Christ, the Word.

**Sally Lam-Phoon**

# When You Ask for the Sun

*"For I know the plans I have for you," declares the Lord, "plans to prosper you and not to harm you, plans to give you hope and a future."*
*Jer. 29:11, NIV.*

IT IS THE DAY AFTER MY SON'S WEDDING in São Paulo, Brazil. All of us know what it takes to prepare and finish every detail for a wedding. Besides all the endless lists, telephones calls, and financial investment, you have to count on the unexpected. My son, Tiago, decided to have a garden wedding. We agreed immediately, knowing that February in Brazil is summertime—beautiful sunny days and no worries about rain. We went to the place several times to make sure we had Plan B, in case it did rain.

The day arrived. My husband and I woke up early and looked at the sky and tried to be confident that the sun would shine till 5:00 that afternoon. In fact, it was a beautiful day! My son said, "Mom, I'm praying for the sun; I know God will not let me down."

When we left the hotel about 4:00, a few dark clouds collected. I became worried not only for the wedding plan but for my son's faith. All the guests arrived on time, and the garden was beautiful. The violins, the music—it was heaven for me. Everything was perfect! Then plans changed. Dark, heavy clouds gathered, and the unexpected happened. Rain. Heavy rain. Our friends left the garden and headed to a shelter. What to do?

The groom and bride talked it over and decided to marry in the rain. The wedding began with the beautiful bride coming down the aisle under a huge umbrella, and a happy groom waiting for her with a big smile on his face. The surprise that made me cry came when my son sang to his bride, "I prayed for my God to send me the sun, but in His mighty plans for my life He sent me rain. But I still believe in this God who, when I ask for the sun, He sends me rain. Thank You, Lord, for my bride, who has married me even under the rain." The wedding was magical and unique. What a memorable day! We are still praising God for the refreshing rain.

Maybe you are asking God for the sun in your life, but somehow you've received a lot of rain. Don't be discouraged. Not only is God in control of our circumstances and plans—He is able to bring good from any situation. Be happy in the sun and enjoy the rain.

**Raquel Costa Arrais**

# God Will Provide

*Abraham answered, "God himself will provide the lamb*
*for the burnt offering, my son." Gen. 22:8, NIV.*

THE YEAR 1983 was one filled with great difficulties for my family. However, once more God fulfilled His promises made in Philippians 4:19: "And my God will meet all your needs according to his glorious riches in Christ Jesus" (NIV).

I was raising my family alone, and bills needed to be paid, so I sold the car, stopped my college course, and gave up a partnership in an X-ray photography institute. All at once I had lost several things that were important in my life. The only thing left was trusting in the Lord to help me feed and educate my four children. The crisis worsened; there wasn't enough food. For the first time I needed to work at night, leaving my children alone.

After a meal I frequently didn't know when the next one would be. In spite of the extreme suffering, I didn't share my concerns with the children, and I didn't allow them to perceive my concern, because I was certain that God would provide a way out. One night when I left for work, the children were alone and hungry. I prayed, telling God that I no longer knew what to do and asking Him to provide food for my children.

As I was closing the door my 12-year-old son, who had a healthy appetite, asked, "Mommy, are we going to go to bed without eating tonight?" The pain that I felt was indescribable. I held back my tears, took his hands, looked right into his eyes, and said, "God will provide, my son." I went down the stairs crying as he waved goodbye.

One of my son's teachers, who lived in our neighborhood, felt a tremendous burden that night as she prepared dinner. She felt as though she needed to go to my home. Quickly she asked her husband to take care of their son and filled a bag with food. When she arrived at my house, my children told her that I had gone to work and that they hadn't had anything to eat. The next day, as soon as I opened the door, my son came running. "Mother, God did provide! God did provide!" And he told me the whole story.

I shall never forget the joy of my child as he witnessed God's power to provide. It is so important to demonstrate to our children how much our God deserves to be trusted.

**Maria Chèvre**

# Ducks in a Row

*Let us walk in the light of the Lord. Isa. 2:5, NIV.*

"I'VE FINALLY GOT MY DUCKS IN A ROW—and I have no energy. Go figure!" In truth, the woman did look exhausted. Dark circles ringed her eyes, and her fingernails were bitten to the quick. Her brown hair hung limply as she moved restlessly, shifting from one foot to the other.

After another "Go figure," I took a deep breath. "Are you sure they're all your ducks?"

She stopped pacing. "Well, whose ducks would they be?" she demanded.

"Maybe some of them were handed over to you from family, school, or church. Perhaps you picked up a few from another's collection."

"Sure, they're all mine," she began, and then her voice trailed off into silence. "Well, that's a new thought!" She laughed nervously. "But they're all good ducks." Defensiveness lurked in her voice inflections. "Some are for home, and some for the job; some involve the community, and lots of them relate to the church and the school."

"They may all be good ducks," I continued, "but are they the right ducks for you?" The woman stopped pacing. "Are they right for your own innate giftedness, for the person God designed you to be? Are they worth the time and energy you are expending? Can you live in balance and still keep them all lined up?"

Silence, followed by a very large sigh. "Not at the rate I'm going," she admitted. A pause, then an even larger sigh. "So what would I do with the ducks that aren't right for me?"

"How about sending them back to their owners," I suggested, "and allowing everyone to be responsible for lining up their own ducks?"

"Now, that's definitely a new thought!" She actually chuckled, a twinkle in her eye.

"Remember," I concluded, "it doesn't matter how well your ducks are lined up if they're not your ducks or not the right ducks for you."

That thought clung to my consciousness over the next few days. After some personal consideration I decided it would be wise to devote some time to an honest evaluation of my own ducks, and to do it on a regular basis. *Lord,* I prayed, *I want my ducks lined up, and I want them to be the right ducks for me. After all, it's the truth that sets us free!*

**Arlene Taylor**

# Bird Housing

*And they shall build houses, and inhabit them; and they shall plant vineyards, and eat the fruit of them. Isa. 65:21.*

FOR THE PAST TWO YEARS we've had bluebirds nesting in our little red bluebird house. Since we have a nice, covered-bridge-style bird feeder, many birds enjoy coming to eat the birdseed that we provide. There are blue jays, cardinals, finches, titmice, chickadees, wrens, and many others. The bluebirds are not seedeaters, so most of the time they find their own insects and grubs, but sometimes we put out special bluebird grub for them, and also provide a birdbath for both drinking and bathing.

This year the bluebirds came back to claim their birdhouse for nesting. Whenever they are away from the birdhouse, two of the chickadees go to the house and look inside. It looked like the bluebirds might lose their house if they failed to stay nearby. This morning at 5:30, the time one of our little dogs decided to tell me it was time to get up, I looked out the kitchen window to see both Mama and Papa Bluebird sitting on top and beside the birdhouse. Evidently they had decided they needed to show the chickadees that this was their house and that they intended to have it all to themselves. Who would win? Only time would tell.

When I watch the chickadees and the bluebirds fighting over their nest site, I think of the text above that tells us how, in the new earth, we will build houses and live in them; we will plant vineyards and gardens and eat the fruit of them. We won't have to build and give the house to someone else. It will be ours forever.

I often think of how I would like to build that home, how many rooms I would want; but to me the most fun would be planning the gardens, both for food and for beauty. I want many fruit trees and flowering shrubs that not only look beautiful but will have fragrant blossoms all year long. I've never seen an orange tree bloom, but I've read that there are both fruit and blossoms on the tree at the same time. I believe this is the way it will be in the new earth. We will have never-fading flowers and fruit in abundance, provided eternally by a loving Father-God and His Son, for us to enjoy. We are even promised one tree that will bear 12 different kinds of fruit. How I long for that day to come!

**Loraine F. Sweetland**

# Was It Worth It?

*Looking unto Jesus the author and finisher of our faith; who for the joy
that was set before him endured the cross, despising the shame,
and is set down at the right hand of the throne of God. Heb. 12:2.*

MY FIRST PREGNANCY was a nightmare. I had nausea, dizziness, and
hunger. I was fortunate to maintain my weight, but what weight I did ac-
crue caused me to wobble as I walked. Everything irritated me, and I'd
break down and cry for no good reason. I found a book titled *What to
Expect When You Are Expecting,* by Arlene Eisenberg, Heidi E. Murkoff, and
Sandee E. Hathaway, the bible of maternity books. It explained what I was
going through and more.

As the delivery neared I felt restless and tired. I would have done anything to speed things along, but the fear of the imminent pain overpowered
me at times. Even so, I was impressed that all would be OK. Then the
thought of finally seeing my baby's face and holding her prompted me to
hasten the process by cleaning my room, moving furniture, walking, and
drinking black cohosh tea. Would it be worth it?

One morning I felt slight cramps in my lower abdomen that continued
every eight minutes, so we proceeded to the hospital. While I was being
transported by wheelchair to the delivery room, the slight cramps evolved
into sharp, knifelike pains so intense and painful that I wanted to be
knocked out. Relief came when the anaesthesiologist administered the
numbing epidural.

After a few big pushes, I was able to gaze upon my baby's face, and the
pain and imposition became a mere memory. Yes, it was worth it.

Imagine how Jesus must have felt when He came to earth and accepted
the pain and suffering He endured to save humanity. He thought it was
worth it. While being beat and spat upon and, ultimately, hung on a cross,
He looked down through the ages and saw each of us and decided that
dying would be worth it to see us in heaven. Jesus, "who for the joy that
was set before him endured the cross."

Just as there are books to prepare us for childbirth, the Bible is our reference to prepare us for Christ's coming. The pain and suffering we'll bear
will become a mere memory, because the joy we'll experience in our new
life will outweigh all that we'll endure for our Savior's sake.

**Larie S. Gray**

# Rejoice With Me

*And when she has found it, she calls her friends and neighbors together, saying, "Rejoice with me, for I've found the piece which I lost!" Luke 15:9, NKJV.*

WHENEVER I'M SCHEDULED to work at the hospital I'm never quite sure what my assignment will be until I arrive on the floor. Some days I'm assigned to care for a group of patients, and on occasion I'm assigned to be charge nurse. One day I was the charge nurse, and my duties were numerous, tasks that helped the floor run smoothly, and occasionally I was involved in direct patient care. It isn't infrequent that near the end of the shift I have to assign the nurses the maximum number of patients they are allowed to care for. Whenever my peers are busy, it's my responsibility to receive all additional admissions, usually one or two.

We had been very busy this particular day with 12 admissions, and the other nurses all had a full load. Three admissions came in rapid succession from the emergency room. The first patient was a very nice gentleman accompanied by his wife. He had a urinary tract problem and was waiting to see the urologist, who was in the operating room. About 30 minutes later the wife suddenly appeared in front of me at the nurses' desk, a look of distress on her face. "My husband needs your help badly!" she said. I quickly followed her to his room.

After getting him settled, his wife gasped, "I've lost my diamond ring!" She looked in his suitcase while I looked around the room, but to no avail. Tears came into her eyes. She said he had given it to her on their fourth anniversary. "I've lost a lot of weight lately, and it's too big. It must have fallen off while I unpacked." I could see both of them felt the loss greatly.

"Jesus knows where your ring is, and He will help us find it," I stated confidently. Quickly I bowed my head and sent up a short prayer for divine help, and the man added a few words to the prayer. As I opened my eyes I immediately saw the ring on the floor at the toe of my shoe. I handed the ring to the patient, who lovingly placed it on his wife's finger, saying, "Dear, I love you even more than I did when I put it on your finger 40 years ago."

All three of us were visibly moved that the dear Lord had helped us find it so quickly. Whenever I think of this incident I know that He will give us opportunities to testify of our trust in Him, and that He is indeed interested in every event in our lives!

**Rose Neff Sikora**

# Living Life to the Full

*But the fruit of the Spirit is love, joy, peace, patience, kindness, goodness, faithfulness, gentleness and self-control. Against such things there is no law. Gal. 5:22, 23, NIV.*

"GENTLENESS IS NOT A WEAKNESS," reads the epitaph on the headstone of a really gentle woman. This woman was an inspiration to many and a wonderful role model to her children.

Sometimes I look back over the years and think of the times the expressions on people's faces revealed what they thought of her, and I cringe and think, *If only they knew!*

Now, five years after she died and some 24 years after the loss of her husband, their many friends and family members still remember them with fondness and much respect. Many people found the Lord as a result of their unstinting devotion to Him. They often worked together selling religious books, bringing the love of Christ to many who may not have otherwise heard the gospel. She was never known to raise her voice, and I can't remember ever seeing her angry, though we had done much to vex her. Despite that, she was a disciplinarian and instilled manners and a sense of duty and responsibility into her children. And surely her children did rise up and called her blessed.

This week two young men in England were found guilty of axing Anthony Walker to death. His mother, Dee, responded that the crime was racially motivated, and her response brought back memories of my mother. I know that like Dee, she would have forgiven the perpetrators. I've listened to many discussions on the radio, and heard different people's views, both Christian and non-Christian, on whether or not to forgive the young men. Some have questioned how Dee could forgive someone who murdered her own flesh and blood, but remembering what my mother taught me, I would have to choose to forgive if only because I would not want anyone to have control over my life as those young men would have over Dee if she didn't forgive them. As Dee demonstrated, we have a perfect example in Jesus when He forgave the people who put Him to death even though He was innocent.

Thank God that we have been given the freedom to live life to the full in Jesus and for the assurance that death is not the end. His promise to each of us is "I have come that [you] may have life, and have it to the full" (John 10:10, NIV).

**Kathy Senessie**

# Betrayed by Appearance

*Man looks at the outward appearance,*
*but the Lord looks at the heart. 1 Sam. 16:7, NIV.*

THE GRAVIOLA, a native fruit from the Amazon, in South America, can be consumed as a fruit, as concentrated pulp, juice, ice cream, fruit preserves, jellies, or jams. Popularly known as "the poor man's jackfruit" because of its appearance, it belongs to the family of the sugar apple (*Annona squamosa*). It contains vitamin C, $B_1$ and $B_2$, besides calcium and iron. The leaves from this tree have been studied recently, and it was discovered that extract from these leaves has an inhibiting action on cancerous cells.

I learned of this fruit only three years ago when a company launched graviola-flavored gelatin. Only two years later, when I moved to a region that is rich in the production of this fruit, we were introduced to each other.

The fruit's appearance is not very attractive. Really, beauty is not its greatest attribute. In fact, this took away my desire to taste the fruit. One day, however, I decided to face this strange appearance, and to my surprise, I must confess that I had wasted opportunity. What a very tasty fruit! Its flavor is pleasant, refreshing, and lightly acid. I really liked it! And to think that just because of its appearance I didn't want to try it.

How many times I have judged people by their appearance? Actually, we do this frequently. We, in our fallen nature, have the tendency to prejudge people. Without knowing them and who they are, we build a profile of each individual in our mind. Our mind allows style and possessions to define people for us. Only when we talk a little with these people, or in some cases we become closer, do we realize that they are very different from what we thought. At times we are disappointed; other times we simply begin to love and admire them.

Have you ever stopped to think what the first impression is that people have of you? Or better, what should be your true identity after someone meets you? Imagine now if God were to judge us through first impressions. What a disaster!

How wonderful it is that God does not see us in this manner. God does not look at our exterior appearance, shriveled and tainted by sin. He looks within us, sees our heart, and knows who we really are. And the best part? He loves us in spite of this!

**Sandra Savaris**

# Little Things

*For who hath despised the day of small things? Zech. 4:10.*

MOST OFTEN we ignore little things in life. We consider them insignificant. Sometimes when my husband sees me troubled over something he remarks, "Why do you always worry over little things?" What he does not realize is that his statement has magnified my little worries instead of helping me to overlook them. Little things are important to me—there is a principle involved with them.

Does any one of us ignore a little dust in our eye? Do we ignore a small thorn in our finger? We are not able to function unless these small things are removed. Cooks know a little pinch of salt makes a difference in a sweet dish, as does a little pinch of sugar in a salty dish. Jesus stated that even a small jot, like a comma, is important in His law.

It doesn't take much to make someone happy. Just a small "Hi there," or even a smile when we are too much in a hurry to talk, can show that we do care. When we do have a little more time, then we can hug someone and say some words of encouragement.

Children are easily made happy by small attentions. Students learn better in class when we say a word of approval rather than a word of rebuke. God takes note of these small things. He even takes note of our thoughts and feelings. When I do my cooking, I find I cook better when I'm happy. I've said many times that if someone annoys me while I'm cooking, it will spoil the dish and make it less nourishing. It's just that I want my dish to be prepared well and with love that will nourish my family.

Ellen White writes, "It is the conscientious attention to what the world calls little things that make the great beauty and success of life. Little deeds of charity, little words of kindness, little acts of self-denial, a wise improvement of little opportunities, a diligent cultivation of little talents, make great [women] in God's sight. If those little things be faithfully attended to, if these graces be in you, and abound, they will make you perfect in every good work" (*Testimonies*, vol. 4, p. 543). "When our work on earth is ended, every one of the little duties performed with fidelity will be treasured as a precious gem before God" (*ibid.*, p. 591).

We need not let the little things of life upset us, but we do need to pay attention to them.

**Birdie Poddar**

# Mr. Independence

*For whoever finds me finds life, and obtains favor from the Lord. Prov. 8:35, NKJV.*

I HAVE THREE GRANDSONS, and I enjoy watching them grow up. They're 6, 14, and 19 years old. Already even the youngest has a desire for more independence. One day after acquiring a $5 bill for helping with a project, he made a profound statement: "Daddy, from now on I don't want you or Mommy to buy me any more toys. I'm going to earn money and buy them for myself." While Clay's dad noted his son's sincere desire to take some pressure off the family budget, he also knew that he would relinquish his independence the first time he came up short at the checkout counter!

I chuckled when I heard this story, but soon discovered my own analogy. Clay's experience could be likened to my telling God, "From now on, Lord, I'll take care of my own needs, leaving one less person for You to be concerned about." However, there have been times I've gone that route and lived to regret it. To be without our heavenly Father's care for even a moment spells disaster. I readily confess to wanting—and needing—His 24-hour involvement in my life.

Eric, the 14-year-old, wants to hurry the growing process by strengthening his muscles. Often he spends time at the local YMCA building up his "abs." After some serious resolve on his part, we're beginning to see real progress. Eric would like a little more girth, and we're quite certain he'll get it—he and the gym equipment have become good friends.

I'm in training too, but it's my spiritual muscles that I'm working on. This requires a time commitment as well, but the dividends pay off in terms of peace of mind and a better understanding of how intimately God wants to be involved in our lives. Now that I'm retired I have more time to devote to spiritual growth. Sometimes I visualize myself "preparing for my finals," and the time commitment is just "senior citizens' homework." While my grandsons are motivated to gain more independence and larger muscles, I'm attempting to be more dependent on my heavenly Father and to grow mentally and spiritually stronger by feeding on His Word and asking for more of His Spirit. "For whoever finds me finds life, and obtains favor from the Lord."

**Rose Otis**

# Faith Counts

*I can do all things through Christ who strengthens me. Phil. 4:13, NKJV.*

MY HUSBAND, Dave, and I traveled with a Maranatha group to Peru. The group planned a white-water rafting trip into the mountains. I was excited—I had never been on a white-water rafting trip, but I wanted to go. I enjoy water very much and can swim well.

After several hours of riding in a bus on a long, hot summer day, we finally arrived and piled out. We followed the rafting leaders down to the water's edge. We listened through a leader's broken English of what to do, how to paddle, how to sit on the raft, and, most important, what to do should we fall out. I happened to be standing in the back of the group and couldn't hear anything. I felt scared. Something kept telling me I should stay behind and not go, but Dave said I should, so I agreed with slight hesitation.

We split into groups; each raft had a leader, with a few more leaders in kayaks. We were given paddles and life jackets that I thought were primitive. We each chose a place to sit and were given a short description of what to do, and then we were off.

Everything went well; we were enjoying ourselves, slapping paddles together and splashing each other. Then the leader motioned to us—we were going through class four rapids. Suddenly our raft went down sideways into a huge wave and rock. Instead of flowing with it, we tipped over. At first I didn't know what had happened. My head popped out of the water, and I saw several others floating. I thought the entire raft was gone. I screamed—the rapids were so strong I couldn't keep my head above water. I swallowed a lot of water and choked. I tried to grab someone, but they went under with me. It knew it was a serious situation. I cried and tried to swim but couldn't, and lost sight of everyone and the other rafts.

I remembered that if we went overboard we were supposed to grab a kayak. I saw one and tried to grab it, but couldn't reach it. I kept going under. I was swallowing too much water. I thought my life was over. Then it hit me: only God could take care of me—I'm nothing without Him. Suddenly someone grabbed me and pulled me into a raft. I continued to cry and shiver. My vision was blurry. We finally made it back to shore and found that everyone was safe.

I'll never forget how God answered my prayer and sent my Dave to save me.

**Rita Back**

# Plan B

*He was chosen before the creation of the world, but was revealed in these last times for your sake. 1 Peter 1:20, NIV.*

MY HUSBAND AND I build rustic log beds. It takes time to pick out trees that have an unusual twist and knotty characteristics yet will fit together. Although it looks like a bunch of firewood at first, with hard work and patience it becomes a work of art; no two beds are alike.

And so it was at the beginning of this earth. The Bible says it was without shape and form. It must have looked like a whole bunch of nothing. Plan A was to create the perfect place with perfect and beautiful inhabitants. Everything from the grass, trees, insects, animals, and birds to Adam and Eve were created to have complete wholeness. Father God and Jesus would create man and woman in the image of themselves, perfect in all of their form and character. There was one drawback, though: because people were created with the freedom of choice, there would be a "What if?" What if people would choose not to obey and thus suffer the dire consequences? There would have to be a Plan B.

God always has a plan. It's called parenting with love and logic. God, our Father, has never wanted anything for us but the very best. He gave guidelines for the good of all creation. We all know that Adam and Eve, through their own choice and disobedience, descended to the level of a fallen angel, and now each of us is born with inherited, sinful tendencies.

The wise Indian saying "Don't judge a man until you have walked a mile in his moccasins" was heaven-sent. Heaven sent God in a Man to walk that mile, and then some, in our sandals.        Plan B, then, would be that Christ, the Creator of the worlds, the universe, would be the Redeemer. That wee baby born so long ago came to save a downfallen world, to shine the light of His truth upon the earth in one of its darkest hours. All of heaven rejoiced at the birth of this miracle child while most people didn't notice. His plan of action was an extreme rescue mission: to restore humanity to perfection and godliness. His love for us knows no bounds.

Your name was on the original draft of Plan B. You were on the heart and mind of God at Gethsemane. Your sins were borne by Jesus at Cavalry. So let Him have your cares, burdens, addictions, thoughts. Plan B is still in effect!

**Karen Fettig**

# Doing Good

*Therefore to him that knoweth to do good, and doeth it not,*
*to him it is sin. James 4:17.*

IT WAS MIDAFTERNOON on a beautiful spring day. I had picked up my 11-year-old son from school and was on the way back home, my 2-year-old son and 6-month-old daughter in the back seat. A yellow school bus had been in front of us for many blocks, and the younger ones were getting restless. I was anxious to get home.

We were about six blocks from home when the red flashers on the school bus came on. I slowed down, then came to a stop, as about 15 teenagers began getting off the bus and milling about. I could tell there was trouble brewing. They were standing in front of my car talking rudely, yelling, calling names, and making threatening motions to one particular girl. She attempted to walk toward the curb, but the teenagers blocked her in. Then one girl reached out and pushed her. The girl pushed back. Others moved closer toward her. I watched, horrified, my heart pounding, as I saw what I knew was going to be an attack on the girl. *This can't happen,* I thought. *It can't!*

Instantly I put my car in park and jumped out. I stepped between the teenagers and the young girl being chastised. I shook my head from side to side and calmly said, "Please, don't do this." Without saying a word, the entire group turned to leave, warning the girl, "We'll get you later! It ain't over yet." She walked off toward home. Relieved, I got back into my car, locked the doors, and drove the last few blocks home.

It's been 23 years since that day, and my oldest son reminds me occasionally of how I put myself—and possibly them—in harm's way. In hindsight I know that's true, but I didn't think about that then. I acted on the spur of the moment and did what I thought was right. I did think that *not* to do something to help would have been a sin. How often we enumerate the deeds that we consider wrong or sinful. But to close our eyes to doing what is good, right, and selfless, especially something critical, such as helping a person in a terrible predicament, is also sinful.

It isn't always easy or comfortable to choose to do good, but God's Holy Spirit prompts and guides us, and His angels will protect us as we seize the opportunities He lays before us.

*Help me, Lord, to open my eyes to doing good as You did when You were here on earth.*

**Iris L. Kitching**

# House Hunting

*I am creating new heavens and a new earth—so wonderful that no one will even think about the old ones anymore. Isa. 65:17, TLB.*

"I THINK WE'D BETTER MOVE closer to town," my radiographer husband said. We lived a half-hour drive out of town in a humble cottage on a sweet little farm. Andrew's job required he sometimes be on call after hours. For him, each call meant an hour on the road, plus worktime. My heart ached for my sleep-deprived husband. I had always refused to consider moving from our little farm overlooking the hills and open plains where our sheep grazed. The cottage was our first home, where our children had spent their babyhoods.

One particularly busy night Andrew was out on his fifth call. He'd had a total of one hour in bed. I awoke with a start, feeling something was wrong. I just had to pray. I didn't know what to pray specifically—I just felt danger was imminent. I got out of bed and checked on our sleeping children. I returned to bed but continued praying. About 15 minutes later Andrew arrived home, clearly shaken. He said he was overtired and his thoughts had been drifting while he drove. Somehow he became abruptly alert just in time to brake hard and swerve to avoid hitting a giant kangaroo. We realized how close I had been to being a widow and our two small children fatherless.

I reluctantly agreed to go house hunting. We inspected numerous houses together. We couldn't agree on even one. "The bedrooms are too small," "It's ugly," "It's too expensive," "The land slopes the wrong way," or "The kitchen bench is pink." Then Andrew suggested I look alone and recommend some for him to inspect. I still didn't find anything. Later he suggested I look for land on which to build a new house. I tried that, but nothing was like our land.

I was jerked into action when our own home sold unexpectedly. I realized that I hadn't genuinely been looking for a house. I had been looking at other people's homes and comparing them to my own. None had trees that I had planted, or little lambs romping together. None of the houses had marks on the walls my toddlers had made. I was holding on to the sentimental, denying the gift of a bigger, better, newer home. Going through the forms and functions of house hunting is inadequate—even spiritually. We need to be prepared to change addresses.

**Bridgid Kilgour**

# First Friends, Then Sisters

*Now therefore ye are no more strangers and foreigners, but fellow-citizens with the saints, and of the household of God. Eph. 2:19.*

WHEN WE MET 11 years ago, we were just two little girls, happy that we each had a playmate. The roads we traveled to this meeting in the coastal town of Douala, Cameroon, were very different. Even though our parents were both church workers, one was a missionary and the other a local pastor. It wasn't long before we were inseparable. We insisted that we travel together and sleep in the same room. We exchanged stories and jokes, and we even told each other our dreams. For more than a year this was our life. We were best friends.

Then the unthinkable happened. Our parents moved, and we were to be separated, possibly for good. We girls realized that this beautiful friendship would end, and our little hearts couldn't bear the separation. Then the best thing happened: it was suggested that we travel together for this trip. For one of us it would be the trip of a lifetime.

The trip was initially supposed to be a vacation for one of us; however, our closeness wasn't unnoticed by others around. It was then suggested and supported that we girls could remain together in Bermuda for another year.

Then the unbelievable happened. A proposition was made to us, and we were asked whether we would like to make this relationship permanent. Our hearts burst into joy—we were no longer going to be just friends, but sisters. This was a dream come true. So in December 1999, Meliseanna Gibbons, and I, Mystere Dipita Guiadem, became sisters.

This is how it is when we come into contact with Jesus, too. He has promised a relationship that will exceed our wildest dreams. We will be able to share our secrets, our dreams, our concerns; and this will make us love Him more as He longs to have this relationship grow. He has always wanted it to be permanent. Jesus is our friend, and He is our elder brother.

Take time today to meditate on this miracle, on all that has happened to make us a part of His family. How wonderful it is to be a member of the family of God! If you don't already consider yourself a part of this family, today is the day to make it happen.

**Meliseanna and Mystere Gibbons**

# Listen and Follow

*Cause me to hear thy loving-kindness in the morning; for in thee do I trust: cause me to know the way wherein I should walk; for I lift up my soul unto thee. Ps. 143:8.*

NOT LONG AGO my husband and I took a trip to the Atlanta area to "scout out the land." He was looking forward to retirement after more than 40 years in gospel ministry, and Atlanta was one of the areas we were considering. When we arrived at the Atlanta airport and went to pick up our rental car, we were informed that it had a navigation system that could assist us in getting around the area. I had never used one before, and the instructions at first seemed vague. I played with it as we drove to Lithonia, where we would be staying. After a day or two the navigation system began to make some sense and did, in fact, prove beneficial.

I entered our destination by area or address, and the system would detect where we were and proceed to give us the directions. Both my husband and I had to admit, "This is pretty neat," and mused that maybe we should get one installed in one of our cars.

After the planned scouting was completed, it was soon time for us to return to New York. After packing and loading, we were off to the airport to return the car and make our way to the airline. The system had an auto button to give directions back to the airport. We engaged it. As we pulled out of the driveway, the voice began giving us step-by-step directions. I was more than fascinated as it directed us exactly to the rental car return area without so much as one wrong turn—as long as we listened and followed.

"How much more on track our lives would be if we determined to listen to and follow God's instructions," I commented to my husband. Too often we insist on doing things our own way, only to end up in trouble and have to return to Him for guidance. Again and again He accepts us and lovingly steers us back in the right direction. His awesome system is programmed to keep us on track as long as we trust and obey His voice. As we continue to follow His leading, we find in Him a friend who wants only what is best for us, a friend whose plan is for us to spend eternity with Him in the home that He is preparing.

*Lord, help me to trust You even when I can't trace Your footsteps. Give me the faith to take Your hand and let You lead me all the way from earth to glory.*

**Gloria Stella Felder**

# A Nickel for Her Life

*Yea, though I walk through the valley of the shadow of death,*
*I will fear no evil. Ps. 23:4, NKJV.*

I'VE KNOWN DESEREÉ since she was a young teenager. She was an occasional babysitter for my vivacious 3-year-old daughter. Desereé thought she was cuter than a button, and she eventually became her godmother. Desereé always seemed older in wisdom than most girls her age. I suppose it was because she had battled sickle-cell anemia all her life. Sickle-cell is a very painful, debilitating—and at times, fatal—disease that strikes without warning. But Desereé was a determined Christian young woman who never let the disease keep her from achieving her goals and dreams. She grew into womanhood, took care of herself, ate healthfully, and dressed impeccably and demurely. She loved the Lord and kept her moral standards above reproach.

When I became director of the Pathfinder Club in our church, she became my deputy director. Although we experienced an age gap, we both shared a love for the youth that went beyond friendship. We were always there for each other in time of need. So it was no surprise that whenever she had a sickle-cell crisis I would be there at her hospital bedside to wipe her brow, keep her company, or just pray for her while she endured the debilitating disease.

It had been years since she'd had a crisis, but when I received the call that she was in ICU, I knew it was serious. I was devastated when I saw she was on a respirator. She was comatose and bloated beyond recognition. "O God," I prayed, "please keep her."

Sisters of faith banded together and prayed on her behalf. The prognosis wasn't good. Her major organs had been attacked and were shutting down. God quietly came to her and kept His promise to be with those who love Him during their near-death experience. Seventeen days later she was out of ICU and on the slow road to recovery. The next year she celebrated her fortieth birthday, and her favorite scripture became Psalm 23, which we all can personally claim.

If only the world would understand what a magnificent God we have the privilege to call Father, the one who values and cares for us. If only we could rejoice as the angels did in the knowledge that Jesus claimed victory over death. If only the world would believe in the true and living God, then each of us could walk through this world without fear!

**Evelyn Greenwade Boltwood**

# Antidote for Fear

*When I am afraid, I will trust in you. Ps. 56:3, NIV.*

DURING A VACATION in Los Angeles, California, my friend asked, "Olga, would you like to go to Tijuana, Mexico?"

"Of course," I replied, "That would be fantastic!" After an enjoyable trip shopping for souvenirs and visiting with her Mexican friends, we started our trip home late in the afternoon. As we drove through the picturesque town of Tijuana, a beautiful souvenir caught my attention.

I excitedly inquired, "Gloria, could we stop a minute at this store? I would like to have a close-up view of this souvenir."

"We'll do better than that," she replied. "I'll drop you off here while I go to the gas station just around the corner and come back for you in a few minutes."

Although there were so many interesting things to see, I quickly made my purchase and hurried back to wait for Gloria. I looked at my watch and realized that 30 minutes had passed. I was surprised when another half hour went by and Gloria still hadn't returned.

As the rays of sun began to sink in the western sky, my heart also felt an uneasy, sinking feeling. Soon the stores started closing, and lights were extinguished as darkness closed in. It became darker and darker. I was apprehensive, thinking something terrible must have happened to my friend, and fear gripped my heart. Then I remembered our text for today: "When I am afraid, I will trust in you." Silently I prayed, *"Dear Lord, please take care of Gloria, and please take care of me."*

The next instant there was my friend, looking concerned, worried, and apologetic, but safe. After we had both offered prayers of gratitude to God, I found out that as Gloria left the gas station a Mexican officer had stopped her because of a traffic violation, and she'd had to travel miles away to pay a fine. Only divine intervention enabled her to return to me before midnight.

Dear friend, today you might encounter unforeseen difficulties, challenges, crises, or trials that might cause fear or concern. Look heavenward! A look to Jesus will cast out fear.

**Olga Corbin de Lindo**

# A Model to Follow

*There was a certain man in Caesarea called Cornelius, a centurion of the band called the Italian band, a devout man, and one that feared God with all his house, which gave much alms to the people, and prayed to God alway. Acts 10:1, 2.*

THE BIBLE CONTAINS many stories that can be of special value to women. This story is about another group the Jews looked down upon. Cornelius was a Roman centurion in charge of a military unit of 100 soldiers in Caesarea, the headquarters of the Roman forces. The home of Cornelius was a model to follow. Today's text talks of these four qualities.

*He was devout.* The Word of God speaks of him as righteous and God-fearing, respected by all the Jewish people. How nice it is to hear people say that a man or woman is devout. How is your relationship with God? Are you a devout person?

*The whole family, not just Cornelius, feared God.* In one family I know, the father is not a God-fearing man—he is a drunkard. He never attends the church or the family worships the mother and the children conduct every day. The father comes in very late in the night and often beats his wife and children. They literally live in fear. They don't have peace of mind. When the whole family loves God, the home will become a heaven.

*Cornelius was a generous man;* he gave much alms. He was a man known for his charity. We should have a concern for the poor. It is our duty to help the poor, the needy, and the unfortunate ones. Dorcas, whose story is told just before Cornelius' story, was also known for helping the poor. Solomon wrote, "Blessed is he who is kind to the needy" (Prov. 14:21, NIV). He adds, "Whoever is kind to the needy honors God" (verse 31, NIV). By helping the poor, we lend to the Lord. Do you have a concern for the poor, and needy?

*Cornelius was a man of prayer.* Israel was a praying community. They used to pray on all occasions. As spiritual Israel we must be constant in prayers. The church should be a praying community. Prayer is a fellowship with God; it will influence our lives day by day. Jesus asked His church to watch and pray. Every home should be a house of prayer.

How much happier we could each be if we followed these godly examples!

**Saramma Stephenson**

# New Every Morning

*Great is his faithfulness; his mercies begin afresh each day.*
*Lam. 3:23, NLT.*

IT WAS SUCH A SIMPLE THING. Just a small, square plastic container with a pump on top, and the words "Gentle Foaming Hand Soap." But it was very special to me, because it was a gift from my youngest daughter, who lives with her husband and four children several thousand miles away. Since I don't get to see her very often, each morning as I used the fragrant soap it reminded me of her caring ways, and I would often offer up a prayer for her and her family. Nothing lasts forever, and after a few months the container was empty. I actually felt a sense of loss without this simple reminder of my daughter.

It was the springtime of the year, and as I looked outside I saw the fields were covered with a multitude of wildflowers of all kinds and colors. There were large showy purple ones and small dainty white flowers. My color-blind son especially enjoyed the yellow flowers, while others of our family saw the red hidden among the green leaves. The reminders of my heavenly Father were there every day. As some flowers finished blooming and faded, other species took their place. Even during the hot summer and into the fall, when the grass was dry and brown on our rain-deprived California hillsides, there were always a few flowers still blooming, still reminding me of my Father's love and care. Every morning I thanked God for His faithfulness.

There were other signs of His faithfulness as we planted our summer garden. We witnessed a miracle as we buried the dry seeds in the soil and within a few days little green shoots began to show. Before long those dry seeds had become large plants bearing tasty squash, tomatoes, cucumbers, green beans, and corn.

Not only in the morning was I reminded of His faithfulness, but also at night when I looked up into the sky at the millions of stars. As the moon shone down it seemed almost like a reflection of His face.

*Thank You, Father, that Your faithfulness does not run out as did my container of hand soap, but that signs are there to remind me, every day, every night, of what a great God You are. Help me to remember to express my thankfulness by sharing with others.*

**Betty J. Adams**

# Something More

*For I know the thoughts that I think toward you, saith the Lord, thoughts of peace, and not of evil, to give you an expected end. Jer. 29:11.*

THERE IS ALWAYS SOMETHING more to our thoughts, our dreams, and our possessions. There are still higher heights and deeper depths to which our heavenly Father wants us—all of us—to go. In deep thought one day, I asked myself this potent question: *Why stand on the seashore picking up pebbles when there are vast oceans to be explored?*

There are oceans of opportunities, career growth and advancement, and just unlimited oceans that are waiting for you and me. In order for us to experience the ocean, we have to leave our comfort zones of drylands—drylands of obstacles, drylands of pain without purpose, drylands of criticism, drylands of mediocrity, drylands of fear and failure, drylands of doubt and defeat. Even drylands of familiarity, despair, discouragement, and poor self-concept.

As you emancipate yourself from your drylands you will realize that you're actually tapping into your divine destiny, where you'll be not just a survivor but a conqueror. Not a victim but a victor, not mastered by your circumstances but mastering your circumstances. A warrior, and not a wimp, realizing that you, through Christ, are greater than your worst encounter. You will then be a direct recipient of the unimaginable, unthinkable reservoirs of blessings God has for His children through His various conduits.

I personally know how it feels to leave my comfort zone. When I accepted a contract with the Bermuda Hospital to work in the emergency room, it launched me into the unknown. The culture was totally different from the ones I was used to in the Caribbean. It was a real test for me, culture shock. The experience taught me that on occasion we have to perform in a show for which we had no rehearsal. Life will not always give us prepared assignments; we might have to do much research. Thank God, I caught the vision, adjusted and discharged my duties, realizing that this experience was designed to strengthen my character and my walk with God.

Today His greatest wish is that you will allow Him to give you a view of the great plans He has for you. His promises are sure, and He is the same yesterday, today, and forever. He has wonderful plans for you! Jesus wants us to explore His vast oceans.

**Althea Y. Boxx**

# Little Blessings

*Not that I speak in regard to need, for I have learned in whatever state I am, to be content. Phil. 4:11, NKJV.*

In order to take care of some company business, my niece's husband had to fly to California from their home in Georgia. We were thrilled when we learned he would be able to bring his family with him. In addition to my niece, their three little girls would be coming too. We attended church together, then went to my older daughter's house for a delicious home-cooked meal. We concluded lunch with a fresh peach cobbler and vanilla ice cream. Everyone was contentedly full (or a better description would be uncomfortably stuffed). However, 5-year-old Ruth still craved another serving of ice cream. Calmly she presented her empty plate to her dad and asked for more. He knew she had eaten enough and gently said, "No."

Now, my niece and her husband are good parents, and their little girls are lovingly well trained, but I guess Ruth felt a bit bolder, since she was surrounded by what she knew was a supportive, extended family. So she increased the volume of her pleading. However, her daddy repeated his "No." She started to pout, and to save the day her mother put a half dip of ice cream on little Ruth's plate. Ruth responded to her mother's kind gesture with "Is that all?" We didn't want to encourage the negative behavior, but because we were amused we all chuckled cautiously.

Then a thought came to me. Isn't that the way we treat God sometimes? Though He gives us blessing after blessing we tend to want more instead of appreciating what we already have. Sometimes God gives us some of the extras, and still we want more.

Of course it's all right to voice our desires and to reach for them when they're practical and possible. God wants us to be happy and to enjoy life as long as we realize it is He who gives us the wisdom and ability to achieve better heights. But Paul reminds us in today's text that he had learned to be contented in whatever state God placed him. He is a good example.

*Dear Lord, help us take time to listen, observe, and see ourselves in little children. Forgive us when we fail to appreciate Your blessings. Please calm our restlessness and love us still. Amen.*

**Mildred C. Williams**

# Be Ye Kind

*And be ye kind one to another, tenderhearted, forgiving one another, even as God for Christ's sake hath forgiven you. Eph. 4:32.*

HOW MUCH ALLOWANCE do we give others, those at home, those who work under us, our friends? It is so easy to be exacting or to draw a line: "You must reach here to be perfect" or "This is how I want it done." What did Jesus do? Jesus patiently allowed Judas to stay on to the end. Jesus never corrected him. He allowed Judas to see for himself when he was wrong. How about us? How kind are we to those who are unable to cope, or do, as well as we do?

We were on a holiday trip to Kodaikanal in India with our son and his family. One afternoon our two grandchildren, Tanisha and Rohit, ages 7 and 6, were bored to the core. They were tired of sitting in the car, and their parents hadn't brought any of their toys or books. So I suggested they go outdoors and play hopscotch. They liked the idea and invited me to join them in the game. To please them, I agreed, and the three of us went out.

Neither of them could draw their lines straight, so I offered to help them. They were amazed at my straight lines, and in no time the job was finished and they started the game. I knew how to play, but the trouble was I couldn't hop as well as they could. Imagine me, at nearly 70 years of age, trying to jump from one square to another using only one leg. It wasn't possible. I stepped on the line so many times the children wondered why I was doing that. Exasperated, one of them cried out, "Nana, you're not supposed to step on the lines." One of them demonstrated how it should be done. Finally I said, "Honey, Nana is too old. She can't hop anymore. You please play by yourselves." Disappointed, one said to the other, "We'll let Nana step on the lines. Let's play. Nana, you can step on the line."

Imagine little children making allowances for me. What an example! What a better world, church, or home it would be if we made room for others to grow, if we gave them the freedom to choose, or provided opportunities to do things for themselves in their own way. How much better if we trusted them with responsibilities, made allowances, and accepted their best when they can't do better, not ridiculing or lecturing when they make mistakes. This is Jesus' way.

**Birol Charlotte Christo**

# My God Cares

*Casting all your care upon Him, for He cares for you.*
*1 Peter 5:7, NKJV.*

ONCE AGAIN IT WAS TIME for the annual 124-mile (200 kilometer) trip to camp meeting. I was faced with a dilemma: travel at night and risk hitting a deer, or travel during the day and risk my health. My multiple sclerosis makes me extremely heat-sensitive. With my pastor-husband already at camp, I consulted my heavenly Father. I felt impressed to leave immediately, so I prayed for courage.

As the miles clicked by, the temperature rose steadily. So did my pain. I stopped at a restaurant, wet a hand towel to cool my shoulders, and again pulled onto the highway. I was thanking God for the relief when I heard a whistling sound and then a pop. I groaned as I imagined a burst salsa jar in the back seat with sauce all over my clothes. Although everything was clean, the problem was soon all too obvious—a flat rear tire.

I called the Canadian Automobile Association. The dispatcher assured me help would be on its way—in 45 minutes. Now I was in trouble: blistering sun, no air-conditioning, no breeze, and stuck on a hot highway. The cloth around my shoulders was drying. I reminded God how I struggled with heat. Suddenly a breeze blew through the window, and again I felt God's care.

When help finally arrived, the attendant fitted the spare and called ahead to reserve two new tires. "Awesome!" he exclaimed into the telephone, and I wondered what he meant. I learned the tire shop didn't stock my tire size. "But," the repairman said, "I ordered this size just in case, and they arrived only this morning." Coincidence? I believe not.

My jubilance was short-lived, however, as two lug nuts broke. The repairman gave no assurance these could be found anywhere in town. Listening to the one-sided telephone conversation, I again heard the word "Awesome!" An hour and a half later I was paying my bill. "Someone is looking out for you, ma'am," he said. "Two tires normally not stocked arrived today; and what's the chance of finding lug nuts in this town?" I assured him that my heavenly Father cares.

Sometimes we resent the irritations, but if we will only relax and let God solve our problems, our faith would grow. Daily we have the assurance that God cares.

**Sharon Ellison**

# Angels Watching Over Me

*For he shall give his angels charge over thee, to keep thee in all thy ways.*
*Ps. 91:11.*

I'VE HAD A FEW BRUSHES with death, but thankfully my guardian angel has been watching over me. My first harrowing experience happened at the age of 7. My younger brother, sister, and I were playing on a freshly blown straw stack. Suddenly I fell into an air pocket and was completely covered with straw. Nothing short of a miracle helped me burrow my way out of a potential tomb.

Another time two friends and I were going to visit a woman who had suffered a stroke. As we crossed a rural railway crossing, the driver didn't see a train coming until we were on the tracks. I was sitting where I'd get the full impact of a collision. Since I'm not one to scream, my eyes froze on the huge monster about to snuff out our lives. In the same instant the driver heard the whistle and stomped on the gas pedal. We cleared the tracks within an inch of our lives. Again God had sent an angel to watch over us.

I recall another time I came close to being a crime victim in California. Coming from a farm in central Alberta, I was rather naïve about life in big cities. One evening I rode a city transit from Glendale to the bus depot in Los Angeles, where I'd board the bus to visit my aunt in Santa Ana. I didn't realize I'd have to walk a block to the depot. I felt edgy as I lugged a big suitcase down the dark street, but I walked briskly with my eyes focused on my destination ahead. Suddenly two men barged out of an alcove, wanting to give me a lift to wherever I was going. One went to get the car while the other tried to divert me. I didn't see how I could get away, so I had to think of something quick. "Why don't we just drop my suitcase off at the depot first?" I suggested. "That way we won't have to mess with it." Once I was safely inside the depot, the man knew he had been duped—I wasn't leaving with him, so he left me alone. Thanks to my angel, I had outwitted the strangers.

I can say, like Peter of old, "Now I know of a surety, that the Lord hath sent his angel, and hath delivered me" (Acts 12:11). But how many times has my angel been protective of me that I'm unaware of? Before each of us begins this day, let's pause for a moment to ask God to send His angels to watch over us.

**Edith Fitch**

# Stopped by the Police

*And will be a Father unto you, and ye shall be my sons and daughters, saith the Lord Almighty. 2 Cor. 6:18.*

I WAS TAKING AN EXTENDED ROAD TRIP alone from Washington State to Texas. Each night I stopped driving in time to be settled in a motel before dark. In the morning I'd decide what town I wanted to get to. I didn't know the area and had no idea what different towns were like. I just did a lot of praying and guessing.

One day I had set my sights on a certain town in New Mexico and was racing through the corner of Colorado. Suddenly I heard the siren and saw red lights flashing. Yes, I had to admit I had been racing a little too fast to get to my destination before dark.

The friendly officer observed that I was alone and unfamiliar with the area. He asked me my plans, and when I shared them with him, he showed me on my map a road that was a good road and would cut off quite a distance. Then he told me that the town I planned to arrive at just before sundown was in an area that wasn't wise for a woman alone to stay in. I felt terrified at the mistake I had almost made. And I felt deep gratitude to God for stopping me. Since it was already afternoon by the time I was stopped, I decided to stay in that town. The policeman assured me it was safe.

At first I'd been upset with myself for being careless enough to get stopped by a policeman, but then I realized God used this incident to save me from danger. So often I speed through life, presuming I'm doing fine. I'm sure that I'm making good decisions. I'm pleased that I'm making good progress down the road I've chosen. Fortunately, each morning I give God permission to interfere with my direction, to interrupt my well-thought-out plans, to change my course through whatever means will get my attention.

God uses so many different ways that I'm always amazed at His ingenuity and creativeness. Not always at the time, but later I chuckle at His sometimes-humorous methods and praise Him for His willingness to take the trouble to keep track of me on all my escapades, and for His wisdom to lead me where I really need to go. *Thank You, Father.*

**Lana Fletcher**

# The Petition

*I can do all things through Christ which strengtheneth me. Phil. 4:13.*

I'M A COLLEGE TEACHER, and most of the time I love my profession. However, at times discouragement takes hold of me. I once scheduled a test for my students well in advance. We agreed to do a review of the material during the three class periods prior to the test. The students came only for the third class of the three review periods because the first two classes were near holidays.

Before the test one of the students told me that the class was going to ask for the test to be rescheduled. This irritated me. I like to plan activities in advance, and changing plans without a valid reason displeases me.

Upon arriving in the classroom, I found a petition on my desk that had been signed by all the students who didn't want to take the test. I felt a wave of indignation take hold of me. *Who do those students think they are? How can they have such irresponsible attitudes—missing classes on purpose, and then not wanting to face the consequences?*

I prayed to the Lord, feeling terribly indignant with the entire situation. *Would facing the class head-on be the best answer, Lord? If I do what they want, won't I be teaching them to flee responsibilities? How can I handle the anger that I feel?* All of these questions came to mind.

I began to talk calmly with the class. I told them that I could postpone the test; however, in professional life they would not always be able to flee from the consequences of their actions. I made a counterproposal: we would postpone the test, but we would have just one test, and they would, in addition to the test, present a book report. We voted, and the test was postponed.

At the end of the class two students talked to me, because they noticed the class uniting only in situations that didn't promote intellectual growth. We had a nice conversation, and I left that classroom feeling that God had allowed me to help that group of students. The experience served as more of a lesson for me than for them.

I understood that when I'm not able to control my feelings, I can ask God to intervene and change what is wrong in me. His intervention is immediate. Only God can remove negative feelings that are within us and replace them with love.

**Iani Dias Lauer-Leite**

# Comfort and Rest Come From God

*Cast your cares on the Lord and he will sustain you; he will never let the righteous fall. Ps. 55:22, NIV.*

THE AUTUMN SAID ITS GOODBYES, and we could feel the approaching winter with its short days and low temperatures bringing a relief from the heat characteristic of the midwest region of Brazil.

I knew that afternoon would touch my life. I was to keep my hospitalized grandmother company for a few hours until the next person arrived to stay for the night. Something told me that this could be the last time I would be with her. As I entered the room I saw Grandmother with a tube in her nose, and she asked, through her gestures, for it to be removed. Squeezing my hand and looking firmly into my eyes, she whispered, "Please, dear, I want to go home. Help me to get out of here. I want to leave."

She had been extremely agitated, I was informed. That situation left me very concerned; I needed to calm her, and I began to pray for God to guide me.

Grandmother would have her 100th birthday the following week. She was struggling against a tumor in her head and serious intestinal problems; however, she was lucid and communicated well. I caressed her face and her hands marked by the years, and almost instinctively, in a soft tone I began to sing hymns about Jesus' love, His return, and the new earth. Slowly she calmed down. She looked at me, squeezed my hand, at times shed a tear, and at times tried to accompany me. All afternoon I sang. When I left that night, she was sleeping peacefully, something she hadn't done for several days.

That night I thanked God for Grandmother and her long life, for the certainty of eternal life, and for the comfort found in the Bible and in the inspired songs that have the power to calm and soften suffering and transport our thoughts to another world.

That was the last time I saw Grandmother; however, I want to embrace her at the resurrection, and together we are going to sing many songs in the new earth. Absolutely nothing—neither suffering nor death—can separate us from this wonderful love if we cast our cares on the Lord.

**Olga Fernandes dos Reis**

# There Is No Substitute for Trust

*Trust in the Lord with all your heart and lean not on your own understanding; in all your ways acknowledge him, and he will make your paths straight. Prov. 3:5, 6, NIV.*

MY HUSBAND ASKED ME to accompany him to get a pickup he had taken 60 miles (97 kilometers) away to have a new engine installed. When we arrived, I waited in the car, leaving it and the air-conditioner running while he finished his transaction. It took longer than I expected.

The route home began on a busy highway. After a short distance the car made a strange noise. Then it stalled in the heavy traffic. After getting it started again, I turned into a nearby parking area. My husband followed me to see why I had stopped. Again the car stalled, and he started it. I got in the truck and drove behind him about a block to an auto parts store. Noticing that the car was running hot, he checked the overflow water container. Discovering the water remaining in it was hot, he added cold water from the outside faucet at the store.

He decided to try to drive the car home with me following in the truck. However, after two tries the truck would not start. Merlin tried, and still no response. He called the garage that installed the engine and received the promise that a mechanic would be sent to our rescue. While Merlin continued to work with the car, I prayed. Upon further checking, he found that the radiator was completely empty, and he filled it.

I continued to pray and at the same time have a pity party. I couldn't believe God was allowing this to happen after we had just gone through a trying experience with another car. My prayer consisted of telling God how I wanted Him to solve our dilemma. Suddenly the Holy Spirit caused me to question my reason for praying. If I knew how our problem needed to be solved, why did I need Him? Immediately I asked for forgiveness. Finally I realized what it really means to put my full trust and faith in Him.

The mechanic came but couldn't start the pickup either. He promised to have a wrecker come and take it back to the garage. Merlin started the car, and it ran beautifully all the rest of the way home.

What a God we serve! When we get out of the way and let Him take charge, He never lets us down!

**Marian M. Hart**

# Hand of Peace

*He stilled the storm to a whisper; the waves of the sea were hushed.*
*They were glad when it grew calm, and he guided them to their*
*desired haven. Let them give thanks to the Lord for his unfailing*
*love and his wonderful deeds for men. Ps. 107:29-31, NIV.*

A WOMAN WALKED INTO MY OFFICE one morning to tell me of a rumor about me that was making the rounds. I laughed it off because nothing could have been further from the truth. I concluded that she was making a joke. A few more minutes of her stay, however, indicated that this was no joke at all. I still dismissed it and told her, "I don't want to hear names, because I would rather continue respecting people around me." Nevertheless, the issue started bothering me. *How can people be so evil?* Why me? Why such a rumor? Little by little it started eating me up. I took it up in prayer and made up my mind that I would stick with God. After all, He and I knew the truth.

A month later the same woman showed up again, and without my consent she just blurted out the names of the people involved. Now I had to deal with feelings of hostility directed toward these individuals. Was the rumor true? No, it wasn't. Did it hurt me? Yes, badly!

There are times in our lives that all sorts of noises, like a storm, start to threaten us: dark clouds, thunder, lightning, strong winds. Even the peaceful trees will start to have fierce hissing noises, and one feels there is no way out. Noises and commotion are the devil's way of putting us into a panic mode so we will give up.

After the dust had settled, I started reflecting on what took place during the ordeal. People who mattered to me sent notes to say they cared and were praying for me. The sermon one Friday night sounded as if it were being preached just for me. A woman stopped me by the roadside and said, "I heard, and I just want to stop here and pray for you. This is an attack from the evil one." My devotional readings seemed to address the turmoil I was going through. I realized I wasn't alone; the Lord was with me through it all!

I don't know what you might be going through in your life, but I urge you, my sister, to look out for the Hand that calms the storm. Call out to Him; He will never turn away from a voice that pleads for His help. You will see that He has been there all along.

Storms by nature are a passing feature! The sun is permanent—as is the Son.

**Judith Musvosvi**

# Courage

*Have I not commanded you? Be strong and courageous. Do not be terrified; do not be discouraged, for the Lord your God will be with you wherever you go. Joshua 1:9, NIV.*

ARE YOU AFRAID of something? Fear can be good if it teaches us about courage. Joshua couldn't have truly understood courage if he hadn't experienced fear. Fear gave him a courageous character and taught him to rely on God.

Early in my life I had to learn about courage, only because God's calls in my life were always bigger than I was. Fear was the first feeling I had before accepting any calls and facing the challenges. Sound familiar? That's why *courage* is my favorite word—and I've learned there is no courage without fear. Fear goes away only when you stop growing, and I truly believe that God works through our fears, saying the same beautiful words He spoke to Joshua.

Have you been challenged lately? Has God commissioned you to do something difficult? Have you been chosen to do a job you never imagined before? Just remember that God promises to equip us with courage, no matter what difficulties we are having. Joshua knew that the task was beyond his natural ability. Can you imagine being in Joshua's sandals, having the responsibility not only to replace Moses but to also face all his enemies? What a task! Understanding Joshua's feelings of inadequacy, God talked to Him about having courage.

It is difficult to be a woman of courage. We can feel courageous from time to time, but true courage is a daily decision, an act of faith. This morning as you face your day, remind yourself that God is always with you. Your situation may be genuinely threatening, but He has not abandoned you, and He promises to stay by your side.

Pray with a thankful heart, asking God to give you what you need to deal with your fears.

Joshua firmly faced his fears, difficulties, and obstacles, knowing God had promised to be with Him. Joshua could move into the land with courage, focusing not on the obstacles but on God, who is completely trustworthy.

God grant you courage enough for today and enough to meet any challenge before you. So be strong and courageous! God will be with you wherever you go.

**Raquel Costa Arrais**

# The Great Banana War

*This is love for God: to obey his commands. 1 John 5:3, NIV.*

WHEN I WAS LITTLE, my mother waged an unsuccessful campaign to get my father to eat a healthier diet. His typical sack lunch consisted of a sandwich, a soda, and a candy bar. Papa refused to give up his sweets, so Mama decided to add a piece of fruit to his lunch.

Trouble was, Papa wouldn't eat the fruit. Every morning Mama packed fruit in his lunch, and every evening he would bring it home, uneaten. This went on for weeks, with neither side giving an inch.

Finally one morning Mama let my sister and me in on a secret. "I've decided to give up on trying to get your father to eat fruit," she announced. "I've bought a plastic banana to put in his lunch. Let's see how long it takes him to figure it out."

The battle went on, except this time with the plastic banana instead of actual fruit. At night Mama would open the bag and scold Papa for bringing home the banana. Then one day he came home with an empty bag. When Mama questioned him, he told her, "I ate the banana, as you wanted me to!"

After much arguing, Papa finally let Mama off the hook by producing the plastic banana from his coat pocket. Papa was the official winner of the banana war, because at this point Mama surrendered.

I'm reminded of this story whenever the question of obedience comes up. God has given us a blueprint in the Holy Bible for how He wants us to live. The Ten Commandments show us how to live a good and moral life—if we obey them. Many of our modern health concerns didn't exist in Bible times, but the teaching that our bodies were created by God, and ultimately belong to Him, certainly encourages us to take care of ourselves. And that, of course, was why Mama wanted Papa to eat more fruit.

But knowing what we should do is a long way from doing it. We have to want to obey. God can provide us with rules for a happy life, but we insist on doing things our own way, even if it is harmful to us. If we truly love God, we will try to obey Him. Like Mama offering my dad fruit day after day, the Lord offers us a rich and bountiful life, if we only choose to accept it.

**Gina Lee**

# A Light in the Night

*The light shines in the darkness, and the darkness has not overcome it.
John 1:5, ESV.*

THERE USED TO BE TWO CHOICES I could make when I needed to get
up during the night. Either I could turn on a light and temporarily blind
myself, or I could grope in the darkness and try not to bump my knee on
the corner of the piano bench.

Now that's all changed. I bought a sensor night-light. I know it's there
all the time, but I notice it a lot more when it's dark. That little device is
very dependable. And because it has a sensor, it doesn't need anyone to
turn it on and off. It just starts glowing when the room begins to get dark.
It has kept me out of harm's way more than once. If I cover that small
beam with my hand, the sensor responds as if the room were dark, and automatically shines. If I find that I'm in total darkness, that little bit of lumi-
nescence will safely guide me to it—if I follow it.

Like my night-light, only far superior, Jesus is always there too.
However, I seem to notice Him more distinctly in the lightless parts of my
life. His gift of hope and love reach out to me like a beacon in the darkness
of my night. I know I can depend on Him. He's always at work in my behalf.

If I try to hide the dark parts of my life from others, or even myself,
Jesus responds immediately. He can sense my situation and knows my innermost feelings when no one else can. The light He gives me can keep me
from falling. Sometimes when I seem to be losing my way, He is there as
my guide, walking me safely through unknown paths. Jesus talked of this
saying: "I am the light of the world. Whoever follows me will not walk in
darkness, but will have the light of life" (John 8:12, ESV).

I have a friend who reminds me of a night-light. She's not the kind who
stands out in a crowd, but when she meets someone who is struggling in
spiritual darkness she lets her light shine. By sharing God's Word, she
makes it possible to keep that person from falling.

Jesus has invited us to be a light for the dark world. He says, "Let your
light shine before others, so that they may see your good works and give
glory to your Father who is in heaven" (Matt. 5:16, ESV). Jesus is pleased
when we share the light He gives us. He is the true light of the world.
Perhaps that's why God calls Him Son.

**Marcia Mollenkopf**

# Lost

*For the Son of man is come to save that which was lost.*
*Matt. 18:11.*

I WAS HELPING MY SON choose a toy in a department store while his father took care of our 10-month-old daughter. When we walked back to my husband, I realized that the baby was gone. She was lost. Since our city is known for children being kidnapped, I desperately ran everywhere in the store. Near the cash register, I asked if they had seen a baby crawling around. A young woman assured me that lost children were taken upstairs to the manager's office. I ran up the stairs, skipping steps as I went. To my relief, I found Carlinha on the lap of a little boy who certainly felt like a hero because he had saved a lost baby.

Another day, in the same store, Carlinha was holding my hand as we looked at the dolls. Meanwhile, her brother looked at cars with his aunt. A little later my sister approached me, somewhat frightened—she had lost my little boy.

I didn't become as desperate this time. Seven-year-old Carlinhos knew how to say his name, address, and his mother's name. Besides, I knew exactly where to look for him. With heart beating rapidly, I zipped up the stairs. I found him there, very frightened, and holding the hand of the store manager.

Later, when my children were grown, we went to the beach. On the sand with my three small nephews, I went near the water to take a picture of my son in a kayak. I had two of the children with me, and the oldest, the 3-year old, stayed with his uncle. When we returned, we discovered that he was no longer there. All the adults desperately searched for Rodriguinho. He didn't know how to speak Portuguese, he didn't know where we were staying, and the beach was full of people. To our relief, he had been found by a lifeguard.

What a horrible sensation to lose a child! What anguish! This helps me begin to understand all Christ's efforts to seek His lost children. The worst part is that many of us, as lost children, don't even know our situation. And it's comforting to know that our Father knows exactly where we are. More than this, He comes to our assistance through the Holy Spirit to show us the way opened by Jesus on the Cross.

*Thank You, Lord, for the high-risk operation that You undertook to save me!*

**Sônia Maria Rigoli Santos**

# God Is Not Finished With Us

*But Jesus beheld them, and said unto them, With men this is impossible; but with God all things are possible. Matt. 19:26.*

SIX YEARS AGO we moved from a busy city to a small community 200 miles (320 kilometers) from our home of 21 years. My husband and I had checked out the boarding high school nearby for our youngest son, but, upon seeing this area, determined that this was a place we would never want to settle. God must have had other plans, however, because we have lived here happily these six years. We bought a house on one and a half acres, with a huge mimosa tree at the front and two beautiful redbud trees at the back and side of the house.

One time we had been away for a few days, and upon arriving home, we saw that one of our redbud trees had been uprooted because of the wind and heavy rain. This was a mature tree, about 15 years old. We cut it up and mourned its loss. The next spring we noticed a redbud growing from the same spot, probably from a small piece of root that was still in the ground where it had lain unnoticed. My husband has been tenderly caring for this little shoot, and six years later we have a beautiful, healthy tree in full bloom.

Sometimes tragedy or hard times come our way. It seems as if these winds of strife just about "do us in," and we can't see how we will ever get back up. But God in His goodness nurtures us, pampers us, and loves us so much that we can't help looking up, smiling, and trying again because we know that God is not finished with us yet. He loves us too much to give up on us. David spoke of this protection that comes only from God: "They saw the works of the Lord, his wonderful deeds in the deep. For he spoke and stirred up a tempest that lifted high the waves. . . . Then they cried out to the Lord in their trouble, and he brought them out of their distress. He stilled the storm to a whisper; the waves of the sea were hushed. They were glad when it grew calm, and he guided them to their desired haven" (Ps. 107:24-30).

*Thank You, Lord, for being with us every step of the way, for Your guiding Spirit, and Your helping hand. Without You by our side we would have no growth or hope. Thank You, Lord.*

**Janet Thornton**

# The Cell Phone

*Are they not all ministering spirits sent forth to minister for those who will inherit salvation? Heb. 1:14, NKJV.*

IT WAS A BEAUTIFUL SUNDAY AFTERNOON, and my family and I were looking forward to a sacred 500-voice concert, "Psalms, Hymns, and Spiritual Songs." After my daughter, Marina, and I arrived at the large cathedral, we started on the self-guided tour of the facility. We were only partway through the tour when we noticed that people were already gathering in the main auditorium, even though it was still more than a half hour until the beginning of the program. Because we wanted to get a good seat, I decided to sit down and save a spot for the three other members of my family, who were still traveling and calling from time to time to ask for directions.

Marina took her phone and went outside for a little while. When she returned, she reached into her pocket and realized her phone wasn't there. Panicking, she rushed back to the place she had used it last.

A very short time later I was glad to see that the rest of my family had arrived. When I told Jennifer what had happened, she said, "But I just talked to her!" Quickly she dialed Marina's cell number and heard it ringing, but no one answered. She decided to put it on redial in the hope that someone would hear it and be kind enough to turn it in to lost and found.

Not more than 10 minutes had passed before Marina appeared at the end of our aisle, holding her phone. She told us she had prayed as she ran, but when she got to the place she had hoped to find the phone, it wasn't there. As she passed an usher in the back of the church, she heard her cell ringing. "That's my phone!" she said out loud. So the usher reached into his coat pocket and showed it to her. After her confirmation, he handed it to her as he added, "Turn it off!"

How grateful we all were for the miracle. There were several hundred people in that building and scores of ushers. Surely an angel had led her to the right place at the right time.

*Dear Lord, thank You for Your wonderful angels and the many ways they bless us day by day. Amen.*

**Mildred C. Williams**

# The Hand of God

*The righteous cry out, and the Lord hears, and delivers them out of all their troubles. The Lord is near to those who have a broken heart, and saves such as have a contrite spirit. Ps. 34:17, 18, NKJV.*

AFTER I GRADUATED from high school, I began an apprenticeship as a lithographer. I got used to the work quickly and enjoyed my work. It was diversified, it never got boring, and I got along very well with my colleagues. Then I started working in the photographic department. I enjoyed work even more, and I asked if I could get training in reprophotography, but I was told that in this job the prospect for the future was rather bad.

So I continued my training in lithography and graduated with a good grade. Since my relationship with the boss wasn't the best, I decided to quit after completing my job training. I found a new company right away where I could work and apply my newly gained knowledge. This company was a short walking distance from my apartment, which I found very positive. I quickly gained essential knowledge and was able to cope with the tasks very well in a pleasant atmosphere.

My boss, however, took on orders that were contrary to my ethical convictions. What should I do? Some colleagues' consciences had become dulled, and they worked as if this kind of thing didn't make a difference to them. Before long I dreaded work when I heard that a new catalogue of this kind was about to be published. One day I decided I was going to tell the head of my department that I wasn't going to do this sort of work anymore.

I prayed for God's guidance and that He would give me the right words to say. And then the moment was there, but I felt unable to move. Just then I felt a hand on my back, pushing me forward. I really felt that hand! I told the boss very frankly that I didn't want to do those jobs anymore. And, lo and behold, it was no problem! From then on I always received "nice" tasks, and I became friends with the head of the department. When he left the company after some time, he asked me if I wanted to join him. He and his friend had founded a new company and needed skilled workers. So I worked another five years in that company.

If we ask and depend on God, He intervenes when we need Him!

**Sandra Widulle**

# God Can Even Use E-mail!

*Praise be to the God and Father of our Lord Jesus Christ,*
*the Father of compassion and the God of all comfort, who*
*comforts us in all our troubles, so that we can comfort those in any*
*trouble with the comfort we ourselves have received from God.*
*2 Cor. 1:3, 4, NIV.*

E-MAILNG IS SOMETHING I truly enjoy doing. My e-mail address book is full of names of folks I've never even met. The reason for this is that I do Bible studies and prayer requests for others. Many people I pray with over the Internet continue to write to me and seem to be encouraged by our online studies. I try not to send many forwards, but sometimes a forward will come to me that just speaks to my heart, and I feel impressed to send it on to someone else. Such was the case this very morning.

A forward arrived that was a parable of a man who had gone to heaven at Jesus' second coming. He was standing in the judgment hall when he noticed that everyone had quilt blocks laid out, representing their lives. Some were beautifully colored with lovely patterns; others had small holes in them. He noticed that his quilt blocks were just shabby and ugly and full of holes. He wondered what was going on.

When he asked the angel about it, the angel held up the pieces, and as he did so, the man could see the light of God shining through all the ugly holes. It was indeed beautiful! The angel assured him that the pieces with the most holes were actually the most lovely of all because they depended upon God's light shining through them.

I was impressed to pass this forward on to several people, and a short time later I received a reply that really made me stop and think, *Lord, what if I hadn't listened to You?*

This person had opened that e-mail in great despair. It came only seconds after he had seriously considered taking his own life. He said he was crying as he wrote, and he had felt that he had absolutely nothing left to offer the Lord anymore. He was so grateful that I had sent the story, and he thanked me again and again. He said his life was exactly like that of the man in the story. God has many ways that He can use us to encourage others. I pray that He will always keep us open to respond to Him, even when it is such a simple thing as sending a forward to someone to encourage them in the Christian way.

**Anna May Radke Waters**

# Witness

*You show that you are a letter from Christ. 2 Cor. 3:3, NIV.*

IT WAS THE DAY BEFORE MOTHER'S DAY. My husband and daughters, Lillian and Cassandra, and I had enjoyed a special Mother's Day program at church. When we got home, the girls raced to the dining room, giggling as they tried to tickle each other. In Cassandra's exuberance to escape her sister's hold, she tripped over her own foot and fell hard. This didn't immediately concern me, as she plays hard, falls often, and is usually fine. After a few seconds, however, she started screaming. This was unexpected. Sending up a mother's silent prayer, I quickly deduced she was seriously hurt and an afternoon trip to the emergency room was warranted.

I grabbed two *Bible Story* books, a few cookies, and Cassandra's favorite thing when life hands her bumps—a cup of chocolate soy milk—and we were on our way to the ER. Cassandra had stopped crying, but she was moaning and favoring her right side, particularly her shoulder and neck areas. While we were waiting for treatment, I read to her a story about Adam and Eve, and then the story of Noah. Just before I started Moses, Cassandra said, "Mommy, I'm scared."

I replied, "Honey, there is no reason to be afraid. The doctor is just going to ask you where hurts, take some pictures, and, hopefully, just send us home."

"But I'm still afraid, Mommy," Cassandra replied softly.

I told her that God is always with us. "Do you think you would feel better if I prayed for you?" I asked.

Cassandra nodded her head yes. After a short prayer, Cassandra smiled at me and said, "Thanks, Mom!"

The pediatric intern evaluated Cassandra, and two X-rays revealed a closed fracture of the clavicle. After a dose of pain medication and a sling, Cassandra was chatting and singing again. As we were leaving, the woman in the curtain area next to Cassandra's stretcher stopped me. She said, "Thank you for your Bible stories and songs—they made me feel better. Please keep me in your prayers as well."

I had no idea this woman was listening. It never dawned on me that we were being witnesses to others. I was just comforting a hurting child and, in the process, comforted a hurting woman.

*Lord, help us each day to be the kind of letter that shows someone Your love.*

**Tamara Marquez de Smith**

# The Most Beautiful Present

*Taste and see that the Lord is good; blessed is the man
who takes refuge in him. Ps. 34:8, NIV.*

IT WAS MOTHER'S DAY, and I wanted to visit my mother who lived in São Paulo, about 110 miles (180 kilometers) from my home. As the church pastor, my husband had his agenda filled for the day, and he wouldn't be able to take me.

Since our boys, Wesley, 3, and Willer, only 5 months old, were very small, it would be impossible for me to travel alone with them. I participated in special Mother's Day festivities in the city plaza and had lunch with some friends from church, but actually I was sad because I couldn't visit my mother.

The day was ending! There was to be a Mother's Day program at church, but my husband had to leave for a commitment he had that night. I began to feel sorry for myself. *What a day! I didn't spend it with my mother, my husband gave me no attention because of his activities, and now I can't even attend the Mother's Day program!*

Depressed, I put the children to bed and soon fell asleep also. Then I was awakened by my husband saying that there was a couple in the living room who wanted to talk to me. Sleepily I went into the living room, and they told me, "We were the first ones to arrive at the accident scene and offer first aid to your husband."

For the first time I really looked at my husband. He was pale and had his arm in a cast. "And the car?" I asked.

"It's better not to see it," he said. "The only thing left are the seats."

If I and the children had been with him, certainly I could have been badly hurt, and perhaps the children would not have survived. Suddenly I woke up, grateful for my wonderful Mother's Day present—the lives of my dear husband and children.

I really didn't understand when my husband didn't want to take me to the program. He knew that I didn't like to miss the special worship service. But I soon understood God was taking care of everything and didn't allow me to leave the house with my little ones that rainy night.

*Thank You, Jesus, for my life and for the lives of the children You have given me.*

Elza C. dos Santos

# Re-Creation

*Behold, I make all things new. Rev. 21:5.*

LAST YEAR I DECIDED to plant spring bulbs in the three long planters on the windowsill. The summer flowers I usually planted there always bloomed when we were away and therefore needed to be cared for by the neighbors. The new plants produced a blaze of breathtaking beauty as yellow and mauve crocuses followed soft-white snowdrops, to be succeeded by multi-colored anemones, freesias, and dwarf irises. They surpassed our every expectation in their loveliness, and beautified the ugliness of our human-made world of concrete and asphalt.

Upon our return several months later, however, the planters were a sad spectacle of cracked, sun baked earth, almost as hard as the concrete yard. Not a single stalk or leaf gave hope that there was any life below the surface. I told myself that the bulbs were probably unharmed, deep in the planters, and decided to dig them up to verify this. But I was very disappointed. Some had disappeared completely, and those that remained were little more than dry husks that crumbled in my hands. I was ready to throw them away when I noticed that some of these skins had tiny pieces of bulb remaining, and I determined to plant them again to see if they could possibly recover.

Weeks came and went before small green shoots began to appear. When the flowers eventually bloomed they were inferior in number, size, and beauty. But they bloomed triumphantly nonetheless. Now I'm feeding them regularly and caring for them tenderly, and when it is time to dig the bulbs up for the summer, I'm confident that they will be well developed and healthy, ready to produce an even more beautiful display next year.

Often, when the Master Gardener takes us under His care, we are like those poor, neglected little bulbs. There is nothing of beauty in our sin-scarred, shriveled, selfish lives, but He who put the spark of life into us originally knows our potential. When warmed by the sunshine of His love and regularly fed by His Word, we reach up to commune with our Creator and Sustainer, and then we start to bloom. Without any effort on our part, the lovely flowers of a Christlike life bring joy to those around us and glory to the Master Gardener, the Creator and Re-Creator of everything beautiful, from a dried-up bulb to a sin-scarred soul.

**Revel Papaioannou**

# A Promise Made Good

*May the Lord our God show us his approval
and make our efforts successful. Ps. 90:17, NLT.*

"This is your chance, Debbie, and you'd better be quick to take it," advised our early intervention caseworker. A young child and her mother had perished in a mobile home fire, thus creating an opportunity for another special-needs child to take her place in school. I didn't hesitate. Sonny began his school career at age 12. This new school was to be a prototype, a lighthouse, for all Canada. It was heralded as "The Beacon of Hope."

Sonny's needs were many. Just keeping him alive was emotionally and physically exhausting for me. He was often sick, or would be awake during the night. Consequently, sometimes we'd stay home, or he'd arrive late for school. I kept the administration staff informed. Still, to this day, our guardian angels help Sonny's dad and me make the 75-mile (120 kilometer) round trip to school and back home through all kinds of weather!

It was in late October 1989 when I was asked to meet with the vice principal. I wasn't prepared for the pain that pierced my heart. "You'd better make more of an effort to get Sonny to school, or he will lose his place here!" Then the unthinkable happened just a few days later. Sonny was airlifted to Edmonton with life-threatening medical concerns.

On my knees beside my child's deathbed, I wept and prayed. Jesus heard my prayers, and Sonny's life was spared. Immediately upon our return home, Sonny was dedicated to the Lord.

A humble thank-you would never do. I owed Jesus much more than that, and I told Him so. "It's my desire to do my best each and every day to tell others about what You have done for me." This is a promise that heaven helps me keep.

In 1990 I felt the Lord instruct me to journal Sonny's and my life. I'm happy that I obeyed. It's through these blessed pages, which I've entitled "Dimensions of Love," that I witness for the Lord. I've made a sincere and honest effort, for my entire family's sake, to be the best Christian that I know how to be, and I believe that God is pleased with me.

It's my hope that you can say the same. I feel that the human race is standing on the threshold of eternity. Christians who shine with love for Jesus are indeed His beacons of hope.

**Deborah Sanders**

# When Bad Things Happen to Good People

*Have pity on me, . . . O you my friends, for the hand of God has touched me! Job 19:21, NRSV.*

THE WHOLE TOWN MOURNED the death of a fallen hero. Dan Snyder, age 25, played forward for the Atlanta Thrashers hockey team before his tragic death in a motor vehicle accident. His best friend, teammate, and namesake was the driver of the Ferrari on that fateful night. Dan was a young man from a Mennonite town not far from where I live who made it big in hockey, Canada's favorite sport. Tributes poured in from family, friends, teammates, hometown folks, and hockey officials. All attested to the good person this young man was. Yet his life was tragically cut short.

Literally hundreds of thousands of stories can be told of "good" people to whom bad things have happened. The example above was recent and given much local media coverage. For many of us, when bad things happen there is no media coverage, no hometown support. We consider ourselves fortunate to have family and friends around. Depending on the circumstances, we may even find ourselves deserted by those we expected to offer support. In spite of our life experiences that should have taught us better, we do a mental search, anxiously trying to uncover the hidden and unconfessed sin that has resulted in this punishment. We know for a fact that Scripture does not support this theology. If God were to punish us for each sin we commit, we would be blotted out of existence before reaching adulthood. Yet we insist on punishing ourselves in this manner.

I'm convinced that while we live in this sinful world bad things will happen, regardless of our personal actions. That's the nature of sin. The evil one will assail us, especially if Satan thinks there's a chance to discourage us, but God's love will prevail. During times of trial let us, like Job, hold fast to these words: "For I know that my Redeemer lives, and that at the last he will stand upon the earth; and after my skin has been thus destroyed, then in my flesh I shall see God" (Job 19:25, 26, NRSV).

Dear sister, be assured that the heavy cross you bear is not a punishment from God. You are being prepared to live in a place where nothing bad will ever happen to you again. Hold fast to this promise!

**Avis Mae Rodney**

# Garbage

*Who can say, "I have kept my heart pure;*
*I am clean and without sin"? Prov. 20:9, NIV.*

THURSDAY IS OUR WEEKLY garbage pickup day. Every Wednesday night after we come home from church, we haul the garbage can, yard waste, and recycle bin out to the curb in front of our house. It's amazing how much trash one family can accumulate in a week's time. Sometimes I'm embarrassed at how huge the pile is! I look around at my neighbors' trash piles, and they don't seem to be as big as ours.

As I was rolling the cans out one night I thought, *Wouldn't it be wonderful if I could just roll myself out to the curb each week and have all the garbage in me removed—from my heart, soul, mind, and body? To have the feeling the woman in the Bible had when she touched Jesus?*

I was thinking of the woman in Mark 5 and Luke 8. She had been bleeding for 12 years and was healed by one touch of the Master's garment. What must that have felt like! Or to be lifted from a state of death, as was Jairus' daughter when Jesus took her hand and raised her out of bed. Or to feel the scales fall from your eyes, as did Bartimaeus when Jesus healed his sight. Just think of how marvelous we would feel to have all the filth, decay, and rot instantly taken away!

This world fills us with so much junk from television, newspapers, video games, music, conversation, selfish thoughts, and hundreds of other things. How can we, with our sinful nature, keep ourselves pure and clean? God doesn't want to have to throw us all away. In fact, He said, "For I did not come to judge the world, but to save it" (John 12:47, NIV). He created us in His image, so He alone can remove the rotten, spoiled debris, recycle what is salvageable, and purify me with His Spirit.

What a great way to experience this by going to church each week. Through worship, prayer, singing, and listening to His Word, we are re-created. No more garbage! No more dirt! This purifying process allows me to be confident in sharing my faith with others. I'm re-created into a new creature.

Do you feel like having all that garbage removed from your life today? Jesus can haul it away. Jesus is waiting for you at the curb!

**Karen Phillips**

# A Map for the Journey

*You have made known to me the path of life; you will fill me with joy in your presence, with eternal pleasures at your right hand. Ps. 16:11, NIV.*

THE WIDE-BODIED TRUCK picked up speed, so I accelerated and stayed close to prevent any other vehicle from coming between it and my Buick Regal. I wasn't tailgating—I just wanted to make sure that I kept up with the driver so that I could catch his signal to me to turn right when I came to the correct exit. Lost again, I was depending on a kind-faced truck driver who had heard my pitiful tale at a service station that I had stopped at for directions. "I'm going that way. Just follow me," he volunteered. By following him, I got to my speaking engagement on time.

Over time I've perfected the art of getting lost, and even with the advent of MapQuest (which I now use regularly), there's no guarantee that I'll get to my destination without making a few wrong turns. If I'm on my way to a new location, it's almost a given that I'll get lost at least once. It sounds as if I'm not a fit candidate for life in today's fast-paced world, in which everyone seems to be going nowhere at breakneck speed. The truth is, not many of us are cut out for this kind of life without a little help. My older son, who is well aware of my flawed sense of direction, became exasperated. "Ma, get a map!" A real estate agent, he is an expert map reader and knows the value of such a skill.

Actually, I do know the value of a map, though I'm not good at using one. I've seen others use it to good advantage. When a group of us women traveled from Maryland to New England to attend a conference, we missed our interstate connection into Massachusetts. But Peggy, our driver, had a map that she immediately used like a pro. Although we had gone many miles out of our way, she was able to read us back onto the right road and to our destination.

Life is a journey, and for those of us who want to get to our destination successfully, the advice is crucial: Get a map! The Bible has all the roads mapped out, and our Lord Himself is eager to steer us down the right path. This map is a safeguard against being lost in this world's maze of conflicting values, and when we open it up we will see that the great Cartographer has given us the full layout of the territory over which we must travel. If we listen, we can hear Him saying, "I'm going your way; follow Me." And if we willingly follow, we will never be lost, but joyfully end up where we need to go.

**Judith P. Nembhard**

# Service Needs No Title

*Serve the Lord with gladness: come before his presence with singing. Ps. 100:2.*

I WAS ONLY 15 and in high school when it was decided I must undergo ear-nose-and-throat surgery. I was scared, afraid—terrified. What if something went wrong? I didn't want to die. As I awaited my turn to be taken to the operating room, I shivered intensely and uncontrollably as I lay on the hospital bed. I decided to bargain with the Lord. "Dear Jesus," I prayed, "I'm very scared; I don't want to die. Could You please make the surgery go well and wake me up? Don't let me die now. If You do this for me, I promise You that I will be Yours in service for the rest of my life."

Sometime later I didn't know whether I was sleeping, dreaming, awake, alive, or dead. I just wasn't sure—it was just a weird feeling. I began to seek for answers by running my hands all over my body. Finally I found the bandaged surgical site. So it did happen, and I was awake and alive! It was a glorious feeling! Immediately I remembered the promise I had made to God earlier that day. I turned my head to face the window, as if to look up at the sky for God so that I could thank Him. Instead I saw a bright and beautifully lit ship out on the ocean, making its way to dock in the harbor. It was indeed a beautiful scene, and I felt peace and happiness inside of me. I just wanted to celebrate life! My prayer began, "Dear God, thank You for waking me up. Now I'm totally Yours. Use me anywhere You want to use me for the rest of my life. Amen."

I'm 45 now, and God has kept me faithful to my vow. I have absolutely no regrets; I believe it was the greatest and the best decision I've ever made. The noblest thing that anyone can do with life is to give it back to God in service. It really doesn't matter what kind of work we do as long as we are in God's service—that's all that matters. Service to God needs no title; it only requires willingness.

A songwriter seems to have captured my experience in God's service when the following song was perfectly penned: "I am happy in the service of the King, I am happy, O so happy! I have peace and joy that nothing else can bring, in the service of the King."

May you find peace, joy, and happiness in God's service today and always.

**Jacqueline Hope HoShing-Clarke**

# Mothers in Israel

*The aged women likewise, that they be in behaviour as becometh holiness . . . . that they may teach the young women. Titus 2:3, 4.*

AS I GREW UP IN THE CHURCH I remember that there were certain elderly women in our congregation who were called "mothers in Israel." The thing I remember most about these women was that all church members, young and old, showed them great respect. Their advice was sought by younger women, and those in need of prayer would also go to them.

As a young person it was difficult to understand just how important these women were in the life of our church. But as I grew older and became a wife and mother, I began to understand the important role "mothers in Israel" would play in my life.

Through the years there have been a number of women who have been my "mothers in Israel." Each of them was a role model to me, an advisor, a teacher—someone who loved me and showed me compassion and sometimes was able to identify with my own struggles because she had walked that way before. These women have taken the time to share with me from their own experience, their hearts, and their pain. I've been so grateful for each woman God has sent into my life, for they have helped to make me the woman I am today.

Paul gives counsel to the older women in our midst. He says that these women must be exemplary in their behavior, and that they should teach the younger women. With each passing year I find myself growing older, and the question I ask myself is *Will I become a "mother in Israel," and will I have to wait until I'm old and gray to do this?*

I've concluded that I've been an "older" woman since I was in my 20s, when I found that to teenagers I was considered old. But the real question is whether I've taken the time through the years to mentor or help my younger sisters as they face life's many challenges. The answer is yes, but I've been more intentional with my assistance since I entered my 40s. Now I'm seeing my 50s. But this hasn't caused me to feel that I no longer need to be mentored.

I believe that God calls all women to be "mothers in Israel" to our younger sisters. It takes time and patience, but the rewards are many as you see these precious flowers bloom and become the women God intended them to be. Will you too take up the challenge?

**Heather-Dawn Small**

145

# Favorite Daughter

*Delight yourself in the Lord and he will give you the desires of your heart. Commit your way to the Lord; trust in him and he will do this: Ps. 37:4, 5, NIV.*

BEING A FAVORITE DAUGHTER is very good—and a privilege. It makes us feel very special, and an immense satisfaction emanates from within us like a light that illuminates all who are around us. This joy overflows through our smile, the way we look at people and things, and through our words, revealing everything within us.

This is how we feel when we understand the love of our heavenly Father, who loves each one of us as His favorite daughter. Each of us is unique. Our omnipotent God can love each one of us, individually and completely, without denying any of His blessings to His other sons and daughters.

I was my father's favorite daughter, and this brought me much joy; however, it also brought me much sadness. I had 14 brothers and sisters, and the three siblings closest to my age were very jealous. This caused them to hit me quite a lot. They broke all the toys and presents that I received, and I never saw my things again. One day I saw them breaking the last doll that I had received. I went up to them, crying, and told them that I was going to tell Daddy and Mommy. My brother said that if I told them he would do away with me and throw me in the weeds that were beside our farmhouse. Fear overtook me, and I told no one.

All of this was because of their jealousy, the result of my being my father's favorite. In spite of this, I never hated them for this; in fact, I love them very much. I have hope that one day Jesus will change their hearts, and they will accept Him as their Savior. And then, when we reach heaven and contemplate the glorious face of Jesus, all that we experienced here will be forgotten forever.

Jealousy or envy will no longer exist in that land where everyone will be treated and loved the same. Everything will be filled with peace and joy such as we have never before felt. If here we have bountiful moments of peace and joy, in heaven we will find an explosion of joy.

*Dear heavenly Father, lead me in Your ways until we reach the eternal home. Don't allow us to take our eyes off our dear Savior, Jesus.*

**Aparecida Bomfim Dornelles**

# Don't Ever Doubt!

*Therefore do not worry, saying, "What shall we eat?" or "What shall we drink?" or "What shall we wear?". . . But seek first the kingdom of God and His righteousness, and all these things shall be added to you. Matt. 6:31-33, NKJV.*

WHEN I REACHED RETIREMENT in 1994, I decided to open my own business instead of continuing to work in the same company. I always enjoyed working, so my husband and I opened an establishment in which children's parties could be held. This undertaking involved a great amount of work, but we were rewarded very well financially.

Since only my husband and I did the work, the profits were ours. After our business had been in operation successfully for four years, a couple befriended us and sometimes visited. Nadir became a close friend, and she began to talk to me about the Bible and about Jesus' return. I grew up in an evangelical home, but I had never heard anyone talk about Jesus' return. Nadir offered a Bible study to me, and I promptly accepted it. She and her husband began to visit us more frequently, and invited us to come to their church. It had been 17 years since I had visited my church, but as I understood the true teaching of Christ I accepted the doctrine she taught.

My work was very intense, especially from Friday through the early hours of the morning on Sunday. However, in one weekend I earned four times what I had received from my retirement for one month.

The Bible studies continued, and when the topic of the Sabbath was studied, I had no doubt that this was God's will. From that day on I didn't schedule another party. The last commitment had been fulfilled. To everyone's surprise—my family, clients, and even the minister and his wife—I closed my business. I was certain that by doing God's will and obeying His commandments, I would not be in need of anything. And I can guarantee that up until today, at no time have I missed that extra money.

I'm happy because I've been chosen by God. I belong to Him, and I know that He cares for me. I will never doubt His promise, and I want to be always ready to do His will.

*Lord, help me today and always to follow Your commandments and Your will for my life.*

**Eliana Nunes Peixoto**

# Love Hearts

*God is love. 1 John 4:8, NIV.*

I COLLECT HEARTS. I'm not sure how the collection started. I think I liked the simple shape, and that they are symbols of love and affection.

I didn't realize how many hearts I had collected until our church teens visited, and as a joke they began to count the hearts on the pictures, those hanging from the Shaker-style peg rails, and the country-style padded hearts on a home-made wreath and coordinating hearth garland. There more than over 150. And that was only the living room. Then they started on the kitchen, where the walls are stenciled with a garland border that has a heart every 10 centimeters.

Many of my hearts are made from different materials—wood, glass, leather, pewter, amber, felt, terra-cotta, porcelain, fabric, and even salt! But they aren't just decorative; the hearts remind me of different aspects of God's love.

The felt heart is soft and warm and reminds me of God's loving care and kindness. The heart made of marbled red stone reminds me of the strength of God's love for me, and that it will last forever. The tiny blackboard heart with its felt eraser reminds me that His forgiving love keeps no record of my wrongs. The needlepoint heart with hundreds of tiny stitches reminds me of God's patient love for me and the way He pays attention to every detail of my life. The crystal glass heart reminds me that God has openly revealed His love for me in a thousand different ways. The heart-shaped wreath of rusty wire is like a crown of thorns that reminds me of the sacrifices God has made because He loves me. The heart made from chicken wire is like a fence that reminds me of God's protection. One smooth metal heart contains a gentle chime that reminds me of the joy that God puts in my life to make my heart sing. A wax candle heart invites me to let the light of God's love in my life shine out to others.

As I look over my hearts again, they don't just remind me of God's love; they inspire me to love others in the extravagant way that God has loved me: kindly, patiently, everlastingly, forgivingly, sacrificially, protectively, and joyously. Some days I need one heart aspect more than another. Which of God's love hearts do you need most? And which of God's love hearts will you most need to share with those you meet today?

**Karen Holford**

# An Angel

*For He shall give His angels charge over you, to keep you in all your ways.*
*Ps. 91:11, NKJV.*

AS A FRESHMAN IN COLLEGE I had the opportunity to reside in the home of a wonderful family. On a beautiful Sunday morning I decided to take a walk around the neighborhood, and, as was my custom, I prayed before leaving. It wasn't long after I closed the front gate and began walking that I heard a shuffle behind me. I instinctively turned, and what I saw froze me in my tracks. Our neighbor's always-in-a-bad-mood rottweiler, Rock, was loose. I knew it would be dangerous to show fear, and I was too far away from home to call for help. I stood still, asking God what my options were, when Rock passed me, advanced a few steps, stopped, patiently waited a few seconds, then looked at me as if asking, "Well, are we going for a walk, or not?"

To my surprise, I started walking, and to my relief Rock started walking too. Ours wasn't the usual owner and pet side-by-side walk, although we were very aware of the other.

Rock was displaying his athletic abilities by jumping over hurdles and chasing after small birds while I tried to breathe and show confidence with each step. We came to a small park, and Rock soon disappeared behind some trees. I kept walking on the road and resumed my conversation with God that had started during my morning worship. Minutes passed, and with no sign of Rock, I became more relaxed—until I saw a strange man walking toward me. Trying to avoid contact, I slowed my pace and crossed the two-lane street to the other sidewalk. To my dismay, the stranger quickened his pace and crossed over too. Each step was closing the gap between us, so I deliberately walked back to the sidewalk beside the park.

As I glanced back, I saw the stranger coming straight toward me with a grin on his face. Just then I caught sight of Rock rolling on the grass. Without hesitating, I whistled to him, and he jumped to his feet and looked directly at me. I then did something I never thought I would do—I patted my knee, beckoning Rock to come to me. Then a threefold race took place: Rock raced toward me, my heart raced faster, and, best of all, the stranger raced away.

Back in my room I praised God from whom all mercies flow, and I thanked Him for His protection that morning. Indeed, before His children call, God will answer, and while they are still speaking, He will hear (Isa. 65:24).

**Evelia R. Cargill**

# Sharing With Those in Need

*Share with God's people who are in need. Practice hospitality. Rom. 12:13, NIV.*

"ARE MY EYES PLAYING TRICKS ON ME, or am I seeing things?" I asked my husband as he drove past a woman and a baby on the side of the road.

"What?" My husband turned his head toward me. "What did you say?"

I pointed to the woman and the baby standing on the side of the road. Neither had much clothing on. Since we were close to our house, I told my husband to drive me home quickly so that I could grab a dress and come back to the mother and child.

When we returned to the place, we again found the woman and the baby boy. After we got her dressed, we invited her to get in the car to go to our home with us. Something wasn't right, but we didn't know just what it was. At home we thought we could find out what was wrong.

The woman, holding her baby in her arms, agreed without talking, and got into the car. Within a few minutes we were home. The baby was hungry, and he cried all the way home. I quickly made him some cereal and gave it to him. To my surprise, the mother began wrestling the cereal plate from the baby's hands. I quickly added some bread and fruit and placed it before them. My husband and I watched them compete for the food, which they finished within minutes.

We later learned that they had been on the road for more than three days and hadn't eaten anything during that time. We packed some extra food for them before my husband took them to where they were going.

My mind was directed to what the Bible says in Romans: "Share with God's people who are in need. Practice hospitality." May the Lord give us eyes to see other people's needs, a heart to respond to those needs, and a deep sense of the suffering of many in this world.

Many times we may not have a lot to give to other people, but whatever we give may make a big difference to someone who has nothing. With one act of kindness we can bring relief to one of God's suffering children.

**Judith Mwansa**

# A Circle of Warm Women

*Who can find a virtuous woman? for her price is far above rubies. . . .*
*Favour is deceitful, and beauty is vain: but a woman that feareth the Lord,*
*she shall be praised. Prov. 31:10-30.*

WHEN WOMEN JOIN TOGETHER as a force to achieve a common goal or fulfill a worthy cause, there most likely will be success, because as a group we are a force to reckon with. Women serve as pillars, a community that comforts, cheers, ministers, and gives of themselves to others, bringing healing and health. Women bring hope where there is despair, and touch the lives of those who mourn.

Whether we are married, single, widowed, mothers, grandmothers, or sisters, women have a great responsibility. We read of the virtuous woman in Proverbs 31, but some of us may say we don't fit this picture, or this is not how we want to live. Whatever our choices are, the important factor is that we play our roles well, because as we move on, we become role models for those who follow.

A few years ago I had to leave the city of my birth and travel to another city to work in a position that would require my being away for a long time. I was concerned that I would be alone and miss my friends and family. The change was necessary, however, so I went.

I gradually adjusted to my job and made new friends, but being a single woman, I wanted to travel to my home city frequently for fellowship. Then one weekend I was introduced to the women's ministries activities at the university church where I work, and was invited to the meetings. This brought about a change in my life.

After attending the first women's ministries meeting, I continued to go, and soon became involved in the different activities. Being multiskilled, I also had a lot to offer. A warm fellowship circle developed among us women, and our ministry was very rewarding. I'm amazed at the goodness of God in supplying our needs and hearing and answering our prayers. The need for fellowship among family, friends, and associates can be a great one, and can have negative consequences if it is taken lightly.

*Thank You, heavenly Father, for a circle of warm women who have helped to fill my need for fellowship. May God continue to bless us as we strive to reach and touch lives for His cause.*

**Elizabeth Ida Cain**

# Standing Strong

*A farmer went out to sow his seed. . . . Some fell along the path, and the birds came and ate it up. Some fell on rocky places, where it did not have much soil. It sprang up quickly, because the soil was shallow. But when the sun came up, the plants were scorched, and they withered because they had no root. Other seed fell among thorns, which grew up and choked the plants. Still other seed fell on good soil, where it produced a crop—a hundred, sixty or thirty times what was sown. Matt. 13:3-8, NIV.*

LARGE BLOSSOMS of bright-yellow, deep-orange, and variegated orange-and-rust marigolds nestled snugly into their crate, awaiting a new home in a garden. They had caught my eye as being perfect for my outdoor patio. Their fresh green leaves hinted of healthy foliage that would grace my garden. Proudly I carried my new purchase home. Flowerpots cradled in French water rocks awaited them.

I planted them in the choicest planting mix and set the pots amid the stones. They had space, felt the wind, and savored the sun. But there was room for only half the crate of flowers in the pots. So I planted them closely together in a corner of the garden like a ground cover.

The ones in the pots didn't do well at first. They didn't like being single plants in the pots. With no support from the other plants, they faced the winds alone. Their heads drooped. Their leaves wilted. I watered and fed and hoped. Gradually, the plants gained strength. Their heads stood up. Their leaves filled out. They were growing! Not only did the marigolds in the pots grow—they flourished and bloomed, like the house built on the rock that absorbed the wind, the sun, the storms, and stood firm (Matt. 7:24-27).

What about the ones planted close together? At first they did well; then they weakened. There was no place to grow. Roots entangled with each other; leaves turned brown. Flowers withered. Soon only a few were alive.

It is comfortable for us to stay in our comfort zone, surrounded by family, friends, money, convenience, and church. We may depend on others for our spiritual growth, and take it all for granted. Often it's when we strike out alone on some venture, or when a crisis sets us apart, that we forge ahead with our life, knowing what God can do for us individually. It's then that we grow, becoming strong and secure, compassionate and mature.

**Edna Maye Gallington**

# Where Will We Go?

*Come to Me, all you who labor and are heavy laden,*
*and I will give you rest. Matt. 11:28, NKJV.*

HERE I AM, seated on a cement bench, in just any square in front of just any church. The night is rainy, and now the clock is showing that it's minutes before midnight. The rain outside has slacked off, but I'm raining on the inside—a rain of complaints, doubts, uncertainties, insecurities, and dislikes. Fear of facing the future. To tell the truth, what I have is a storm within me. At times it seems as though I will drown.

Why am I so vulnerable? Where is my self-sufficiency? I feel an incredible attraction to difficult, impossible, unique things. I like challenges; however, here I am, seated on this bench in the square as though I have no place to go, yet conscious that I need to go. Although the sun doesn't appear, even though the water overflows, I need to go.

Is there anyone who understands me? I need to go, but where will I go? To the security of a happy home? Does this exist? To a place of peace and comfort? Where can I find this? To the arms of someone who loves me more than life itself? Would this make me happy? Shall I go to the agitated life of those who take advantage of each second of existence in orgies and pleasures? Here within me there is just a sea of tears. After all, live for what?

When I find no solution in any of these alternatives, when the emptiness continues in the heart of someone who has experienced everything, when I've been disappointed with everything and no longer want to live, I need to admit that Christ on that cross is the only thing that motivates me to keep going. I go on in spite of the summer thunderstorms that temporarily cloud the brightness of my life.

Without the sun, nature dies; and without Christ, hope vanishes. He is the Sun of righteousness, the Sun that warms me!

The multitudes move from one place to the other, in a hurry to reach where I've arrived. But I'm certain that I would not reach any place if I hadn't recognized Christ as the only way. I didn't know that it was useless to run along the paths of the world until the storm came and I needed to take His hand, which was always there reaching out to me. It is through the grace of the Father that we can walk along holding hands with Jesus during the storms of life!

**Judete Soares de Andrade**

# My Life

*How great is your goodness. Ps. 31:19, NIV.*

AFTER GROWING UP in a small town in the interior of the country, I moved to the capital city for college. I was enchanted with new friends and the freedom of living by myself. I tried everything. For four and a half years this was my way of life. I didn't believe in God. I didn't even think about attending church. The Bible was foreign to me, and I knew very little about Jesus and had no idea that He would return.

Growing tired of the parties, I began to think of suicide. What would happen if I killed myself? Would I go to hell? In spite of learning this in my childhood, I didn't believe it. What should I believe in? I knew nothing about life. A great emptiness overtook me because I lived far from my parents. They didn't know of my needs.

One Friday night I called my friend Vanessa and told her everything that I was experiencing. She had just returned from a Bible study and said that the people she studied with were praying for me. I knew that I hadn't called by chance. God had answered their prayers and extended mercy to me.

I didn't believe in God, but she invited me to learn about Him, and I accepted. She introduced me to Margarete, who told me of a God that I didn't know—a God who is an intimate, loving, kind friend. This was exactly what I needed! We began the studies the following day. Our studies lasted for almost four hours, because we talked of the many things happening in our lives. I invited all my friends from the parties to the studies. Many began, but unfortunately, they didn't continue. A true transformation took place in my life. I lost interest in things that had occupied me before, and I began to truly love the things of God. After three months of intensive Bible studies I gave my life to Christ.

My family was against my decision until they recognized that I had changed for the better. God gave me a wonderful husband and new friends who today bring joy to my life. Today my greatest desire is my salvation and that of the people who surround me. For this reason I do as much as possible to witness in the best manner, sharing what I believe. I have great pleasure in working for God!

**Renata Panini Nadaline**

# Miracle on the Puente de las Américas

*The angel of the Lord encampeth round about them that fear him, and delivereth them. Ps. 34:7.*

I WAS RETURNING from work that beautiful June Sunday. As my husband and I drove along, enjoying the beauties of nature, we engaged in an interesting discussion. We were almost midway across the bridge Puente de las Américas when our conversation came to an unexpected halt. To our horror, a car traveling in the opposite lane careened, then zigzagged across the double lanes and came directly at us.

My husband exclaimed, "Father, have mercy!" I was too numb even to breathe a prayer. I simply closed my eyes. He slammed on the brakes, and we both waited for the impending crash.

The few seconds that elapsed seemed like hours before I heard my husband whisper, "Thank You, Jesus." Only then did I open my eyes. Where was the car that had been rushing to crash into us? How did it get back across the double lines into the correct lane? These unanswered questions and the miracle that occurred will be explained by our guardian angel when we get to heaven and he tells us the rest of the story.

Experiences such as this reassure us that God is indeed a loving, watchful, and caring Father who constantly cares for His children. I hear someone say, "But Sister Lindo, sometimes bad things happen. What about the accident that took the life of Barbra's nephew? Or the tragedy in which three members of the Da Costa family perished? My answer is simply "I cannot explain, because I don't know." What I do know is the unalterable fact that God's love is so great that He died for us.

Permit me to share an anonymous quotation I read a few days ago that has helped me to cope with some of these trials and the sadness we face daily. The author states, "God does not shield us from pain that sin has spread throughout the race, for if He did, how could we know the depths of wisdom, love, and grace of God. God does not keep us from life's storms; He walks through them with us."

*Dear Father, grant us faith to trust that You are always with us, even though we cannot understand everything.*

Olga Corbin de Lindo

# A Satisfying Answer

*Before they call I will answer; while they are still speaking
I will hear. Isa. 65:24, NIV.*

ONE WELL-REMEMBERED EXPERIENCE marked my childhood.
My mother, a beautiful and strong woman, began to have pain in
her abdomen. Because the pain was so intense, she couldn't sleep at
night. Many times I saw my father kneeling at the foot of her bed,
praying night after night, asking our heavenly Father to take away my
mother's pain. For a child, witnessing your mother in such a weakened
condition wasn't something very encouraging or reassuring.

Friends and relatives formed a prayer circle, interceding for my mother.
Within six months she underwent surgery twice to discover the origin of
her pain; however, the cause wasn't found.

No physician could discover the cause of her suffering. When we no
longer understood why God permitted this situation, a doctor and family
friend said that it would be necessary to perform a hysterectomy. Several
days before my mother's surgery, a biopsy disclosed that there were small
tumors in the uterus. Because they were located on the organ's wall, it had
been impossible to see these tumors previously. Then we understood the
reason for the pain that signaled a problem. Perhaps without pain my
mother would not have sought medical advice, and the small tumors might
have grown and become something more complicated.

Sometimes we suffer, and want the discomfort removed immediately.
We ask God for something, and we want things to happen in our way and
in our time. However, God's clock is much better than ours. If we place our
lives—and everything else—in His hands, He is faithful and just to fulfill
His promises. As He has promised, He will grant what our heart desires.
We need to respect His silence and wait for Him to intervene in our life; He
cares for our happiness and peace. Even though our prayer may not be answered in our time, it is because God knows the right time to pour out His
blessings. After giving your life to the Lord, trust in His answer, even if you
don't understand what is happening at the moment. In the future you will
certainly understand, because before you call, He will answer.

*Today, Lord, give me patience to understand that You have the best
answer for me in Your time.*

**Priscila Ferri Sarmento Martins**

# The Master's Touch

*Be not ye therefore like unto them: for your Father knoweth
what things ye have need of, before ye ask him. Matt. 6:8.*

AS I WAS VISITING with a sister in Christ, she told me about the trials and
tribulations that she had been going through. As I listened, one testimony
got my attention.

She said she had changed her way of praying a while back. Every morning when she awoke, she would fall down on her knees to pray. Her first
and foremost prayer was of thanksgiving, especially for keeping her through
the night and waking her up, clothed in her right mind.

The second thanks to God was for forgiving the sins that she might
have committed unknowingly. Because of the many things she was going
through, the Holy Spirit impressed her that she should start out her day
with giving thanks, no matter what trial she was going through.

A short while after she started giving thanks for good times and bad,
things began to happen. As the Sabbath began to roll in, she gave God the
praise for seeing her through the week. She was still out of a job, and the
only money she had to her name was $2. With her last $2 in her hand she
went to church, believing, "But my God shall supply all your needs according to his riches in glory by Christ Jesus" (Phil. 4:19). She wasn't worried,
nor did she fret. As the day went on, she received three gifts. One of the
members of the church said she was impressed by the Holy Spirit to give her
$20. The next gift she received in a tithe envelope that had a $20 bill in it.

The third and last gift was given to her in a thinking-of-you card. As
she opened the card, a $100 bill fell out. She was so taken back with grati-
tude and thanksgiving she didn't know what to say. She asked the young
woman who gave her the $100 why she did what she did. The young
woman said that the Holy Spirit had impressed her to give a gift of love,
and she happened to be the recipient.

Little becomes much when you place it in the Master's hand. She
was convinced that she received the Master's touch that day, all because
she decided to change her way of praying, and she would always express
her thanksgiving.

**Olive Lewis**

# God Is in Control

*The Lord will keep you from all harm—he will watch over your life; the Lord will watch over your coming and going both now and forevermore. Ps. 121:7, 8, NIV.*

OUR CHURCH WANTED to have evangelistic meetings, so we decided to take advantage of some satellite programs that were going to be broadcast for nine nights. We signed up to present this series at our church in Belgreen. On the last night my son, Terry, also was beginning evangelistic meetings at Urbandale, so my daughter, Katy, and I decided we would attend Terry's meetings. We decided on the time we would leave so we would be on time. Then Kathy's daughter decided she wanted to go too, and they quickly finished up the horse chores. Ashley wanted to shower before dressing, which took more time, so we could see we were going to be late.

As we were finally ready to leave, it began to rain. My sister from next door ran over to tell us that the tornado warning sirens had gone off in Rockford, and a tornado had touched down in Caledonia on Highway 37.

By now it was raining very hard, and it turned really black about two miles from home. It was difficult driving in the downpour, so I said to Kathy, "I feel we shouldn't try to go on. Let's go back home." I turned the car down another road to head back. We made it home safely, even though I couldn't see much of the road.

Later that evening we heard a report on the news about a tornado that had hit Caledonia, damaging some businesses and a cattle ranch. When they gave the time it had happened, I realized that if we had left when we had planned to, we would have been going through there right when that tornado touched down. I really felt blessed! God had taken care of us and worked it all out. "God is good all the time—all the time, God is good."

I'm so glad that we have a heavenly Father who is in control of everything that happens. He has the power to keep us safe every day, and He keeps us in His care when we allow Him to control our lives. Isn't it a comfort to know that we have His protection in all we do and everywhere we go?

**Anne Elaine Nelson**

# Judged!

*And the king will answer them, "Truly I tell you, just as you did it to one of the least of these who are members of my family, you did it to me." Matt. 25:40, NRSV.*

MY FATHER-IN-LAW, Harry, was long ago laid to rest. He was the best father-in-law anyone could ask for. I'm convinced that when Jesus returns, Harry will be among those who are awakened from the sleep of death to meet King Jesus in the clouds of heaven, and he will go home to live with Him.

Harry never joined the church. He was an upright man who was honest in everything he did. He was kindhearted, helping others in times of need. He faithfully visited aged, ailing friends who needed some extra help from time to time. He had no time to waste on fretful, unkind, dishonest people.

Unfortunately, some of these people were in the church, which is probably why he never joined. They stood in the way of his seeing Jesus there. It is sad but true that the exhibitions of dishonest, unkind people stand out and speak loudly to people looking on. I know there were many goodhearted people in that church, but how sad that the example of several who were not soured the whole church experience for Harry. Their actions spoke louder to him than any other words he heard. It has been said that one bad apple can ruin the whole barrel, and that describes Harry's experience with the church. It wasn't just one church but several over the years of his life.

Maybe if those thoughtless, uncaring "Christians" had let God into their hearts and then tried to make things right, Harry would have seen the difference. It could have inspired him that they had something that changed their lives that might have helped him to see God more clearly.

Are we blocking the view of Jesus for others? Through our actions, do we discourage people from seeing the hope and light of heaven in a connection to God? It's often the little things we do, or don't do, that block out the view of Jesus to someone standing in our path.

God forgive us for being stumbling blocks. Help us, God, to be stepping-stones for others to find the clear picture of God.

**Peggy Curtice Harris**

# My New Curtains

*Every good gift and every perfect gift is from above,
and cometh down from the Father of lights. James 1:17.*

I DECIDED I WANTED to put up some new curtains in our bedroom because the ones I had made years before were faded and thin. I looked at the curtains in Wal-Mart, but I didn't see anything I liked. Nothing I found in the fabric aisle suited me either. There's a fabric store on Sand Mountain, and I decided to drive down and look at their large selection of material. I saw material for quilting, crafts, weddings, and dresses. But browsing through the three rooms didn't turn up anything that struck me as suitable to match the blue paint of our bedroom walls or my personal tastes.

I was about to leave when the owner handed me a bolt of fabric she'd just gotten in. The pattern of birds and flowers in bright, cheerful colors really caught my eye. I unrolled a length, liking the nature look with a Scripture verse. Perfect! I had her measure off several yards, dug out some money I'd been given for Christmas, and, clutching the plastic bag with the fabric, I left the store with a feeling of satisfaction and joy.

Last evening I sat down at my grandmother's old Singer sewing machine and stitched up curtains from the bird fabric. As I looked at my new curtains I realized that if I had gone to the store several weeks earlier, as I had thought of doing, I would not have found my bird curtains with God's reminder of His care for me. Printed among the various birds are these words of Jesus: "Look at the birds of the air; they do not sow or reap or store away in barns, and yet your heavenly Father feeds them." "Therefore do not worry about tomorrow" (Matt. 6:26, 34).

God let me look all through the store before He gave me the best—the bolt of cloth saved for last, with a personal message of love. I'm delighted how the curtains brighten our bedroom, and I'm inspired at how God enjoys blessing me. My Father has the very best in mind for me. He knows what I like, even when I don't know what I'm looking for. As I look at the sparrows, chickadees, finches, and wrens among the daisies, thistles, hibiscus, and sunflowers, I see God's message to me: "Wait for the best; I'll give it to you."

**Barbara Ann Kay**

# My Driving Angels

*For he shall give his angels charge over thee, to keep thee in all thy ways.*
*Ps. 91:11.*

LATE ONE NIGHT I was driving from St. Petersburg to Orlando, Florida, after a long day of moving my sister Bernie. Many members of my family were there to make sure that the move went smoothly. Now it was late, but I still needed to get home. My youngest sister, Nat, began to worry about me because I have a history of being terrified of driving, especially at night. She promised to follow right behind to make sure that I was safe. I whispered a prayer and started on my way, grateful to those who promised to help me.

As I took Interstate 4, which leads to Orlando, it suddenly seemed to me that I had veered too far left and had exited the highway. It was dark, and my van was so packed with Bernie's belongings that I couldn't see whether or not Nat was behind me. What should I do? I was wondering where to turn and what to do when my cell phone rang. *Who could that be?* I wondered, since Nat didn't have her cell phone. I picked up, and a voice I recognized so well yelled, "Keep straight, and you'll get right back on track!" The voice belonged to my cousin Gina. I hadn't realized that she was following me too. I obeyed gratefully and soon found myself back on the highway that would lead me home. I drove on with the assurance that Jesus was with me and that I had two precious angels driving uncharacteristically slow behind me. Sometimes we can see and hear our angels, sometimes we can't—but they are there!

As I drove I remembered the many times that I had pointed the way to my cousin and my sister, who were now following me to make sure that I was safe. Both young adults had lived with us, and we were very close. I realized more than ever that in this life we all sometimes need someone to direct us. "Keep straight," "Turn around," "Yield," and "Stop" are some of the directions that I had to give and that I had to take. How wonderful it is that God has provided us with supportive family members who can guide us when we lose our way! It is more humbling, though, that the Lord in heaven would give me my own driving angels to lead me safely home.

*Lord, today please give me an opportunity to point someone to You, the perfect direction.*

**Rose Joseph Thomas**

# The Election

*I will instruct thee and teach thee in the way which thou shalt go:*
*I will guide thee with mine eye. Ps. 32:8.*

I SURPRISED MYSELF at the end of my first semester at the community college by qualifying for the National Community College Honor Society, Alpha Gamma Sigma. On top of that, I was elected to the office of vice president! The vice president's only duty, other than chairing meetings in the president's absence, was to organize the annual fund-raiser book sale. Basically, that meant I had to schedule every member of the society for a time slot to sell books. Because of this duty I became well acquainted with everyone in the society.

New officers were to be elected the next semester. The society president led out in the nominating and election process as I wrote the names on the board. The election was conducted in reverse order, starting with treasurer and ending with president. As the president called the first nominated name for the office of treasurer, I became aware that everyone was looking at me. No, not looking—staring intently at me. As the names were called, no hands went up until I voted—then everyone voted for the same person. Evidently they were waiting to find out the person I voted for! What was going on? Then I realized that from my work with people in the book sale the semester before, the society members knew that I knew which members were people who carried through on their responsibilities. Once I realized that, all I had to do was look at the voter, then at my choice for the office, and they elected my choice for the office! It was amazing. My eye guided them to the person I would vote for.

I had always wondered how God could guide me with His eye, since I couldn't see Him. Now I understood. To be guided by God's eye, I had to look to God for direction, then look where He looked. His eye did guide me when I looked to Him for guidance, then looked at the path He wanted me to follow. Of course, I had to be looking for His teaching and His direction. If I watched, He would definitely guide me with His eye!

*Beloved heavenly Father, thank You for guiding me with Your eye. May I always look for Your guidance and teaching. May I be so close to You that I can see the path You have chosen for my life's journey, and may I always choose that path. In Jesus' name, amen.*

**Darlenejoan McKibbin Rhine**

# The Day of Reckoning

*Then the King will say to those on His right hand, "Come, you blessed of My Father, inherit the kingdom prepared for you from the foundation of the world: for I was hungry and you gave Me food; I was thirsty and you gave Me drink; I was a stranger and you took Me in." . . . "Assuredly, I say to you, inasmuch as you did it to one of the least of these My brethren, you did it to Me." Matt. 25:34-40, NKJV.*

A SUMMONS ARRIVED, telling me that on a certain date I must report for jury duty. My second daughter had served on a jury and said that it would be a good experience for me. She further mentioned that it would be excellent to learn how some of our taxes were spent. Since this was the second summons, I couldn't make another excuse.

On the appointed day I went to the Superior Court, where the process of choosing the jurors was to take place. The designated room was filling up, and I observed that there were people of different races and, from their names, from different countries of origin. I looked at their different features. Of course, they could tell that I wasn't originally from the United States either. It was going to be quite interesting how the jury was to be chosen from among these men and women, young and old.

We were asked questions such as Are you an American citizen? Are you 18 years or older? Do you understand English well? Have you been convicted of a crime? I thought about the judgment day, when we will appear before the Judge of the universe. Books will be opened. Questions will be asked. Deeds, good and bad, will be revealed. What a day that will be!

From all the world people will have to face the great Judge. What will they hear from Him? "'I was hungry and you gave Me food; I was thirsty and you gave Me drink; I was a stranger and you took Me in.' . . . 'Inasmuch as you did it to one of the least of these My brethren, you did it to Me.'" Or will we hear Him say, "'Assuredly, I say to you, inasmuch as you did not do it to one of the least of these, you did not do it to Me'" (Matt. 25:45, NKJV).

Then the most important question will be "Are you a citizen of My kingdom?" Have we fully accepted Jesus Christ as our Savior and accepted a place in His kingdom?

**Ofelia A. Pangan**

# My Hammock

*Come to me, all you who are weary and burdened,*
*and I will give you rest. Matt. 11:28, NIV.*

I BROUGHT TWO HAMMOCKS back from our holiday in
Mexico, hoping that they will remind me of my need to rest a little.
I'm a person who always finds something that needs to be done, and
it's very difficult for me to sit still and rest.

I loved to watch the lifestyle in the area of Mexico where we vaca-
tioned. The more relaxed attitude became something I learned to appreciate. Many live in simple houses; often the whole family lives in one
room. It is their kitchen and living room, and when night comes, they hang
up their hammocks, and it becomes a bedroom. The families I saw didn't
seem to need so many things, just a gas cooker, a refrigerator, a TV set, a
table, and a hammock. If you don't have to finance all the rest of the things
we consider necessities, life isn't so exhausting. You don't need to work all
the time.

I've learned a few Spanish words typical for this lifestyle: *mañana* (tomorrow), *más o menos* (more or less), *no se preocupe* (don't worry).

God, of course, knew from the beginning that people could not, should
not, work the whole time, so He gave us the Sabbath—a kind of a hammock in time, a time for us to rest and get away from it all.

But we even tend to fill the Sabbath hours with holy busyness. I wonder
if holy stress is any better than everyday stress.

Why are we so busy? Where does my inner unrest come from that
makes me want to do something all the time? Is it just something to keep
my thoughts occupied so that I won't realize what I really need, that I need
peace and rest to be able to communicate with my God?

When I've finished all my projects, I will get into my hammock and
rest. But if I wait until all my projects are finished, I will never find the time
for my hammock. You see, my work seems to multiply quicker than I can
get it done.

And that is why I wanted these hammocks. When I see them, I will be
reminded that even I should get some rest, that I need to rest. And so I
must get into my hammock and let others take over for a while. And maybe
I will realize that things will get done, even without me.

**Hannele Ottschofski**

# From House to Home

*He who has begun a good work in you will complete it until the day of Jesus Christ. Phil. 1:6, NKJV.*

I HAVE A FRIEND who is a gifted craftsman. He takes houses that are plain, dull, and often uninteresting, and makes them unique, bright, and useful. Every house he has lived in has been beautifully transformed. I didn't think there was a house couldn't improve—until he and his family bought their latest domicile.

It was an old two-story farm-style dwelling, located (from my perspective) a few miles east of nowhere. The unfinished upstairs rooms were rough lumber with supporting wall studs being the center of interest. The kitchen, badly in need of cupboards, had layers of flooring material randomly placed. I could see four different patterns. I'm sure the quaint bathroom fixtures were genuine antiques. The three well-used outbuildings blended with the interior of the house perfectly. I would have given up even before learning that water for the house had to be hauled from a lake more than a mile away. I saw the problems. My friends saw the possibilities. As they shared their plans with me, my thoughts changed. I knew then that they could make it happen. I just figured it would take a long time, because remodeling is often more difficult and more time-consuming than building a new house.

On my next visit I saw impressive improvements. The last time I dropped by, the metamorphosis was complete. What I once thought was an impossible undertaking had become a beautiful home. With the hard work behind them, I could tell by their faces that my friends felt that without a doubt, any sacrifices they'd made hadn't been in vain.

Perhaps the Lord looks at us a bit like my friends looked at their house—full of possibilities but needing lots of work. With godly love and patience Jesus has been remodeling people for a long time, hammering out bad habits, grinding away pride, nailing down lessons in meekness and humility, and rewiring so tempers won't short-circuit.

When His work is completed, Jesus is coming back to take us to heaven, to the home He has prepared for us. When He sees the glowing faces of those He has redeemed, I hope He will know without a doubt that His sacrifice wasn't in vain.

**Marcia Mollenkopf**

# Marian High— Elsies River

*Fear thou not; for I am with thee: be not dismayed; for I am thy God: I will strengthen thee; yea, I will help thee; yea, I will uphold thee with the right hand of my righteousness. Isa. 41:10.*

SOMETIMES I WONDER why God allowed me to move from Bethel to Marian, the school where I now teach in Elsies River in Cape Town, South Africa. The area around my school is a dangerous, high-crime area. We are getting used to the sound of gunshots. Believe me, the death of a child—a child being shot—is something I can never fathom. My school is safe—high fences, gates, and a security system—but sometimes these criminals find a way to get inside, which means that we are not really safe. In spite of that, our staff is very happy, treating each other like family. We also have a wonderful principal.

When I first came to Marian, I thought I would just stay for a term, but I'm still here today. Even though I don't plan to spend my life here, I believe that God sent me here for a reason, and it's my wish to do what He has for me to do. This is a special school for Black and Coloured girls who have been the victim of rape, abuse, and other horrific crimes. But they are still children who need love and attention, and most of them don't get that at home. Some do share their stories with me. Painful as they are, I always remind the girls of the power of prayer. I tell them that God cares for them no matter what situations they come from, and that God has a plan for them. I tell them that I came from a place where, for most of the people, life is about stealing, fighting, drinking, and having babies at an early age. I was born there, but I chose to be who I am today. I'm proud of who I've become, but I still pray and care for those I left behind. I believe that if you forget where you came from, you will also lose sight of where you are going in life.

Each day before I go to school (and on my way) I pray, because I can never be sure if I will come back safely. We Christians need not be afraid— our lives are in His hands. He has kept me for the past several years in Marian. Because I trust Him, He will surely carry me through. I'm just the clay, and He is the potter: "Yet, O Lord, you are our Father. We are the clay, you are the potter; we are all the work of your hand" (Isa. 64:8, NIV). He directs my life—I invite you to trust Him as well.

**Deborah Matshaya**

# The Rain Stopped

*In the day of my trouble I will call to you, for you will answer me.*
*Ps. 86:7, NIV.*

IT HAD BEEN RAINING cats and dogs, but I was unaware of it until Maggie came to relieve me at the cash register when it was time for me to take my lunch break. As I rushed out, she called, "Take your umbrella—it's been raining hard."

I didn't have my umbrella with me, so she gave me hers to use at lunch. As the afternoon wore on, the rain never stopped. When we finished work at 3:30, I wondered how I would be able to walk the mile and a half home in such rain without an umbrella. I'd been sick and didn't want to get wet and be sick again. Neither did I know anyone who could give me a ride home, but I had to leave the premises by 5:00, before the gates were locked.

With fear I gave the entire situation all to God in a silent prayer. I knew He could do things that no one around me could do. And sure enough, within minutes I realized that the rain had stopped. I quickly walked home without getting a drop of water on me. I was so grateful to God!

When I walked into the house, my daughter was amazed that I wasn't wet. She shouted, "Thank God," because she had been praying that I'd be able to get a ride home when she saw that I'd left my umbrella behind. When I told her that I had walked, all she said was "Clap for Jesus." As far as she had seen, it had been raining all day, and it was still raining when I entered the house.

Though I was taken aback, I related it to what happened in the times of old when God did the same thing for the Israelites in Goshen. Yes, the 10 plagues came upon all Egypt—except Goshen (Ex. 8:22; 9:26). He is the same God who stopped the sun from setting for the Israelites as long as Aaron and Hur held up the prophet's arm. The Lord is still near us just as He was then, and all we need is faith. To my daughter it was a miracle, so she gave a testimony about it in church; but even then the people couldn't believe it. How did God do that for me? I don't know how or why, other than I had asked and believed.

*My able Father, I wish I could thank You enough for Your faithfulness. I say with the poet, "Even eternity is too short to extol thee."*

**Mabel Kwei**

# Why Is the Grass Always Greener?

*Be content with such things as you have. Heb. 13:5, NKJV.*

AS I STAND IN MY BACKYARD overlooking my neighbors' yards, their grass always looks greener than mine. But once I step into their yard and look back over at my yard, my grass looks greener. Funny, isn't it, how life seems?

Take, for example, my life. My home is far from perfect. Robert and I disagree more than we seem to agree. We seldom go on vacation, and the house is more cluttered than straightened up and organized. The front door handle falls off when you touch it. And if you stand in the middle of the kitchen floor, you would almost think the house is a little lopsided. On rainy days the basement has a funny odor. The house is in obvious need of repair, but then so is my car. On the other hand, my girlfriend Susan seems to have it all: a new home in a great neighborhood, new furniture, and, most of all, a husband who seems to adore her. At least I thought so until one day.

That day Susan's two boys wanted to come over to my house after church. When we arrived at my home and started up the stairs, Brian declared, "This is my second family. I love to come to your house." This puzzled me a little. Later that afternoon, when Susan came to pick Brian up, I told her what Brian had said. She laughed and explained, "Yeah, the boys love to come to your house. They say it's so peaceful, and that this is what a real home is like." Susan said that her home was seldom peaceful. Brian's dad was always arguing, and the police had often been called to their home. Susan said that Tom, her husband, never wanted to spend time with her or the boys. Because of this, they seldom went on vacation. I told her I thought Tom was so affectionate. She said that was just a show for people. Then she told me that, in fact, Tom was very abusive. I was so saddened by all this.

I told Susan that I would pray for Tom; I would pray that one day he would be real, and his affection for her and his family would be real as well. I also tried to encourage her.

How many times we look at others and envy what they have—or what we think they have. But as many have learned, things don't make us happy. Our happiness, or contentment, comes from our relationship with Jesus. And where there is love, there is happiness.

**Avis M. Jackson**

# Lightning

*For as the lightning cometh out of the east, and shineth even unto the west; so shall also the coming of the Son of man be. Matt. 24:27.*

WORLD WAR II WAS ON. My husband was stationed at Fort Francis E. Warren in Cheyenne, Wyoming. At that time the city's population had been nearly doubled by military families. Housing was difficult to secure, and we felt indeed fortunate to have a small apartment that was attached to a large greenhouse.

I was working in my little kitchen one morning when a severe storm developed. The elevation is high in that area, and electrical storms were frequent. It wasn't unusual to learn of someone being struck by lightning. I watched dark, angry clouds form, then torrential rain fell in sheets on the sloping glass greenhouse roof that joined my kitchen. Suddenly a blinding bolt of lightning flashed simultaneously with a deafening clap of thunder. What appeared to be an enormous ball of fire struck the greenhouse roof and descended toward my window. In an instant I found myself standing in the open front door, frozen with fear. I cannot remember how I got there. I felt I couldn't move, and not until the storm had abated did I try.

*I'm sure I must be white*, I mused as I reached for a mirror, but my hand shook so hard I couldn't see my image. I thought of the trips my husband and a soldier friend frequently made for the local county coroner to assist in retrieving lightning victims, and I shuddered. This was much too close.

As blinding as it was, I'm confident that that bolt of lightning was but a candle in comparison with the magnificent shining spectacle we will one day see, not in angry storm clouds, but surrounded by a white cloud of glorious angels. And in a moment, victims of earth's tragedies will be retrieved from this sinful planet. I expect to be watching for that cloud even as I watched that day long ago in Cheyenne. But please, God, I will not be afraid, and when my Savior invites me to glance in His heavenly mirror, I will see a face filled, not with terror, but with youthful perfection and joyful excitement. I pray each day that my resurrected husband and my children will surround me when God's "lightning" strikes and we rise to meet Him, ready for our trip home.

**Lorraine Hudgins-Hirsch**

# Validation

*May he give you the desire of your heart and make all your plans succeed. Ps. 20:4, NIV.*

I FIRST DREAMED OF GOING as a student missionary my freshman year of college. During vesper programs at college, former missionaries shared their experiences, and future missionaries were dedicated before their year of service began. I watched from my pew, thinking, *I want to do that!* More than once I spoke to those in charge and browsed the call books. However, it seemed so outside the box of anything my family had ever done, and I wasn't sure that I wanted to teach. During my final year of college the dream still lurked in the back of my mind. And college graduates could participate in the student missions program the year following their graduation. Knowing it was my last chance, I learned that I could likely find a position to utilize my interest and education in health. So I began the application process.

Around the same time, I determined to join a short-term mission trip to Kenya—visiting Africa had been a longtime dream. Going as a student missionary cost $2,500; the Kenya trip cost $1,800. Committing to either project stressed me out. Like most college students, I had little extra cash. Nevertheless, I told God my dreams, asking Him to provide according to His will.

The Kenya trip was the most immediate need, so I listed everyone I could think of to ask for sponsorship, enough so that each needed to send only $10. I mailed batch after batch of letters to family, friends, friends' parents, former teachers, former work supervisors and coworkers. The first $1,000 deadline arrived, but at the end of the day I lacked $200.

"Wait a minute," Sherrie Norton said, "another check for $200 was just brought in!" After that I waited until the end to check how much money I had. It was too stressful!

Shortly before our scheduled departure, I questioned God: *Do you really want me to go to Kenya* and *go as a student missionary the following year? Do my dreams really match Your will?*

That afternoon Mrs. Norton added up the money. Yes, the $1,800 was there! I was going to Kenya! But there was more. We looked at each other, eyes wide. In all, more than $3,700 was in hand—Kenya, plus more than half required for my year as a student missionary. Did God want me to serve Him on these short-term and long-term mission projects? The answer was pretty clear.

**Emily Thomsen**

# Cross-country

*I will instruct thee and teach thee in the way which thou shalt go:*
*I will guide thee with mine eye. Ps. 32:8.*

IN JUNE, at the start of summer, a traveler can expect drastic changes of weather and other circumstances, especially if that person is an inexperienced traveler. Our first day of driving began with a very calm, cool morning; it promised to be a bright and sunny day. But not too long after the beginning of our journey, we experienced a very heavy rainfall. We thought that to avoid endangering ourselves we really needed to stop and let the rain pass. It was too easy to have accidents because of zero visibility. But before we could pull off the road, the clouds and fog had cleared, the rain and thunderclaps had stopped. The sun was bright again. Praise God! That was something we could be really thankful for. We paused for a few moments at the end of this first day to plan strategies for a better next day.

The second day promised to be another bright and sunny day. As we entered another state and saw new scenery, the new weather forecast indicated an approaching storm. Dark, heavy clouds loomed ahead, and in a few minutes the rain poured down. Fortunately, it didn't take long, at our speed, to leave the drastic weather behind. The sun's rays were back again, and we felt it safe to continue.

We encountered other obstacles on our journey. Road construction slowed down the traffic, as there were several detours that delayed all vehicles moving on the road. Then there were the scary encounters with huge trucks. Some drivers didn't signal, which made it dangerous for the drivers and passengers following them. The extreme temperature in the desert areas of New Mexico, Arizona, and California also required that we take precautions against the possibility of dehydration.

The Lord was wonderful. We completed our journey safely and arrived on the expected day. With preparation before the trip, the plans were carried out with trust and guidance from God.

As we travel through life, unexpected storms are sure to come. We must keep our eyes to the heavens, watching for the Son to shine once again.

**Esperanza Aquino Mopera**

# A Recipe for Happiness

*Therefore all things whatsoever ye would that men should do to you, do ye even so to them. Matt. 7:12.*

MY PATIENCE WAS GONE! I had explained twice to the woman at the computer store what was going on with my new laptop computer, but she didn't seem to be listening. When another person arrived, she began to tell them about it, but she had it all mixed up. I impatiently said, "Excuse me! Please let *me* explain!" She kept interrupting me, so I didn't mind interrupting her.

She looked at me as if I were sprouting horns, but I didn't really care. After I told my version to the man, he informed me there wasn't anything they could do there in the store; they would have to ship the computer out. I was fairly certain it would be a simple thing to correct with tech support. I had purchased their in-house warranty at the time I got the computer, but hadn't been able to get through to them. He told me their in-house warranty was actually no good for tech support, only parts and labor for a broken computer, even though the sales rep who had sold it to me had said something completely different.

In the meantime I noticed that the woman had slipped away for a bit, but I really didn't care where she had gone. Then suddenly she was back with a manager, and she said that since I hadn't had the computer for 90 days they were going to switch my warranty over to the manufacturer's warranty, where I could get free tech support any time.

I was so surprised at her doing this after the way she had acted, but very quickly made the decision to go ahead and make the switch, at no cost to me.

When all the paperwork was finished and she had returned to her desk, I told my husband to wait for just a moment while I went over and thanked her for what she had done. As I approached her desk she looked up, and an almost fearful look crossed her face. When I told her I just wanted to thank her so much for her help to me in getting the warranty changed, her eyes suddenly became bright with tears as she quietly said, "Thank *you!*"

The problem was resolved with one phone call, and my heart sang as I realized that I was able to bring joy to the woman who at first had caused me so much frustration. We both felt so much better now. The golden rule still applies.

**Anna May Radke Waters**

# In the Dark

*Yea, though I walk through the valley of the shadow of death, I will fear no evil: for thou art with me; thy rod and thy staff they comfort me. Ps. 23:4.*

MY AUNT HAD GIVEN ME the responsibility to do a few errands in town, and, at the age of 12, I knew this would be my greatest task ever—a big responsibility. I beamed, thrilled that my aunt considered me mature enough to handle this job. I determined not to fail. I checked my list twice in order to get everything completed. I selected each item with care, just as my aunt would have done. I was feeling good about how everything came together nicely. I hadn't encountered any problems. Preoccupied with getting everything done on my list, I hadn't noticed that the time had quickly passed, and it was now dark. Once this realization kicked in, my heart skipped a few beats. Now I didn't feel very adult-like. To make matters worse, the bus service was no longer running. I had no choice. I had to walk through the dimly lit and lonely park to get home. As I began to walk, my legs felt wobbly, my stomach felt weak, and my head throbbed. However, I was determined not to cry or give up. I repeated memory texts for courage. I prayed, and I hummed songs. However, as I got deeper into the park, even these things didn't help my fear. Close to tears, I begged God to rescue me. I started walking faster. In my mind the faster I walked, the less time I would be afraid.

Suddenly the lights in the park seemed brighter. I also saw the figure of a man walking in front of me. I was told never to talk to strangers, so I hung back, determined not to let this man out of my sight. As I watched this stranger walk in front of me, I couldn't believe we both were heading in the same direction. By the time I finally got home, the stranger had somehow disappeared.

I had made it home safe and sound. I was too emotional for words. When I told my grandmother of all that had happened, she said that God had answered my prayers. I never did see my companion again. God personally brightened my path and sent His angel to walk with me. That night, before going to bed, I was so grateful; I repeated Psalm 23 again and again. God had been watching over me all along the way.

We sometimes get into dark times and circumstances, but no matter what we fear, God is our shepherd, walking with us. May you be blessed by that rod and that staff too.

**Diantha Hall-Smith**

# Rainbow Light

*You are the light of the world. Matt. 5:14, NIV.*

I'VE A LITTLE RAINBOW MAKER on one of my windows. Solar power shines on a tiny panel and creates enough energy to rotate a glass prism. When the sun shines, light passes through the prism and scatters gently moving rainbows all around the room. The prism is pretty on its own, even without any sunlight shining through it, but the sun gives it the energy to move and enables it to scatter the full spectrum of colors rather than just a shiny whiteness.

As I sat watching the rainbows one peaceful early morning, I wondered what kind of light God wanted me to be in the world. I remembered from a physics class that without light we can't see any colors. How could my light show up the God-colors in the worlds of those around me? I thought about the different colors of lights in my world and what they could help me to understand about being a rainbow-colored light for God. These were some of my ideas:

Red lights—traffic lights and the warning lights on some of my appliances. Perhaps I could protect others and offer warning signals to them. Perhaps sometimes I need to know when to stop and hold back for a while.

Orange lights—safety lights. I need to know when to wait and when to be patient with others.

Yellow lights—twinkling strings of party lights. I can think about ways of adding sparkling joy to others' lives.

Green lights—traffic lights. Knowing when to get up and go. I can be active in my love for others and be inspired to choose the best moments to take action.

Blue lights—flashing blue lights on rescue vehicles. I can put my needs aside for a while and make myself available to support others in their emergencies.

Purple lights—ultraviolet light. Perhaps the light of my love can show up the purity of God's glowing love in even the darkest places.

Today, turn your energy panel toward God's light. Move by absorbing His energy and scatter rainbows of His loving light wherever you go. Let Him shine His colors into the world through you, so that you can be a rainbow of His love too.

**Karen Holford**

# Nena

*Let us fix our eyes on Jesus, the author and perfecter of our faith.*
*Heb. 12:2, NIV.*

DURING OUR ENGAGEMENT my fiancé, Roy, and I visited a pet store. We found a cute little rabbit. A small white ball with black spots, long eyelashes, and big, light-blue eyes—she was irresistible. We named her Nena.

However, the sweet little ball soon became an enormous rabbit that had outgrown its box. When she stayed alone at Roy's apartment, mischief was on her agenda. One day the refrigerator cords were cut. Then it was the telephone cords. Now I wasn't certain I wanted this rabbit, at least in a place without a patio or yard. We were each about to move our furniture into an apartment and get married. I had images of gnawed chair legs and lamps that didn't work. Fortunately, our friends who lived in a house with an enormous patio agreed to adopt her.

After several months we visited Nena. She lived in a chicken pen with her very nice chicken friends. When our friend scattered grain to feed the chickens, who do you think appeared to eat grain along with the chickens? Nena, the rabbit. When the time came to rest, several chickens climbed on their perch to sleep. Nena also jumped up to her place and settled down quietly, just like all her roommates. This rabbit was just another chicken!

How incredible! The influence of continually observing other types of conduct and habits had changed her. What power observation has! So I ask: What are we observing? What nutrients are we using to feed our minds? What are the influences that surround us?

If we accept Christ in our heart, eternal life is already ours through faith and the grace of Jesus. Our heart has been renewed, our motives are now pure, and our conduct is identified with the will of God. But at times, immersed in a materialistic, competitive society with diluted principles, we may copy what we observe, and we may not act according to our spiritual nature.

How important to observe what fills our mind and our thoughts! We need to care for the avenues of the soul, because our actions and what our mouth speaks are guided according to what is in our heart. Today you can choose what you will allow to control your thoughts. Let your friendship with Jesus influence your actions. Speak with His words, look with His eyes, and may you have the mind of Jesus today.

**Cyntia de Graf**

# Free at Last

*If your law had not been my delight, I would have perished in my affliction. Ps. 119:92, NIV.*

"MOTHER! Didn't you hear what they said on the television? Why are you smoking?" my son asked, surprised.

My heart shrank from the blow. How could I explain to a 5-year-old my desperate struggle to give up smoking? I was well aware of the media messages: cigarettes drastically cut your life span and life quality. Since childhood I had been impressed by a familiar story—a warning. My uncle Vicente, a hardened smoker, contracted terminal cancer. During his last days he repeated continually, "Now, yes, I can stop smoking. Why couldn't I stop before?"

For about a year, using various methods, I tried to quit. I felt guilty and impotent as I failed time after time. I was leaving a terrible example for my children. At that moment someone knocked at the door. A neighbor invited me to some meetings where slides about interesting current topics would be presented. I went to only one meeting; however, I accepted the Bible studies that were offered later, and my life began to change. By the third study in the series I was able to give up smoking forever. Nevermore would I poison my body or feel like a slave to this habit.

Years later, when I led a group of teens who participated in a temperance march, I had the opportunity to express my gratitude and my witness of the power of God to free those who sincerely seek Him. For 24 years my lungs have breathed freely. During this period nine of my relatives have been taken because of tobacco. Had I not quit when I did, I'm certain that I would have been the tenth.

Between the years 1950 and 2000, 50 million people throughout the world died of causes related to smoking. Many of them were intelligent, educated people who knew the risks. Nevertheless, they didn't recognize their problem until it was too late to change the situation.

If you have a problem of tobacco addiction, or any addiction to any substance, remember that God is powerful and is willing to free you, although He will not force your will. Give yourself to Him and the study of His Word. Soon you will find a way to cut this implacable chain that prohibits you from advancing toward a future filled with freedom.

**María Susana Mistretta de Golubizky**

# The God Who Sees Me

*She gave this name to the Lord who spoke to her: "You are the God who sees me," for she said, "I have now seen the One who sees me."*
*Gen. 16:13, NIV.*

DO YOU EVER HAVE DAYS when you feel as if you must have become invisible? Days when people seem to ignore your very existence? I certainly do. I recall one occasion when I was walking through a department store and noticed a woman and her small daughter coming toward me. The child, who was carrying a container of popcorn, turned just before she reached me to look back and speak to her mother, but kept on walking. Despite my attempted sidestep, the girl collided with me and trod on my foot. "Are you all right?" asked the mother immediately. As I took a breath, ready to respond graciously to the anticipated apology, the woman continued, "You didn't spill any of your popcorn did you, darling?" In fact, neither mother nor daughter looked at me or spoke to me at all—I might as well have been a post or a piece of furniture. As they moved away I found myself muttering crossly, "No, please don't apologize—I'm sure my foot will be just fine!"

On the days when you feel invisible, unnoticed, unappreciated, or even unloved, it is so good to know that although our fellow humans may ignore or ill-treat us, there is a God who sees and hears and cares. God saw pregnant Hagar out in the desert as she fled from Sarai's mistreatment; He felt for her in her misery and brought her a message of hope and reassurance (Gen. 16). Hagar then named God "The God who sees me." God saw barren Hannah as she wept and prayed near the tabernacle door. He heard her silent anguish and granted her heart's desire (1 Sam. 1). God saw exhausted Elijah as he hid from Jezebel's wrath, and encouraged him with a glimpse of Himself (1 Kings 19). Jesus saw despised Zacchaeus, perched inelegantly up a tree, and offered him salvation in exchange for a home-cooked meal (Luke 19). Jesus saw a poor widow at the Temple as she put in her tiny offering, and acknowledged the true value of both her and her gift (Luke 21).

*Dear Lord, thank You for seeing, hearing, and caring for me. And today, as I come across people who are disregarded, discouraged, tired, lost, or hurting, help me to be the kind of person who looks, listens, and loves as You do.*

**Jennifer M. Baldwin**

# Unexpected Blessing

*For the Lord God is a sun and shield; the Lord bestows favor and honor; No good thing does he withhold from those whose walk is blameless. O Lord Almighty, blessed is the man who trusts in you. Ps. 84:11, 12, NIV.*

SINCE MY HUSBAND WORKED within walking distance from our home, we hadn't looked for a bigger place. We stayed in the weekend house that he had bought when he was a bachelor. It is small, but it has a large yard with grass and trees. We both loved the house and the area, but years passed and stuff accumulated, for we are both collectors. My husband loves to collect old stuff: radios, computers, telephones—everything electronic—and we found ourselves unable to move except in a narrow path between piles. Boxes lay everywhere. It became uncomfortable to live in.

Then it was time for my husband to look for another job, and he was hired by a company 19 miles (30 kilometers) away. I prayed for a long time that we would find a house that we could afford to buy closer to his work. Even though we didn't have much money, I kept on looking at the ads in the newspaper. Martin kept saying, "Start looking when you have enough money in your hand."

I just replied, "God will provide," and this was what I put in my mind.

As usual, I looked again in the Sunday newspaper, and an advertisement caught my attention. I asked Martin if he would look at the house—the price was good, it was more than double the size of our current place, and within walking distance to his new workplace. We learned that another couple was interested in buying it. I kept on praying, *Lord, if this house is really meant for us, please make it possible for us to get it through Your help*. It turned out that the other couple were both tall, and the low basement's height was perfect for me and my husband, so they looked for another house.

We showed the picture of the house to my husband's parents, and we were surprised that they gave us a big sum to buy that house. We didn't expect that much, and we thank the Lord for the blessings He bestowed upon us. Even in my wildest dreams I couldn't believe that we would be living in that house, since we didn't have the money. I reminded my husband, "Walk in faith; trust in God and believe in His Word—He has prepared a blessing and is ready to pour it out."

**Loida Gulaja Lehmann**

# Whose Prayer Gets Answered?

*He went to the house of Mary, the mother of John whose other name was Mark, where many had gathered and were praying. Acts 12:12, NRSV.*

THE KNOCKING WAS LOUD and persistent, but it also interrupted the prayer meeting, so the church members tried to ignore it. Finally Rhoda, the maid, went to the door. And there was Peter. When he was finally allowed in, he "described for them how the Lord had brought him out of the prison" (Acts 12:17, NRSV). An obvious answer to prayer, right? It seems so.

But in the first part of Acts 12, Scripture tells us that "about that time King Herod laid violent hands upon some who belonged to the church. He had James, the brother of John, killed with the sword. After he saw that it pleased the Jews, he proceeded to arrest Peter also" (verses 1-3, NRSV). James died, Peter lived on. Do you suppose the church prayed when King Herod arrested James? I cannot imagine that they didn't—after all, he was the church leader. But their prayers weren't answered. James was killed. Is God capricious? Did He love Peter but not James? Did the members not pray hard enough, or use the right words? What was going on?

We read stories of miraculous happenings, of people saved from certain death. We read that God promises to help us. We read: "A thousand may fall at your side, ten thousand at your right hand, but it will not come near you. . . . For he will command his angels concerning you to guard you in all your ways. . . . Those who love me, I will deliver; I will protect those who know my name. When they call to me, I will answer them; I will be with them in trouble" (Ps. 91:7-15, NRSV). But we have prayers that haven't been answered. Loved ones die. Accidents happen. People suffer diseases and tragedy. We become discouraged and depressed. What is going on?

What is going on is that we live in a world full of sin. God does answer prayers, but not always as we think He should—sometimes He has to say, "Because of sin, bad things happen. But I'm always with you. Sometime soon I'm coming back, and nothing bad will happen again. That is when all My promises can be fulfilled." It is not about how much we pray, about how good or bad we are, nor what words we use. It is that God knows best, and He is still taking care of us. We pray and we praise Him for the times we escape harm; we must also thank Him that someday He will be able to answer all our prayers.

**Ardis Dick Stenbakken**

# What God Must Be Like

*He loveth him that followeth after righteousness. Prov. 15:9.*

I ALWAYS CALLED MY FATHER DADDY, even though I was in my 40s when he passed away. I think it was because I lost my mother when I was 4. Daddy was the only real parent I had. I had two stepmothers, one at age 5, and another at age 14. My first step-mother knew all the four-letter words that I was taught not to repeat. By the time Daddy married my second stepmother, who was a well-meaning person, I had been on my own too much. It was too late.

Daddy never went to high school; he never even went through all the lower grades. His father died when he was young, so he worked to finish raising his younger brother. Daddy was a garage mechanic, and later a welder. I still remember spelling words for Daddy whenever he wrote letters.

Daddy may have had little formal education, but he loved to read and learn. In the 1940s some of the grocery stores gave out encyclopedias, one book a week, for about $1. Daddy thought that that would be a good way to learn, so each week he bought another book in the set. He began reading them, and soon he knew things that I had yet to learn about geography, travel, animals, and people.

It was from Daddy that I gained my love of reading. The first books I ever read were garage mechanic's books with little bears in them—for Bear wheel alignments. Daddy saw I had an interest in reading, so he found me some secondhand books. I still have those books today. Daddy valued education; he was disappointed when I failed to graduate from high school, choosing to gain a husband instead. I later went to college, after completing my GED tests, and graduated. My father was happy to see me get the education he'd never had. I then went on to obtain my master's degree in library science, all because of the love for reading instilled in me from my father when I was a little girl.

Many say that our view of God comes from what our father was like. My father was strict, but I knew he loved me, and I learned good moral values from him. I think God is much like that—strict for our protection, but merciful and long-suffering because He loves us. My prayer for you today, dear reader, is that you will follow that God.

**Loraine F. Sweetland**

# Mama and the Mama Bear

*For He shall give His angels charge over you, to keep you in all your ways. Ps. 91:11, NKJV.*

WE WERE ON A TRIP in Alaska with our three daughters and had just seen Mount McKinley from our campsite nearby. Before walking to the lake, I picked up a big red towel that would be handy for washing up. We took a shortcut through a trail in the woods and soon reached the lake, but missed the signs regarding bears and other natural disasters. As we reached the lake I stopped. Prakash, my husband, continued on around the lake, leading our three girls.

Suddenly I heard Prakash shout, "Bear!" I thought that he was only trying to scare the girls, but the unusual urgency in his voice made me look up. There, directly in front of him, was a mother black bear, reared up on her hind legs. Two cubs hid in the bushes. All had been disturbed from their blueberry supper by our evening walk. Forgetting the directives we'd heard about not running, all four turned and raced back down the trail right toward me.

I joined the retreat, but I couldn't run as fast as even my 8-year-old. My family was far ahead, but the bear, who couldn't resist chasing the unruly mob that had disturbed her, was now in hot pursuit right behind me!

My first thought was *I'm going to die. I guess that's OK, because I know my Lord—but it sure is gonna hurt when that bear chomps down!* The next thought quickly followed the first:

*You haven't prayed*!

*Help me, Lord!* I prayed as I continued to run, wild-eyed, up the path. Likely that was the shortest prayer in history—next to Jonah's.

Suddenly I realized that in our flight no one had made a sound, and the rangers had said to make a lot of noise in bear country. I screamed, "Help! Help! Bear!" At the same time my husband threw the red towel at the bear. Again I glanced over my shoulder. Mama Bear was gone! To this day Prakash declares that throwing the towel scared her away. I tell him that my shining knight ran so far ahead of me that the bear couldn't even see the towel without binoculars. We both know that but for the grace of God I would have died that day.

*Thank You, God, for prolonging our earthly lives. Now make our family instruments You can use to help others as long as we live.*

**Sherry Shrestha**

# Prayers Answered

*Ask, and it will be given to you; seek, and you will find. . . .*
*For everyone who asks receives, and he who seeks, finds. . . .*
*If you then, being evil, know how to give good gifts to your*
*children, how much more will your Father who is in heaven*
*give good things to those who ask Him! Matt. 7:7-11, NKJV.*

IT WAS MY OLDEST DAUGHTER'S BIRTHDAY. The family had gathered together at the lake for a picnic celebration that beautiful June day. The sun glistened on the water. We enjoyed waterskiing, riding the Sea-Doos, and watching the children have water fights in the swimming area. As the sun sank below the horizon, we gathered around the picnic tables for a birthday supper.

As everyone brought out their gifts, our daughter gave one small, square box to her father, and one to me. I had often teased the children, saying, "You know, it really should be the parents receiving the gifts on their children's birthdays, because it is really us who remembers their birth." So my quick remark was "Well, finally, one of you agreed with what I've always said."

She looked at me, and I could see tears forming in her eyes. She came and put her arms around me and whispered quietly, "Mom, this gift is not only because you first gave me life. Remember calling and telling me about the new diabetic studies at Vanderbilt? I resisted; I didn't want to even acknowledge that I was a diabetic, let alone become a part of an experimental study. I told you no, but you didn't give up. Then we moved back to Nashville after the study had begun. Once again you asked me to at least call. Just to please you, I did, and was accepted into the program. Now, 10 years later, they are announcing to the medical world the results of the experimental treatment. The doctors have told me that the treatment I had been receiving has proven to be a major breakthrough."

Because I had insisted that she become a part of it, years had been added to her life. Her gifts were her way of thanking us. And so it was that we were all here together at the lake. My prayer that night was "Thank You, Lord, for hearing my prayer and answering in Your way in Your time. And for not giving up on any of us."

**Barbara Smith Morris**

# Sparing, Sharing, and Caring

*Other seed fell on good soil. . . . It . . . yielded a crop, a hundred times more than was sown. Luke 8:8, NIV.*

EVEN BEFORE THE FIRST spring flowers bloom, the gardening catalogs arrive with their beautiful pictures of perfect produce and coupons to tempt me to take advantage of $25 off on an order of $50 or more. And I always do!

Eagerly I turn the pages, looking for old favorites and to see what new products are offered. We'll want three kinds of corn: early, midseason, and late. Then there are beans, squash, cucumbers, okra, radishes, lettuce, various greens, and other seeds. Tomato and pepper plants will be bought locally.

This year I bought only 20 tomato plants, although I like to have plenty to eat, preserve, and share. Then the volunteer tomatoes started coming up. Now, a real farmer would plow them under, but I started transplanting them. One row held 15 of them, another seven or so. I took a box of them to church on Wednesday night and found willing takers. Another friend took a few more, but after counting more than 70 left, including the ones I bought, I gave up. My patient husband put stakes up for the transplanted ones; the rest sprawled on the ground among the corn and beans. But they too are bearing lots of good fruit. Some have grape tomatoes, which are expensive in the supermarkets; some have bigger "tommy-toes," some have plum tomatoes, and some have big, beautiful ones. And, yes, we've had plenty to eat, preserve, and share. I'm glad we could rescue these plants instead of plowing them under, even though they didn't fit into the plan we had. We would have missed the variety and wonderful extras they have provided.

I believe we can learn a lesson from those plants that popped up unexpectedly and in the wrong places. We have probably all known people who "march to a different drummer." There were those in Bible times as well as today. Saul, who became Paul, was zealous, although misguided. But instead of "plowing him under," Jesus spoke to him on the road to Damascus, and he became a mighty plant in God's garden, bearing much fruit for the kingdom.

Let's be willing to nurture some of those who pop up unexpectedly and in what seems to be the wrong places. They might be the very ones needed to add variety to our garden of friends!

**Mary Jane Graves**

# Crowns and Hopes

*And you will not know what hour I will come upon you.*
*Rev. 3:3, NKJV.*

THE SECOND WEEK in June had been set aside to celebrate the twentieth anniversary of our church's high school. From the beginning of the week, special events brought back memories of past struggles and sacrifices, and friends regaled us with stories of joys and achievements.

On Wednesday the school opened her arms to welcome her alumni with a reunion party. One such alumnus was Stephanie DeRoux, Miss Panama 2003, who came along with Justine Pasek, Miss Universe 2002.

My science class had been proceeding as usual until one of my boys, on his return from the bathroom, gave us the news that Miss Universe and Miss Panama were on campus. We were ecstatic, and I immediately received many requests from students to "go to the bathroom." Soon the bell for recess rang, and we all raced to the reception hall, where the celebrities gave autographs, graciously took pictures with us, and shared a few moments. Since everyone wasn't able to approach them in the hall, a classroom-to-classroom visit was arranged for after-recess periods.

I was in one of my fourth-grade classes when we heard the kids in the classroom next door clapping and screaming, unable to contain their happiness. We knew the guests were on their way. We were ready. My students had made small posters welcoming the beauty queens. They even picked up the trash from the floor and perfumed the air with Lysol! Moreover, they wore ear-to-ear smiles that expressed their pride in being Panamanians, as well as students of the Inter-American Academy of Panama.

Seconds turned into long minutes as we waited for the arrival of our guests. Where were they? A quick check confirmed our suspicions—they had had to cut their visit short, leaving us and other classrooms disappointed. I tried to resume the lesson, but it was no use; the sadness on the faces of my students was heartbreaking.

As I reminisce on the events of that day my thoughts are drawn to the great arrival of the King of kings, of which the whole world will be a witness. My prayer is that we will be eager, as my students were, and also ready to meet our King in peace.

Evelia R. Cargill

# An Answer in Time

*Call to me and I will answer you and tell you great and unsearchable things you do not know. Jer. 33:3, NIV.*

JUNE 26, 2006, marked 30 years since I had given my life to Jesus. I'm pleased to follow God's teachings. Five of my 10 children were raised according to God's principles, but to my dismay, some of them, especially my son, in their adolescence abandoned these teachings. He was the object of my prayers for more than 20 years. I prayed, fasted, and cried out to God, never ceasing, certain that God would bring him back one day. His attitudes distanced him more and more from God, and friends led him into alcohol, smoking, and questionable relationships.

Whenever a special program was held in church, he and his girlfriend were my special guests. There were even times he answered an appeal, but soon he forgot the commitment made, and continued in his old life without much enthusiasm.

One day the gospel reached his girlfriend's heart, and she became interested in getting to know Jesus. He also became encouraged; they began Bible studies and gave up smoking. However, when they realized that they would have to make their marriage relationship official, there was another problem. Apparently, the situation had no solution. However, as a persistent mother, I never became discouraged, and continued to plead with God for their salvation.

Then a great tragedy occurred. Without explanation my son's girlfriend was suddenly attacked with a fatal cerebral aneurism. Shocked by her death, my son and his little 4-year-old came to live in our home. Working and taking care of his child alone, especially facing the pain of this tragic death, would be impossible.

With my limited comprehension I could ask God only, "Why?" The answer I didn't know. A sermon I heard during that year, however, helped me to understand that the answers from God are in His time and according to His way.

Today my son has joined my church. He has married, and his family praises God together. And we who suffered the loss of such a dear person can thank God that He gives us comfort, if not all the answers to why things happen. May the Lord give us discernment to accept His will and to be ready for that glorious morning when we meet our beloved ones again.

**Marlene Martins dos Santos**

# Blessings

*All these blessings will come upon you and accompany you if you obey the Lord your God. Deut. 28:2, NIV.*

HAVE YOU EVER CONSIDERED the many blessings the Lord tucks into each corner of your day? I've come to think of His blessings as touches of grace in my life. The more I recognize and appreciate them, the more joyful my walk with Jesus becomes.

Recently I was asked to speak at a prayer breakfast. I had just accepted the invitation when my husband and I received another invitation to attend a graduation ceremony. You guessed it—they were both on the same day. I really wanted to be at both, so I asked the Lord to work out His will. A week before the prayer breakfast the women's ministries leader called to say they had scheduled the breakfast an hour earlier. Now I could make it to both functions. I was so thankful!

As I left home that morning my husband reminded me to stop for gasoline. I didn't want to be late, so I drove straight to the prayer breakfast, planning to stop on the way back. Soon, however, I noticed the fuel light come on. When I called to tell him about my dilemma, he told me to drive slowly to the next filling station. To my relief, it was only nine miles (15 kilometers) away.

At the same time, the airtime on my cell phone ran out, and I knew my husband would worry if I didn't keep in touch with him. As I was about to pay the service station attendant, I realized I didn't have any cash with me. I hurried to the auto bank only to find it was out of order, and the attendant had already filled the gas tank.

When I explained the situation, he cheerfully went to ask management to swipe my card (not a normal procedure with a debit card). I left the service station with a heart overflowing with gratitude. As I drove down the road, I received a text message to say my airtime had been topped up—I could contact my husband.

I remembered God's promise that "before they call I will answer" (Isa. 65:24, NIV). We have a Father who cares about every detail of our lives, and He is waiting to shower us with the blessings we need. All we have to do is ask.

**Cordell Liebrandt**

# Miss Perfect and Me

*Do not judge, or you too will be judged. Matt. 7:1, NIV.*

I HATED HER. As I looked at her, my heart was scorched with jealousy. She knew everything! Or at least it seemed as though she did. I had been out of college for two years, but once again I had entered into the life of homework and study. I was scared. Scared I wouldn't make the grade, that I wouldn't remember how to study, wouldn't be liked by the teachers or accepted by my peers.

She was perfect. Always cheery and positive, she remained only seconds away from a good-natured laugh. Hers was the only voice answering the teacher's questions in my accounting class, and it was to her the classmates went for help—she knew it all. If putting up with Miss-Perfect-Know-It-All in accounting wasn't enough, I had to sit directly behind her in a second class as well. I stared at her blond ponytail. *Why, God, are some people so blessed? And then there's me. Please take away this jealousy. Help me to like her.* Struggling to be nice one day, I started talking with Miss Perfect. "Is this your first time at college?" I asked.

"No; I have a degree in nursing, but decided I didn't like it," she replied. "I'm in the secondary education program now."

"Oh! How come you're in accounting, then?" I questioned further.

"My specialization is business. Actually, I've taken accounting before, but it's been a few years, so I decided to take it again. One of the students in accounting said they were jealous of my knowing all the answers. I had to explain to him that I had already taken this class." Her comment made me smile. *He wasn't the only one!* I sheepishly admitted to myself.

Come to find out, Miss-Perfect-Know-It-All had a name, Cindy. She was just as human as I was, and a good student despite her previous knowledge. Chatting with her became an everyday thing. By the end of the term the two of us were coordinating which subjects we would take together the next semester, and even the following school year.

Thinking about Cindy has led me to wonder how many other people I've presumptuously judged. I may have missed out on a really great friendship. Friends come in all kinds of packages. Just ask me—or Cindy.

**Kristi Geraci**

# An Encounter With God— at the Clothesline

*God is our refuge and strength, a very present help in trouble.
Ps. 46:1.*

I'M INTRIGUED at the places God chooses to meet me. There are days God seems to be very silent (or even absent), to the extent that I would ask, *So God, where are You now?* But I've come to discover that God is neither absent nor uncaring. God is indeed a very present help.

It seems that God enjoys meeting me as I do domestic chores. I vividly recall hanging clothes on the clothesline in my backyard one usually sunny Sunday morning when I noticed that there was no sunshine. In fact, the skies were dark with rain clouds. What compounded the situation was that among the wash loads were clothes my husband needed for overseas travel the next day. I must get them dry. I looked helplessly at the sky. When I tried to figure out a solution and found none, my spirit was broken. When I finally realized I couldn't help the situation I sought God's help. (It's a shame that we have to feel so helpless before we look to God.)

I continued hanging the clothes on the line while I prayed. *God,* I said, *Could You please make the sun shine?* In the midst of the prayer the voice of discouragement came to me. It went like this: "You really believe that God is going to make the sun shine just for you to dry your clothes?" Immediately I knew it was the voice of the evil one, and just as soon as he spoke, God gave me a song. And this is what it said: "O for a faith that will not shrink, though pressed by many a foe; that will not tremble on the brink of poverty, of poverty or woe; of poverty or woe. . . . Lord give me such a faith as this."

I lifted up my voice and sang loudly and mightily, as if to say to the devil, "My God is much more powerful than you are, so get away from here!" As I sang, I felt encouraged and strengthened, and my broken spirit felt restored. For a moment I forgot that the day was unsuitable for laundry. I was caught up singing as I continued putting garment after garment on the line. Then I began to feel hot. I paused and looked up. Yes! It was the sun, brightly shining, and all the rain clouds had disappeared.

God gave me more than the sunshine; He gave me more than lines of dry clothes. My God gave me more faith to trust in Him, and He gave me a song as well.

**Jacqueline Hope HoShing-Clarke**

# Choices We Make

*For as the heavens are higher than the earth, so are my ways higher than your ways, and my thoughts than your thoughts. Isa. 55:9.*

SOME OF US HAVE CHILDREN and grandchildren who choose not to follow the beliefs they were taught while at home. It is sometimes very difficult for us to decide whether to be a stickler to our values, or to be supportive of their school events and other activities.

One such incident took place recently. One Sabbath afternoon my daughter, Julie, phoned to invite me to attend the local band competition. "Mama, I believe the kids' band plays just after sundown; would you like to come and hear them?" I was hesitant for two reasons: I would have to travel before sundown, and my knee was still weak and painful from recent knee surgery.

After talking it over with my husband, we decided I should go. I had to park some distance from the ballfield. I limped from the parking lot to the side of a small tent where teenage girls poured ice water. One of the girls shouted, "Here comes our band!" I glanced over to see the blue-and-white uniforms of the band as they marched by. Water was handed to them as they passed. My "grandmother" eyes scanned the faces, searching for my grandson, Tyler, now a proud senior, and his younger sister, Olivia, a freshman. Finally I spotted Tyler, carrying his trumpet. Soon I saw the sweet face of Olivia, proudly wearing her new band uniform, her blue eyes bright with excitement. She carried her saxophone carefully as she took her cold drink.

After the band passed, a nice young man took me to the stadium in a golf cart. I arrived just in time to hear the band play their first number. I made my way up the steep cement steps to the place my daughter, her husband, and my youngest grandson, Grant, were seated. Grant told me he was so excited because his dad had entered his name for the drawing of six prizes. His father hastened to tell him he might not win, but over the loudspeaker came a voice: "The winner of prize number one—Grant Herren." His dad proudly accompanied him to claim his first-place price: $1,224 worth of sports equipment. We were all impressed and snapped several pictures.

After the golf cart took me back to my car, I sat there for a few minutes, thinking over the events of the evening. My heart was overwhelmed with love and reassurance from my heavenly Father. I knew I had made the right choice to be with them on this special occasion.

**Rose Neff Sikora**

# Cheering Up Agnes

*In every thing give thanks. 1 Thess. 5:18.*

VISITS TO AGNES frustrated me to no end. Agnes was a small, thin woman with bent shoulders and a wrinkled brow. A frown seemed to be permanently etched on her face, and her lips pinched tight with disapproval.

"Hi, Agnes!" I bounced into her tiny apartment with a piece of freshly baked cake, hoping to see her eyes light up with appreciation. On my last visit she had moaned about her desire for cake. Surely she would be pleased! Instead she sighed and said, "Why did you bring me cake? I was so longing for cheese. I can't afford it on my small pension."

So, on the next visit, I took a sack of groceries and set them down on her table. "See what I brought you!" I said, taking the tin of cheese out of the bag. The frown lines grew deeper as she complained, "I don't think that will agree with my stomach. It's been upset a lot lately."

"What can I do to make you happy?" I asked. "There must be something you want."

She thought a moment and said, "Look at these sheets on my bed. They are the last ones I own; see the holes. I need new sheets—not old castoffs, mind you, but some new sheets."

I checked my closet and found a pair of pastel-striped sheets that were yet unopened. This would be just the thing to make Agnes happy. They were good quality. Surely I would get a smile of appreciation. But there was no way to make Agnes happy. She fingered them a moment, and said in her saddest voice, "I don't like colored sheets—never did. I only like white sheets."

I gave up trying to please Agnes and began to find it a source of humor to see how she could find something negative in every gift I brought. But since then I've thought how often I am like Agnes when it comes to the lovely gifts God showers on me day by day.

How often do I take for granted what He gives? How often do I complain to God, "Why did it have to rain today when I wanted to work in the garden?" Or when the day is warm and sunny I'm likely to complain, "Lord, I've so much to do today, and it is much too hot. Couldn't You send some rain to cool things down a bit?" I pray for a job and then gripe about the one I get. I can think of a long list of complaints I have made when I should have been praising God with thankfulness for what He has given instead of complaining about what I didn't get.

**Dorothy Eaton Watts**

# U-turn

*He restoreth my soul: he leadeth me in the paths of righteousness for his name's sake. Ps. 23:3.*

UPON RELOCATING TO MARYLAND, I was more determined than ever to follow one of my longstanding household rules: All newly purchased items *must* be paid for in full prior to delivery.

It was a late Friday afternoon in July when I decided to make a payment on my layaway plan. I hurriedly finished preparing Sabbath's dinner and rushed out to pay on my carpet. After assisting Mother to the vehicle, I quickly got in, fastened my seat belt, and said a prayer, and off we went. Thanking God for longer hours during the days in summer, I calmly drove past two lights and turned onto the winding road that was most crucial in getting me to my destination. Mother seemed to be enjoying the scenery as we passed condos, new construction sites, trees, service stations, churches, and private homes. Traffic flowed smoothly as both Mother and I listened to beautiful hymns on the radio.

After several miles I noticed the traffic gradually slowing down. Eventually it came to a complete stop. I could see a police officer standing adjacent to his cruiser, directing traffic. *Oh, boy! Things were going so well—and now this*, I thought to myself. There wasn't an accident, so why was he directing us to detour? As I approached him, he instructed me to make a choice. I could turn either right or left. I turned right, thinking it would bring me closer to my destination. *This should be simple. There must be roads ahead that will allow me to continue my journey, and maybe I will even get there sooner than I had anticipated.* To my amazement, I drove a good two miles, and there wasn't one road that allowed me to make the turn I needed to make. So Mother and I turned around and went home—the layaway payment would have to be made on another day.

Sometimes I think I'm on the right road to heaven, and suddenly I find myself having to make a U-turn. You see, Satan has a way of trying to block my path. He makes it look as if I can't reach my destination. Thank God for Jesus, who has given me a choice—I can continue going in the wrong direction, or I can make a U-turn. My destination is heaven. I hope yours is too! *Father, please help me to make as many U-turns as necessary to meet You in the air.*

**Cora A. Walker**

# Just Do It!

*Do not merely listen to the word, and so deceive yourselves.*
*Do what it says. James 1:22, NIV.*

IN OUT OF THE HOT TUB, INTO THE WORLD the author tells a great story about a hospital patient who inadvertently knocked over a glass of water onto the floor. Fearful that someone might slip and fall, he courteously asked a passing nurse's aide to mop it up. The aide explained that hospital policy required that only small spills be mopped up by an aide. She classified this spill as large, but would be happy to call the housekeeping and have them care for the spill.

Eventually housekeeping arrived, but declared the spill too small for her services. "Small spills," she argued, "must be taken care of by aides."

"In a pig's eye," the aide barked. "It's not my responsibility—it's a large puddle."

The housekeeping staffer disagreed. "The puddle is too small for my services. It is not my responsibility," she stated adamantly. Potshots were fired back and forth between the two.

The exasperated patient took a pitcher of water from the nightstand and emptied it onto the floor. "There," he said with finality. "Is the spill big enough now for one of you to mop it up?"

Ever notice how frequently people try to shirk their responsibilities? I hear it when asking people to assist with ladies' night out, a group I host in my home once a month. Ask someone to bring refreshments, serve on the committee, or come early and help set up chairs, and they all with one accord begin to make excuses!

Current plans include our annual mission fund-raiser—the biggest event of the year—which takes massive planning and many willing hands. One woman read the announcement and said she wasn't working outside the home and offered her services! Another responded, "Oh, I'd be happy to help. Is there anything else I can do?" Such responses were music to my ears.

We have enough shirkers in the world—grumbling, complaining, quibbling saints. The truth is, we all carry responsibility to help God's work move forward. This requires willing servants who not only *hear* His voice but respond as *doers* of the word. This verse calls us beyond *hearing* into action, taking responsibility for whatever God calls us to do. I want to be part of that group, don't you? Whatever God calls you to do on this day, just do it!

**Nancy Van Pelt**

# Where Is It? Oh, No!

*Rejoice in the Lord always. I will say it again: Rejoice! . . .*
*Do not be anxious about anything, but in everything, by prayer and*
*petition, with thanksgiving, present your requests to God. Phil. 4:4-6, NIV.*

I HAD JUST ARRIVED in the Guam airport on my brief layover en route to Bali, Indonesia, when I looked through my purse for my passport. It was missing. Unable to go any farther in my trip without my passport, I prayed and called my sister, who was back in New York, for assistance. She phoned the taxi company that had taken me to the airport almost 22 hours before, and they confirmed that my passport had been found in the back seat of the taxi. Arrangements were made for the passport to be sent on the next plane coming to Guam—in three days. In Guam I was told that it would be impossible to get my passport and get on a plane the same day going to Bali. The passport would need to clear customs, which could take hours, and the time between the landing of the New York plane and takeoff of the Bali plane would be about 30 minutes.

I started praying and claiming God's promise of making miracles happen out of impossibilities. As I watched the flight from New York land, I heard the announcement for all passengers to board the flight to Bali. As the final boarding call was heard over the loudspeaker, I was still without a passport. The next flight to Bali would be in three days, and I had already been delayed for three days of my 10-day vacation.

As the plane to Bali pulled away from the gate, I prayed and praised louder that even as God closed the mouths of the lions, He could bring the plane back to the closed door once I received my passport. As the flight attendant at the gate apologized, I heard the pilot tell her through the radio to open up the door because he was coming back to the gate. He told her that he had been informed that the passport had cleared customs—in record time—and that the passenger would be able to make the trip to Bali. As my prayers went up, the "impossible" blessing came down. As I hurried onto the plane, I could not contain my excitement at how God had increased my faith in that very moment. All during the flight I let everyone on the plane know about God's goodness, and that He comes through when you need Him most.

**Nicole Reid Johnson**

# Our Awesome God

*How awesome is the Lord Most High, the great King over all the earth! Ps. 47:2, NIV.*

I REMEMBER being about 10 years old and returning to school after lunch. I had rushed through my meal in order to return to my two best friends—or so I thought.

Arriving at the playground, my friends decided they had something they needed to tell me; the problem was, who was going to do the telling? They appeared to have real difficulty deciding who should tell me. Eventually we ended up outside the bathroom, and in a while the girls ran into it together to have a whisper. Finally it appeared they had come to a decision—which was that they would tell me together. In anticipation I waited, always the slow one. They started off one word at time, each taking turns. "We–have–decided–that–we–do–not–want–to–be–your–friend–anymore."

Earth-shattering news for a 10-year-old! *What did I do? Why don't they like me anymore, if they ever did?* After the torment of self-evaluation, depression set in. But it lasted only the afternoon. The following day my eyes were opened, because now instead of two friends I had a whole bundle. It was as if losing my very select group of friends had freed me to spread my wings. Now I could talk to anyone I wished and did not have to concern myself with what the others thought.

I believe as far back as that early age, God was preparing me for the type of service He had in mind for me. When I look back on the path my life has taken, I know that I serve an awesome God. He really has every stage of your life in control, and it really doesn't matter if you mess up, because He can make it all right again. He has done it so many times for me.

He truly is awesome, and it is for real. As the author Ellen G. White states: "We have nothing to fear for the future, except as we shall forget the way the Lord has led us, and His teaching in our past history" (*Life Sketches,* p. 196).

*Thank You, awesome Father, for the way that You have led out in my life, for the people whose lives You have allowed me to touch in a positive way. Continue to do Your refining; as painful as the process can be, as You promised, I would love to shine like pure gold.*

**Kathy Senessie**

# The Adoption

*For you did not receive a spirit that makes you a slave again to fear,*
*but you received the Spirit of sonship. And by him we cry, "Abba, Father."*
*Rom. 8:15, NIV.*

SEATED IN THE WAITING ROOM in a doctor's office, I saw a middle-aged couple arrive with a handsome 8-year-old boy who was going to have corrective surgery on his ears. My admiration grew when I saw that courageous boy walk by himself to the surgery area. His mother proudly stated with joy, "We adopted him before he was born. He was expected as though I carried him within me."

"Guilherme is a very valuable treasure for us," his father added. "The other day I said to a very rich friend, who is somewhat selfish, that one of Guilherme's fingernails is worth more to us than his 400 apartments and the millions that he has in the bank. We love him very much. He is truly ours from within our hearts. His biological mother did not even want to see him. To us, he is beautiful, inside and out," stated his father. "He knows that he is adopted. The other day, while we were playing, he said, 'Dad, have you ever thought that you might give me to another family in the future?'"

The father said that Guilherme was frightened and began to cry. "Why, son?" he asked, hugging him. "Why would we give you to another person if you are everything to us and someone we love so much?"

We are also adopted. By God the Father. He loves us very much too, even more than Guilherme's parents love him—or any other earthly father or mother loves their child. And this adoptive Father does everything for us. He takes care of our deformities—He is a great plastic surgeon. He takes a little from here, and a little from there; we just have to allow Him to do what is best. He also understands neurosurgery and cardiology, and is willing to change our bad thoughts and wrong attitudes. He has even promised us a place in His kingdom and an inheritance with His Son, Jesus.

Pausing to consider, I am impressed. He does not want to give us away. He wants us to be His adopted children forever. And we can always be with Him.

What a wonderful God is our adoptive Father!

**Zuila Vila Nova Rodrigues**

# Riding Out the Waves

*Unto thee, O Lord, do I lift up my soul. O my God, I trust in thee:
let me not be ashamed, let not mine enemies triumph over me. . . .
Shew me thy ways, O Lord; teach me thy paths. Lead me in thy
truth, and teach me: for thou art the God of my salvation; on thee
do I wait all the day. Ps. 25:1-5.*

I ONCE WAS GIVEN a box of miscellaneous ocean-related goodies. In
the box were some seashells, baleen (whalebone), floatable glass balls,
dried seaweed, starfish, and fishing net. Also in the box were some intriguing items that looked like nuts. I was eager to find out what they were,
so I studied up on them in *National Geographic World* magazine at the library. I was happy to learn that some people call them "sea hearts." They
often fall into rivers and float out to the sea. The heart-shaped seeds are
highly prized by beachcombers. Sea hearts drifting off the east coast of
Florida may ride the Gulf Stream and North Atlantic currents to northern
Europe. Studies conducted by the U.S. Coast and Geodetic Survey have
found that a journey from Yucatan to Ireland may take about one year. In
the ocean they may ride the currents for many years before washing ashore,
taking root, and sprouting into a plant.

This life-bearing, time-enduring, wave-riding seed illustrates a basic
spiritual principle. God's plans may include extended times of waiting for
Him to act on our behalf. This was true of Noah, who endured ridicule
while spending 120 years building a ship. Abraham and his wife, Sarah,
waited for the fulfillment of God's promise that they would have a son in
their old age. David, God's anointed, chose to wait for God's timing rather
than to take the life of envious King Saul.

Sea hearts cannot choose to be patient, but I can. Sometimes circumstances make it hard to wait for the Lord, and I become anxious for Him to
do something about my situation. And I can become disappointed as I wait
for Him. It seems as though I pray and pray and nothing happens. But God
stretches my patience to enlarge my soul.

Nothing is harder—or better—for us than to follow the example of
David, who wrote Psalm 25. By waiting on the Lord, we can have peace
among our trials, and our faith will grow, even while we are riding out
the waves.

**Vidella McClellan**

# No Place Like Home

*Do not let your hearts be troubled. Trust in God; trust also in me. In my Father's house are many rooms; if it were not so, I would have told you. I am going there to prepare a place for you. And if I go and prepare a place for you, I will come back and take you to be with me that you also may be where I am. John 14:1-3, NIV.*

LAST NIGHT MY HUSBAND and I packed the car with a small bag apiece, our pillows, two dogs, and headed to my parents' house. Granted, it's not that far—we live only about a half hour away, so it's not like we were going on a grand trek or anything. But since the water was temporarily off at our house, we were going to spend the night at my mom and dad's.

Now, you have to understand, this is the house they've lived in for the past 12 or13 years. It's the house I lived in when I broke up with my first serious boyfriend; the house I lived in when I graduated from high school and college; the house I came to when I moved back to Maryland in 2000. It's where my husband and I first met in person, and where we still go for tacos almost every Friday night. It's a very familiar place. A warm and welcome place. A loving, friendly place. But it's no longer home.

We stayed in the guest bedroom, which is very comfortable, but the bed wasn't our bed. We knew where to find what we needed and that we were welcome to whatever that might be. But it wasn't our stuff. Although the accommodations were great, and we were both very comfortable, neither of us slept well. Even the dogs didn't sleep well. We love visiting, but it's just not home.

This morning when I got ready for work in what used to be my old bathroom I thought that I should feel more like this about earth and about heaven. Earth is a nice place to visit—it's familiar. Comfortable, in a way. I have friends and loved ones here who are so special to me, and I love being here—but it's not home. It's not where I want to stay.

There's a place Jesus is preparing for me that is my real home. He says, "I am going there to prepare a place for you. And if I go and prepare a place for you, I will come back and take you to be with me." Although I'm enjoying my time here "visiting" with loved ones, it's just not the same. I don't want to get too comfortable. I want to go home. Don't you?

**Vicki Redden**

# Lost and Found

*Rejoice with me; for I have found my sheep which was lost!*
*Luke 15:6.*

I HAD WANTED to take my children to Disneyland for a long time. My brother was visiting from Montreal and the timing was perfect, as he could help me drive. We left about 4:00 one Sunday morning and arrived at the Canada-United States border about 11:00.

Everyone cleared immigration except for my brother; he did not have his passport. Either he remained in Canada, or we all did. I was petrified at the thought of making the long drive by myself. My brother was the only man in the vehicle. After consulting God and my mother, we left without him.

We had a wonderful vacation, and the day came to head home to Alberta. In Montana there was a brushfire, and everyone had to detour. Somewhat nervous, I followed the cars ahead, no longer sure where we were heading. After a while we came to a fork in the road. I didn't know if I should turn left or right. I turned to the left, stopped under a bridge, and pulled out the map to find out our location. Nothing made sense to me, so I quietly prayed to God. I didn't want the children to know how scared I was.

Immediately after I uttered the prayer, a law enforcement vehicle appeared from the opposite direction and pulled up beside me. The officer asked if we were lost. (A woman parked under a bridge with a map in her hand must have been his first clue.) He asked where we were headed, then informed me that I was never going to reach Canada the way I was headed. The officer directed me to our destination for the night via secondary roads. He told me to follow him, and our "angel" made sure we were on the right road before turning off.

I thanked God because before I uttered the prayer He had dispatched an "angel" to show us the way. He looked down and saw my need. I thought of the parable of the lost sheep. What a joy and comfort to know that God would move heaven and earth to save me, His daughter.

If ever you find yourself in a situation in which you feel lost, scared, and alone, remember that God has given His angels charge over you. He has promised to never leave you nor forsake you. Praise God and hold on to His promises, for they are sure. Why not prove Him today? And He will rejoice with you.

**Sharon Long (Brown)**

# A Call in the Middle of the Night

*The Lord upholds all those who fall and lifts up all who are bowed down.*
*Ps. 145:14, NIV.*

THAT INSISTENT VOICE WOKE ME UP: "Pray for Salete! Pray for Salete!" Still half asleep, I thought, *I don't know any Salete. So whom should I pray for?* Had this just been a dream? But I couldn't get these words out of my mind: "Pray for Salete."

On Saturday I had scheduled a women's retreat 62 miles (100 kilometers) away. I would spend the day presenting the program to the group. Everything went as planned, with a dynamic and motivating program. After the meeting there was a potluck dinner, and we enjoyed ourselves together.

Then the time came to wash dishes—an activity not everyone enjoys. The most enthusiastic women took the lead, and soon the area was much neater. As I was carrying some plates I heard someone call out, "Salete!" A chill ran up my spine. I couldn't believe what I had heard. So there *was* someone named Salete, and she was here!

Calling the host, I asked if there was really someone present by the name of Salete. To my surprise, I learned that there were two women with that name. Soon I located the Salete whose name I had heard first. I asked if she was facing some particular problems.

"Oh, yes," she responded, "I have a lot of difficulties and am certainly in the need of much prayer."

She couldn't hold back the tears, and I couldn't keep my secret. I shared with the women that I'd been impressed to pray for Salete. Touched, we all joined together to pray for her. When we knelt in prayer, we become the link between heaven and earth; through us, God could pour out His blessings. He was ready to hear our requests. "Ministering angels are waiting about the throne to instantly obey the mandate of Jesus Christ to answer every prayer offered in earnest, living faith" (*Selected Messages,* book 2, p. 377).

Let's pray more! Let's pray as a family. Let's pray with our friends. Let's pray in church, and above all, let's spend time alone with God each day. We need to be intercessors and pray for the people whom God places in our lives, then we will discover that there is no greater force than the power of prayer.

**Nelci de Rocco Lima**

# Patience in Suffering

*As an example of patience in the face of suffering, take the prophets who spoke in the name of the Lord. James 5:10, NIV.*

LAST WEEK I VISITED A FRIEND who was very sick. All that week before I saw her, I was complaining and depressed about not finding a job. I was kicking and screaming as if I were an infant needing to be changed. Yes, I needed to be changed—but in the way the Lord was working on my self-centered heart.

It was the beginning of the Sabbath. I was to go to someone else's home for a Bible study, but instead I ended up staying with my friend and others reading the Psalms, Isaiah, and parts from Jeremiah. The Word of God is the hope of the hopeless, the joy of the sorrowful, the healing balm of the sick. Here I had been complaining all that week about my frustrations, while my friend was suffering with a much bigger issue. She had what I had clouded. She had (and has) the determination to live. She had not lost hope because of her circumstance. She is trusting in the Lord. No visible depression or oppression. Yes, I could see concern. But she isn't allowing herself to fall and be flattened by depression. She's focused on Christ, the God of the impossible, making things possible. Her attitude was in stark contrast to the attitude I had been exhibiting all week. I needed to see that.

Psalm 9:9 and 10 says, "The Lord is a refuge for the oppressed, a stronghold in times of trouble. Those who know your name will trust in you, for you, Lord, have never forsaken those who seek you" (NIV).

Yes, dear friends, the psalmist is talking to us. Get up! Stretch forth your feet and put them into the water. Trust Him; the water will part if we do our part and trust Him. And yes, I'm talking to me first!

Psalm 146:5 and 6 is a blessing to me as well: "Blessed is he whose help is the God of Jacob, whose hope is in the Lord his God, the Maker of heaven and earth, the sea, and everything in them—the Lord, who remains faithful forever"(NIV).

The Comforter, the Counselor of the depressed and oppressed is on the throne. Give Him honor and praise!

**Teri Deangelia Roulhac-Lazaro**

# Love Letters From God

*Behold what manner of love the Father has bestowed on us,*
*that we should be called children of God! 1 John 3:1, NKJV.*

WHEN MY MOTHER LIVED WITH US for a few months, I always tried to find something to lift her spirits, so we began pointing out "love letters from God"—counting our blessings. We walked in the park and saw a family of ducks bobbing in the stream when the babies were just little balls of fluff. We watched a snake slowly winding its way up a tree trunk, and even caught a glimpse of a black squirrel—an unusual sight in our area. Other times we observed the daffodils sprinkled throughout the woods, or tried to count the minnows in the stream before they dashed under a slippery rock. Or we'd find a box turtle and take his picture. Our favorite thing was looking for bird nests, where we could spy on the family without disturbing them.

Today I decided to eat breakfast by my dining room windows, which provide a clear, panoramic view of the backyard and my husband's garden. As I ate, I opened my heart to God. *Lord, I need some love letters, and I'll give You all the praise.*

He sent me love letters, sharing the abundant life I have so longed for. First, there was a hummingbird dancing at the feeder, its feathers iridescent in the sunlight, its beady eyes bright with mischief. Mourning doves pecked at the seeds falling from the tray feeder. Then three catbirds and a mockingbird paraded among the tomato vines, one vigorously preening after a dip in the pool. A robin pulled breakfast from under the mulch, gobbled it down, and hopped away. A squirrel filled up on cantaloupe seeds at the lower feeder. Christmassy cardinals chased each other across the yard while a goldfinch waited its turn at the black-eyed Susan. Three butterflies busily worked the butterfly bush. Such opulence! Such extravagant colors in the four different kinds of peppers! I saw marigolds to keep away the ants, yellow and green squash, zinnias in rainbow shades, velvety pink and blue morning glories, and three pretty good-sized deep-orange pumpkins that mysteriously grew on the garden fence.

God is so good. He said, "Good morning, My child. Come see what I found in your backyard and garden!" I answered, "How great Thou art!" and started my day. May your love letters come in abundance today!

**Carol Wiggins Gigante**

# Camp Meeting Memories

*For the Lord thy God walketh in the midst of thy camp,*
*to deliver thee, and to give up thine enemies before thee;*
*therefore shall thy camp be holy. Deut. 23:14.*

I'VE BEEN REMINISCING this morning about long-ago camp meetings. How special the memories are! We all pitched tents to live in (no RVs then), and had large tents for all general meetings. Camp meeting, when I was a child, was held at Anoka, Minnesota. To us who lived in the middle of busy Minneapolis, Anoka seemed like a faraway country place. It was a special, quiet time.

After moving into our tents, we took our slipcovers to the straw tent and filled them with clean straw for mattresses. As children, we thought this was quite exciting.

Then there was Joe, who rang the big iron bell for all meetings and mealtimes. The bell was also rung at night for quiet time. I'll never forget the sound of pounding rain on canvas after a long day of meetings and visits with friends.

I remember waking early to the sound of Norwegian songs and sermons from the Scandinavian tent. Our tent was always close, because Mom and Grandma came from Norway.

At the children's tent there was fresh sawdust on the floor for little feet to walk on. I recall the sound of tent flaps in the wind as we had lessons at the sand table.

One day while Mom was napping I washed my dolly clothes and hug them on the tent ropes to dry. Then when evening came, I remember sitting in the evening meetings with Mom and Dad at the big tent, listening to beautiful music and sermons from God's Word. At bedtime I remember hearing train whistles in the distance, a peaceful sound to fall asleep by.

Quite a few times, while at camp, tornadoes were in the area. Joe rang the big camp bell, and we all went to the cafeteria building and sang hymns till the storm threat was over. Once, though, the tailwinds of a tornado picked up the big tent, ripped it end to end, and set it down, while we were all singing in the cafeteria. No one was hurt. The memories I have always showed that God's hand was over the camp and that even as a child I dreaded when the last day of camp would come.

*Thank You, Lord, for the precious spiritual times and the memories*
*they bring.*

**Darlene Ytredal Burgeson**

# Like the Periwinkle

*"Return to Me with all your heart...."* *Return to the Lord your God,*
*for He is full of loving-kindness and loving-pity. Joel 2:12, 13, NLV.*

ONE DAY MY HUSBAND visited an old friend of ours and returned with
many plants. Among these plants was what we call periwinkles, a pinkish,
five-petaled flower that needs no special attention. We planted them beside
the path within the garden area. Later we noticed that some were growing
between the pavers in the path, and everywhere else they were not supposed
to grow. They needed to be uprooted with a strong hand.

It was discovered by accident that I was suffering from hypertension.
My diet had to change. I discovered that certain things I have always loved
were not the best for my health. These had to be avoided, or I'd have to
face the consequences later on. I still find myself yielding to temptation on
certain things. A candy bar? No big deal, I say. What harm can a small
candy bar do? So I hide it. I yearn for something that eventually could be
detrimental to my life. I feel I'm like the periwinkle, growing where it
shouldn't be growing, wanting my own way.

I need to repent of my old habits. But on my own I am helpless. Like
the periwinkle, I need a strong hand to uproot me from the wrong places
and set me in the right direction. I need to repent. To repent is to face up to
my problem and the fact that I can't do anything about solving it on my
own. We have to acknowledge our disobedience and stubborn ways and repent. The first time we repent is often the worst—and the best. It is the
worst because of the sting of pain and sin is at its strongest. It's best because
there's no joy in the world like being forgiven.

" ' Even now,' declares the Lord, 'return to me with all your heart. . . .'
Return to the Lord your God, for he is gracious and compassionate, slow to
anger and abounding in love" (Joel 2:12, 13, NIV).

So no matter how disobedient and stubborn the habits you have may
be, or in what undesirable places you find yourself, or what temptations
may have have befallen you—no matter how small—you cannot hide
from God. God loves you unconditionally, as no one else does. Father
God waits to welcome you back into His heart of love. Will you respond
to His call today?

**Priscilla E. Adonis**

# Fiery Frances

*If we are thrown into the blazing furnace, the God we serve is able to save us from it, and he will rescue us from your hand, O king. Dan. 3:17, NIV.*

IT WAS TEST GRADING TIME, and I was exhausted. For two weeks I'd been responsible for entertaining a new missionary family who was waiting for their house to be repainted so they could move in. In addition to all my other missionary responsibilities, I had written the tests—and now I needed to grade them all and turn in the grades. I loved my Ethiopian eighth-grade Bible class, but it was challenging since their knowledge of English was very limited. They found it hard to express themselves in English, and I tried hard to read through their misspellings and bad grammar to get to the ideas they were trying to express. I encouraged them to try their best, and I told them I wouldn't grade their English. I wanted to know how much they understood the lesson and to do their best to express themselves.

I decided to take the test papers and go over to the school to work, where it was quieter. We had spent the whole quarter discussing many Bible heroes. My test was for them to choose three of their favorite heroes, tell the story, and quote the memory verse that went with each one. I found the papers to be very typical. Most of the students struggled with spelling and grammar, and I was finding it very tiring to decipher their stories. However, I could tell that many of them had understood the questions and had received the messages I had tried to get across.

Just as I was about to quit for the day, I came across the test of one of my best students. His English was good, and I had no trouble understanding his story. He had chosen to tell of Daniel's three friends who refused to bow down to the idol. The story was well done, but his memory verse sent a shock through me. Then I laughed and laughed—it released all the tension that had built up inside for many days. I could just picture my students praying this prayer when I would become impatient with them in class. I knew this boy meant no harm. He had seen my name on the blackboard many times, and it certainly resembled the word he was trying to spell. He had written: "Our God whom we serve is able to deliver us from the burning, fiery Frances."

Not only did it relieve my stress, but I wondered if God was trying to teach me a lesson as well.

**Frances Morford**

# Where Are They?

*Fear thou not; for I am with thee: be not dismayed; for I am thy God:*
*I will strengthen thee; yea, I will help thee; yea, I will uphold thee with*
*the right hand of my righteousness. Isa. 41:10.*

PEOPLE OFTEN SAY, "The high school years are the happiest time." But
for me, high school years were my worst experience.

I was in my second year of high school when I almost gave up on life.
My mother went to Manila to find a job, and stayed there for almost four
months. It was hard for me to replace her work as a mother. Among other
chores, every Friday I ironed our clothes and prepared for the Sabbath. I
really missed my mother, so I used to cry every evening. My father also was
very lonely, because that was the first time my parents had been apart from
each other. But as members of a family, we strengthened each other even if
our mother was not with us.

One time my father decided to accompany my brothers to catch fish.
They went *payaw*, meaning that they would go out to sea to catch fish.
There were eight in the boat, including my grandfather and some other
church members. As they reached the middle of their fishing area, the
weather changed suddenly. There was a low pressure causing squalls; strong
winds blew and high waves rolled. The men panicked, because in the midst
of the storm their engine stopped, water got inside the boat, and rain
poured down. They raised a sail on the boat so that it could add balance.
Some of them were trembling because of cold, especially my grandfather;
others were seasick. At they same time, they were very hungry. They prayed
for God to calm the angry weather. After two days and one night at sea,
their boat was still afloat, but they still didn't expect to be able to reach
shore. However, they did eventually reach Polillo Island, also a dangerous
area. They found safety there with Christians who helped them, giving
them clothes and food. All this time I had no idea where they were.

In life we face more than one type of storm. Our family has faced both
emotional and literal storms. When you face a storm, you too can claim
the promise in today's text. I was very thankful to God for protecting and
sustaining all of us. Indeed, God can calm life's sea when sorrows come.
He is our refuge and strength, a very present help in times of trouble. He
always knows where we are and what our needs are.

**Michelle Engcoy Golle**

# Be Still— a Sweet Reminder

*Be still, and know that I am God: I will be exalted among the heathen, I will be exalted in the earth. Ps. 46:10.*

I CONSIDER MOTHERHOOD A PRIVILEGE. Have you seen the energy kids have? We envy their energy even as it wears us out! Kids can go on and on for the longest time without realizing their need for rest. "Please, be still" is the plea of parents all over the world. "But Mom, why?" is their usual objection. Parents know best! We understand it's beneficial for all to stop awhile and be calm—not because activity isn't good, but because we all need time to relax, to recuperate from the strenuous activities that wear us down. We all need the opportunity to rest a bit.

Our heavenly Father knows what's best too. He knows how much we need solitude and rest, even when we don't willingly recognize it. In the hustle and bustle of our daily lives our heavenly Father calls for us to be still so that we may know Him better and understand that He is in control. He calls us to sit at His feet and listen to His words of wisdom and encouragement. He invites us to be still and rest in Him, to rely on Him, and to trust Him. He asks us to be still and allow the Holy Spirit to work in our lives; be still, that we may praise Him and exalt His name.

Jesus even invited His disciples to "come with me by yourselves to a quiet place and get some rest" (Mark 6:31, NIV). Won't you accept His invitation to be still and trust Him? Bring to Him your concerns, your dilemmas, your questions, your needs, or anything that troubles you. You will realize that He cares for you in a very special way. Alone, in the stillness of God's presence, you will get to know Him so well that your doubts and worries will vanish. In the stillness of His presence, you will be safe from the troubles around you. Be still and know that God is with you. The Captain of the heavenly host is on your side. He is your refuge. When you praise Him in the stillness of His presence, your life will be renewed and strengthened. Give honor and glory to His name and testify that He is Lord! Your life will never be the same, for the Lord is your God. He knows you, and you know Him.

"Be still, and know that I am God." What a sweet reminder of His loving care for you and for me!

**Rhodi Alers de Lopez**

# God Cares for Me

*And it shall come to pass, that before they call, I will answer;*
*and while they are yet speaking, I will hear. Isa. 65:24.*

IT WAS AUGUST 18, 1976, and I was on my way from Seoul, South Korea, to our tiny village of Sanjuri. My husband was stationed at Camp Pelham, a stone's throw from Panmunjom, the Demilitarized Zone that separates North and South Korea. At the United States Embassy I had received a passport for our 2-month-old son and 4-year-old daughter.

Before getting off the train, I could sense tension in the air. Since I couldn't understand the language, I hurriedly walked the short distance to our house. Once there, I learned that two American servicemen, who had been on a tree detail, were brutally hacked to death by North Korean soldiers in the Demilitarized Zone. United States Armed Forces around the world were put on high alert. Several questions began to circulate. Would the United States and North Korea go to war? Would civilians have adequate time to evacuate? Would we see our loved ones again? Would negotiations prevail?

A dusk-to-dawn curfew was enforced, and all villages were blacked out at night. It was such an eerie feeling! We prayed to the Lord for our safety and asked that His will be done. The following morning my husband put us on a train to Seoul to stay at our church's military center. He said, "Yvonne, if I do not see you again, take care of yourself and the children." At the center I was privileged to visit with other church families. We knew that if an evacuation were ordered, we would be close to the airport. The next days we huddled together, grabbing at every bit of news.

By August 21 tensions began to subside. Operation Paul Bunyan describes the incident as follows: "The North Korean government caused a tree at Panmunjom to become a symbol of brutality and oppression. For three days it stood as a challenge to free men everywhere . . . a group of free men rose up and cut it down." What a relief!

We were able to return to Sanjuri once again. Through this experience I learned that the Lord—not just a group of free men—answered our prayers. My family was spared, and an entire nation still enjoys freedom.

**Yvonne Donatto**

# Light and Sound Show

*And I saw the glory of the God of Israel coming from the east.*
*His voice was like the roar of rushing waters, and the land*
*was radiant with his glory. Eze. 43:2, NIV.*

A FEW WEEKS AGO the Indian community here in Kenya celebrated what they call *diwali,* which marks the end of the old year and
the beginning of a new year. I switched the kitchen lights off and called
my husband. Together we watched the beautiful display of fireworks
from our kitchen window. Every burst of color and light was accompanied by sound. Although the sounds were muted from where we watched,
I was sure it was almost deafening at the actual site.

We'd been to a couple of light and sound shows when we worked and
lived in Egypt. One was at the Great Pyramids of Giza. The show is usually
held during the evenings when there is no moon, and all is in total darkness. Considered among the eight wonders of the ancient world, the
Pyramids, made of blocks of solid rock that weigh about two tons each that
were placed one on top of the other, look quite amazing during the day.
But at night, as the history of the Pyramids is narrated and bright laser
lights are directed to them, these magnificent wonders of architecture are
spectacular beyond words.

A similar show is held at the Karnak Temple in the Valley of the Kings,
also in Egypt. The various temples, built some 4,000 years ago, are show-
cased in a magnificent light and sound show. We left the show in silence,
too overwhelmed with wonder.

These human-made shows are spectacular, but there is another light and
sound show that is to come. "Then I heard what sounded like a great multitude, like the roar of rushing waters and like loud peals of thunder, shouting:
'Hallelujah! For our Lord God Almighty reigns' " (Rev. 19:6, NIV).

The sound of trumpets played by thousands of angels and the blazing
light of glory radiating from the throne of the Son of God as He comes
down to earth from heaven will leave every being in awe: "For as lightning
that comes from the east is visible even in the west, so will be the coming of
the Son of Man" (Matt. 24:27, NIV). It will be the ultimate light and sound
show all humankind will ever see. I pray that when the day comes, I will be
there—and that I won't be silent. I yearn to sing with all the saints,
"Hallelujah! For our Lord God Almighty reigns!"

**Mercy M. Ferrer**

# God Values Me as a Woman

*And many women were there beholding afar off, which followed Jesus from Galilee, ministering unto him. Matt. 27:55.*

JESUS TREATED EVERYONE AS SPECIAL, and because the Jews didn't value women, He spent extra time showing that He valued them.

He honored His mother throughout His life and was subject to her for 30 years. His first miracle was to make wine at her request, and at the cross He made arrangements for her to be cared for. He welcomed the mothers who came to have their children blessed. He surprised the woman at the well by speaking to her, a Samaritan woman, and He a Jewish man. He shared with her more openly than any of the men that He was the Messiah, and she believed Him. He took time because He wanted the crowd to listen to the hemorrhaging woman's story. He went all the way up to Syro-Phoenicia to heal the Canaanite mother's daughter. At first He treated her as His disciples expected, then He showed them God's love in the way He responded to her.

The message was clear. He valued all women. He defended the woman caught in adultery when the chief priests first brought her to Jesus. He comforted Mary and Martha when Lazarus died, and spoke first to Mary after the resurrection. He didn't have to choose women as disciples or bid them follow Him—they just did, all the way to the cross.

For several years I began my devotional time with the prayer "Lead me to the scripture that will show me what You want to change in me today." I expected Him to point out this flaw or that sinful behavior—or at least a wrong attitude. But again and again the message the Holy Spirit spoke to me through God's Word was surprising. The attitude He wanted to change was what I thought He thought of me. He wanted me to believe that His promises of unconditional love and acceptance to women included me.

I would argue, *Lord, isn't there a negative thought I am having that You want to work on?* But He would put His arms around me and say, "What I want to talk about today is your need to believe I love you for real and for sure and for always." I was amazed. That was His only message for me that day. *Father, thank You that throughout Scripture You acknowledge my value as a woman in the way You deal with women.*

**Lana Fletcher**

# 'Tis the Blessed Hour of Prayer

*For his anger lasts only a moment, but his favor lasts a lifetime;
weeping may remain for a night, but rejoicing comes in the
morning. Ps. 30:5, NIV.*

HE WORE MANY HATS and possessed many wonderful qualities: a
people magnet, vibrant and full of life; the life of every party; a preacher; a
deacon; a principal; a friend; a father; a brother; a husband; a Christian; an
encourager; a joker; a politician. You name it, and that was Charles. He was
my big brother, who carried joy and laughter wherever he went.

Then Charles became ill. A massive heart attack left him with very little
strength. I, along with Mom and my siblings, were at his bedside nearly
full-time to help take care of him. We loved him dearly. He never complained despite the sometimes painful medical procedures. He never lost
his vibrant, pleasant, talkative demeanor. Everything that could be done to
make him well was done, but he steadily grew worse. We had him anointed
according to James 5:13-15, and waited for the miracle, but he just did not
improve physically. Instead, his faith in God increased and never wavered.
He was open for the will of God to be done in his life. I, on the other hand,
wanted him to be healed, and nothing else would do. So my prayers were
only about getting him well. From my perspective he deserved to live because he was so good.

When multiple system failure became obvious and the inevitable was
staring everyone in the face, I denied it. I was daring enough to tell him to
keep hope alive, but he was ahead of me. Unlike me, he was ready, and he
was unafraid. When I spoke of hope, he supported me kindly but pointed me
to another hope—the hope of eternal life found in Jesus our Lord. I finally
understood; today I reflect on what God allowed, and how He gently took
him from us—but gave us enough time with each other to build ourselves up
spiritually. We spent precious moments in Bible readings, prayer, and
singing. Our favorite prayer song was "'Tis the Blessed Hour of Prayer." Just
before he fell asleep in Jesus, he was heard by the medical team singing. My
guess is that he was singing about the blessed hour of prayer.

I know that when Jesus returns with resurrection power we will be reunited with Charles and all our other loved ones. We shall sing throughout
eternity because every hour in heaven will be a blessed hour of prayer.

**Jacqueline Hope HoShing-Clarke**

# Learning to Trust

*Wait on the Lord. Ps. 27:14.*

MY FAMILY was experiencing a certain drama, and during those 477 days we learned the meaning of Paul's words in 1 Thessalonians 5:17: "Pray without ceasing." Friends, and even strangers, joined us in prayer.

My brother had a problem. He didn't have a chance to choose, and at the same time, he was unable to solve his case. His future was in the hands of others, and only the Lord could intervene. We trusted in this!

Every day I called my mother to learn the news. When I found out that my brother was encouraged and trusting, I praised God. But when he was discouraged or in despair, my anguish grew to the point that many times I didn't even have the energy to carry out simple tasks around the house. Ever since I was a child I had been his protector. Being eight years older, I defended him from friends when disagreements came about. Almost always, my brother got the worst end of the situation because he was small and thin. Now, however, there was nothing that I could do.

How difficult it is to learn to live by faith! We trust in God when we know that the remedy is efficient and the surgeon is competent. We trust when we have someone to ask for a loan, or when a friend can offer us a new job. We trust when we study enough. However, when we lose control of the situation or when there is no medical solution, when the financial resources run out or when we do not see the light at the end of the tunnel, we feel totally alone, and our faith is shaken. We forget that when we are alone God is still with us. Often we do not remember that when we can do nothing more, He is the one who intervenes.

*Thank You, Lord; You gave me this opportunity to learn total dependence on You in times of relative peace so that when difficult days come my faith may be strengthened, and I will be able to survive the unexpected.*

Today, if you are also facing problems or situations to which you see no solution, wait on the Lord, and He will strengthen your heart. We can say with the psalmist, "And they that know thy name will put their trust in thee: for thou, Lord, hast not forsaken them that seek thee" (Ps. 9:10).

**Sônia Maria Rigoli Santos**

# My Prejudice

*Then I heard the voice of the Lord saying, "Whom shall I send? And who will go for us?" And I said, "Here am I. Send me!" Isa. 6:8, NIV.*

WHEN I SAW THE PREACHER up in the front of the church, ready to present a sermon, I became discouraged. I recognized this young man by sight, but I had an aversion for him, for no reason. But when I realized my prejudice was taking hold of my mind, I remembered my aunt, who once said, "When I go to church, no matter how much I do not like the sermon, I attempt to find something in it that serves for my life. I always remember the idea that it is of value for someone. After all, God allowed this sermon to be preached!" With this thought in mind, I asked God to take away my prejudice and show me what I needed to learn that morning.

The sermon was about the call of Isaiah to be a prophet (Isa. 6). As the preacher presented the message, I forgot the dislike I had for him and concentrated on the ideas in his sermon and marveled. When I arrived home, I wrote a small outline that summarized the main ideas and how they applied to my life:

**1. Isaiah saw God and became conscious of how small he was before God.** When I stop to see God, to pray and read the Bible, I understand that I am a sinner. But this only takes place if I am willing to "see God."

**2. God granted forgiveness to Isaiah, sending an angel with coals from God's altar to purify his lips.** This showed Isaiah that he was forgiven. Lesson for me? God forgives me. He comes to me when I am too weak to go to Him, and He grants me His forgiveness.

**3. God asked, "Whom can I send?" Isaiah answered, "Here am I. Send me."** One more lesson to learn: Besides God forgiving me, He gives me proof—confidence—as He gives a mission, a purpose in life. When God asks about whom He is going to send to carry out something, it is up to me to respond, "I am ready."

I should not concentrate on the human instrument; I should concentrate on what God is telling me through the instrument. I should not disdain people for any reason; I should be concerned about what my mission is.

What is your purpose in life?

Iani Dias Lauer-Leite

# Under His Wings

*Be merciful and gracious to me, O God, be merciful and gracious to me,*
*for my soul takes refuge and finds shelter and confidence in You;*
*yes, in the shadow of Your wings will I take refuge and be confident*
*until calamities and destructive storms are passed. Ps. 57:1, Amplified.*

ONE BLISTERING HOT JULY NOON I drove down our street and saw them a few blocks from my home. An 8- or 10-year-old-girl was seated on the curb. In front of her was a little girl, probably her younger sister, who was about 4 years old. The older girl had her little sister's head covered with her skirt so that just her face showed, lovingly shading her from the sun. They seemed to be waiting for someone to pick them up, to take them to lunch or perhaps on an outing to the park for a picnic. The little sister appeared relaxed and confident in her big sister's shadow. She obviously found refuge in her sister's caring gesture, trusting and comfortable.

When calamities, sickness, or storms assail us, we also may have a helpful big sister. However, if we aren't blessed with a big sister, we all have a big brother, Jesus, Who longs to cover and protect us through every challenging situation.

One of my mother's favorite hymns was "Under His Wings," written by W. O. Cushing in the 1800s. Two verses state: "Under His wings I am safely abiding; though the night deepens and tempests are wild, still I can trust Him; I know He will keep me; He has redeemed me, and I am His child." "Under His wings, what a refuge in sorrow! How the heart yearningly turns to its rest! Often when earth has no balm for my healing, there I find comfort, and there I am blest."

Indeed, we can always find shelter and courage to face tomorrow with confidence, because Jesus covers and cares for us just as the big sister covered her little sister with her skirt and shadow that hot July day.

From my favorite author's pen I've often read and shared the following promise with friends who needed encouragement: "Not only does Christ know every soul, and the peculiar needs and trials of that soul, but He knows all the circumstances that chafe and perplex the spirit. His hand is outstretched in pitying tenderness to every suffering child" (*The Ministry of Healing*, p. 249). What a promise for each of us!

**Nathalie Ladner-Bischoff**

# He's Waiting

*Come to Me. Matt.11:28, NKJV.*
*His father saw him and had compassion, and ran*
*and fell on his neck and kissed him. Luke 15:20, NKJV.*

WHILE I WAS REREADING THE STORY of the prodigal son (Luke 15), the Holy Spirit impressed on my mind and heart something I hadn't seen before—the eager anticipation of the father in looking for his son. Now, it's true the passage doesn't say anything about this, but it's implied in the father's actions when he does see the son. My thoughts were concerned with what is written between the lines of the story.

Here is a father who greeted his long-lost son with much excitement, compassion, and joy. He saw the son as he was approaching home, which implies he was looking for the son. I want to think that the father looked every day for his son's return. I can see him standing outside his home, his aged eyes eagerly searching the horizon for the son he loved so dearly. And I can also feel his disappointment when the day would pass and his son had not come home.

Why was this so intriguing to me? Because I saw myself as the son and God as the father in this story. Each day He eagerly looks for my coming to spend time with Him, anticipating the joys we will share. The truth is that some days I don't come; some days I don't take the time from my busy schedule to meet my heavenly Father, yet He still waits. I do know from the story that every time a day passes and I don't spend time with my Father, His heart is broken.

The story also tells me that when the father saw the son, he ran to him with open arms and rejoiced. But more than that, he blessed him with a kiss, with a ring, sandals, and the best robe. And he held a party to show his joy at his son's return and to let the son know how precious he was to the father. Which makes me wonder: What blessings have I missed in times past when I didn't meet my Father?

So what are you waiting for? There's someone who's eagerly waiting to spend time with you. He's been waiting for a long time—don't disappoint Him today. Make the time now to meet the Father. He is eagerly waiting for you, to embrace you and bless you abundantly.

**Heather-Dawn Small**

# "Test Me," Said the Lord

*"Bring the whole tithe into the storehouse, that there may be food in my house. Test me in this," says the Lord Almighty, "and see if I will not throw open the floodgates of heaven and pour out so much blessing that you will not have room enough for it." Mal. 3:10, NIV.*

I HAVE KNOWN my husband for 35 years, and he has always had faith capable of moving mountains and total trust in God and in His promises. While he studied theology in a seminary in Collonges, France, he had a classmate from Austria who had financial difficulties. His wife worked, and he worked as a night security guard several times each week. They had no children, but they still had financial problems. One day my husband saw that his friend was very, very worried. So my husband asked him, "Karl, tell me, are you returning tithe to the Lord?"

"You are crazy. I can't; I earn very little. I don't have money for anything."

In spite of that, my husband told him that he should do it to test God, that God would not abandon him. But Karl responded, "No, we are counting every cent, and there is nothing left. I will return tithe when I have a steady job, when I have money."

"Look," said my husband, "I want to make a deal with you. This month you are going to give your tithe faithfully, and at the end of the month, if you lack money, I will give it to you."

"You have gone totally beyond good judgment," stated Karl. "I'm certain we're going to be short of money, and you don't have money to give me."

My husband had to agree, but he assured Karl, "I know that God is going to bless you, and you'll have enough money." Karl would not agree. But after several more minutes of argument, the two made the deal, each one promising to fulfill his part, and they went their own ways.

The weeks passed, the month ended, and again Karl spoke with my husband. "You know, Eric, I can't believe it. I don't know what happened to us this time. We didn't save, we lived the same as all other months, and for the first time in years we didn't come up short. To the contrary, we had money left over. Without a doubt, God poured out His blessings because we were faithful to Him. How wonderful that you reminded me of this! I won't forget. Thank you."

*Lord, help us to always put You first, returning what already belongs to You.*

**Françoise Monnier**

# Victory

*So do not fear, for I am with you; do not be dismayed,*
*for I am your God. I will strengthen you and help you;*
*I will uphold you with my righteous right hand. Isa. 41:10, NIV.*

I HAD POWER OF ATTORNEY for Mrs. Lucivan, who was entitled to receive a predetermined amount of money in a lump sum.

According to the instructions there was to be no commission or surcharge taken from the amount. Although the bank said they would pay the amount in several installments, they would still make the surcharge. So as her representative, I went to the special court of the federal justice system and filed a claim. On the day of the conciliation court appearance I went alone, because I could represent Mrs. Lucivan without the presence of a lawyer. During the court appearance, I explained my point of view to the bank's lawyer. She coldly looked at me and stated that I was wrong; Mrs. Lucivan did not have the right to receive the lump sum without a surcharge. I sought advice from a lawyer, and after analyzing the process, she reached the same conclusion. However, I didn't give up, and I began to pray until the court date came up because I was confident that God could change that situation.

The day for the case arrived. As we waited, my lawyer advised me to give up because loss was certain, but I prayed, and God impressed me that the victory was assured. Now the lawyer was asking me to give up? I thought, *Lord, why did she say this?*

The case began, and my lawyer stated, "This is your last chance—give up." However, totally confident, I told her that I would go to the end, because God had told me to do so. The negotiator then asked about an agreement, and both parties stated that there was none, and then we went in for the audience with the judge. The judge stated that I really had no right to a lump sum and gave the floor to my lawyer, who, through divine inspiration, contested with an argument that at no time had we thought of. The judge agreed with this argument, and gave the floor to the bank's lawyer, who was speechless. I won! The bank paid the entire lump sum and without any charges.

When we trust in God, pray, and give Him our request, He will never leave us without an answer. Give God your request; do your part, and He will answer. "The secret of success is the union of divine power with human effort" (*Patriarchs and Prophets*, p. 509).

**Cristiane Morais dos Santos**

# Praise the God of Love

*For God so loved the world, that he gave his only begotten Son,*
*that whosoever believeth in him should not perish, but have everlasting life.*
*John 3:16.*

HUMAN BEINGS will do almost anything for love. People have murdered for the sake of love. People have risked their lives for the sake of winning someone's love. Indeed, God created us with a great capacity to love and receive love. Even an infant, who has not yet learned the ways of people, demands his or her mother's attention.

You are in the minority if your love life is fulfilling and meaningful. Most of us look for love in our families, but we get disagreements and squabbles with our brothers, sisters, and parents. We look for love among our friends, but we get misunderstandings and betrayals. We look for love at church, but we face established cliques that are hard to penetrate. We look for love from our spouses, but we get disappointments, betrayals, and pain. Some of us look for love from our children, but we get ungratefulness and more pain. Our lives are empty and lonely.

The only true source of love is God Himself. Human love relationships are usually based on selfishness; they are heavily tainted with sin. We are not willing to give love as much as we would like to receive it. Sin robs us of the ability to give and receive true love. Sin creates a strong give-and-take, earn-it situation. God's love is very different. God so loved the world that He "gave." Giving is the basic ingredient of love. The best way to experience love is to give it, not to receive it.

The second ingredient is the gift itself. God gave the very best He had—His own Son. He didn't give perishable things. Many of us don't love enough to die for someone. But God did! O what manner of love this is! God already gave that love—all we have to do is embrace it and make it real in our lives. Though our human folk may disappoint and hurt us, God's love is always available.

Embrace God's love today and make it real in your life. Call upon the Father, whose arms are always outstretched to embrace you into His abundant love. Get on your knees; thank Him for this free gift. Ask Him to teach you how to love the way He loves. Pray that God may teach you to love the God way.

**Earlymay Chibende**

# Saving Avocados and Saving Souls

*In the same way, let your light shine before men, that they may see your good deeds and praise your Father in heaven. Matt. 5:16, NIV.*

OUR FRIEND Margaret Gill, who lives at Pine Lake Retreat Center in Groveland, Florida, was having her 100th birthday on August 11, and my husband and I decided we could not miss the occasion, even though we were living in Tennessee. My eighty-fifth birthday was on August 8, so for my birthday present my daughter and her husband offered to drive us to Florida. We had a good trip and enjoyed our visit with Margaret.

While we were there in Florida, we visited a fruit stand that offered avocados for sale for an unusually low price. But they were very ripe. The next day we were leaving for Tennessee, and we wondered if they would hold up for the trip. My son-in-law very patiently packed them in our cooler, using his own clothing for cushioning, and off we went for the 500-mile trip home. Each time we made a stop for gas or to eat, we checked the avocados to be sure they were all right.

When we reached Laurelbrook, our home, we soon found many people who loved avocados, and we didn't have any trouble selling them, cautioning everyone that they were ripe and ready. A staff supper was scheduled for the following Wednesday, so the host for that occasion needed five. Someone else was serving supper for the students, and she wanted two to make something special for them. We made quite a few friends—and disappointed a few—with the avocados.

While thinking of our concern and continual watchcare over the avocados, I began to reflect on how much concern we exhibit for those who need to be fed the gospel story. Are we as anxious to see these wandering ones saved? Are we taking advantage of every opportunity to share the good news of salvation with all whom we meet?

Daily I am praying that we may not only be faithful ourselves, but that we may be looking for others with whom to share what our wonderful Savior has done for us and is doing every day in our lives, that we will let our light shine. May we all be gathered in safely to our heavenly home when Jesus comes soon.

**Rubye Sue**

# Be Not Deceived

*Many deceivers, who do not acknowledge Jesus Christ as coming in the flesh, have gone out into the world. Any such person is the deceiver and the antichrist. Watch out that you do not lose what you have worked for, but that you may be rewarded fully. 2 John 7, 8, NIV.*

PACIFIC ADVENTIST UNIVERSITY is a bird sanctuary for Papua New Guinea. Many bird-watchers visit this campus to watch some of the rare birds of the world. One of the interesting and well-known birds on this campus is the bowerbird. The male bower is a skilled dancer and builder who can build a great castle on the grass. This castle has a firm and strong platform, pillars made from branches and the platform woven with grass. The construction can stand as high as two or three feet and covers an area of three feet square. It's intriguing how this small bird works on such an intricate and complicated bower castle. On the platform of his castle he will dance and sing in his bid to entertain the female bowers and attract one of them as his mate.

Another special skill of the bower is its ability to imitate voices, noises, and tunes—many are deceived by it. Bowerbirds love to perch and sing and play around our yard. There are lots of trees and foliage that provide sanctuary for them.

One morning as the children and I were having family worship, we heard what sounded like my nephew Simione, from Fiji, calling me. We had been expecting him to return to finish his Bachelor of Science course. The call sounded urgent as he repeated, "Nei, Nei, Nei!" which is Fijian for aunty. We stopped worship, and Josua, my son, rushed downstairs to open the door.

To his disappointment, there was no Simi at the door. Then he was surprised to hear the call change. The call was a mimic of the special call that Josua and his two friends had developed. The imitation was so much like Josua's call that the two boys next door returned the call. Josua stopped and looked up in the direction of the call. There was the bower, singing his call loud and clear, facing the direction of our neighbor's house where the boys were replying. All of us were amazed by the skill of the bower and how it had tricked all of us. Our verse reminds us that we should be alert because there will be deceivers who will work to mislead us. Let's be on the alert and not be misled—we don't want to miss heaven!

**Fulori Bola**

# Lesson From Mankau

*Then said Jesus unto his disciples, If any man will come after me,
let him deny himself, and take up his cross, and follow me.
Matt. 16:24.*

FINALLY THE MOST AWAITED time had come—we were bound
for Kenya, Africa! It was July 31, 2005, and a group of 30 daring and
committed men and women began their journey to Kenya to do a mission project. The trip alone required 20 hours by plane and eight hours
on a bumpy bus. We really didn't need to exercise that day, because the
eight-hour drive from Nairobi to Mankau, a tiny village in the eastern
Kenyan province of Meru, feels like a day of nonstop workout.

We were there not only to build a women's community center but to
foster women's awareness to a community in which women are regarded as
second-class citizens. We also included in our programs health and religious evangelism.

One late evening, after a long day of hard labor, I laid my head on my
twig-made bed, feeling tired and homesick. I battled deep inside: *Lord, why?
Why do I have to do this? Or do I have to do this? This not only is very hard
work, but is also costing me a lot of needed financial resources. And think
about the inconvenience of this place, Lord.*

Then in my heart I heard the Lord saying, "My child, if you love Me
you will not even think of all the inconvenience and hardship that this mission trip is causing you. You can make it, and you will come out victorious
and happy."

As I lay there, wide awake, the scene of the cross flashed into my mind.
I felt embarrassed. My Lord did everything for me. He gave up heaven for
me. He went to the agony of the cross for me. He was homesick. He used
rocks for His pillow.

True to His promise, the mission trip was a success. Not only were we
happy to see the women's center building stand (this is the only building in
the community), but we had made friends and had helped bring 80 precious
souls to Christ. And yes, the members of this group, coming from different
parts of the United States and from all walks of life, had become a family.

Christ did so much because He loves me, and I pray that I will be given
another chance to do mission work for Him again, anywhere—I want to
live for Him every day.

Jemima D. Orillosa

# Teacher or Evangelist?

*You are the light of the world. A city on a hill cannot be hidden. Neither do people light a lamp and put it under a bowl. Instead they put it on its stand, and it gives light to everyone in the house. Matt. 5:14, 15, NIV.*

TWENTY YEARS AGO I began to work as a science teacher for the fifth through eighth grades in a public school. I had recently graduated and had no experience in leading a class. On the first day I felt completely insecure about what to do to capture the attention of those teens.

As I thought about those adolescents, I felt a great responsibility toward them. I remembered that Jesus never missed an opportunity to speak of His kingdom. I prayed silently, asking for wisdom to transmit Jesus' love to the students.

One day the opportunity came to ask a question: "What is the difference between a house and a home?" The class quieted. No one answered. I explained, "A house is restricted to just the constructed area, while a home, regardless of how it is built, is formed where there is love, communication, and mutual respect."

Speechless, they said that they had never heard of such a thing and would like the opportunity to learn more. I offered them a Bible course, and they all decided to participate. When the first course ended, I offered another, and once again all the students were involved.

As the course progressed, great changes took place in their lives. Parents thanked me. They were grateful for my concern with the spiritual lives of their children. Other employees in the school requested the studies.

At the end of that year we held a ceremony to distribute completion certificates for all the students, their families, and the employees in the school. The minister I invited presented a sermon about Joseph in Egypt. A total of 826 certificates for the two Bible courses were presented. The school principal, commenting on the event, stated that she had made a mistake at the time she hired me. She thought she had hired a teacher, but in reality she had hired an evangelist. The following five years in that school God granted me the privilege of teaching more than 3,000 students, who also finished some type of Bible study. The results of this work will only be known in eternity. May God be praised.

**Maria Chèvre**

221

# Pansy Panther

*Be sober, be vigilant; because your adversary the devil walks about . . . , seeking whom he may devour. 1 Peter 5:8, NKJV.*

TWO YEARS AGO we and our two cats, Billy Bob and Priscilla, moved to a rural neighborhood. Three weeks later Billy Bob simply disappeared. We called. We drove around the area. We inquired of neighbors if they'd seen a mellow yellow cat. They had not. "But because of the coyote population in these hills, cats often don't last too long around here," they warned.

A short time later I brought home a long-haired black kitten to keep the lonely Priscilla company. The newcomer loved to play and play hard, often so engrossed in her play that she seemed oblivious to anything else. In fact, she played so aggressively that my husband named her Panther. When she began shredding his flowers, we expanded her name to Pansy Panther.

Late one summer afternoon we were sitting on the back porch, visiting with friends and laughing at Pansy's antics. My husband kept calling whenever she strayed too far away (and she strayed often). Sometimes she returned to him—usually she didn't. Above the pleasant conversation and friendly laughter, I began to hear something else. The sound came from only a few yards away in the area of scraggly trees at the base of our little pine-covered hill. Turning slightly, I saw beneath the underbrush two long, skinny legs—and then two more. The yellow eyes of a lean, mean coyote were locked on Pansy as she joyfully played. "There's a coyote!" I said in a low voice to my husband before running down the porch steps in the direction of the intruder. The coyote simply faded into the shadowy forest, while behind me my husband scooped the clueless Pansy into the safety of his strong hands.

How like our deadly enemy was that coyote! And, like Pansy, we are often unaware that the adversary of our souls waits and watches as we stray more deeply into our play, work, worry, self-pity, or bitterness. Stealthily he draws near, prepared to pounce and destroy. The apostle Peter warns us to be ever aware of what's going on in our lives, to be constantly vigilant if we are to avoid falling victim to the enemy of our souls. The apostle James reminds us to "draw near to God and He will draw near to you" (James 4:8, NKJV). Only the safety of God's strong hands can keep us out of the hands of the arch-predator.

**Carolyn Rathbun Sutton**

# Delivered From Fear

*Fear not, for I am with you; be not dismayed, for I am your God.*
*I will strengthen you, yes, I will help you, I will uphold you with*
*My righteous right hand. Isa. 41:10, NKJV.*

WHEN MY TWO CHILDREN WERE YOUNG, I began to think about what life would be for them if I were gone. I'm not sure how it happened, but I became obsessed about protecting my children from harm, hurt, and heartbreak. Between my fears and the endless news of car accidents on the road, I developed a severe case of panic attack. I seldom drove on the highways, and when I did I trembled, perspired, and feared. For the next five years I was terrified of driving. *What if I had an accident? What if my children got hurt?* My heart beat wildly, and I could scarcely breathe because of terror. Often I had to pull over to regain my composure. The attacks were so severe that sometimes I would panic just at the thought of having an attack. The fear was so suffocating and unreasonable that it blinded me. I couldn't explain the change to myself or to others. My close family adjusted their expectations, and I dejectedly assumed the role of passenger during trips. Fear had stolen my joy!

The children grew, and we moved to a nearby city where my son would attend high school. It was a two-hour drive that I hadn't taken for years. One day I had to make the drive, and the hot, gripping fear whispered thoughts of death and horrible accidents. Slapping the thoughts away, I began to talk to God. I claimed Isaiah 41:10 as my own. As I claimed the promise I felt peace for the first time, and quietly an old voice spoke from within. Fear had silenced the voice of the Holy Spirit since I had decided to protect my children alone. It directed me to pray a prayer of repentance. I repented that I had not given my children completely to the Lord's care. What if I were gone? Would the Lord not care for His children? I cried and confessed that the Lord was in control, and the small voice seemed to cheer me on. I drove with the assurance that I was delivered from fear.

Sometimes the enemy reminds me of my old fright, but I still drive on. I no longer fear that an accident will claim my life and leave my children motherless. I know that whatever happens, Jesus has my children in His righteous hands.

This knowledge urges me to drive on—not only on the highways, but through life.

**Rose Joseph Thomas**

# A Cry Heard by God

*Ask and it will be given to you; seek and you will find; knock and the door will be opened to you. For everyone who asks receives; he who seeks finds; and to him who knocks, the door will be opened. Matt. 7:7, 8, NIV.*

SEVERAL YEARS AGO I became seriously depressed; the depression took joy from my life. It had been three years that I'd been without work, and I felt guilty because I couldn't help my parents or accomplish my dreams. It seemed to me that all doors were closed.

Lost in tears, the pain in my heart was great; I didn't see the light of hope in any corner. Opportunities for employment appeared, but I would have to work during the Sabbath hours. Locked in my room, I knelt and opened my heart to God, telling Him everything that was happening, and my feelings and my dreams. I didn't want to disobey His commandments.

I don't know how long I stayed there; I only know that my weeping reached my heavenly Father. "What about Your promise—knock on the door, and it will be opened?" I asked. I had been knocking with both hands, and the door seemed tightly closed, and now I had begun to reject myself.

Anguish was my experience. I struggled with God as Jacob did. One night I asked God permission to go to sleep; however, I needed His lap—the pain was just so great. That night I slept peacefully, and I dreamed I was sleeping in Jesus' arms. I didn't realize what Jesus was trying to tell me, but it didn't take long to discover.

That very week the telephone rang; my local church headquarters invited me to take a test, giving me a chance for employment as a telephone operator. I fell on the sofa and broke out crying, knowing that this was God's answer to my prayer. I was certain that that job was for me. The interview was quick and uneventful. I was concerned with the computer test—it had been five years since I'd turned a computer on, and I didn't remember how it worked. But God showed me that what He gives no one can take away. I've been working in this office for five years, and not as the telephone operator, but as a secretary.

Praise the name of our God, who wipes away our tears and gives us a lap when we need comfort!

**Luciana Barbosa Freitas da Silva**

# One of Those Days

*But seek ye first the kingdom of God, and his righteousness;*
*and all these things shall be added unto you. Matt. 6:33.*

WHAT A GOOD DAY to stay in bed; I struggled with the idea of getting up. The minutes slipped by, and now it was time to leave for work. When I realized the late hour, I jumped from the bed, put on my clothes as quickly as I could, prayed with my hand on the doorknob, and left quickly—without breakfast, and without my morning devotion. The next bus would be coming in a few minutes. What a way to begin the day!

I made it to work on time, but because I began my day rushing, I was not able to concentrate. I made several mistakes, and to make things worse, I forgot to transfer my money from my other purse, so I went without lunch. My work didn't get done, so I had to stay late. Besides that, I had to borrow money from a colleague for the bus ride home. On the way home the bus broke down, and when I finally got home it was almost dark. I fell into bed exhausted. Nothing had gone right that day.

Since I couldn't sleep, my thoughts took me over the day's events, and I realized it hadn't begun well. I had started my day without God. Because of just a few minutes more in bed, I faced a lot of stress and tribulation. I then remembered what Jesus said: "Seek ye first the kingdom of God, and his righteousness." What perfect counsel for the beginning of the day!

We should seek God early, when we get up, taking time to pray, read the Bible, and meditate. No Christian should think that they will have a beneficial day if they don't put God first.

God doesn't want us to have a turbulent day, filled with unpleasant things. He wants us to go to Him during the first hours of the day so that we may find strength in Him for the tasks that we have to fulfill. Then we can rest in His arms in the certainty that we will have a day filled with heavenly blessings that only a loving God can offer us.

As you get up each day, remember that God has many blessings for you, and He renews them each morning. Begin your day seeking God first; by so doing, "all these things shall be added unto you."

**Sandra Savaris**

# Guardian Angels

*The angel of the Lord encamps around those who fear him, and delivers them. Ps. 34:7, NRSV.*

SHE MUST HAVE BEEN 2 years old on that blessed Sabbath day, one of those very special Canadian summer days. The sun shone brightly, but a gentle breeze kept the temperature at a comfortable level. I felt especially enriched by the spiritual blessings of the Sabbath services. As was customary, the adults gathered outside the church, greeting each other and exchanging pleasantries. The children played safely in the large open spaces at the back.

The church is very nicely situated, offset from busy Highway 2, which crosses the entire province of Ontario. The church sits on a lovely piece of real estate that overlooks the Bay of Quinte. The yard is nicely landscaped and well maintained. I enjoyed being a member of the congregation.

The happiness of that Sabbath afternoon was shattered when someone screamed our daughter's name. Instinctively I turned to face the road. My brain froze. My body stiffened. Time stood still for what seemed an eternity. To our horror, our toddler stood in the middle of the road. On hearing her name, Karimah turned and ran back across the road toward a shocked crowd. For a fleeting moment I was jolted back to reality. I reasoned that although God spared her life going across the road, it was improbable that she would be spared certain death coming back across that extremely busy road. I couldn't move. I couldn't speak. I simply waited for the impending impact. Then she was safely in her father's arms, and everyone breathed a sigh of relief, gave thanks to God, and commented on the miracle we had just witnessed.

No one could recall a time when there had been no traffic on Highway 2 at this location. Yet for those of us who witnessed this incident, that was what had happened—traffic briefly stood still, allowing our daughter to cross the road in both directions safely. We were left with no uncertainty that God sent His guardian angels on a specific mission to rescue Karimah. We cannot explain how she got from the backyard, past the adults, and darted into the road unnoticed. This we do know: God can—and does—send His angels to protect us when we need them most. Let us praise God when we witness this protection!

**Avis Mae Rodney**

# The Incomplete Reference

*Not that I speak in respect of want: for I have learned,*
*in whatsoever state I am, therewith to be content. Phil. 4:11.*

IT WAS DEADLINE, and every typist in the Los Angeles *Times* composing room was typing as fast as they could to get the copy into the system. I was coming back from the desk, news story in hand, when Kathie stopped me. "I've been watching you," she said. "I know you're a widow with a handicapped child to raise and a semi-invalid mother to care for, and your medical bills have to be horrendous. Yet you are always smiling and happy. With the problems you have, why are you happy all the time?"

I smiled. "Kathie, I'll answer you after deadline." I returned to my computer, praying desperately, *God, You have to help me with this. Please give me the right answer!*

The minute the deadline passed, Kathie was at my shoulder. "Well?"

"Kathie, as the Bible says, 'I have learned, in whatsoever state I am, therewith to be content.' "

"Where does it say that?"

My memory failed me. "Somewhere in Romans, I think," I stammered, "but don't quote me." I felt guilty. I had been trained to always memorize texts with the reference.

Months later Kathie came to say she'd given up her night job, joined a local church, and just had been baptized. She said, "That verse you quoted wasn't in Romans. I went home that night and, starting with Romans 1:1, I read my mother's Bible until I found the verse you quoted in Philippians 4:11. By the time I reached that verse I had met Christ and given Him my life."

Kathie had been a prostitute whose day job was a typist for the *Times*. Now she was a Christian, full of joy in her new life, all because I had forgotten the chapter and verse of a Bible reference. I had asked God for guidance in my answer. He gave me just what I needed—the words of the verse without the reference, knowing that Kathie's curiosity would drive her to her mother's Bible, and that in reading He could introduce Himself to her and win her to Himself.

*Dear God, thank You for immediately hearing. May I always trust Your answer when You give it.*

**Darlenejoan McKibbin Rhine**

# My Walking Partner

*The Lord is my shepherd; I shall not want. Ps. 23:1.*

SEVERAL YEARS AGO I was a long way from the familiar surroundings of my little home church. I settled into a new class with the anticipation of an interesting study from the Bible lesson guide. The teacher had a different and innovative idea for us that morning. His assignment was for us to consider personalizing Psalm 23 to fit each individual need. At first the task intimidated me, for it included the possibility of reading my composition before the class. After I gathered my composure, I began to formulate words in my mind.

David wrote this beautiful psalm, and it is frequently quoted from memory. David, the shepherd boy, could readily identify with sheep and shepherds. I chose another avenue of identity that would fit my needs. I like to walk, so I chose to write about my walking partner. Quickly I jotted down my thoughts and felt myself being drawn closer to the Lord as I explored new dimensions and words for Psalm 23. No doubt that was the intent of the teacher, and it worked for me—it really did personalize it for me. I hoped the others in the class would feel the same way while they were completing their literary compositions that would be unique to them.

This is my paraphrased edition of Psalm 23: "The Lord is my walking companion. He provides comfortable walking conditions for me. He lets me walk in green pastures, and He leads me beside the quiet streams. He restores hope in my soul. He takes me along paths of righteousness. Even when I must walk in the dark valley and face death, my companion is with me. He protects me from fear of the unknown walking trails. He prepares a wonderful picnic for me while my enemies linger near. My heart is full of gratitude. His goodness and mercy never ends and will continue till we walk together in the house of the Lord."

Now, as I walk in the park, these thoughts frequently run through my mind, and a smile forms on my face. Sometimes the people I meet will smile back, totally unaware that I am walking with my Lord.

You may want to spend some time in personalizing this psalm and feel the Lord draw near, according to your personal needs. After all, His messages *are* for us personally.

Retha McCarty

# The Sky Is the Limit

*Be of good courage, and he shall strengthen your heart,*
*all ye that hope in the Lord. Ps. 31:24.*

AUGUST 9 IS NATIONAL WOMEN'S DAY in South Africa, and August 9, 2004, was one of the days I will always remember. That rainy day I first ran a six-mile (10-kilometer) women's marathon in Cape Town. I woke up at 5:00 feeling hungry, and I knew that if I didn't eat, my ulcer would complain, so I decided to eat cereal, hoping that by 8:00, when the race was to begin, the food would already be digested. I was nervous and scared as the hour drew near. I phoned my friend Benny, who had my race number, and she said she would meet me at the entrance to the race start at 7:20.

At 6:55 I stood there, nervous and anxious. I remember feeling a pain in my stomach by 7:30; I wasn't sure whether it was the cereal or the ulcer. The scary part was that the rain wasn't stopping, and I wasn't sure if I was going to make it in my first marathon.

I prayed a lot, and I had very good support from my boyfriend, my mother, and friends; I knew they were praying for me. I also knew I was fit because I'd been training every day and ran three miles (five kilometers) every Sunday morning. But six miles was a bit too much, I thought.

We made it to the starting point, where some schoolchildren sang the national anthem, and off we ran. As we ran, it encouraged me that so many people enjoyed the race, so I also relaxed. The first five kilometers went well, but I worried about the next five because of the approaching hill. I didn't pause or stop—I was enjoying my pace.

When I approached the finish line, people cheered, photos were taken, and I got my bronze medal. I cried with excitement. I was not position one, two, or three, but the fact that I finished the race on time meant a lot to me. I realized that all things are possible in life if only one believes and is determined—and has God's help.

Some of us born during the Bantu education days never had an opportunity to recognize our talents because we had no resources at school. When I came to Cape Town, I realized that I had a second chance to live my dreams. Now I know that I am a strong Black woman who can take a challenge and turn it into an opportunity. The sky is the limit now—with God on my side, who, or what, can be against me! Life is too short to sit and mourn. Happy Women's Day!

**Deborah Matshaya**

# The Lord Opened the Windows of Heaven

*Bring ye all the tithes into the storehouse, that there may be meat in mine house, and prove me now herewith, saith the Lord of hosts, if I will not open you the windows of heaven, and pour you out a blessing, that there shall not be room enough to receive it. Mal. 3:10.*

ON THE DAY that I was supposed to pay my bills I made some calculations and realized that I wouldn't be able to pay everything that I owed. Right there I knelt and prayed to the Lord, asking for His help. Then I went to the bank to withdraw my direct-deposited paycheck. While in line, all I could think about was what I could do to pay my remaining debts, and once more asked God to guide me.

I withdrew the money, separated out my tithe and tucked it away, and went to pay the remaining bills. As expected, I had no more money. There was nothing more I could do. What I was unable to pay with the little salary that I earned would have to wait until the next month. I returned home tired, thanked God for what I had been able to do, and went to bed.

Several days later I remembered a debt that I had incurred on the credit card of a friend. I felt despair, because I wouldn't have any money to cover that amount. What should I do? I knew, however, that the money for my tithe was still in my drawer, waiting to be given at church. An enormous struggle took place in my mind. Next week I would have to meet my commitment to my friend and pay that debt. I was also aware of Romans 13:8: "Let no debt remain outstanding, except the continuing debt to love one another" (NIV). So would I return the tithe, or pay my friend so as not to cause a problem between us? Although apprehensive, I decided to return the tithe, and I prayed that God would give me courage to tell my friend that I didn't have the money at this time.

The days went by, and two days before I was to make the payment to my friend, I opened one of my purses. To my surprise, I found the amount necessary to pay the debt that I owed my friend. I had forgotten that I still had that money.

I thanked God, first for having kept me strong in doing my part in returning the tithe, and then for His giving His promise of pouring out His blessings on those who are faithful to Him.

*Each day, Lord, may You help us choose to be permanently faithful to You. Amen!*

**Carmem Virgínia**

# Waiting and Watching

*Watch therefore—for you do not know when the master of the house will come. Mark 13:35, RSV.*

MY HUSBAND HAD BEEN called away to attend some church meetings in another province. The transport that was organized for the trip came at 6:00 Friday morning. It would take more than 16 hours to reach his destination. The meetings would be held on Sunday, and very early Monday morning he would be homeward bound.

We had been married 32 years, but my husband is not a fellow who likes phoning. If I say, "Why didn't you phone me? Most husbands phone their wives; why don't you?" he'll say, "You know where I am; why worry?" So I didn't expect a phone call.

On Monday morning while I was answering my correspondence the phone rang, and I rushed to answer it. It was my husband! He said he'd be home by lunchtime. I completed my letter writing at 11:00 and rushed to the post office. I was planning to go to the shop as well, but decided to go straight home to prepare a special welcome-home meal, knowing he would be hungry and tired from his long journey.

Lunchtime came. I set the table and tried to keep the food warm. I made a nourishing and colorful salad, too. I even had strawberries and ice cream waiting to be enjoyed as dessert.

Time ticked by. I paced up and down. I looked through the window. I took several walks down the path to the front gate, hoping to see the vehicle coming down the road. I was restless and couldn't get myself occupied with anything else. I wanted to be ready to welcome my husband as he arrived home.

More time passed. I switched the stove off so the food wouldn't dry out, and refrigerated the salad. I was becoming more and more anxious as I noticed it was 3:30 already.

Then, when I did do something else and wasn't watching, I heard voices. And there he was! In that very moment, when I was occupied with other business, he arrived!

I'm also watching and waiting for my heavenly Bridegroom. He has given us signs of His coming (Luke 21). After waiting so long, will I again be caught up doing other business? I hope not. I want to be ready, don't you?

**Priscilla E. Adonis**

# The Glad Game

*Be joyful always; pray continually; give thanks in all circumstances, for this is God's will for you in Christ Jesus. 1 Thess. 5:16-18, NIV.*

I WONDER HOW MANY of the present generation have heard of Pollyanna? For those unacquainted with the story, Pollyanna was the only child of a poor ministerial couple. After their tragic death, Pollyanna was sent across America to live with her only relative, a wealthy maiden aunt whose strict sense of duty forced her to take the child.

Approaching her aunt's splendid house, Pollyanna imagined the prettily decorated room she would have. Instead, a maid showed her to a stuffy attic room with a tiny window, no pictures on the walls, no curtains at the window, and no mirror in the dresser. Shocked and disappointed, Pollyanna brushed away her tears and tried to play the glad game her father had taught her.

"I'm glad there are no curtains at the window," she told the maid, "because now I can see the beautiful trees and clouds and fields, and they're real, better than any picture on the wall."

"I'm glad there's no mirror in the dresser too, because now I can't see my freckles or how straight my hair is, and if I can't see them, they won't worry me."

And so the story continued. It made a deep impression on my sister and me. We particularly liked the episode in which one of Pollyanna's many adult friends tripped and broke his leg. Rendered helpless, he angrily challenged Pollyanna to tell him something he could be glad about under the circumstances. She thought deeply for a few minutes and finally burst out, "You can be glad you're not a centipede."

Mother used the book too. Whenever we began to fret about something, she told us to play the glad game. It became a guideline throughout our growing-up years and is still often mentioned.

"Stress" is the buzzword nowadays. We work and play under such great pressure that we take our delays and disappointments too seriously. When things get tough, try playing Pollyanna's glad game. You'll always find something to be glad about, especially if God is in charge of your life.

**Goldie Down**

# My Provider

*But my God shall supply all your need according to his riches in glory by Christ Jesus. Phil. 4:19.*

FINALLY! Our long-awaited vacation was due, and the four of us were excited that we would spend it under the Spanish sun. After a two-hour flight the plane landed, we rented a car, and drove off to Barcelona. We circled around, looking for a place to park our car so we could eat something in the nearby McDonald's. My husband, Martin, sat at a table to secure the space for the rest of us, while we went to select the food. Martin had gathered our passports from immigration at the time of our arrival and had forgotten to return them to us. As we returned to our table I saw Martin searching around, looking for something, and he looked very pale. We were shocked to learn that his bag, which he had put down right beside him, had been taken. He recalled a woman sitting down beside him. Soon after she left he noticed that the camera bag was gone too.

We went to the police to make a report stating that our documents had been stolen so that we would have something to show to the airline on our return home to Germany. The report would serve as replacement for the actual documents. We didn't want to ruin our vacation, so we set aside the problem and had some fun. Then after too short a time we headed again to the airport.

Our airline wouldn't let us board the plane without passports; neither would they honor the police report with all the stamps on it. Another airline accepted the report, but we would have to buy new tickets. We collected our remaining cash, but even after they reduced the price for our sake, we were still short 50 Euros. We kept praying, asking the Lord to solve our problem. In my despair I went to show the agent my purse, which was already empty. But as I opened it up, there was a neatly folded 50-Euro bill—just the amount we needed to buy our tickets to fly back home.

We couldn't say a word. We just looked at each other, and the tears started to flow. We don't know how the money got in there, for I had opened my purse up many times and there had been only a few coins in there. For us, one thing was sure: God had shown again a miracle to His children who trusted in Him. He provides for our needs in times of trouble.

*O Lord Jesus, thank You for looking after our needs. You are worthy to be praised!*

**Loida Gulaja Lehmann**

233

# My Unclean Lips

*I said, "There is no hope for me! I am doomed because every*
*word that passes my lips is sinful, and I live among a people*
*whose every word is sinful. And yet, with my own eyes*
*I have seen the King, the Lord Almighty." Isa. 6:5, TEV.*

THROUGHOUT MY CHILDHOOD bad language was not tolerated, and I was punished for every violation. Because my father swore profusely, it was very easy for me to pick it up. My mother punished me by washing my mouth out with soap.

I went to boarding school while in primary school. Bad language was frowned upon there, too. Some of the boarders swore occasionally, but the friends I chose didn't swear, and the habit was more easily broken. I was easily influenced and needed to choose my friends carefully.

In my adult life the problem resurfaced in a most unpredictable way. I was appointed children's ministries leader at our church, soon discovered the lack of resources, and began writing my own plays. One play was the story of the innkeeper in Bethlehem who turned Mary and Joseph away because he was booked up. I wrote about the numerous travelers who asked for rooms and how annoyed the innkeeper became. He muttered "Bother, bother, bother" every time someone knocked on his door asking for a room. During rehearsals the words stuck in my mind. The words weren't blasphemous or crude, but to me they were expletives nonetheless. God soon showed me that He didn't want any such utterances. I felt my own sinfulness but remembered the great prophet Isaiah, who struggled with the same temptations. Isaiah had seen God and believed he would die for his sinfulness. Similarly, I ask God to be with me throughout every day. As with Isaiah, realizing God's greatness would help me overcome temptations. An angel took a burning coal of fire with a pair of tongs and placed it against Isaiah's lips to purify them. Ouch! I prayed for a less-painful solution.

Acknowledging who God is has helped overcome my temptations. I repent whenever expletives enter my mind. I may not have said the words, but God heard them. I want to be alert to His presence all the time. I want to think of my God as a companion, not only a judge. He knows I am human, but He has told me what saddens Him. I am committed to cooperate with Him in overcoming any bad habits.

**Bridgid Kilgour**

# A Lesson From Caros

*Suffer little children, and forbid them not, to come unto me.*
*Matt. 19:14.*

THE BLISTERING SUN had lingered overhead far too long, blanketing the area with stifling humidity that sucked the oxygen from the air. A brief stop at Taco Bell would surely offer me and two of my granddaughters a respite from the heat. I felt my blood boil as I wrestled with 4-year-old Carolina's seat belt. By the time I got them seated inside, I was sweating profusely and becoming nauseated.

"Caros," I said, "be careful with your drink before you spill—" Too late. The juice cascaded from her chair like a waterfall, forming a red puddle on the floor. I glanced over at her, and she too seemed hot and bothered. I quickly snatched my napkins from the table and bent down to clean up her mess. "Here, let me clean up this mess you've made."

As I wondered how she managed to spill her drink before taking one sip, she said softly, "Grandma Amy, when you were little like me, did you ever spill your drink?"

Without making eye contact I said, "Yes, many times." But my admission was not in answer to her question, for while I was on my knees cleaning up the mess she'd made, I could clearly see Jesus cleaning up mine, and my heart was broken. He stoops at our feet and says ever so gently, "Here, let Me clean up the mess you've made of your life." Time and time again He has knelt so lovingly at our feet, His red blood, like a waterfall, pooling at the foot of the cross, cleansing us from the guilt of our sins. He so willingly drank from our cup so that we might enjoy the delights of His righteousness.

I handed Caros my full cup, only to receive her empty cup. My love for that little girl quenched my thirst. Her lesson warmed my heart. Jesus loves to exchange His righteousness for our filthy rags. It is His love for us that keeps Him at our feet, especially delighted when we accept the offer of His cup of infinite mercy. He knows that we, like little children, are so eager to taste of the pleasures of the world that in our haste to drink, we make a mess of everything.

*Dear Jesus, how often have we spilled our cup of foolishness at Your feet, only to have You clean it up? Thank You for seeing us as little children. Please give us Your grace so that when we are tempted to drink again, it will remind us of Your sacrifice. Amen.*

**Amy Smith Mapp**

# Greener Pastures

*Behold, I give unto you power to tread on serpents and scorpions, and over all the power of the enemy: and nothing shall by any means hurt you. Luke 10:19.*

SOMETIMES WHEN WE'RE in a dangerous or stressful situation our first reaction is to do something without prayer or much thought, just to get out of "harm's way." Then, after it's all over, we're actually in disbelief.

A couple years ago my husband, who is legally blind, and our grand-daughter were working on our goat pen. We couldn't seem to keep the goats inside the electric fence. They always wanted what looked greener on the other side, which was our beautiful garden. My husband was kneeling down on the ground, hammering a post. Our granddaughter looked up and saw a snake over her granddad's head, hanging from the goat shelter. Arielle said, "Granddad, there's a snake hanging over your head." He thought she was joking because of the calmness in her voice. When she said it again, he realized he was in danger. He slowly eased away from the fence post, then told Arielle to run and tell me to get his gun. In the meantime our dog, Celtae, held the snake's attention. I came running with the shot-gun in my hand, but I was afraid because I'm a city girl! My husband proceeded to take care of the snake, with me warning him to be careful because the snake was fighting for its life.

My husband still tells the story about his close call with the snake that was hanging over his head, and his ability to see well enough visually to get rid of it. He says he knows his angels were with him that day.

You know that old serpent, the devil, is sneaking around, just waiting for his chance to strike. Just as our dog was holding the snake at bay, our guardian angels are there to protect us. Just as Arielle was there to warn her granddad of unforeseen danger, we have the Scriptures to warn us about unforeseen dangers when we disobey.

Sometimes we're blindsided as to what is happening, but the Holy Spirit gave my husband the eyesight to see the snake and dispose of it. Let us not be spiritually blind so that the devil convinces us of a greener pasture on his side, or that we're not in danger. With the devil around, we are in peril.

Elaine J. Johnson

# God Cares

*O Lord, our Lord, how majestic is your name in all the earth!*
*You have set your glory above the heavens. Ps. 8:1, NIV.*

THE SKY WAS BEAUTIFUL, the ocean breathtaking, and the summer breeze gentle. Yet my heart was heavy. As I sat on the bench on the dockside I kept questioning the Lord as to how I was going to continue paying for my older daughter's college tuition. It seemed as though the world was falling in on me. As a single parent of two children, I was constantly agonizing with the Lord. My mental conversation with Him was suddenly interrupted by the sound of a rushing speedboat. As I gazed at this machine gliding across the blue waters, my attention was taken up with the speed at which it was going.

Then my thoughts shifted, and I continued conversing. Again I was abruptly interrupted by the sight and sound of a flock of birds. What a nuisance these creatures seem to be! Seconds later several came close to where I was seated. They seemed to be telling me something. I continued watching as their other feathered companions gathered around. "Why are these birds flocking around me?" I asked God. With intense admiration I delighted in their precision. Walking in one straight line, as in a military parade, these creatures showed such poise.

Of course, by now my thoughts weren't on how I was going to make that tuition payment but on how organized and precise God's creatures are. They pecked on morsels, flapped their wings, cocked their tiny necks, and walked with their chest high in the air. They seemed to be saying, "We have no worries in the world; our Creator has given us breath. He supplies food for us every day, and He has given us the ability to fly—so why should we worry?" It was truly a lesson to be learned.

As I continued to watch my new friends take their flight, I gazed toward the high hills that surround our beautiful island. I realized that I've never taken time to truly admire the Creator's handiwork. These hills are indeed a display of God's majestic creation.

I left the dock that day filled with assurance that my heavenly Father would provide the finances. Surely, if He cares for the sparrows, how much more will He care for me and meet my all my needs?

**Naomi J. Penn**

# The Reunion

*God himself shall be with them, and be their God. Rev. 21:3.*

I HAD JUST RETURNED from our annual retired church workers' convocation and was still in a state of euphoria as I reflected on the wonderful friends with whom I had mingled over the weekend. They had come from everywhere—friends who in one way or another had made an impact on my life. Many I had not seen for decades. Familiar, smiling faces appeared around every corner, and hugs were freely exchanged as we met along the walks.

Our days were packed. Morning devotions, breakout sessions on topics such as grief recovery, health, aging gracefully, and others, enriched our lives. A watermelon feed, musical programs, tours, a banquet, and the divine worship hour filled our days with happy fellowship. Tears were shed, too, as we recalled losses among our number. Declining health among longtime friends was inescapably taking its toll, and we were reluctant to bid goodbye on that last morning, knowing we were most likely seeing some of these dearly loved friends for the last time on this earth.

Every moment had been precious. But a happier reunion is coming, and I don't want to miss it! My reservation has already been acknowledged for another retired workers' convocation, this time at God's own Celestial City, if you please. There again, we will joyfully greet long-lost loved ones. There at last we'll flourish in the atmosphere of heaven and sit at that glorious banquet table where our Redeemer is host. There, our devotional periods are conducted by the very object of our long years of worship, and we fall at His nail-pierced feet in joyful adoration.

There will be no graying heads, no twisted bodies, no canes, no blind eyes or deaf ears, no memory loss, no pain, no sorrow, no guilt-laden baggage. We will walk with youthful alacrity and steady gait. We will tour heaven's cosmic attractions with abandon, visit other worlds, and share our experiences. And yes, there will be hugs—many of them. And tears! Oh, yes, there will be tears. I can see them freely coursing down our cheeks—tears of gratitude as Jesus embraces us individually, wipes them all away, and assures us that indeed we are worth His sacrifice! What a God! What a Savior! What a Friend! We will be home at last with our heavenly family.

I can hardly wait for that wonderful day. How about you?

**Lorraine Hudgins-Hirsch**

# A New Way of Loving

*When Enoch had lived 65 years, he became the father of Methuselah. And after he became the father of Methuselah, Enoch walked with God 300 years and had other sons and daughters. Gen. 5:21, 22, NIV.*

I HAVE ALWAYS HAD ADMIRATION, gratitude, and respect for my parents for the hard work, time, money, and love that they always gave me. However, when maternity reached my life, a new feeling toward them appeared. Not really new, but everything I already felt toward them increased. Each time that I got up in the middle of the night, or during the hours that I spent caring for my children, I remembered my parents. Some things that I had not comprehended, I began to understand better.

Today, for example, in choosing between buying clothes for my children or for me, it is easy to choose to buy things for them. This choice doesn't make me sad; rather, I feel happy to see them beautiful and well-dressed.

My feelings changed not only in relation to my parents but also in relation to God. I think of the marvelous Father we have who loved us so much that He gave His Son to die for us.

Christian author Ellen White writes: "During these earlier years Enoch had loved and feared God and had kept His commandments. . . . From the lips of Adam he had learned the dark story of the Fall, and the cheering one of God's grace as seen in the promise; and he relied upon the Redeemer to come. But after the birth of his first son, Enoch reached a higher experience; he was drawn into a closer relationship with God. He realized more fully his own obligations and responsibility as a son of God. And as he saw the child's love for its father, its simple trust in his protection; as he felt the deep, yearning tenderness of his own heart for that firstborn son, he learned a precious lesson of the wonderful love of God to men in the gift of His Son, and the confidence which the children of God may repose in their heavenly Father. The infinite, unfathomable love of God through Christ became the subject of his meditations day and night" (*Patriarchs and Prophets*, p. 84).

May God give you a greater vision of His love for you today!

**Luciana Ribeiro de Mattos**

# Danger in the Air

*For in the day of trouble he will keep me safe in his dwelling;*
*he will hide me in the shelter of his tabernacle. Ps. 27:5, NIV.*

I WAS JUST 14 AND FLYING INTO THE BIRMINGHAM AIRPORT IN ENGLAND. We were about to land and had almost touched the runway when the plane took off again, rising steeply into the night sky. As we began to circle the airport, I looked down to see fire engines and ambulances racing onto the runway and into a special waiting area.

The pilot announced, "I'm afraid we have a slight technical hitch, and we'll be circling for a while to use up as much fuel as possible before we land. The control tower has told us that there's a fault with our undercarriage. It may have been damaged on takeoff."

Everyone was silent. I knew my parents were waiting in the airport to meet me. I wondered about the "slight technical hitch." A damaged undercarriage seemed to be a serious problem. The atmosphere was tense and sharp. A woman began to cry.

Up there in the night sky there was absolutely nothing I, in my human strength, could do. I was alone, inexperienced, and shy, and I knew nothing about airplanes. So I prayed. Even the pilot was limited in what he could do. No human could go out there and mend the damage while we were still flying. I wondered what it would be like to die. It took a long time to burn the fuel down—a long time to think, and a long time to pray. But I felt wrapped in a comforting sense of peacefulness.

Finally the pilot announced that it was time to attempt the landing, and we prepared ourselves for whatever might happen. I watched the ground come closer, and prayed harder.

We glided onto the runway with one of the smoothest landings I had ever experienced, and finally came to rest on a stretch of runway farthest from the terminal. Everyone cheered and laughed! The emergency vehicles headed back to the depot as we finally exited the plane.

Now older (but perhaps not so much wiser), I sometimes think I can fix my own undercarriage, and forget that God can mend anything much better than I can. I need to take a seat in His plane, no matter how dark the night, how alone I feel, or whatever fears and dangers I may face, and be totally dependent on Him to bring me to a safe place. And He always does.

**Karen Holford**

# Reflection of Christ

*In the same way, let your light shine before others, so that they may see your good works and give glory to your Father in heaven. Matt. 5:16, NRSV.*

I SAT IN THE LOBBY of my county's school board at one of the computers in the employment area, trying to update my personal profile. Before I had left my apartment that morning, I prayed that my day would go well. "Lord, I want my life to be a reflection of Your life. I want Your beauty to be seen in my walking, speech, and deportment today." I especially prayed this prayer because several weeks before that morning I'd gone to that same building and had an unpleasant experience. I was hoping I wouldn't see that woman again. As I pulled into the parking lot I was still praying that I wouldn't see her.

My prayer was answered. I didn't see her, and I was feeling really happy. I continued praying that my day would finish on a positive note. "I just want the beauty of Jesus to be seen in me."

I watched as many people walked by, people from all walks of life. I continued to watch the behavior of many until I became engrossed in what I was doing. Then I saw a young man walking back and forth, looking into the faces of the people who were sitting around the computers. He stopped a few feet away and said to me, "Miss, can you give me 50 cents?" I asked him a few questions to make sure that he was sincere about wanting the money to buy food. I gave him more than what he had asked for, and he thanked me and went on his way.

There were many people sitting around those computers, but he chose to ask me for the money. I wonder many times what difference he saw in me. Did he see the beauty of Jesus in me? Was my appearance different? Only God and that young man knew. I felt good for the rest of the day, knowing that I could help someone, and also knowing that someone saw something different in me. Isn't that what letting our light shine is all about?

*Lord, I continue daily to ask: please let my life be a reflection of Your life. Let the beauty of Jesus be seen in each of us this day.*

**Patricia Hines**

# Trust in God

*If you believe, you will receive whatever you ask for in prayer.*
*Matt. 21:22, NIV.*

THERE WAS A MEETING in the city that morning, but I woke up feeling sick and didn't know what to do, because I lived almost 15 miles (25 kilometers) from downtown. If I went by bus, I'd get home very late. My husband suggested that I go by motorcycle.

Even though I was apprehensive about the dangers along the way, I went by motorbike. I participated in the meeting, then ran several errands downtown. As I was returning home, already on the highway, I felt one of the tires going flat. I immediately attempted to return to town so that I could get the tire fixed, but soon the tire was totally flat and beginning to come off the wheel. I couldn't go back—or forward. Now I had to wait for someone to stop and offer to help me.

Already tired, I parked the motorcycle on the shoulder of the road, and right there I prayed to God, asking His help. There was nothing I could do but wait for divine intervention.

Several cars and motorcycles passed, but no one stopped. However, I knew that the Lord wouldn't abandon me there in that deserted area. He knew my motives and the reason I came to the city, and why I was willing to go to the meeting. I waited patiently and confidently in His providence. He would send the best person to help me.

I waited a little longer, and then a motorcycle stopped beside me. Soon I realized that the biker was our friend. He helped me remove the tire, and took it to a tire repair in the city while I waited with the motorcycle. When he returned with the repaired tire, he put it back on the motorcycle, and I made the return trip home.

It was a difficult day; however, each time I remember the difficulties I faced, I turn my thoughts to God and thank Him for the providence and the care He provided. He sent our friend to help. "The Lord will hear when I call unto him" (Ps. 4:3). I called out in a moment of anguish and need, and He heard me.

Remember that God treats those who are faithful to Him with special care. He fulfilled His promise, and He will fulfill His promise to you. Give yourself to Him today and wait, trusting His divine providence.

**Joana D'arc O. da Silva Hemerly**

# God's Amazing Rosebush

*The One enthroned in heaven laughs. Ps. 2:4, NIV.*

THE GOLD AND TAN HUES of the Brass Band rose immediately caught my eye. How exquisitely they would blend with the beige brick of our church. The perfect place for the bush would be just to the right of the top of the steps leading up from the parking lot. These musings went through my mind at the Annual Master Gardener Show as I admired the various rosebushes. I ordered a Brass Band for our church and waited two months for the nursery to call me with the news that my order had arrived.

At last! When I purchased it, I had thought, *How nice that rosebush would look in the newly planted rose garden at home!* After a few more selfish thoughts (*What difference would it make? I could buy another one for the church?*), I thought of Sapphira and Ananias, who had promised the disciples that they would give all their profits to the new church from a piece of property they were selling—and then kept some of the money for themselves. And with what tragic consequences! (See Acts 5.)

Although I didn't think God would strike me dead, I nevertheless planted the Brass Band at the church. God surely smiled down on His rosebush. Never has a rosebush produced such an abundance of blossoms—dozens at a time, month after month. So very beautiful! I was so glad I had planted it there at the church.

Soon thereafter I acquired the same kind of rosebush for my own garden and planted it with the same OK-Lord-I-planted-it-You-make-it-grow attitude.

I sometimes think I can hear God laugh. I'm sure He has a great sense of humor (it's all right if you don't agree with me) as I check out my bush and find only one or two blooms a month. I wonder if He is reminding me that He blesses what is cheerfully given to Him. The difference between the bushes could only be called funny.

I enjoy watching members walk past on Sabbath mornings and admire the beautiful roses at the church. Many shut-ins have received bouquets from God's special rosebush. I can (almost) hear Him whisper, "What do you think of My glorious bush?" I smile and remember that the One enthroned in heaven laughs.

**Dorothy Wainwright Carey**

# The Right Person

*Be careful for nothing; but in every thing by prayer and supplication with thanksgiving let your requests be made known unto God. Phil. 4:6.*

"LORD, LEAD ME to the right person today," I prayed one summer day in 2002. Months earlier my mother had begun some business transactions. The company with which she was dealing required a letter from another agency by a specific date. The problem was that Mother was now hospitalized. Dad didn't see a problem; he would get the letter. He returned empty-handed; Mother was the only person who could be given the letter. Dad suggested that I try. *But if they wouldn't give the letter to Dad, they aren't going to give it to me,* I thought. However, I would try.

I explained the situation to my supervisor and asked for some time off the next morning. Then I placed the problem before the Lord, asking Him to lead me to the right person, a secretary or supervisor who would understand the problem and help me.

I arrived at the agency at 7:30 to find out that the agency didn't open until 9:00, but I could wait in the foyer. While waiting, a woman arrived and told the officer why she was there. He directed her to another location. Just then the Spirit said to me, "Tell him why you are here." When I did, he said, "They aren't going to give you that letter; your mother is the only one who can receive it." I continued to pray quietly, thinking the security officer wasn't the right person I'd prayed for. Five minutes later the officer asked if I had a notepad. When I said I did, he dictated a letter to me with specific facts. I signed the letter, and he took it and went into the office. *Well, at least my letter will be the first one to receive attention*, I thought.

Minutes went by, and the officer returned and handed me an envelope. I opened it, and there was the letter Mother needed! The agency was not yet open for business, I had not met with a secretary or supervisor, yet here I was with the needed letter! The only person I had spoken to was a security officer, who in God's plan for my family *was* the right person! I thanked the officer profusely and walked out into the street praising God.

Sisters, whatever problem you may face today, present it to God with thanksgiving. He will take care of it in His own way.

Maureen O. Burke

# What Do I Wish for My Enemy?

*And so we know and rely on the love God has for us. God is love.*
*Whoever lives in love lives in God, and God in him. 1 John 4:16, NIV.*

LET'S TALK ABOUT LOVE. Today I read something wonderful about this precious gift that we receive from Jesus. This gift is not just a feeling, but a principle. Love is each individual promoting the happiness of the other, whether the other individual values this or not. How difficult it is to love like this!

One day I discovered my inability to love when I came upon the divine command "Love your enemies and pray for those who persecute you" (Matt. 5:44, NIV). I thought, *I am not going to be able to do this. No, no, this is impossible! I know myself, Lord, and I will never be able to love like this! Why do You ask me to do this if You know everything about my fallen nature?*

An enemy is someone capable of taking your peace, turning you inside out, causing dormant instincts to be revealed in you, and bringing about reactions that you thought you were incapable of possessing. Then it happened to me. I was tested and needed to choose between obeying the divine commandment or reacting according to my instincts. My enemy was real, with skin and bones, and I was the only one who knew.

One day I went to the extreme of kneeling and wishing terrible things on my enemy. I wanted a terrible cancer to consume my enemy; my hate was lethal, until I heard the soft, calm voice of the Father, and I chose to obey Him.

After a crises of depression, tears of desperation, a desire to flee, I finally discovered what dependence on God meant. I learned by remaining at His feet, in complete submission, conscious that I would receive from Him the power to overcome as He had overcome, walk as He had walked, and love with His heart, since my heart was incapable of doing this.

After several years of relating to my enemy, I learned from my failure the immense love of the Almighty. If you love those who love you, what reward shall you have? Anyone can love those who love them; however, you will be rewarded when you learn from the Father to give your life for those who have wanted to destroy you!

**Judete Soares de Andrade**

# My Kitty-Cat Escort

*The angel of the Lord encamps all around those who*
*fear Him, and delivers them. Ps. 34:7, NKJV.*

WHEN MY MOTHER-IN-LAW became terminally ill with cancer, our family had to make special plans for taking care of her in her home for as long as possible. Friends and relatives helped some, but most of the responsibility fell on my and my husband's shoulders.

Fortunately, Mom lived within walking distance of our home. I took the day shift. Julie, our high school-age daughter, helped afternoons and early evenings, so I could go to my part-time school custodial job. Carl did the night shift.

Carl and I needed some one-on-one time together. So after I'd gotten things done at our house, about 9:30 p.m., I'd walk to Mom's to be with him. She was usually asleep by then. I'd walk back home about 11:00. Carl worried about my safety and wished that he could walk me back and forth, but he couldn't leave Mom alone.

One of the couples who lived next door to us had several large dogs that they allowed to roam free. And those dogs were definitely more aggressive after dark! I told Carl not to worry, that as well as having God to protect me, I had a kitty-cat escort.

Carl looked out Mom's living-room window. On her deck sat our three tabby-striped cats, Georgette, Tigerette, and Beastie Boy. Each evening the cats walked with me to Mom's, stayed on the deck until I was ready to leave, and then accompanied me home. Our cats cheered my heart during those dark, trying days. The dogs never bothered me during the nine months that we followed this routine.

I've heard it said that "cats are little angels in fur." And it certainly seemed that our three were. Maybe God thought we would feel better if I also had an escort that we could see. I thank Him for impressing their feline hearts to do what they did. How good that He was able to use our furry friends to show us how much He cared about us and what was happening to us.

The cats have since grown old and died. But the love and kindness that led them to help make our ordeal more bearable will always live on in my memory.

**Bonnie Moyers**

# A House for God's Child

*A true friend sticks closer than one's nearest kin. Prov. 18:24, NRSV.*

LONG AGO SOLOMON wrote about a friend who sticks closer than family. It was like that with my girlfriend. We stuck together. When her call came at minutes to midnight, we talked, unburdening our distresses. Then I heard her say, "Madge, I need a change for Marla." I knew that her daughter was giving her problems, and I heard myself say, "I will help you."

When I put down the phone, I wondered, *Where am I going to put her*? I had just moved to Florida and had only a tiny one-bedroom apartment. "Dear Lord," I prayed. "Please find me a bigger apartment and some sturdy furniture so Marla will feel comfortable here."

Each time I prayed, a strange thing happened—I got the same direction. "Go to Meadowood Loop." I knew that area because I have a friend who lives there, but those were houses, not apartments. Eventually I came to my senses. The Holy Spirit was speaking to me.

I called a real estate agent and asked her to take me house hunting. My request was specific: "Just Meadowood Loop. Nowhere else." The first house she showed me was one I had never liked, but if this was the house the Lord wanted me to have, I determined to accept it. On our way out, however, the agent said, "There is another house you could see." Then she took me to a house I had always liked, even though I knew it was out of my price range.

The owner told me that because her husband was very sick, she wanted to return to France before he died. As I started to leave, she mentioned that the house was being sold furnished. I turned around and took a second look, reminding myself that I had asked God for furniture. Was this His answer?

Now I became more confused than ever. I had found the house I liked but had no down payment. I hadn't been in the United States long enough to qualify for even a Federal Housing Administration mortgage. What did God want for me? But traveling through a maze of impossibilities, I found that God wanted me to bring glory to His name. Within six weeks I got the FHA mortgage on that three-bedroom house. (And it even had a double garage!)

God gave me the house for His child. He promised to go before and make the crooked places straight so that I might know He was the Lord (Isa. 45:2, 3). And He did just that!

**Madge S. May**

# In Brokenness You Shine

*The Lord upholds all who fall, and raises up all those who are bowed down. . . . The Lord is near to all who call upon Him, to all who call upon Him in truth. Ps. 145:14-18, NKJV.*

MY SON AND HIS FAMILY came to visit for a week. We had a marvelous time getting to know his three little ones better and catching up on the family news with his wife. What I will never forget, however, is a song my minister-son introduced to me. It's a song that contemporary Christian artist Steve Green wrote: "In Brokenness You Shine."

The song made quite an impact on me. The words are beautiful. A few lines of the chorus say it all: "Help me believe/And trust You one more time/ In brokenness You shine."

Then I thought about one of the reasons for my son's visit—to pick up a car my husband had fixed up. One of my husband's clients had given him a car headed for the wrecking yard. It was no beauty—the engine was shot, one door had dents, and paint was coming off the hood. Yet my husband saw potential in it. After a few trips to the wrecking yard for parts from like models, a new engine, and a complete paint job, the car was shining.

In prayerful amazement, I wondered, *If my husband can make a wreck of a car shine like this one, how much more can our heavenly Father make us shine in our brokenness?*

Thinking of the words of the Steve Green song gives me a lot of encouragement. Sometimes our lives become a shattered dream, and we can't find the words to speak, but this is when our heavenly Father sees and hears our pain and will come and pour His mercy on us. The song reminds me that even in our brokenness Jesus can shine through us.

During the course of our lives we make many mistakes, but as we saw in the story of Mary Magdalene, Jesus is there to help us. He will shine through our brokenness if we will just trust Him.

Jesus is no stranger to sorrows. He was known as the Man of Sorrows. No matter what brokenness we find in ourselves, our heavenly Father understands. He will always find some good that can come out of our situation, good that will encourage others to trust Him also.

*Thank You, Jesus, for reminding us that no matter how shattered our lives may be, if we only trust You, You will shine through.*

**Marion Newman Chin**

# The Wondrous Works of God

*Stand still and consider the wondrous works of God. Job 37:14, NKJV.*

THIS MORNING I awoke very early, feeling very miserable with pain, so I arose, took some medication, and made myself a hot drink. I then opened the curtains in the back room and sat in my easy chair to wait until I got some ease. I didn't put the light on so that I wouldn't disturb my husband.

It was very dark. I stared down the street, and soon I could see dark shapes in the darkness and decided they were trees. I hadn't noticed before how many and varied kinds there were. Later I noticed a pale pink glow in the eastern sky, and I could see the trees more clearly silhouetted against the pale glow. Some were tall and spread out, others tall and stately. I noticed a palm tree and a pine tree that I could clearly recognize.

I saw a man in the dim light, hurrying from house to house with what looked like a shopping basket in his hand. I wondered what was happening, but as he came closer I could see he was the milkman delivering milk.

A few cars drove by, and I noticed a rather small gray cloud on the horizon. As I watched, the cloud became scalloped around the edge with pale gold that quickly turned to bright gold. Occasionally the cloud would open, and the gold showed through. It quickly changed shape, but always with the brightest gold all around the outline.

Suddenly the sun burst through so bright and beautiful that I couldn't watch anymore—it was too bright. I felt I had had a spiritual experience—and the pain had eased. Immediately my mind began to think also of the sunset. The sun doesn't just drop out of the sky and then darkness falls. Who hasn't seen a spectacular sunset with its play of clouds and color? We have that lovely period we call twilight; the color lingers in the sky and so softly the light fades to blackness.

I was impressed with how kind God is to make a gradual change from the blackness of night to the brightness of day, and the opposite at the end of the day. The change is comforting and gentle, loving and beautiful, because He loves us so much. "Stand still and consider the wondrous works of God."

**Muriel Cross**

# The Desires
# of Your Heart

*What things soever ye desire, when ye pray, believe that
ye receive them, and ye shall have them. Mark 11:24.*

MY VAN, with almost 200,000 miles on it, was wearing out. One
thing after another had started going wrong with it. It was time to get
another van for sure. I asked my son, Larry, if he would look at the auction for one for around $3,000, because I didn't want a car payment. He
came back with the news that any car around that price wasn't worth
much. However, the man he goes to the auction with said he had one down
in Florida that was similar to what I was looking for.

He said he would drive it back up in a month. Meanwhile, I continued
with my old van, saving money for the new one. Near the end of May,
Larry said the man had brought up the minivan, a Chrysler New Yorker,
that had only 78,000 miles on it. I'd been praying about this, asking God if
this was the right one for me.

I hadn't asked what color it was. I guess you're thinking, *Who cares the
color as long as it has four wheels and a good engine that runs?* Maybe it's a
woman thing, but I began to wonder about the color. I even prayed about
it: *I don't care what color it is, just so it's not green.* Then I added, *Purple
would be nice.* (My favorite color.) *But I don't care—just don't let it be green.*
There was also an outside temperature gauge on my old van that I had enjoyed, and I thought I'd miss that.

Larry set up an appointment to get the van on Friday. At noon I went
down to the bank to get a cashier check. Again I prayed, *Please let me know
that I'm doing the right thing—this is a lot of money for me.* Before I went
into the bank, I called Larry. He said the appointment was for 4:30, after
my work. He told me he had driven the van. Then he said, "And Mom,
you're going to love it—it's purple." I could hardly believe it! Right away I
thought of the text that says, "He shall give you the desires of your heart"
(Ps. 37:4, NKJV).

After work I went to see my new van, knowing indeed it was for me. It
even had a temperature gauge, just like the one on my old van.

*Thank You, Lord, for looking after me each day and supplying all my
needs—and even my desires. I want to serve You better each day.*

**Anne Elaine Nelson**

# With All of Me

*Love the Lord your God with all your heart and with all your soul
and with all your mind and with all your strength. Mark 12:30, NIV.*

"ANNALEESE GOT A TATTOO. A butterfly on her ankle!" Melissa shouted
the news before my car had come to a complete stop. She was in the middle
of the driveway, hands on her adolescent hips, gesturing at the house across
the street. "So, what do you think about it? Is it wrong?"

I just looked at her, not really in the mood to tackle a tough topic. But
Melissa was nothing if not persistent. She climbed into the front seat and
adjusted her seat belt. "Well, is it?" Her voice sounded so serious that I
wiped the smile from my face.

As we backed out of the driveway I took a deep breath and plunged in.
"Many things in life are not necessarily wrong. It's more of personal prefer-
ence and what we believe is prudent." *Prudent.* She repeated the word to
herself. I knew I'd be hearing that word again soon!

"But would you get one?"

"No, I wouldn't." In response to the question mark on her face I continued, "At this stage of my life I try to ask myself, Does this choice show
that I love God with my entire being? Will it enhance, or deface, my body
temple? For me, inking a pattern onto the largest organ of my body—my
skin—would not be honoring."

"Is that why you don't recommend"—she drew out the word—"nose,
and tongue, and navel, and eyebrow piercing?"

"That, and the risk of potential infection and injury," I replied.

"The text doesn't say 'body,'" Melissa mused. "It says heart, soul,
and mind."

"I know. But research by Dr. Candace Pert strongly suggests that the
body can be thought of as our subconscious mind. The body acts out,
often at a subconscious level, what begins in the brain. That means our
mind is all of us."

Melissa's eyes were huge in her lovely little freckled face. "Oh," she said
softly. "That's a new thought, but I get it. I want to love God with all of
me!" After a moment she added, "And I was just asking, you know. I don't
want a tattoo or a piercing. The butterfly looks a trifle gross."

I had to laugh! And yes, Melissa, I want to love God with all of
me, too.

**Arlene Taylor**

# Heavenly Sandpaper

*Casting all your care upon Him, for He cares for you.*
*1 Peter 5:7, NKJV.*

LORD, IF I'M CALLED TO TEACH GRADE 1, I'm going to quit on the spot! These were the words of an impetuous young teacher who had discovered that every time she taught grade 1, her demonstration lessons or practice teaching was a complete disaster.

I had found that my teaching abilities were quite acceptable for grades 2-7, but grade 1? Well, that was another story. No matter what valuable help I was given from my lecturers, there was little improvement.

My carefree college days passed too quickly, and following graduation there was great excitement among the graduates as we each received our teaching appointments. When I learned that I would be returning to my home state of Queensland, Australia, I said, *Thank You, Lord, for hearing my prayers.*

New teachers were required to contact their future headmaster; it was then that I ventured the question "Do you know which grade I will be teaching?" You have probably guessed by now what the answer was!

*O Lord, why? You know how inadequate I feel teaching the little ones. Remember what I said? Do You want me to quit? Lord, I really thought that You had opened all the avenues to show me that teaching was where You wanted me. So why have I been called to teach grade 1?*

When I look back now on the six wonderful years I spent teaching grade 1, I'm able to say, "Thank You, Lord; You really knew what You were doing. I was very confident of my abilities to succeed in grades 2-7, and therefore I would not have felt the need to be dependent on You for continued guidance."

This experience proved to be my "heavenly sandpaper." God was using this time in my life to remove some of the rough edges. He wanted me not to run ahead of Him and to try to do everything in my own strength. He wanted me to commit my new day to Him every morning and to seek His guidance in every difficult situation. He wanted me to learn patience and to be loving and lovable. *Dear Lord, thank You for leading in my life. I love You.*

**Lynn Howell**

# A Single Toothbrush

*Now I will rescue you and make you both a symbol
and a source of blessing. Zech. 8:13, NLT.*

ONE AFTERNOON I hosted a conversation dinner for a group of young
university couples, 10 articulate graduate scholars. One couple had brought
their young daughter along. As the hours flew by, the young child grew
restless. I granted her permission to explore my home. Sauntering through
the house, the little miss began her exploration, her beaded braids as perky
as her attention to detail.

Minutes later she returned and threw herself into her mother's arms.
"Oh, Mommy," she said. "It's so sad." The 4-year-old's voice was woeful.
Suddenly there was silence. We all had to know what had happened. "I
went into that pretty bathroom," she said, pointing to the guest bath. I
waited to hear about what she had accidentally broken. "And there was
only one toothbrush. It looked so lonely. So sad." And, eloquent in her
tearfulness, she began to weep.

I had never before thought about the solitary toothbrush as a symbol of
my singleness. I knew I had taken pains to get all the accessories in that
bathroom to match—the shower curtain matched the tissue paper holder,
as did the towels, the wall hangings, and the floral arrangements. Even the
tangerine soap matched that lone toothbrush. But that was not what the little child saw. What she noticed was what she thought was a mournful symbol of my aloneness.

As soon as my guests left, I found three other toothbrushes, still
wrapped in cellophane, to add to the holder. Then I had an unexpected
rendezvous with my Savior. Some contemporary theologians would call it a
divine "somehow."

Somehow, with each toothbrush, it seemed that I heard a gentle question: "What have you been doing that matches a life you say you shun?
What have you been saying that echoes with the harshness you don't try to
soften? What have you been wearing that could symbolize something other
than the Christianity you try to project?" Now, each time I change toothbrushes, I look for the special blessing I had received from a guest. Each
time I try to learn a new Bible text that matches that blessing.

*Thank You, God, for precious children who point out what adults
don't see. Thank You for the privilege of being a symbol for You. May my
actions match Your words.*

**Glenda-mae Greene**

# Productive Waiting

*And we know that all things work together for good to them that love God, to them who are the called according to his purpose. Rom. 8:28.*

A FEW YEARS AGO the Lord and I wrangled over the conviction that I should become a stay-at-home mom. I prayed for God's will in my life and to trust the direction He had planned for me. When I knew that being a stay-at-home mom was God's plan, I decided to change my work schedule from full-time to one day a week. The schedule change was planned to occur that summer, but in the meantime a coworker and I had a major disagreement. I was so hurt and angry that I contemplated changing my schedule sooner so as not to bear any more of the harassment I was receiving. I prayed for guidance and healing. My answer was a strong conviction to stay rather than to leave early. I questioned the Lord on this, but the conviction was very loud and clear, although the reason was not to be so clear at that moment.

As time went on, the awkwardness and hurt feelings eased up. My coworker and I were getting along again. It was not until my schedule changed that I realized exactly how much God was working in my life. The person I had had the conflict with was my main contact. She was easy to deal with and granted most requests I made. She even actually stood up for me when I was at the disadvantage of not having information I needed at my job. Not only had things improved on a work level, but I felt more connected with God.

Since that time I've had a lot of time to reflect, and I'm glad I listened to God's leading. Whether I was right or wrong regarding the conflict didn't matter. The main concern was the hurt I was holding in my heart. What seemed a long waiting period was an important cooling-off period that I evidently needed. God blessed me in spite of myself.

*Lord, thank You for making a bad situation a whole lot better. I need to be in constant communication with You, or I will rely on my own understanding and miss the blessings You have planned for me. Help me, Lord, to understand that waiting can be productive if it is part of Your purpose for me.*

Friends, things do work together for good. Let us each wait patiently to see how God works things out according to His purposes. I'm glad I did.

**Mary M. J. Wagoner-Angelin**

# Look Upward With Faith

*O Lord, you have searched me and you know me. You know when I sit and when I rise; you perceive my thoughts from afar. Ps. 139:1, 2, NIV.*

"WHEN SADNESS COMES UPON YOU, and pain comes to your heart/ Look upward with faith; God gives comfort./ You have a secret pain that no one can see./ Look upward with faith; you will have relief./ Do not put your head down to sadden yourself more./ Look upward with faith; attempt to see Christ."*

The 9-year-old girl had just read these words when her mother entered the room. She exclaimed, "Look, Mother! What beautiful words in this poem—they apply to me." And she read it again for her mother to hear.

This girl, very ill, and with a physical pain in her heart, didn't know that that poem was a beautiful and inspiring hymn. She heard it again some years later in a religious boarding school in São Paulo when she was a teenager. It was there that she gave her "sick heart" to Jesus.

What a wonderful God who saw me in that little straw bed in a mud house on a small farm! God threw out His bait of salvation through the words of that hymn, and He also cured me. And not only me, but my mother as well. We both suffered from the same coronary problem.

How did He heal us? By showing us the way to healthy living, which gave us abundant life. Mother is now 90 years old, filled with joy and much faith in our Lord Jesus Christ.

I do not tire of thanking my God for such great salvation. Psalm 139 is one of my favorites. When I read it and meditate, I see myself! Verse 13 states: "For you created my inmost being; you knit me together in my mother's womb" (NIV). And verse 16 says, "Your eyes saw my unformed body" (NIV). Finally, verse 14 sums it up: "I praise you because I am fearfully and wonderfully made; your works are wonderful" (NIV).

Dear friend! Open your Bible and meditate on this beautiful poem in Psalm 139, and together we shall thank this wonderful God who gave us such great salvation. And at the end of each day we can say, "Search me, O God, and know my heart; test me and know my anxious thoughts. See if there is any offensive way in me, and lead me in the way everlasting" (verses 23, 24, NIV).

**Jaci da Silva Vôos**

*Literal translation of Portuguese version of the hymn "Beautiful Isle of Somewhere."

# Come Apart and Rest

*And he said unto them, Come ye yourselves apart into*
*a desert place, and rest a while. Mark 6:31.*

THAT SEPTEMBER 5, the first Monday after Labor Day, was a momentous day. It was the beginning of school, and my lastborn, Janna, was off to join my other children and to make her separation from Mother. I was up early, fixing lunches for the three children, another for me, and one more for my dog, Cindy, our Labrador retriever. My husband smiled fondly, as he was in on my secret.

I had curled Janna's obstinately straight hair, but a night sleeping on the curlers hadn't helped the curling process much. Tufts of hair just sort of stuck out here and there. I worked on it as much as I could, hoping that the new dress for the occasion would make up for the so-so curls. I gathered up the lunch bags and shooed kids and dog out of the house and into the car. A quick stop at the school, a tearful goodbye, and Cindy and I headed down the turnpike that would lead us to our day of freedom—or maybe consolation.

An hour later I parked my car in the almost-empty parking lot at Walden's Pond. I gathered my things, including my copy of Thoreau's *Walden*, and called Cindy. We began our day by walking the three-mile trail around the pond, me shuffling through the first downed leaves of fall, and Cindy running hither and yon, sniffing. I found a comfortable place at the ruins of Thoreau's cabin and became engrossed in the book of his life, living in nature at this very spot. A few of the season's last tourists hiked past me.

At lunchtime I brought out our lunches. Cindy enjoyed hers as much as I did mine. Then I walked around again, admiring the reflections in the pond and the colored leaves floating peacefully away. When it was time to pick up the children from school, I had read half the book. I called Cindy to my side and returned to the parking lot.

I picked up the children and enjoyed Janna's excitement about her first day. There even seemed to be a smile on the dog's face as the children enjoyed the tale of our adventure. It had been good to be alone in God's beautiful creation and in the joy of its silence. Come apart and rest and see that it is good.

**Dessa Weisz Hardin**

# Ernest

*For a man's ways are in full view of the Lord, and he examines all his paths. Prov. 5:21, NIV.*

THAT LABOR DAY WEEKEND my kids and I were having a garage sale. It was time to get rid of all the unwanted stuff that could become someone else's treasure. We started early in the morning, setting out all the collected items in the driveway so prospective buyers could look them over and, hopefully, take them off our hands. Though still early morning, the day held promise it would be warm and beautiful.

With little sales activity, I decided to bring our pets outside to enjoy the fresh air—the cat, the dog, and the two guinea pigs, Ernest and Sneakers. When taking the guinea pigs outside, we would remove the pigs from their cage and place them in the yard. They normally would huddle close together, squeak a little, and nibble on the grass. So when the phone rang, I thought nothing of leaving them there and running into the house to answer it. But when I returned, Ernest was nowhere to be found. He was small and had short legs. How far could he go in such a short period of time?

Then I realized what he'd done. Much to my dismay, Ernest had crawled into a nine-foot landscaping drainage pipe. He sensed no danger; the pipe was dark and cozy—a nice little spot to rest for a while. Never mind that the pipe was covered with a black tarp and rock—lots of rock! We tried coaxing him out with carrots and greens. Ernest wouldn't budge. Finally we had to remove the rock, dig out the pipe, and stand it on its end. It took considerable time and effort to accomplish all this. Then we shook and shook the pipe until Ernest plopped onto the ground, covered with muck and dirt.

How many times are we lured into what looks like a nice, cozy place in our lives? We settle in and think all is fine, unaware of the looming danger. And sometimes, as with Ernest, it doesn't take long to get into trouble. However, it often takes a lot of time and effort and work to get out of trouble. Thankfully, we have a heavenly Father who holds His watchful hand over us and has our lives in His full view. When we panic and realize we're stuck, all we have to do is call on His name, and He is there to rescue us. *Thank You, Lord!*

**Karen Phillips**

# Is Anything Too Hard for God?

*Is any thing too hard for the Lord? At the time appointed I will return unto thee, according to the time of life, and Sarah shall have a son. Gen. 18:14.*

I WAS GOING TO GIVE BIRTH, but not to a human baby. I was about to deliver my first research project that had to be completed by Wednesday. I didn't have time to become ill, but just a week and a day before my project's deadline my husband returned home with what we thought was food poisoning. By Sabbath he was well enough to attend church, but our son Charles had the stomach virus. So I stayed home to take care of him.

By Sunday I began feeling ill, but I had to continue typing my paper. On Monday morning I had the virus, and all I could do was carry my trash can around and pray. I finally took the medication my husband offered and the illness was gone, but I felt too weak to keep typing.

Tuesday morning I went to work on some classroom-related projects that also had to be completed by Wednesday. Then I requested a personal business day for Wednesday. The next morning I was feeling fine and finished up a portion of the paper, but I began having severe muscle spasms in my legs, back pain, and cramps. When the pain became too great, I began to pray. When I felt better, I would get up and type. This cycle continued for several hours until I went to take some pain medication and a nap.

After the nap I had three hours before I had to drive to Detroit to attend my 5:00 class and then defend my research project at 6:00. I live about an hour and a half from Wayne State University, and the traffic on I-75 can be very challenging. I finished typing the paper at 3:00. My husband picked up the children from school and returned at 3:45 to drive me to my classes.

We made it to Detroit in record time. I completed my final class assignment and walked to my next class. My appointment was at 6:00, but the instructor didn't have anyone in her office, so I was able to defend my project and return to my awaiting family by 6:12.

Do you have some projects to give birth to? Have faith in Jesus, for only He can help you to deliver them!

*Dear Jesus, I have so much to do, and sometimes obstacles get in my way. Please help me to have the faith, love, joy, peace, and wisdom in You that I need. Amen.*

**Quetah Sackie-Osborne**

# Soft Words

*A soft answer turneth away wrath: but grievous words stir up anger. Prov. 15:1.*

SOME PEOPLE SEEM TO HAVE a knack for dealing with difficult people, while others (including me) find themselves biting their tongues to keep from antagonizing others. When I was younger, I believed that I needed to be truthful, whether my words hurt others or not. Someone has well said, "Politeness is to do and say the kindest thing in the kindest way." Not following this advice has often caused me much anguish over the years.

I remember an incident when teaching parochial school my first year. One of the parents, the wife of another teacher, was helping to varnish some chairs. There were spots of paint on the chair, and the varnish was stirring up the paint, producing a very unpleasant end product. When she showed me what it was doing, I immediately said, "Well, don't keep doing it." She was rather upset with me and felt that I was blaming her for what was happening to the chair—after all, she was donating her time to help get things ready for school. Such a little thing, but it caused a rift between us that might have been prevented had I chosen different words to encourage her to do the job another way and prevent what was happening. What was needed—and should have been expressed—was to clean the chair with turpentine and/or paint remover, let it dry, and then varnish the chair. But I didn't say that, and feelings were hurt.

As school board chair and volunteer treasurer for a local food co-op, I've learned to deal with many people and to choose my words before I speak. I try to use neutral words. Because I grew up without a mother, this has not been the easiest thing to learn. I envy those who seem to have that talent or who have been encouraged to learn that ability with the help of parents. Whether dealing with peers or with an almost-99-year-old mother-in-law who has Alzheimer-type dementia, I've learned that it takes a sanctified, divine sympathy for others—and that comes only by the grace of the Lord. Day by day, with prayer, this too can be a learned accomplishment. Are you learning that lesson as I am? How much better this world would be if we all treated each other in kind and polite ways.

*Thank You, Lord, for helping us.*

**Loraine F. Sweetland**

# Why Didn't You Tell Me?

*He will bring you a message through which you*
*and all your household will be saved. Acts 11:14, NIV.*

GERMANY HAS MANY GOOD MOTORWAYS, and traveling on them should be a pleasure. But because of heavy traffic and maintenance work in the summer months, we cringe at the thought of driving across the country. The Autobahn is often congested, and driving becomes a strain.

Recently we visited our daughter in northern Germany. On our way back we came to the Hattenbach interchange, where we had to choose one of two directions—either Frankfurt or Munich. Just at this point there was road work, and the left lane was diverted onto the lane for oncoming traffic. I knew that I'd have to turn off to the right, but as there were no signs to the contrary, I supposed this would be made possible even from the faster, left-hand lane. However, there was no such sign. So I drove on, then realized that I wouldn't be able to turn to the right in my chosen direction. I passed the exit, wondering what to do. A bit further on there was a sign: "Those wanting to turn back in the direction of Munich, please use the next exit and turn."

I couldn't believe it! They had put up a sign for people like me who had driven in the wrong direction. Why hadn't they put up a sign earlier, preventing this from happening? Or had I missed the sign? My son-in-law's parents had passed the same interchange a couple days before and had taken the same detour. There were no signs, and no one had thought to tell anybody about it.

Our daughter and family came south a week later, and yes, they took the detour as well. None of us had thought to tell them about it. We had lost about 10 minutes, but they lost an hour. When they got back onto the right motorway, there had been an accident and the road was blocked. Had we told them of the interchange problem, they would have passed the place before the accident happened. My daughter said later, "Why didn't you tell us?" Well, why didn't we?

Why don't we tell people about what is ahead of us? Are we so immersed in other things—or so thoughtless—that we don't tell the world the good news that Jesus wants to guide them home if they will only let Him? We let people take detours instead of telling them the best way home. Tell the world about your experience with God. That's all it takes.

**Hannele Ottschofski**

# Through the Open Door

*I know thy works: behold, I have set before thee an open door,*
*and no man can shut it; for thou hast a little strength, and hast kept*
*my word, and hast not denied my name. Rev. 3:8.*

IT WAS TIME TO PACK and go away to a boarding school. It seems my visiting sister had discussed my future with our dad. Yes, he had agreed that I should go.

My new blue luggage, a present for eighth-grade graduation, was quickly filling up under the watchful eyes of my sister. There was my favorite pink-beaded necklace that I tucked into one corner of my case. "You will not need that necklace at the school," my sister said. I didn't argue, and left it behind. She had attended college at that school for a year and was certainly familiar with the rules and regulations. I must trust her judgment.

As we made that 60-mile (97-kilometer) trip, my thoughts ran the whole gamut of emotions between excitement and anxiety, sadness and fear of the unknown. These emotions, coupled with my extreme shyness, made my whole body shudder. Past memories flooded my mind as I thought of my childhood. My mother had died when I was 4, and my brother and I had gone to live with relatives on a farm. My sisters had gone with relatives to a farm in another state, and I hadn't had much contact with them till now. Dad had remarried, and his new wife didn't always understand my quietness and shyness. Little did I know that my stepmother's pork chop dinners would no longer be a part of my life, as the school didn't serve meat.

I'd be starting high school while living in the dormitory with college students. It was as if Jesus Himself held the door open for me to enter into a whole new world of Christianity. Life at the boarding school opened a new door, and all I had to do was to go through and follow where Jesus would lead me. Bible class was a wonderful experience. I had never owned a Bible and had never before read any of the beautiful words it contained. Prayer was completely foreign to my daily routine, but soon became an added benefit to my life.

Two months after I turned 16 my dad died. God knew that I would need a place of refuge, and He had prepared a place for me. The school became my home and my family. The door was opened, and the Lord drew me in with loving-kindness. Praise God, He has a door for each of us!

**Retha McCarty**

# To Measure Unto His Stature

*Till we all come in the unity of the faith, and of the knowledge of the Son of God, unto a perfect man, unto the measure of the stature of the fulness of Christ. Eph. 4:13.*

"DEAR JESUS, I want to be like you. I do not want to scream. But I scream. I scream because Mark makes me scream. So I scream. It is disgusting. Amen." Little 4-year-old John consoled himself with this prayer when he realized his helplessness to stop screaming. I could understand, because "what I would, that do I not; but what I hate, that do I" (Rom. 7:15). During our visit to Michigan, my husband and I observed keenly how our grandsons, Mark (7) and John (4), grow. Little John had a habit of screaming. Whenever he was left under our care, he would excuse himself by saying, "You are not family members." If he couldn't have his own way, he would end up screaming.

One day, however, after a screaming tantrum, he sobered down and said to us, "Please do not tell Mommy and Daddy." Yet when his dad came home, John ran to his open arms. Looking into his dad's eyes, he related his story of screaming from A to Z. And then he said, "Daddy, I'm sorry. What punishment will you give me?" Yes, that was the beginning for John to grow out of screaming.

One day while I was sewing, I suddenly heard a thud and the abrupt shutting of the refrigerator door. It was John. He had taken a scoop of cottage cheese to gobble up. I reprimanded him, and he immediately said, "I took it because I'm always hungry, and I have asked Mommy." I calmly said, "Please don't tell a lie." With that he walked away to his bedroom. But after a moment he came back and said, "I'm sorry, Grandma." His repentance touched me. I hugged him and prayed, "Loving Father, thank You for helping John to say he is sorry. May I too learn to do just that. Amen."

Observing little John taught me a great lesson in daily spiritual growth. One day while I was playing with him building houses with blocks, John asked, "When is Jesus going to get it done and take us home?" I had to ask myself, "Am I homesick for heaven?"

*Loving Father, help us to daily grow "unto the measure of the stature of the fulness of Christ." And thus someday we will live in those mansions You have gone to prepare for us.*

**Annie M. Kujur**

# Just Get Him Some Grapes!

*Watch and pray, that ye enter not into temptation:*
*the spirit indeed is willing, but the flesh is weak. Matt. 26:41.*

A FEW DAYS AGO I made an early-morning trip to the grocery store to pick up a few items to bring to work. Within minutes I was finished, and went to the self-checkout to scan my items. I noticed a young girl about 8 years old asking a grocery clerk walking by for at least eight brown grocery bags. The clerk obliged and handed her some bags, and the girl quickly left the store. I chuckled to myself, remembering the days when it was mandatory that all school books be covered, and I, as well as many others, had used brown bags. No doubt this girl could proudly tell her teacher that day that she had covers for all her books.

I completed my checkout, thankful that all items had scanned without a problem and that I didn't need to find a clerk for assistance. I lifted my bag and headed for the door. Once outside, I saw the same little girl standing at a car parked in the pickup lane. A small toddler was fussing inside the vehicle as the mother exited the car and began talking to the girl. "Did you get them?" the mother asked. Her tone was sharp and argumentative.

"I didn't know where they were!" the girl replied sheepishly as she put the brown bags in the car.

"What do you mean, you didn't know where they were? They are over in that area," the mother said, pointing to the part of the store where the produce was. "Go back in there. There's no one in the store right now. Just get him some grapes! And hurry, so you can get to school."

At her mother's insistence, the girl turned immediately and headed back into the store, this time to get grapes for the toddler, who was now crying uncontrollably. Flabbergasted, I continued to my car. I couldn't believe that this mother had ordered her daughter to steal grapes. Surely she wasn't thinking of the impact of her request! I felt embarrassed and sorry for the young girl and irritated at the mother for encouraging her child to do wrong.

*Lord, every day we have the choice of making right and wrong decisions. Help us not to be led into temptation or to lead others into temptation. May our lives influence others not for evil, but for good. Amen.*

**Iris L. Kitching**

# Mommy, Can You Give Me a Hug?

*Where can I go from your Spirit? Where can I flee from your presence? Ps. 139:7, NIV.*

AFTER ATTENDING THE CHURCH SERVICE my 9-year-old daughter, Rebeca, asked if she could spend the afternoon in the home of her friend Mariana. I confess the request irritated me because I'd have to catch the bus and cross the city to pick her up. I was very tired, but finally gave in to her request.

Late in the afternoon I went to pick her up. During the ride I began to think about my life, which had fallen into an unpleasant situation. Many struggles and trials afflicted me and robbed my peace.

When I reached her friend's home, I hardly greeted Mariana's parents, got my daughter by the arm, and immediately started back home. For a few moments we walked together in silence because I was in a very bad mood.

By my side, my innocent daughter felt the tension because of my facial expression and my attitude. There we were, mother and daughter, in silence that broke the ties of love. At this moment my daughter, as though screaming for help and not understanding the situation, said, "Mommy, can you give me a hug?"

I immediately crumbled and realized how cruel and unjust I was acting toward my little girl, and how far I had gone from God. That request opened my heart, and I understood that she wasn't to blame for my problems. I understood in her words the burning desire to change the situation. We hugged, with my heart cut to pieces but happy because God used my little daughter to help break the hardness of my heart.

Many times the Lord requests an embrace from us when we face daily struggles and we forget Him. When He sees our situation, He says, "My daughter, will you give Me a hug?"

Nothing is better to calm our affliction and to resolve our problems than to fall into His arms.

"Each is tenderly watched by the heavenly Father. No tears are shed that God does not notice. There is no smile that He does not mark. If we would but fully believe this, all undue anxieties would be dismissed" (*Steps to Christ*, p. 86).

*Today I ask You, Lord, to embrace me and guide me with Your loving hand.*

Angela Maria Vargas Peres

# To Work or Not

*For the Lord God is a sun and shield; the Lord bestows favor and honor; no good thing does he withhold from those whose walk is blameless. Ps. 84:11, NIV.*

SHORTLY AFTER OUR DAUGHTER, Monique, got married and moved across the country to California, I finally realized that my nest was empty and retirement was nearer than ever. I became bored. I volunteered for several more things in our church and community, and still had time left over. My pastor-husband, Samuel, and I had made our last move to be in our retirement home, and of course he found many things to do. I had always been gainfully employed but was not always happy; the hours were often very long—and sometimes tense—so that I actually dreamed about being retired.

I asked the Lord to show me what would be the best job for me at this point; the only paid work I'd ever done was 42 years in health care. So I busied myself with résumés and the classifieds, and then interviews, but I wasn't satisfied with what was being offered. I imagined the children of Israel, wandering in the desert, comparing what they had with what they'd had back in Egypt. I remembered that God has always led me in the past, and I had no doubt that He would not forsake me now. Therefore I did what He told me to do: "Stand still and see the salvation of the Lord" (2 Chron. 20:17, NKJV).

I sought the Lord for the right job, the right hours, and the right distance from home. Then I started to job hunt again and sent résumés. Then I received a call from a prospective employer who was very interested in me, but had one reservation. She ended up referring me to a similar job that could use me and my experiences, and in that very hour she made a phone call and sent me over! After beautiful interviews, everything that I had requested was granted—plus some. If you ask God for directions, there is no need to worry; He will do it in His time, if it is good for you. If you want to worry about it, then don't pray about it, as prayer and worry don't blend. Throughout our ministry in different states and cities, we've lived in the Lord, and He has always granted the job that I needed for that time.

*Dear Lord, help us, Your children, to wait on You. You have told us You will not withhold any good thing from us. Remind me, Lord, to wait on You.*

**Betty G. Perry**

# Choosing the Right Thing to Wear

*The Lord looketh on the heart. 1 Sam. 16:7.*

HAVE YOU EVER HAD the embarrassing experience of going to a social gathering and finding that you were not dressed appropriately? During his senior year in college, my husband became an assistant pastor of our large church. We were a young family, but, as pastoral staff, we were included in a ministers' meeting at a local camp. Not having any information about the activities planned, Ted dressed in a nice suit and tie, and I wore a dress. When we arrived, we were dismayed to find everyone else dressed for outdoor activities. The next gathering took place at a city church. Having learned the ropes, Ted wore a sport shirt with an open collar. Guess what? All the other men were in suits and ties! We survived, however, and he continued to serve the college church for two more years before going on to pastor our own churches.

Nowadays we live in a more casual society in which it seems that anything goes, even for church. Although that can be distressing for some of us, we must remember that while we look on the outward appearance, the Lord looks on the heart.

In Matthew 22 Jesus told about a king who made a special dinner to celebrate the marriage of his son. He sent his servants to invite many guests, but they all made excuses. Some of the servants were mistreated, and some were even killed. Then the king sent out other servants to gather in both good and bad people to furnish guests for the wedding.

Obviously, these hastily rounded-up guests would have had no opportunity to go shopping or look through their closets to find something to wear; but that wasn't necessary, as the host provided suitable clothing. No doubt when the king entered the hall he was pleased to see his guests—until he noticed one who was not wearing the wedding garment. The man had no excuse, and the king had his servants evict him.

Our King has special cloths for guests to wear at the marriage of His Son—the robes of Christ's righteousness. We don't have to go shopping or search our closets for something to wear, but we must put on the wedding garment, lest we be evicted from the celebration. I may not see if you are wearing it, and you may not see if I'm wearing it, but remember, while we look on the outward appearance, the Lord looks on the heart, and that makes all the difference!

**Mary Jane Graves**

# Like a Mother

*Can a mother forget the baby at her breast and have no compassion on the child she has borne? Though she may forget, I will not forget you! Isa. 49:15, NIV.*

I HAVE ALWAYS LIKED SWINGS. Even today I can't resist the enchantment of the long chains, and the dizzy sensation that swinging produces. When my sisters and I were children, my father had a wonderful idea—build a swing on our patio. Of course, we were all excited and "helped" however we could so he could finish quickly.

Finally the swing was ready. The new wooden seat and the shiny chains extended their invitation to everyone. Mother was the first to try it out, enjoying it as she went flying higher and higher. Then suddenly—*zap!* The chain snapped, and Mother landed on the ground. Quickly we ran to her rescue. Her words, as she lifted herself off the ground, were "I'm glad that this happened to me and not to one of the girls."

I was barely 6 years old, but this moment touched my life. My mother loved me so much that she preferred to suffer in my place! This feeling reached my child's heart with a sweet warmth, giving a certainty of love that has been with me always, and even today brings tears to my eyes. Such immense love from my parents has, without a doubt, helped me to understand the infinite love of God more completely. Always by precept and example, my parents taught my sisters and me to make Jesus our best Friend. I have a profound gratitude to the Lord for giving me the opportunity of growing up in a Christina home.

The Word of God, through the prophet Isaiah, provides hope and comfort for everyone. Perhaps your childhood wasn't happy; maybe your first experiences taught you not to trust and love but rather to doubt and fear. Perhaps your parents made mistakes that have affected your life, your decisions. But God promises us that His love is greater than that of a mother's.

Fathers and mothers in this world can fail; they can forget; they can make mistakes. But our loving God doesn't make mistakes; He doesn't forget any of His daughters. Fathers and mothers in this world can't be chosen, but today you can choose to make God your Father, your Mother, your Friend, your Savior. Always know, with eternal certainty, that this Father does not fail, He makes no mistakes, He does not forget.

**Cyntia de Graf**

# The Dead Pullet

*Agree with thine adversary quickly. Matt. 5:25.*

I WAS IN THE CLASSROOM teaching when suddenly my neighbor appeared at the door with a dead chicken dangling from her hand. Burning with rage, she blurted out, "See what your dog has done to my chicken! I want a replacement." Silence struck the class as they stared wide-eyed at their teacher and the woman at the door. Somehow managing to keep my composure, I said, "I am so sorry; I will see you later." She then walked away with the dead pullet.

One of our Alsatian pups had killed her Barred Plymouth Rock pullet, most probably playfully, but the chicken was dead nevertheless. Too "chickenhearted" to face my adversary, I wrote her a note instead, expressing my sorrow and regret. I suggested that she go to the school's poultry farm and pick out whatever she would like to replace her loss, and I would pay for it.

Thoughts of the dead chicken and its owner tormented me day and night. My husband was away traveling, or he would have taken care of the matter. I worried about what I would say should she confront me again. The next day I went to the farm, told the manager what had happened, and explained that the woman would come to the farm to make her pick and that I would pay for it.

A few days later, on my way to school, the neighbor and I crossed paths. I smiled at her, and she smiled back at me. Then we exchanged pleasantries. Neither of us mentioned the chicken. I found out later that she never went to the farm to get her replacement. I had known that I needed to be calm in order to agree with my adversary. Even though I hadn't witnessed the incident, I agreed with her that my dog had killed her chicken. I didn't question her. To prevent ill feelings, I had done all I could to replace her loss.

Many times, out of selfishness, we get into arguments and find it difficult to give in. This brings misery to both parties. The Bible says to agree with our adversaries and to do it quickly. The word "quickly" gives us no time to doubt. No time to argue or question. If we keep this biblical commandment, a lot of agony, ill feelings, and distress can be avoided. This is God's way, and it is the easier—and better—way.

**Birol Charlotte Christo**

# Praise the God of Creation

*In the beginning God created the heaven and the earth. Gen. 1:1.*

THE STORY OF CREATION fascinates Christians and challenges nonbe-lievers. The very concept of creation is beyond human comprehension. When we think of creation, we automatically have some raw materials in mind, yet God created from nothing.

The very idea of a God who creates is good news for God's children. If God could create the trees, rivers, mountains, animals, birds, and fish—if God could create a human being from nothing, surely He can create solutions to all your challenges in life.

Many times we try hard to solve problems on our own. We spend sleepless nights toying with our burdens. We spend long sorrowful days carrying challenges we know we can't solve. We turn to research and human intelligence. All this fails us because all human ideas have limitations. We run in many directions in search of answers. We live stressful lives; some of us sink into depression, and some even commit suicide. Why? Because life's challenges can be overwhelming indeed! There is one, and only one, solution to all our burdens—the God of creation.

Today, stop and think of how powerful God is. If God created you and all that is in this world from nothing, don't you think He can create solutions to your challenges? If God created the human mind, don't you think it's God who can create ideas that will solve your problems? If God created your heart, can't He create a solution to mend it when it's broken?

God created, and this same God is standing at the door of your heart today. He wants to create in you a new smile. He wants to create in you a new way of thinking. He wants to create in you a new body. He wants to create in you peace of mind. He wants to create in you happiness. He wants to create in you true joy. He wants to create solutions for your life.

What is your burden today? What is your challenge today? What are your questions today? What are your needs today? You have a God who created, and the same God is still able to create. He wants to create a new you, who will be in touch with His heart; a you who will depend on God's ability to create.

Open your heart and let God create solutions in your heart today.

**Earlymay Chibende**

# Themba

*And if I go and prepare a place for you, I will come again, and receive you unto myself; that where I am, there ye may be also. John 14:3.*

*THEMBA* HAS TWO MEANINGS in the Xhosa language: "trust" or "hope." Themba was also the name of our local church-related school in Peddie. The word weaves well into my experience of hope.

The long summer school holidays would soon begin, and I was eager to get home. This time I would not be traveling alone—Inet was joining me. The route wasn't going to be the same, either, but it still would get me home. I stayed at Inet's place the day before, and early in the morning we began our journey on a donkey cart that would take us to the railway bus.

I didn't mind the transport—I just wanted to get home. With excitement we boarded the donkey cart—riding on that cart in the early morning was fun! But halfway between Peddie and Themba the donkey stopped and refused to walk. The driver did all within his knowledge to make it move, but it just would not. Because time waits for no person, I began to panic. We climbed down from the cart and started off on foot. After a long walk on the main road, we spotted a car next to a hut. We prayed and hoped that it was in good working order.

When we knocked at the door, the owner welcomed us, and we negotiated with him to get us to the bus. The problem was that there was no sight of the cart with our luggage. At that moment I learned a lesson of trust in God, because somehow that cart appeared in the distance, the donkey trotting as fast as it could. My spirits were buoyed! We would get to the bus!

We headed for town, finally arriving at the railway station. The bus was still there, its motor idling, ready to leave. Someone shouted, "Hurry up, ladies, it's getting late!" I was relieved to know that the Lord had delayed the bus till we arrived. I sank into the seat. The only thing in my mind was "I am going home!" Hope had kept me going.

Yes, I'm going home—my Father is waiting to meet me at the other end. Are you, too, looking forward—in the blessed hope—to meeting your heavenly Father?

**Ethel Doris Msuseni**

# Thoughts About Heaven

*Eye hath not seen, nor ear heard, neither have entered into the heart of man, the things which God hath prepared for them that love him. 1 Cor. 2:9.*

IT WAS FRIDAY MORNING at our little self-supporting mission, and a very important member of our staff had not come by our home at his usual time. We had dutifully put our garbage can at the end of the driveway, and our neighbor had placed several black plastic bags across from it, waiting for him to pick them up.

Then it was lunchtime, and still no sign of Jim in his white dump truck. Late afternoon came, and I called his home. His wife informed me that he had started on the other end of his route, intending to come by us later. Then the president of the school pointed out to Jim a need to do some cleanup in front of the sanitarium, which Jim dutifully did. On his arrival home, he said, "Oh, I forgot to pick up trash out in front."

Now, we live near the woods and have several nocturnal visitors that have learned how to take the lid off our garbage can and scatter the contents all over the yard, searching for food. So after bringing our can into the safety of the laundry room, I called our neighbors to tell them what had happened so they could do likewise.

This morning as I knelt to thank God for His many, many blessings, I fast-forwarded my thinking to our blessed hope and that glorious city where there will be no unclean thing.

Years ago I was privileged to be secretary to Pastor M. L. Andreasen, and sat at times in his classroom as he told his students the differences between our sinful world and that celestial abode. In heaven, he said, our ears and eyes will be perfect. We will be able to see all the way to the end of that bountiful table that Jesus has prepared in the new earth. Then, jokingly, he told the students that it wouldn't work for us to have that kind of vision in this world—you might see around the corner where your husband is hugging another woman!

We often talk about and look forward to that world where there will be no more sorrow, no more sickness, and no more death. But what about no more garbage? no more traffic? no more bugs? no more unfaithful spouses? Won't that be heavenly? Truly it will be beyond anything that has entered into our hearts or minds. I can't wait!

**Rubye Sue**

# God Has a Thousand Ways

*Be kindly affectioned one to another. Rom. 12:10.*

CLOUDS HUNG LOW that September 21 when an e-mail came that helped sweep them away: "Just know that I have appreciated you from the moment I saw you in the store so many years ago. Your kindness showed on your face, and you weren't afraid of me, and had such a big heart to let a total stranger approach you. Then you prayed with and for me. You are a truly great person, never doubt it. . . . You are one of the rare few who takes her religion to heart and wears it daily. Sylvia."

I sent a quick reply: "Sylvia, you made my day!" and asked if she remembered what year it was that we first met.

"In l982—the twins were still in diapers but walking and getting around and into everything! And later that same year you lent me money for school that made it possible for me to get my nursing education. I deeply appreciate having a wonderful, sincere "older sis" with whom I can communicate at all levels, and who really has a kind, understanding heart. Hugs, Sylvia."

Summer 1982, Tappahannock, Virginia. We stepped in almost simultaneously as the automatic grocery store doors opened. Giving her a side glance, I saw an anxious, weepy, worried young face. I flashed her a smile. She responded by saying softly, "Please pray for me." We walked into an empty corner and bowed our heads. Without prying into details, I prayed earnestly for the Lord, who knew her problems, to bless her and help her over her downheartedness. It was a brief prayer that started a friendship that has lasted to this day. She confided that her franchise had failed, and she was attempting to get on her feet again. Then we parted after we introduced ourselves.

Then in her mid-20s, Sylvia surprised me the next week by bringing her twins, Faith and Hope, to church. She also opened her life to me, confiding her struggles to support herself and her twins. We developed a friendship, and Sylvia has since kept in touch by occasional phone calls, letters, and, recently, by e-mails. Friends can be made in surprising ways. Are you ready to respond when God places one in your path?

**Consuelo Roda Jackson**

# Appreciation

*And let the peace of God rule in your hearts, to the which also ye are called in one body; and be ye thankful. Col. 3:15.*

WHEN I WAS A TEENAGER and my younger brother was of preschool age, a woman came to our house to take care of my brother after kindergarten. Little by little she became more involved in our family life. She began to take over some tasks in our household and was a great help to my mother. As my brother grew older and no longer needed a babysitter, my mother's "Pearl" (that's what my mother called her) continued to come to our house on a regular basis to do the cleaning, laundry, and ironing. I vividly remember my mother greeting her every time she came to our home, and saying goodbye to her, always with words of appreciation. I sometimes wondered if that was really necessary. After all, wasn't she just doing her job? *Wouldn't it be enough to thank her just once in a while?* I used to ask myself.

My mother's example raised important questions in my mind: Do we thank one another enough? Do we appreciate what others do for us, or do we take everything for granted? I remember a minister telling of an incident that happened in one of the churches he used to pastor. One Sabbath morning, in front of the whole congregation, he expressed his gratitude to the woman who was responsible for the floral arrangements. The woman was overwhelmed by his gesture, as she had never been recognized for her contribution to the church in her 20 years of performing this very same task!

So do we want to wait 20 years before expressing our appreciation to somebody? We often tend to be thankful without expressing it: we enjoy a nice, clean house, the beautiful floral arrangements at church, a delicious meal, etc., but we often fail to express our gratitude to God and to those through whom He provides us with these blessings. But shouldn't we encourage each other and express our appreciation to one another?

In almost every one of Paul's epistles he gave thanks for the people to whom he was writing, as well as for their faith (Rom. 1:8), God's grace for them (1 Cor. 1:4), their partnership in the gospel (Phil. 1:3), and the love and faith that they showed to others (Col. 1:3, 4). What an example! To whom can we say "Thank you" today?

**Daniela Weichhold**

# The Corn Maze

*Thou wilt shew me the path of life: in thy presence is fulness of joy; at thy right hand there are pleasures for evermore. Ps. 16:11.*

WHEN I THINK of the word "maze," I always think of puzzles in a magazine that you trace your way to the end with a pencil. I had never been inside a real maze—a delightful labyrinth of tall greenery, winding paths, blind alleys, and wrong turns. Then last summer I visited a corn maze with my grandson. I learned that a maze is like a swimming pool. You can't appreciate it without actually plunging in. Towering hedges of corn walled me in. Paths seemed to lead in every direction. There was no turning back; I would have to thread my way in and out in order to escape.

From the entrance I ran straight into a wall of foliage. By peering through it, I could glimpse the center of the maze with its high lookout for those who want to cheat. So near—and yet so far away. Unless a person were to push her way right through the hedge, reaching the center takes time. This confusing jumble of paths and poor visibility was testing my skills in a way I had not experienced before. I forgot the outside world and happily lost myself, having a good time with my grandson.

Hampton Court in London is one of the most famous mazes in the world. And like any good maze, it packs the most paths into the smallest area in order to compound the confusion. At the same time, a maze seems to hold a profound meaning. Treading a maze is like our path through life, complete with wrong turns, dead ends, and a seemingly elusive goal.

As I look back on my own life I remember times that it felt as if I had gotten myself into a maze that I couldn't get out of. But I thank my Lord that He didn't give up on me. When we're faced with some mazelike impossibility, we can call upon the wonder-working God who will provide us with a way out. When I'm being tested, I try to remember that there are many promises in the Bible. Generations have proven them true, and so can I.

If you're experiencing some high walls and curving mazes, never hesitate to pour out your heart to God. You will find that prayer is the shortest route between your heart and God's. You're on the right path!

**Vidella McClellan**

274

# Give Thanks Forever

*You turned my wailing into dancing; you removed my sackcloth and clothed me with joy, that my heart may sing to you and not be silent. O Lord my God, I will give you thanks forever. Ps. 30:11, 12, NIV.*

YESTERDAY WE WENT out in the canoe for perhaps the last time this season. I had hoped to hear the loons. Maybe there would be a pelican or great blue heron. For the past two summers I had been too weak to paddle the canoe. But it appeared that the cancer was gone now. I had enjoyed canoeing several times this summer. My arms seemed to be getting a little stronger each time, although my husband figured he did most of the work.

There were only the very common gulls and mudhens on the water. But I was happy to be out on the lake again. Each season brings different vistas, different evidences of God's love. I watched the shoreline. The leaves were starting to turn color, and there were a few splashes of gold from the birch trees. The browns, rusts, and oranges contrasted with the evergreens, the spruce and pine. Occasionally there was a bright-red shrub. Even the bare dead branches added to the kaleidoscope of color.

Then I noticed something I had never seen before. I had noticed the rushes along the shoreline. We usually could count on seeing several yellow-headed blackbirds perching on the bending grass. One day we'd seen a deer bounding through the low area where the rushes were. But not today. The rushes were starting to dry out, changing their bright-green color to a yellowish-brown. They were waving slightly in the breeze, and as I watched, I saw the reflection of the wave ripples shimmering and dancing through the gently moving reeds. "Do you see that?" I exclaimed. No one could have orchestrated the movement and light except my heavenly Father. I thanked Him for the beauty I saw. I thanked Him that I could see. I thanked Him that I was alive.

How is it with you? Are you thanking and praising God for the beauty you find around you? God has given us so much! All are evidences of His love for us. I pray that today I will remember to be in a thankful attitude all the time, whether things are going smoothly or not.

**Carol Nicks**

# Who Touched Me?

*But Jesus said, "Someone touched me; I know that power*
*has gone out from me." Luke 8:46, NIV.*

ONE OF THE BIBLE STORIES I enjoy reading most is about the
women who suffered from a 12-year blood disease. Then, upon
touching the hem of Jesus' garment, she was completely healed.

Jesus' miracles while here on earth leave us in awe. How consider-
ate and kind He was to everyone! He saw the longing of an afflicted person and felt the pain of those who were suffering. This story pleases me
because I can apply it to my life.

Many times sin, stress, or an inversion of values and evil leave my heart
spiritually ill. I become weak and discouraged, and none of the earthly solutions that I seek seems to give any results. I continue to feel bad, as though
a spiritual blood disease is taking all of my strength.

Then I decide to go to Jesus. I push through the multitude of problems
that insist in keeping me far away from the Savior, and finally I am able—
even as weak as I am—to fall on my knees at the feet of the Savior and spiritually touch the hem of His garment. In that instant Christ realizes that I
have touched Him. He looks at me tenderly, extends His hand, and listens
to me. In faith I give myself to Him, tell Him what I feel, and ask for
strength to come from Him to help me. And He smilingly tells me, "Be of
good courage, daughter. Go in peace!"

As I get up from my meeting with the Lord I feel healed, relieved of all
my burdens, and I can smile again. His hand blesses, His hand lightens my
burdens, heals the wounds of my soul, and gives me the certainty of His
company on the path of life.

God is the creator of the universe. He is powerful, omnipotent, and
omniscient, and sustains the heavenly bodies through His power. You and
I, although so small, are as important to Him as the cosmos, which by His
laws perfectly follow their path in the direction of infinity. His love is as
large and as broad as the universe; He gave His son to save those little ones
who approach Him with faith. None of our concerns, no tear that is shed,
causes Him to be indifferent.

When we go to Him with confidence, He heals us from the disease of sin
and gives us strength to continue. We can leave His presence certain of His
blessing because He tells us, "Be of good courage, daughter. Go in peace!"

**Juliane P. de Oliveira Caetano**

# View From My Office

*I will lift up mine eyes unto the hills, from whence cometh my help.*
*My help cometh from the Lord, which made heaven and earth. Ps. 121:1, 2.*

EVERY WORKDAY as I enter my office and pull back the curtains I am awed by a spectacular view that seems to say, "Welcome to a brand-new day!" This powerful display of God's handiwork is majestic and awe-inspiring. People who visit my office often remark that I have the best view on campus.

The sparkling sun with its golden halo bathes the earth with warm rays. The bright-blue sky is covered with clouds that look like waves on the sea. Stretched out in the distance are majestic undulating mountaintops that line the horizon. Evergreen trees stand tall and stately. Other trees, covered with thick green foliage, form a protective barrier against the outside world. Near the library three flags sway gently in the breeze, a vivid reminder of my allegiance to my God, my church, and my country.

From this vantage point I see young people wending their way to the library, classrooms, café, and other places of interest. To my right is the church—a place of worship and praise, a quiet place where saints and sinners alike come to find solace and renewal for their troubled souls, a place where lasting friendships are formed and sometimes culminate in holy matrimony. Nestled between the church and the library are two residence halls that house our future leaders, God's precious possessions.

That's the view from my office. More important, though, what does the view of my life say to my coworkers, the students, and other people with whom I interact daily? Will they see that I am a person of integrity, a loving and caring Christian? If they recorded my conversation of the day, would I be ashamed or embarrassed to listen to the tape? Would my words portray the fruits of the Spirit, or be words of gossip and criticism? Would my attitude help or hinder someone in their Christian growth? Would my life point them to Jesus, or would it disappoint them? What a solemn responsibility rests on my shoulders.

*As Christians our lives are viewed constantly. Lord, I pray that mine will reveal that I love You, and that You are the center of my joy.*

**Shirley C. Iheanacho**

# A Good Time Dishwashing

*God has given gifts to each of you from his great variety of spiritual gifts. Manage them well so that God's generosity can flow through you. 1 Peter 4:10, NLT.*

THERE IS NOTHING I can think of that is less exciting than a bunch of dirty dishes standing in the sink and sitting all over the counter. If I say to myself, *I will just let them go and do them in the morning,* then for sure they greet me the first thing upon getting out of bed.

Almost everyone I know dislikes dishwashing—that is, everyone but Charles and Jan, two people from a very small church in our town. (They don't have an automatic dishwasher either.) The pastor gets to their church only twice a month. When he comes, there is always a very nice fellowship dinner.

On the weeks the pastor isn't there, Jan and Charles have everyone from the church over to their house for dinner after services. Their house is so small that the tables reach from the dining room and on through most of the living room. Many times there are 20 people, or more, there, and Jan and Charles are always able to put on a delicious meal for everyone. You won't find paper plates or cups there either. They set the table with their good china—white with gold edges. They use their gold-rimmed stemware. A banquet is really more what it looks like.

I can't imagine how these two can plan all that hospitality when they are both employed full-time. If you ask Jan how they do all that, she chuckles and says, "The Lord helps!" And surely He does.

Over dinner we enjoy good food and the opportunity to know one another better. When it's time to go home, several of the women offer to stay and help with the dishwashing. Jan says, "No! Charles and I will do the dishes this evening. We enjoy doing them. It's our time to do something special together while we have a good time communicating."

What a wonderful attitude! They make a fun time out of an unpleasant chore. May God richly bless both of them for being so caring and sharing.

*Lord, show each of us what we can do to serve You even though we may be very tired and feel unable—or we just don't like doing the job.*

**Darlene Ytredal Burgeson**

# The Receiving End

*I will instruct thee and teach thee in the way which thou shalt go:*
*I will guide thee with mine eye. Ps. 32:8.*

EXPERIENCE IS A GREAT TEACHER, and it is fair to say that she who has never walked in another person's shoes would have little or no experience to share about those shoes. The same principle applies to life in general. We are actually shaped by our personal experiences. Each person's experience is unique and different.

I once decided to do some freelance nursing for a while. During this time I accompanied a family member to the hospital to have a surgical procedure. This was new for us on a personal level since no one in our family had ever had any similar procedure.

It dawned on me that, for the first time, I wasn't on the giving end but on the receiving end. I had traded places not by choice but by circumstance. I was not giving the orders but was receiving them. This role change taught me humility, patience, and trust—I had to depend on other nurses' knowledge and expertise. One's performance at the giving end could easily dictate what you'll get at the receiving end. This experience brought vivid memories of many patients and their families I had come in contact with during the discharge of my duties, and the professional demeanor I have always tried to exhibit. Jesus expects no less from us since we are always accountable first to Him and then to others.

Being on the receiving end can result in great rewards. It allowed Queen Esther to play a critical role in the deliverance of her people. It provided much-needed food for Ruth and Naomi following their return from Moab after the death of their husbands. It empowered Mary Magdalene to wipe Jesus' feet with choice perfume in spite of Judas's murmuring. It elevated Joseph from prison to palace, and allowed Sarah's womb to be opened to give birth to Isaac, the child of promise. It allowed Daniel to escape the mouths of lions. It permitted David—of all persons—to be called a man after God's own heart. It handpicked Rebekah for Isaac. And finally, it invites all peoples of the world to receive the ultimate—Jesus, the Savior of the world.

The receiving end can open new channels of blessings that you will not have room enough to receive.

**Althea Y. Boxx**

# One Letter Can Make a Huge Difference

*A word fitly spoken is like apples of gold in pictures of silver.
Prov. 25:11.*

THE MINDS OF YOUNG CHILDREN never cease to amaze me. They are so creative and intriguing—and say the unexpected at the most inappropriate time, hearing and reciting differently from that which was said.

Many stories have been told about children mutilating the Pledge of Allegiance. The final product varies with each child. Some say "to the public" when it should be "to the republic." Some say "witches stand" when it should be "for which it stands." Others say "invisible" when it should be "indivisible." Their statements are certainly innocent and are based upon the children's limited yet ever-growing vocabulary.

The other day my 4-year-old niece came to spend a few days with me. Of course, each hour—or even each minute—was filled with an unexpected surprise. Needless to say, I walk and talk gingerly in her presence. Well, most of the time. We made a day of baking cookies, having a tea party with storytelling, and then, of course, dress up. She donned the elongated gloves, boas, beads, and a glorious hat to top it off.

One of the latest words added to her repertoire was "gorgeous." "That's gorgeous" and "You're gorgeous" was what I heard from her for 10 minutes straight. In my attempt to take the focus off her newfound word and add yet another to her ever-increasing vocabulary, I told her, "You're elegant."

She poked her lips out, folded her arms across her chest, and said with a forceful voice, "I'm not an elephant!"

Whew. Moments later, after my attempts to clarify, she said, "Auntie, you're antastic!" Of course, I asked her to repeat herself, and again I heard, "Auntie, you're antastic!" Even without the "f" at the beginning of her word, I smiled and said, "Thank you. I think you're antastic too!" Don't you just love them! Every now and then one letter can make a huge difference.

Give someone a compliment today! Don't worry too much about the words—be sincere and just do it! And let me not let this moment go by without letting you know: You're antastic!

**Lady Dana Austin**

# Monarch

*Not even a sparrow. . . can fall to the ground without your Father knowing it. . . . So don't be afraid; you are more valuable to him than a whole flock of sparrows. Matt. 10:29-31, NLT.*

IT'S FALL HERE IN MISSOURI, and lately I've noticed so many monarch butterflies. It must be their migration time. Just this morning one seemed to follow us as we took our walk. We watched as it lazily floated before us, then beside us, then over the road. Sadly we watched as a truck blew past and brought it to its end. God cares about the sparrow when it falls—does He also care about a monarch?

I think the entire creation process is so fascinating! Just think—God didn't simply speak the word; first, He had to think through and design the intricate systems of each species. He did the same with the monarch. He planned how the butterfly lays its microscopic eggs on the underside of a milkweed leaf. He planned how the caterpillar emerges, eats voraciously, and forms a chrysalis with beautiful gold specks, similar to a crown. Miraculously—and according to plan—the regal monarch then emerges. So God thought through this whole process, and yes, He cares when one of His creatures falls.

What I love about monarchs and their transformation process is how beautifully it parallels our life as Christians. As the caterpillar gets ready for the next stage, it must stop feeding and attach itself to a twig. In this position it lies perfectly still, submitting to the preordained process. In the same way, we submit to Christ and are also changed.

This summer I had dug some lovely orange-blossomed butterfly weed from along country roads for my wildflower garden. Later I noticed some pretty caterpillars eating it. Recognizing them as monarchs-to-be, I brought several inside, along with plenty of the weed for them to eat. They didn't survive. There were more caterpillars, and I watched for chrysalises, but saw none. It was only later that I noticed some "fruit" on the butterfly weed that looked remarkably like milkweed. My butterfly weed is a relative to milkweed; and yes, monarchs eat it. Next year I'll enjoy more caterpillars and more monarchs.

*Praise You, Father, for the miracles of transformation in the life cycle of your monarch butterflies and for Your changes in me, too.*

**Becki Knobloch**

# Blessed and Blest

*The blessing of the Lord makes one rich, And He adds*
*no sorrow with it. Prov. 10:22, NKJV.*

I WAS ABOUT TO GRADUATE from the university with a degree
in accounting. However, I really wanted to keep on studying for an
advanced degree, with no interruptions on the way. That would involve taking some mastery subjects to keep up my skills. Then after
graduation I'd need to contact a lawyer to start the process of acquiring
my accountant's license. All this, plus the extra expenses connected with
graduation, put me in a financial predicament.

I started to worry. How was I going to pay for my studies and other expenses when I had no money? I thought about dropping the subjects to pay
for my license. Then I realized that I was trying to solve everything by myself. The same God who has been with me all the time, blessing me and answering my prayers, was still there, letting me know that He loves me no
matter what. I asked God to guide me and show me what I had to do.
Letting Him know what I wanted and what I needed, I turned my problems
over to the Lord.

Two weeks before graduation my cousin said she had a "little gift" for
me. I assumed it was just what she said it was: a little gift. But God knew
what I needed! When I picked up the pretty pink box covered with
flowers, I knew something good was in it. And there was—the exact
amount of money I needed to pay for my accountant's license.

By sharing this with you I'm letting you and other people know how
great God is! Test Him, try Him. I can testify that He is a God of blessing.
God knew what I needed. He answered my prayer in an unexpected way
and through another person. Thanks to Him, I can keep on studying—and
my license is already in process.

Never doubt the power of God, because He knows the exact time to
answer our prayers. As it says in Psalms: "Put your hope in God, for I will
yet praise him, my Savior and my God" (Ps. 42:11, NIV). Blessed be the
Lord—I've been blessed. I know that God wants to do the same for you
when you turn to Him for help.

**Ingrid Itzel Hines**

# Puppy-sitter Wanted

*In my Father's house are many mansions: if it were not so, I would have told you. I go to prepare a place for you. And if I go and prepare a place for you, I will come again, and receive you unto myself; that where I am, there ye may be also. John 14:2, 3.*

THE CLASSIFIED AD CAUGHT MY ATTENTION. A woman was advertising for a puppy-sitter, someone to watch her "baby," an 8-month-old Pomeranian named Lea. Out of concern and love for her pet, she was seeking someone to take her puppy into their home and provide a warm, loving haven while she was away on vacation. She was particularly sad to leave her puppy for this time period, because the puppy would celebrate her first birthday a few days after her mistress's departure. The owner, of course, wanted to screen prospective pet-sitters carefully and introduce the chosen sitter to the puppy well in advance of her departure date, to ensure that both the puppy and the sitter were comfortable with each other. Since Lea would be living with this person for two weeks, it was important that they were established friends when the time came for her to be separated from her beloved baby.

If a person is not an animal lover they will probably think this scenario is terribly frivolous. "Just put the dog in a kennel," they might say. It may not seem to make much difference where the dog spends the two weeks— it's just an animal. As a dog lover, I don't enter into such debate. I can, however, empathize with the puppy owner. If her puppy is going to live with someone for two weeks, she wants to be certain they have a relationship first.

As mediator between God and human beings, Jesus wants us to develop a relationship with God so that we can spend eternity with Him in His home. Jesus assures us that He is preparing a place for us in His Father's house (John 14:2, 3), and He wants us to establish a relationship with the Father through Him: "No man cometh unto the Father, but by me" (verse 6). Imagine how uncomfortable you'd feel if you had to live with someone you didn't even know, in a place you'd never been before. College freshmen must know how it feels. It takes awhile to build a relationship with a new roommate. For each of us that time to build a relationship with God is now. Out of love and concern for us God sent His Son, Jesus, to redeem us to Himself (John 3:16), not just temporarily, but for eternity.

**Sherma Webbe Clarke**

# The Runaway Trailer

*He shall call upon me, and I will answer him. Ps. 91:15.*

THE SUBURBAN SPRAWL in Auckland had increased immensely in the 17 years I was away. So much had changed. A few weeks ago, however, I did see one very familiar sight—a tennis club that has been in an eastern suburb for many, many years. There used to be a field beside it, with two or three horses always grazing. There was also a sealed area, which was used as a car park. Just a short distance past the tennis club is an estuary flowing into the beautiful Waitemata Harbour, where there were—and still are —public boat ramps. But now, of course, houses have crowded in; both the field and parking area are gone.

Seeing the tennis club brought the following incident flooding back to my memory. One public holiday long weekend more than 30 years ago, my husband and father-in-law launched their boat there. Like so many men, they spent many happy hours fishing, and that weekend they had decided to stay out overnight. So I towed the boat trailer home and disconnected it from the car. The next day, in the early afternoon, I towed the trailer back to the boat ramp. As I drove past the tennis club I saw, to my utter shock, the boat trailer flying past my car on the inside of the road. It had come off the coupling! "Please stop it, God!" I cried out. As I watched, the trailer tow bar plowed into a high grassy mound that halted it in full flight. God had instantly answered my plea, as immediately past the mound were many parked cars, their owners playing tennis.

If the trailer hadn't been stopped, there is no doubt it would have hit one or more of those cars. Even worse, there could have been somebody walking there! *Thank You, God*, I breathed. When I inspected the trailer and the hitch, it was obvious that the trailer had come off the coupling simply because I hadn't attached it properly.

Whenever I'm separated from Jesus, I am headed straight for danger. Jesus talked about this in the parable of the vine. He said, "Abide in me, and I in you. . . . I am the vine, ye are the branches: He that abideth in me, and I in him, the same bringeth forth much fruit: for without me ye can do nothing" (John 15:4, 5). The most important thing you and I can ever do is to make sure our connection to Him is secure.

**Leonie Donald**

# Perfume That Lasts

*She put this perfume on My body to make it ready for the grave.*
*Matt. 26:12, NLV.*

I REALLY LIKE PERFUME—I think that all women should always use perfume. And why not men, too? If you don't own French perfume, use a fragrance that emanates when you walk past someone. My daughters-in-law, Alesandra and Belinda, like to give me perfume. They always find something that meets my taste.

One day I was visiting one of them, and, after doing some chores, I went window shopping in a large mall. As I was leaving, Belinda opened her purse and generously took out some money and placed it in my hands. She smiled and said, "Take this money and buy some perfume for yourself."

I'm sure my face was radiant as I came out of the store with my favorite perfume in my hands. "Thank you, Belinda; thank you very much," I said, meaning every word of it.

There are expensive and very good perfumes that remain impregnated in clothing and/or on the body for a long time. This is what happened during the festivities held at the home of the former leper Simon. A short time later Jesus would be crucified. But here was Mary—the disenfranchised, rejected, mistreated one—pouring perfume that would last for hours on the head and the feet of the Master. It was a very special perfume, prepared in the most elite perfumery in Jerusalem. It was the best that she had to offer Him.

His entire body was covered with the fragrance, and I'm certain that later, after He was beaten as He was taken to the cross to be crucified, the fragrance of that perfume that had been given to Him by Mary emanated from His body with the blood that flowed.

In His blood-saturated hair there was perfume. At the foot of the cross as His clothing was being divided the fragrance of the perfume still remained on the garments.

When we are offended, criticized, discriminated against, do we emanate the perfume that is long-lasting—the perfume of forgiveness, kindness, patience, and self-control?

The offended, beaten, and crucified One emanated perfume, and when He came out of the tomb He left there His clothing, folded and perfumed with the essence of love for us, a fragrance that lasts even to this day.

**Zuila Vila Nova Rodrigues**

# God's Police Officer

*Before they call I will answer; while they are still speaking
I will hear. Isa. 65:24, NIV.*

ABOUT 7:00 one Sunday evening we were driving to a beautiful
church in the interior of the state of São Paulo, Brazil, to attend the
worship service. A special musical group was to make a presentation,
and my husband didn't want to arrive even one minute late, so he was
driving faster than he normally did.

Our teenage sons, very aware of his speed, were saying, "Accelerate,
Dad!" "Pass the car!" "Go, Dad; go, Dad!" "Faster, faster!" each time he
passed a car. They looked at their watches and counted the minutes because
they too wanted to arrive for the opening of the program.

I confess that I was afraid. I'm frightened about traveling at night, and
especially under these conditions. When I attempted to calm them down,
they all got angry at me, because they wanted to get there quickly. Very
concerned and frightened about the situation, I closed my eyes and prayed,
*Lord, I can do nothing, but You can. Amen.*

When I opened my eyes, I saw a light from a flashlight signaling our car
to stop on the shoulder of the road. Everyone saw it. And everyone was
silent. We stopped, and the police officer approached. As my husband lowered the window, the officer warned him with a calm but firm voice: "Sir,
you need to be more careful, because you have your family in the car. You
cannot continue driving the way you were; you were going very fast. What
is your address?"

My husband gave him the information, and then the officer said, "The
ticket will be mailed to your residence. You may continue. Good night, and
have a good trip!"

Silence reigned in the car. How I wanted to thank the police officer, but
how? It certainly wasn't a state police officer—he didn't even have a car. I
knew it was an angel who had been sent to protect us that night. And the
ticket? No ticket ever arrived in the mail. Even with the stop, we arrived on
time for the musical presentation.

How can one not believe in this wonderful God? Through experience I
can say, "The angel of the Lord encamps around those who fear him, and
he delivers them" (Ps. 34:7, NIV).

Elza C. dos Santos

# A Butterfly Card

*Now ye are clean through the word which I have spoken unto you.*
*John 15:3.*

THERE ARE TIMES IN OUR LIVES that we have failed God, so we feel guilty and don't recognize His presence. Nevertheless, we ask Him, "Lord, please listen to me."

My cousin and I were having some misunderstanding, and we hadn't talked for months. I prayed, "Lord, I've already forgiven her, but I don't want to talk to her anymore." I knew in the back of my mind that I had a wrong attitude.

I asked something of God, but it seemed He wasn't listening to me. I didn't feel His presence at my side; I knew I had to do something. In my heart I knew that I should ask first for God's forgiveness. So I prayed again and asked Him to forgive me. "I know it's not easy to totally forgive someone who has hurt you, but because I love You, Lord, I will do it for You. I want to ask for Your forgiveness, Lord; please give me a sign that You've already forgiven me, Father. I do not want to be far from You, because I can do nothing without You by my side."

After attending a vesper prayer meeting, I went back to the dormitory. As I walked past my bed I saw a cut paper butterfly on which was written, "Happy Sabbath, Kathy. John 15:3." It was from one of my roommates. I opened my Bible and read today's text: "Now ye are clean through the word which I have spoken unto you." I knew right then that He had used my roommate to let me know that even if we may have failed Him, He is always there for us, ready to forgive us when with a sincere heart we ask for it.

God will never leave us; it is our sin that separates us from our Lord. He loves us, and I am grateful to have Him in my life. I treasure the additional promise found in Philippians 4:13: "I can do all things through Christ which strengtheneth me."

I will always thank God for coming into my life and accepting me as His daughter. I know for a fact that He will never leave me—or you! Friend, do you too have someone you need to forgive? Maybe it wasn't even easy for Jesus to forgive those who were hurting Him. I can tell you it isn't easy, but with Jesus it can be done. And oh, it feels so wonderful!

*I love You, Lord, and I will always love and praise You all the days of my life.*

**Kathy Sonio Zausa**

# Will You Hold My Hand?

*Though he fall, he shall not be utterly cast down:*
*for the Lord upholdeth him with his hand. Ps. 37:24.*

IT WAS ONE OF THOSE SABBATH AFTERNOONS that I would have preferred to relax at home. Having come through the hustle and bustle of a busy week, I yearned for the inviting comfort of my old green recliner. But there was something special I had to do. I needed to join the team for our weekly visit to the prison.

Wending our way through the various units at the jail, we finally arrived at the solitary confinement block. After the usual preliminaries, we listened as the speaker told about the love of God for us all. "Always remember," she said, "the eternal God is your refuge and strength, and underneath you are the everlasting arms."

All of a sudden my reflections were interrupted by a request that almost broke my mother heart. "Will you hold my hand?" Automatically I turned toward the person whose petition had pulled at my heartstrings. Sitting on the edge of a cot in his lonely cell was Robbie, a 17-year-old boy who had, in a fit of rage, used an ax to commit heinous crimes against his grandparents just that week. Instinctively I reached for the outstretched arm. I could only imagine the cauldron of raw emotions that had caused Robbie to be imprisoned. As my fingers grasped his hand, my tears melded with his as I prayed, "Dear God, help us to remember that down in the human heart, crushed by the tempter, feelings are buried that Your grace can restore."

I've often thought about that precious boy. I don't understand the disconnected images in his brain that prompted his murderous acts, but I know God had a reason for my being at that place at that time. I think of a powerful passage that Ellen G. White once penned: "Christ was treated as we deserve, that we might be treated as He deserves. He was condemned for our sins, in which He had no share, that we might be justified by His righteousness, in which we had no share. . . . 'With His stripes we are healed' " (*The Desire of Ages*, p. 25).

I've settled into a sense of peaceful anguish as I think of that young boy. Fanny Crosby's hymn still rings in my ears: "Rescue the perishing, care for the dying; Jesus is merciful, Jesus will save."

**Iralyn Haig Trott**

# Lessons From a Pumpkin Patch

*Like the new-born infants you are, you must crave for pure milk (spiritual milk, I mean), so that you may thrive upon it to your souls' health. 1 Peter 2:2, NEB.*

LAST SUMMER someone gave me a pumpkin seedling that I planted in my backyard. Soon a pumpkin vine was running riotously across the yard. In a short time large yellow flowers decorated the vine. When they fell off, several tiny pumpkins took their places.

I excitedly counted and watched the pumpkins as they grew. These pumpkins would be my mission investment project for the year, and I carefully tended them to be sure each would grow to perfection. Then one week there were several rainy days, and I was unable to visit my pumpkin patch. Imagine my surprise when I inspected the vine to find that the latest pumpkin on the vine was bigger than the others! I couldn't understand why this was so, and kept telling my family about how fast this particular pumpkin was growing. One day I noticed that it was lying in a puddle of water. I attempted to support it with a piece of board to prevent it from rotting in the excess moisture. It was then that I discovered the secret for that particular pumpkin's rapid growth.

While all the other pumpkins depended on nutrients from the root of the vine to grow, this pumpkin had developed an additional source. What had originally been a tendril directly across from the pumpkin's stem had somehow become a root which sank down into the soil and became a direct source of nutrients for that pumpkin. When it was reaping time, my prized pumpkin was twice the size of the others on the vine.

As I considered the pumpkin, I thought about how frequently we Christians depend on the pastor or Bible class teacher to feed us with the Word of God instead of making quality time for personal Bible study. We become malnourished spiritually when there is opportunity to be spiritual giants. We wait for handouts from other people's research when we can be mining the Scriptures for ourselves. The apostle Peter counsels us to desire the Word with the same intensity that a newborn craves mother's milk. Then, like healthy infants, we will grow up in Christ and mature in our Christian experience. Let us eagerly crave the precious Word of God, that our souls may thrive and develop to their fullest potential.

**Candace Sprauve**

# Stay in Your Box

*As water reflects a face, so a man's heart reflects the man.*
*Prov. 27:19, NIV.*

HARMONIOUS AND SWEET, mellow tones graced the enormous space of the Patriot Center. Tiny lights scattered and blinked throughout the audience like sparkling stars. It seemed to me as if a bit of heaven had settled in as the Gaither Vocal Band and a host of friends shared their hearts, voices, and joy in the Lord during a four-hour concert. My husband and I had been graciously invited to share an anniversary evening with friends.

I can't carry a tune in a bucket, as they say, but, oh, how I love music! And how I enjoyed the concert! The Gaithers opened the concert with their signature song: "If you want more happy than you heart will hold," "when the day is done, throw your heart wide open and give it away."

My husband sang a song at church recently and said he was stepping "out of his box" to sing a song for the Lord. But he loves to sing, so it seemed as though he had more happy than his heart could hold, and he threw open his heart and gave it away.

What about that "box" and what the Lord expects from each of us? I think we are prone to think that the Lord likes to watch us squirm and make us do something clearly out of our element. I am inclined to think He wants to give us strength to do the things that He has already designed to be a unique part of our original personalities. C. S. Lewis explains this in his book *Mere Christianity:* "The more we get what we now call 'ourselves' out of the way and let Him take us over, the more truly ourselves we become. . . . It is when I turn to Christ, when I give myself up to His personality, that I first begin to have a real personality of my own."

Abide in Him. Ask the Lord for strength to be stripped of your inhibitions. Discover and enjoy the talents He has given you within your own box. Paul tells us regarding these gifts, "Now to each one the manifestation of the Spirit is given for the common good. . . . And he gives them to each one, just as he determines" (1 Cor. 12:7-11, NIV).

Make doors and windows in your box; decorate it, and invite others to come in and see it. Above all, sing in your box. Talents of every sort will spill from your heart as you "throw your heart wide open and give it away." Share yourself—your true self, your God-given self.

**Judy Good Silver**

# When No One Wanted First Place

*But many who are first will be last, and many who are last will be first. Matt. 19:30, NIV.*

WHEN I WAS 12, I participated in a children's cooking contest promoted by a food company in a special fair celebrating Children's Week. Nearly 200 children had registered and had gone through the first and second elimination stages. We were now in the final competition. The premiums were on display: first place, a gold watch; second place, a bicycle; third place, a record player. The fourth-place winner would receive a tape recorder, and everyone else would receive a gift certificate from a department store.

One of the boys ran to the bicycle, sat on it, and declared, "This bicycle will be mine!" I thought how much *I* wanted to win the bicycle! A girl began to cry and sobbed that *she* wanted the bicycle. I suddenly realized that no one wanted to win first prize.

Everyone went to the mini-kitchens, and the recipe was distributed to each competitor. I looked at the recipe in despair: chicken with green pepper. My mother was vegetarian, and I had never prepared any meat. My mother, brothers, sisters, and neighbor watched from the stands. After learning of my difficulty, the neighbor shouted a few instructions to me.

Everyone else had finished and were serving their dishes to the judges while I continued to wait for my chicken to bake. I had seen advertisements in magazines showing glistening baked chicken, and I wanted mine to look like that. Finally one of the event organizers entered my kitchen to say that my time was up; I should serve my finished dish immediately. When I took the chicken from the oven, I realized that the skin had started to burn. Somewhat discouraged, I removed the skin and served my chicken with green pepper to the judges.

To my surprise, I received second place and won the bicycle! The boy who placed first cried and screamed because he didn't want the gold watch. His mother attempted to convince me to trade with him, saying I could sell the watch and buy another bicycle, but her arguments did not convince me.

Have I sometimes chosen things of lesser value while forgetting that Christ offers me something of much greater value—eternal life? May my choices today be what God has made for me!

**Sônia Maria Rigoli Santos**

# The Wisdom of Kindness

*Now that I am old and gray, do not abandon me, O God.*
*Let me proclaim your power to this new generation, your*
*mighty miracles to all who come after me. Ps. 71:18, NLT.*

ONE OCTOBER DAY I was invited to take part in a panel discussion with a third-year University of Alberta inclusive education class. Being the mother of Sonny, an 18-year-old man/child, qualifies me to have some authority on such matters. I felt the Lord guiding me to accept this challenge. I was given a list of topics, and in advance I wrote out my answers to serve as my guideline.

I was the first of the five panel members to speak. I told the class that public speaking wasn't my cup of tea—even though I felt that my job as a demo person at Costco for the past two years had prepared me for this special day. (We all laughed!) The students were receptive, so I just read word for word from my guideline.

"What makes inclusion successful?" was one of the topics for discussion. My answer: "It's not what, but *who*: purpose-driven people who are determined to make a positive difference in changing attitudes and enlightening those around them. People need to come to the realization that they themselves, or others whom they love, are not guaranteed immunity from immeasurable life-changing disabilities."

Unless there is a sincere, genuine willingness and desire for people to have respect, tolerance, patience, and honest and open lines of communication (with thoughtful gestures of uplifting acts of kindness and compassion toward one another), the challenges of inclusion become mountains. However, with faith and the right team of people, these mountains can be removed.

For the betterment of everyone, we need to learn to walk together in love even if we don't see eye to eye. We all need to develop an attitude with gratitude. Teachers need to respect and acknowledge that the job of parenting a severely mentally challenged child is a tough go that never becomes easier. Teachers must be patient with these special parents; unkind words could send their world into a disastrous tailspin. Always be looking for the win/win solution to every challenge you face. What wisdom can you find greater than kindness?

**Deborah Sanders**

# Prepared for Trouble

*And there shall be a time of trouble, such as never was . . . . : and at that time thy people shall be delivered, every one that shall be found written in the book. Dan. 12:1.*

WHEN I WAS A TODDLER, my dad practiced calisthenics with me. Along with the tumbling exercises, I was taught to fall safely. By the time I went to school, I could perform complicated maneuvers as easily as I could walk across the room. Heights didn't frighten me. In fact, I had only two fears: the sudden appearance of a barking dog or a spider. These could cause me to stop breathing or to faint.

As I grew up, other activities and interests entered my life, and I no longer did calisthenics or tumbling. By the time I married, I had completely forgotten about those early exercises I so enjoyed with Daddy.

I was sick the entire time of my first pregnancy, and slept with a night-light on for emergencies. One night as I just drifted off to sleep, I heard a plop next to my head. Sleepily I turned to see what had made the noise and saw a spider the size of a quarter!

*"Eeek!"* I screamed, then stopped breathing. The terror caused by the sight of this big spider, less than two inches from my face, caused muscle memory to kick in, and, in spite of the fact that I was in my seventh month of pregnancy, I executed a calisthenic maneuver I hadn't used in more than 20 years, leaping eight feet in a somersault to land facing the bed. I stood staring across the room at the bed pillow where the spider sat.

I have thought back in wonder to that night almost 40 years ago. My dad practiced those moves with me nightly from babyhood until I started grade school. My body had been trained, through practice, to respond automatically. Twenty years after the last time I had practiced those moves, my body reacted automatically—under stress, and in terror— to "save" me from the perceived danger.

We're going to go through a time of trouble in the last days of earth's history when we shall be tried for our belief in God. The practice of being faithful now, when not under end-times stress, prepares us to react automatically when those dangerous times occur in our lives and we have no time to plan how we are to move, act, or pray.

**Darlenejoan McKibbin Rhine**

# Mercy Extended

*For thy mercy is great above the heavens. Ps. 108:4.*
*He is ever merciful. Ps. 37:26.*

CASSIE AND I TRAVELED from the East Coast to the West Coast of the United States. We came from Virginia and passed through several states with green trees and cool, fresh air. As we traveled, we tried to make sure that we never ran low on fuel.

On our fourth day of travel we entered the last state we had to cross. We left the hotel in Flagstaff and headed toward the border of Arizona and California, planning to gas up at the nearest station. But we missed the turn. Since we still had about a half tank, we drove on. What we didn't realize was that it would be a very long distance before we'd reach the next gas station. After about 60 more miles (97 kilometers), we were running low on gas.

About 40 miles from the next gas station and in the middle of the desert, the fuel indicator showed red. We were in real trouble. We were driving along the side of a mountain; the road was high, and the temperature was 104° F (40° C). I worried about dehydration if we had to stop in the desert. I instructed Cassie to drive slowly in the right lane to economize on the gas and to be prepared to stop by the roadside. This would also help the troopers notice us and help us. Cassie was reluctant to slow down, because all the other motorists were driving at least 75 miles (120 kilometers) per hour. Most were driving 80-100 miles (130-160 kilometers) per hour. Slowing down would be a hazard; we couldn't slow down.

We exited toward a small community, hoping to find some gas. Instead we met a couple. The man told us we had two choices: return to the freeway and drive 40 miles east, or proceed west to Ludlow, about 36 miles. Cassie noticed I was extremely worried. She tried to comfort me. "Relax; go to sleep. I don't want you to get sick. We'll be fine."

Three miles before we were to come to a station, I heard the empty tank sound, but I also noticed the Union 76 sign. We would make it—with God's help.

I felt the extended mercy of God. He provided just enough fuel for us until we could get more. God's mercy is everlasting and extends from the beginning to the end.

**Esperanza Aquino Mopera**

# Feelings

*Thou wilt keep him in perfect peace, whose mind is stayed on thee: because he trusteth in thee. Isa. 26:3.*

FEELINGS! How do we handle them?

Have you ever had the feeling of aloneness? Have you ever felt that no one understands you? Have you ever felt that you didn't have a friend in this world? Have you ever felt like getting in a car and just driving away? Have you ever been on the verge of tears and didn't know why? Have you ever felt that no one loves you, not even Jesus?

If so, remember to always pray. With God you are never alone. "I love them that love me; and those that seek me early shall find me" (Prov. 8:17).

If you've ever experienced any one of those feelings, you aren't alone! You aren't crazy, you aren't losing it, because God is love. First John 4:7 says, "Beloved, let us love one another: for love is of God; and every one that loveth is born of God, and knoweth God."

When you put your trust in the Lord when these feelings come, Jesus will put His loving arms around you and give you peace, perfect peace—wonderful peace! "Finally, brethren, farewell. Be perfect, be of good comfort, be of one mind, live in peace; and the God of love and peace shall be with you" (2 Cor. 13:11).

In the future, when those feelings come, read Psalm 27:7: "Hear, O Lord, when I cry with my voice: have mercy also upon me, and answer me." Psalms 28:8 is a great help as well: "The Lord is their strength, and he is the saving strength of his anointed." God understands all our feelings and can help us handle them.

*Lord, Thank You for Your compassion and care for my life. When I feel weary from the stresses of life, help me to remember that I can find rest and comfort in You. "In my distress I called upon the Lord, and cried unto my God: he heard my voice out of his temple, and my cry came before him, even into his ears" (Ps. 18:6). Give me peace within myself. When I am depressed, give me peace, unspeakable peace. Help me to love myself and to trust and love You, because You said, "I love them that love me; and those that seek me early shall find me" (Prov. 8:17). In Jesus' name, amen.*

**Hattie R. Logan**

# The Power of Music

*Speak to one another with psalms, hymns and spiritual songs. Sing and make music in your heart to the Lord, always giving thanks to God the Father for everything, in the name of our Lord Jesus Christ. Eph. 5:19, 20, NIV.*

THE MEMORY IS STILL CLEAR to me even now when I hear the sacred hymns such as "Rock of Ages," "The Old Rugged Cross," and "What a Friend We Have in Jesus." They remind me of the time I was a young school girl in the mid-1930s, walking along the dusty streets, carrying the Ingathering can to solicit the simple homes of the little town where we lived. It was always in the fall of the year, and we called it Harvest Ingathering, a means of gathering funds for world missions and welfare work.

The church had a flatbed truck on which the members placed a pump organ and a few chairs. The older members sat on these and played and sang the good old hymns as the truck drove slowly down each street. We schoolchildren had learned our little speech, and we knocked on doors to ask for mission offerings. It was hard for people to resist the sight of children doing this, and we could gather significant amounts of money that way. In those days people were not all watching television or listening to iPods, and I'm sure the sound of the music from the street had a powerful appeal in the process. It really did for me, because to this day the impression returns.

Music has the power to build memories and bring back memories. Godly music draws me into God's presence, where I feel safe and loved. Sacred music has the power to heal, inspire, and quiet my soul. When I hear the songs again, the memory becomes part of the present, and I once more feel the comforting love of Jesus.

I like this thought: "Singing, as a part of religious service, is as much an act of worship as is prayer" (*Patriarchs and Prophets*, p. 594). Ellen White further writes: "Song is one of the most effective means of impressing spiritual truth upon the heart" (*Evangelism,* p. 500). It certainly was for me in those long-ago Ingathering days, and again as the memories return when I hear those songs once more.

*Dear Lord, let me draw nearer to You today as I hear again the wonderful words of life in the familiar sacred hymns.*

**Bessie Siemens Lobsien**

# I Had to Pray About It

*Casting all your care upon Him, for He cares for you. 1 Peter 5:7, NKJV.*

MY HUSBAND AND I had just moved back to Florida from Texas, so I went to the Department of Motor Vehicles to get my driver's license changed over to our new address. It was a simple procedure—or so I thought until I came face to face with a rather stern officer. "No, ma'am, you can't do that," he told me brusquely. "You'll need evidence that your Florida insurance was reinstated, or you'll have to pay $150." And then he softened slightly. "But check with the agent at the desk in line 2. She might be able to help you."

Relieved, I hurried to the woman and explained my dilemma. "Oh, yes," she said kindly. "You can do that if you have your Texas insurance papers with you." I knew I had those documents, but they were in the car. "All you have to do is get them," she told me, and I rushed to the car.

Returning to the office a few minutes later, I was surprised to find that I couldn't get in. The officer at the door, the same one who had refused my request before, wouldn't let me in. "Your papers say Texas, not Florida," he pointed out. "You'll have to come back tomorrow."

I prayed about my problem all night, and then I got more specific in my praying. *Dear Lord, please let me not have to deal with that grumpy man again, and please let everything work out.*

Bright and early the next morning I went back to the office and joined the line. Heartened, I noted that the unhelpful agent was not at the door. *Thank You, Lord,* I whispered as the line inched slowly toward the desk of another man.

When I reached his desk, however, he sent me to the desk of the man I'd worked with before. *Dear Lord,* I prayed fervently, *please work things out for me, even if I must deal with this grouchy man.* And then a marvelous thing happened, something only God could do. When there were only two people in the line ahead of me, the agent was called away. When I got to the front of the line, another friendly man was there. My business was arranged smoothly and quickly.

Sometimes in this life we worry so much that we forget to pray. God wants us to acknowledge that we need His help. When we ask Him, He will help us. He cares for us!

**Naomi Liptrot**

# Messages

*Make your light shine, so that others will see the good that you do and will praise your Father in heaven. Matt. 5:16, CEV.*

ON THE STREET where I live it is a tradition to hang a pink or blue balloon on the fence when anyone has a new grandchild.

Most of us moved here when the suburb was built, and our children grew up together. The years have sped by, and my four (two boys and two girls) now have families of their own, blessing me with eight treasured grandchildren. On September 24, 2003, it was my turn to proudly hang a pink balloon on the fence, heralding the arrival of Jasmine. Then exactly one week later, a blue one announced the arrival of Bradley. The neighbors next door were quick to note the change of color only days apart. Not knowing we were expecting two so close together, they asked quite sincerely whether I'd made a mistake. I promptly and proudly translated the balloon messages.

There are countless ways we send and receive messages, and they all seem to demand our attention. My mobile phone reminds me of this with its text messages. Modern technology speeds messages from one side of the world to the other via satellite. There are answering machines, fax machines, e-mail, phones—and let's not forget that little machine called a pager.

Some of the nicest messages I've received warm the heart: "I love you," "Keep courage," "Thinking of you," "Praying for you," and many more. May we use these little phrases as precious gifts to give those around us, for memories of sweet words cheer the heart in a world that gives many sad messages.

The Bible offers messages of hope and comfort, others of instruction or warning, all of which God has sent with love. After accepting His messages, it's important to remember that my words and actions are visible messages given to all whom I meet each day. I pray my neighbors are able to interpret me as a true witness, unlike the confused message the change in colored balloons gave.

*Dear Jesus, text Your messages upon my heart today so that I may be guided in truth. Bless each sister as she witnesses too through her daily messages. "Your word is a lamp to my feet and a light for my path" (Ps. 119:105, NIV).*

**Lyn Welk-Sandy**

# The Message From the Kiskadee

*The eyes of the Lord are on the righteous and his ears are attentive to their cry. Ps. 34:15, NIV.*

I READ A STORY about a woman who watched a bird singing in her bathroom windowsill. Paying closer attention, she soon saw that it was a small kiskadee. Then the idea came to her: *Every time that I hear the kiskadee singing, I will offer an intercessory pray in favor of someone.*

Thinking that this was an interesting idea, I decided to do the same—but I doubted that I'd hear a kiskadee singing, because the area in which I lived was very busy. I didn't remember ever seeing one of them around my house. However, as soon as I woke up on Saturday morning, the first sound I heard was "Kis-ka-dee! Kis-ka-dee!."

*Interesting,* I thought. *It has  probably always been there, but I just ignored it.* I'd heard his song, but his beautiful chirping didn't say anything to me. At that moment, however, the name of someone I should pray for came to mind. I offered that prayer and have continued to do this whenever I hear the beautiful kiskadee song.

A few days later, while I was traveling to a neighboring town with my husband, I told him of the experience. He thought it would be difficult to hear a kiskadee at our home; but then, as though we were being tested at that exact moment, we looked up and saw a large sign in front of us that read "Kiskadee Paints." We laughed as we realized the creative ways that God uses to reveal Himself to us. We knew that we should pray for someone.

I continue to do this whenever I hear a kiskadee, but more important, I pass this idea on wherever I go. Recently, as I held an evangelism program, I explained the idea to the church with a slight adaptation. Every time that we heard a kiskadee sing, we would pray for the evangelistic meetings and the people who were attending.

Praise God, the week of evangelism was marvelous! Many people participated, and a number of them have already given their hearts to Jesus.

Sharpen your ears! Listen for the song of a special bird, then pray for someone. Spread this idea around, and be certain that God will hear your prayers. He will begin to accomplish marvelous things that go beyond your expectations.

**Nelci de Rocco Lima**

*October 19*

# The Burning Bush

*Thou shalt not covet thy neighbour's house . . .
nor any thing that is thy neighbour's. Ex. 20:17.*

I WAS ABOUT TO GET IN MY CAR when I caught a glimpse of my neighbor packing away his garden pots for another season. I called out to him with compliments on the brilliant color of his burning bushes. Since Bill is a horticulturist, I asked him to take a look at mine. Except for a few leaves, my shrubs were still very green in color, while his were a beautiful deep red. Mine were so far removed in appearance from my neighbor's that while standing only a few feet away from them, he asked what they were. My shrubs were planted a couple years before my neighbor's. We had chosen them specifically for the bright orange-red hue they are supposed to display in autumn. On closer examination Bill confirmed what we suspected—the bushes lacked moisture because of their location in the garden. As he walked away, he tossed a friendly tease in my husband's direction about his bushes being better than ours.

Herein lies the lesson. I've always considered myself to be a covetous person only with respect to good things. After all, we are encouraged in 1 Corinthians 12:31 to covet the best gifts. I interpreted this to mean "desire the best things," but not in a hateful or jealous way. In this instance I must admit to feeling some jealousy toward my neighbor for his obvious success with these shrubs. The result of this experience is that I have learned that it's a very slippery slope we're on when we use self as the yardstick by which we measure our Christian standards and behavior.

It took a very simple incident for this covetous human nature of mine to rise to the forefront. The remedy for the lack of color in my burning bushes is also simple. I've learned that consistent watering of the plants during the summer months will yield brilliant colors in autumn. I'm committed to doing what is necessary to obtain the desired results in my garden next autumn. I'm also committed to using Christ as my only standard from now on.

If you can identify with this lesson, I sincerely invite you to make the same commitment today. And remember: do not covet anything that is your neighbor's, not even the shrubs in your neighbor's garden.

**Avis Mae Rodney**

# Saved by His Blood

*In him we have redemption through his blood. Eph. 1:7, NIV.*

OCTOBER 20. Today I am scheduled to receive the bone marrow stem cells. It's been two years since I was diagnosed with chronic lymphocytic leukemia. At that time the doctor told me I should go home and just forget about the diagnosis. He said that this usually was not a fast-growing cancer, and I would probably die of something else. He indicated that I might need chemotherapy some time in the future, but that I was too old to be considered for a bone marrow transplant.

Within the first year my white blood count had gone so high that the doctor prescribed the chemotherapy. This worked several times, but the results didn't last.

Two years after the diagnosis I developed an ear infection that wouldn't go away, no matter how strong the antibiotics used or how many poultices I applied. My blood counts and bone marrow biopsy indicated that the cancer had become very aggressive and that I didn't have much longer to live. The doctor then said that my only hope was a bone marrow stem cell transplant. He knew I had five siblings and said that the chance of a match from one of them was good. My siblings all came to give blood, and it was sent to the lab for matching. Each of my four sisters thought she might be the match. But it turned out that my brother was an almost perfect match.

I was finally admitted to the hospital and underwent one week of strong chemotherapy to get rid of all the cancer in my bone marrow. And today my brother's stem cells are being dripped into my veins.

I watch for one hour as the blood flows in. I wonder if it will "take," if it will do what it's supposed to do. I wonder if it will find its way to the bone marrow and start making the blood cells I need to live. As I watch I'm reminded of the blood of Jesus—how it saves. It is only the blood of Christ that washes away our sins.

And now it is two weeks later, and my blood is checked every day. Finally, the counts are starting to go up. Thank you, Raymond, for the gift of your blood. *Thank You, dear Jesus, for the gift of Your blood on Calvary so that I might enjoy eternal life.*

**Carol Nicks**

# The Good Part

*Mary has chosen what is better. Luke 10:42, NIV.*

I ATTENDED A CAMP MEETING in South Carolina recently. As I walked toward the doors of the pavilion, I tripped accidentally and fell prostrate on the cement entrance. Very embarrassed when someone said, "Call 911," I opened my eyes and looked around. I heard a young man say, "Let's get her up." Out of nowhere came about six young men—angels, really—who lifted me to my feet and asked about my physical condition. Still stunned, I thanked them and proceeded to walk into the pavilion to the restroom to adjust my clothes. My husband, and others, urged me to go to the hospital to seek medical attention. After about 30 minutes I agreed, and my husband took me to the hospital. There I was diagnosed with a fractured right arm. It was placed in a cast, and I spent the next five days in bed.

With my arm in a cast and sling, I finally went back to the pavilion and enjoyed the messages and thanked my Lord for the trials that strengthen us. The adversary, the devil, is waiting for an opportunity to trip us up. The Lord allows only so much so that we will know that He is Lord. God had angels encamped about to assist me so that permanent injury didn't result from such a hard fall. This experience actually drew me closer to my Lord and Savior.

When Sabbath morning arrived, I was eager to get to church, but getting dressed was a much slower process with only the use of one arm. I became discouraged, because putting on hose was too difficult. The enemy tried to discourage me by saying, "You've never gone to church without hose." For many years I've always paid attention to what my family wore, as I believe we should put our best food forward and wear our best clothes for Sabbath. This time, though, I went to church without paying attention to all the little details—I was thankful to have a desire to go to church and worship. Some things that we think are so important are not. Think about Mary and Martha of biblical times. Martha was paying attention to all the little details, but Mary chose to sit at Jesus' feet to listen and be blessed.

*Dear Lord, so many times we pay attention to unimportant details. We know they need attention, but give us the holy discernment to choose the good part and be blessed.*

**Betty G. Perry**

# House Wrens

*But for you who revere my name, the sun of righteousness will rise
with healing in its wings. Mal. 4:2, NIV.*

JUST OUTSIDE MY OFFICE WINDOW at home hangs an artificial plant
that our local house wrens have taken over. Wrens, I've learned, are fiercely
territorial, and if they feel themselves being crowded, they will destroy the
eggs of competing species of birds.

In the spring Daddy wren establishes his territory. Then there's the ro-
mantic and noisy music of their mating. I love to hear the chatter between
Mom and Dad as they watch over their young, and the cheep-cheep of the
newly hatched eggs. Wrens are diligent caretakers of their young, but something happened the other day that taught me just how generous they can be.

My daughter, Carmen, came into the house distraught at the sight of a
baby wren that had fallen out of another nest. She figured she could put the
little thing into the nest in the artificial plant, but I wasn't so sure. I reminded her that some mother birds will abandon their young if a foreign
entity enters its nest. Never mind, she was determined to give this baby a
chance to live. We grabbed newspaper and gently placed the wounded bird
in the nest just outside my window.

I found myself doing something I hadn't done since childhood—I
prayed for that little bird with all my might! Happily, the next morning I
saw one of the wrens circling the nest and going about its business of feeding the flock. Then the other parent joined in. I could see the tiny beaks
reaching up for the food. Baby bird had been happily adopted.

This experience made me think about how generous God is with us. Our
sins caused us to fall from our self-made nest, and we were near death. But
Jesus came by and gently picked us up and put us back into His nest and nurtured us back to health with the combined strength and tenderness of a
mother and father. He didn't care if we fell from a distant nest—He took us
in and mothered and fathered us until we were strong enough to fly.

The analogy breaks down here, however. Unlike those baby wrens, we
can never fly on our own. God's parenting continues throughout our lives.
Christians can fly only if they continue to depend on their heavenly
Parents—Father, Son, and Holy Spirit. When we forget that, we fall out
of the nest and have to learn how to fly again, sustained daily by God's
everlasting wings.

**Lourdes E. Morales-Gudmundsson**

# Just in Time

*Be anxious for nothing, but in everything by prayer and supplication, with thanksgiving, let your requests be made known to God. Phil. 4:6, NKJV.*

WE WERE OUT OF VACUUM BAGS, and I needed some right away. I couldn't compromise the Thursday cleaning in preparation for church. Since my husband was taking the twins to their respective jobs, that meant I had to get across town to the store before it closed at 5:00. I had a meeting at 3:30, which I anticipated would go until 4:30. If all went well, I'd have time.

However, when I arrived at my destination I discovered that the parking lot was closed, so I headed to a familiar spot about three blocks away. I attended my meeting and rushed out of the building about 4:35.

I prayed that God would get me to the store in time. While I was waiting to cross the street, a friend drove up. He was on the way home and had just picked his wife up at work, so they gave me a ride to my car. *Wow*, I thought, *I didn't specifically pray for a ride to my car, but God knew what I needed just when I needed it.*

The pressure was on as I had 15 minutes to get to the store. I maneuvered through the traffic while maintaining the speed limit, and my heavenly Father coordinated the lights just right. At 4:51 I stopped at a red light, but I kept on praying. I didn't feel anxious at all, as I knew that I would make it. And I did, with a few minutes to spare.

This incident showed me that God works out every detail to meet my needs. Everything worked in harmony so that I could arrive at my destination quickly and safely. That was not by chance but by design. God takes care of not only the big hurdles in our lives, but the little ones as well. Sometimes we think that we don't want to bother God with little things, as He is busy, so we wait until we have something major—like cancer—to call on Him.

God is interested in every aspect of my life, and for God nothing is too insignificant when it comes to me. He provides parking when I need it, a phone call to cheer me up when I am down, laughter to take away sadness, calm after the storm, and devotionals such as these to remind me that I am not alone. God feels the same way about you and will come through for you, too, just in time.

**Sharon Long (Brown)**

# Stretching Class

*He came to that which was his own, but his own did not receive him.*
*John 1:11, NIV.*

WHEN I REACHED ADULTHOOD, I became conscious of the necessity to do physical exercise. Since I don't have enough self-discipline to carry out these exercises on my own, I became a member of a sports gym. One morning during the stretching class I heard the song "Jesu, Joy of Man's Desiring." This composition was very well known to me—I even know how to play it on the piano. In fact, it was one of the first songs that I learned to play, and I always thought it was very beautiful. As I paid attention to it, I realized that the instruments harmonized perfectly, making listening to it something sublime. In the back of my mind only one phrase echoed and repeated throughout the song: "Jesu, joy of man's desiring."

I asked myself if Jesus was really my joy, my encouragement, my only hope. As the song continued to play, I thought about how often I've put Jesus aside in my life, how easily I forget to be thankful to Him for everything good that He gives me. How many times I forget to share my life with Him. It's easy to leave Jesus, and all spiritual things, in second place. I imagined Jesus making the salvation of the world a priority and coming to the world because of His love for people—to give you and me the joy of salvation; and then He was rejected by people. I remembered John 1:10, 11, which states, "He was in the world, and though the world was made through him, the world did not recognize him. He came to that which was his own, but his own did not receive him." Jesus came to offer the most precious gift that exists throughout the universe—eternal life—which had been lost by humankind. But people did not desire Him, did not recognize Him as their Savior.

Why is Christ not our greatest joy, the hope that sustains us in the midst of suffering, the thought that keeps us alive and vibrant? A warm feeling filled my heart as I realized that there, with my classmates doing exercises, God had sent me such a simple yet beautiful message. The fact that God is concerned about teaching little lessons in common moments of life made me understand that He is concerned about me more than I had imagined.

Each day since then, I have sought to make Jesus the reason for my joy. Is Jesus your joy as well?

**Iani Dias Lauer-Leite**

# Fathomless Billows of Love

*And I am convinced that nothing can ever separate us from [God's] love. Death can't, and life can't. The angels can't, and the demons can't. Our fears for today, our worries about tomorrow, and even the powers of hell can't keep God's love away. Whether we are high above the sky or in the deepest ocean, nothing in all creation will ever be able to separate us from the love of God that is revealed in Christ Jesus our Lord. Rom. 8:38, 39, NLT.*

ONCE AGAIN I felt that old stab of inadequacy. My peace of mind was disturbed; I felt let down all evening. The next morning as I read my New Testament chapter, the last two verses were today's text. I realized how appropriate they were to my state of mind. If I really was loved by Jesus and felt His love, then nothing could take away my peace. I needed again to apply His love to me in my heart, not just my head.

Just as this was sinking in, some words floated into my head. At first I couldn't place their origin: "fathomless billows of love." Then I remembered the title of the song: "Wonderful Peace." Finding our hymnal, I wrote out all the verses, meditating quietly on the words. All my life I've sung this song, but those last words of the chorus had never sunk in. Fathomless billows of love—what are they? Fathomless means something that can't be understood; a billow is like a cloud or fog bank being blown over me. God's love for me is that strong, that deep, that enduring? I can't comprehend it. And nothing will separate it from me. Nothing can take it away. I began to feel its intensity in my heart. I let those fathomless billows of love pour over me, bathing me in their warmth and abundance. The tears were also abundant as I applied the love of my heavenly Daddy and Jesus Christ to myself.

The second verse spoke deeply to me: "What a treasure I have in this wonderful peace, buried deep in my innermost soul, so secure that no power can mine it away, while the years of eternity roll!" And the last verse is so relevant to my current situation: "Weary soul, without gladness or comfort or rest, passing down the rough pathway of time! Make the Savior your friend ere the shadows grow dark; O accept of this peace so sublime."

*Thank You, Jesus, for Your Word that reminds me of Your personal love for me. And thank You for fathomless billows of love.*

**Becki Knobloch**

# A Glow on My Face

*When thou passeth through the waters, I will be with thee; and through the rivers, they shall not overflow thee: when thou walkest through the fire, thou shalt not be burned; neither shall the flame kindle upon thee. Isa. 43:2.*

A FEW YEARS AGO I was scheduled for outpatient surgery. Honestly, I was terrified—the future seemed uncertain. The lab report indicated that there was a possibility of cancer. The word *cancer* struck fear in me. Several times I asked myself, *What if the results come back, and I have cancer or some other debilitating disease? What will happen to me?*

I was scheduled to be at the hospital by 6:00 a.m. After getting settled in the outpatient room, I pulled out my devotional book and opened it to the reading for the day. To my amazement, the title read, "Lord, Help Me!" Deep in my heart that was my cry. The text said: "He shall call upon me, and I will answer him: I will be with him in trouble; I will deliver him, and honour him" (Ps. 91:15). When I read this verse, I felt as if God's hand had reached down and touched me. I felt a calm assurance—all would be well. His words were comforting and stated clearly that He would rescue and honor me. Immediately I experienced a feeling of peace that only He could give. My fears and anxieties dissipated. My God had heard my cry for help.

Just before I was wheeled into the operating room, two church leaders came to pray with me and my husband. It felt good to know they cared and had taken the time to come to the hospital to assure me of their love, prayers, and support. One of them remarked, "Do you know that you have a glow on your face?" When I looked in the mirror nearby, it was quite visible. My loving heavenly Father had placed it there.

The surgery went well, and doctor assured me that there was no evidence of cancer. I shouted, "Thank You, Jesus. To God be the glory!"

When you face what seem like insurmountable challenges, I encourage you to trust God to see you through; He specializes in the impossible. He promises that when we call upon Him, He will answer us; He will be with us in trouble and will rescue and honor us. He is a God of miracles, and nothing is too hard for Him. I pray that His sweet peace and the warmth of His love will fill your soul today.

**Shirley C. Iheanacho**

# My Best Angel Through Him

*Your word is a lamp to my feet and a light to my path.*
*Ps. 119:105, NKJV.*

R-R-I-ING! R-R-I-ING! Very early in the morning I pressed the buzzer for our worship in the women's dormitory. After worship I cooked, cleaned, and swept around the dorm. This was my routine as a working student. For me there could be no wasted time—every moment counted!

During our Week of Prayer, our speaker, Pastor Abdolmasin, stayed in the guest house, next to our dormitory. He loves to jog every morning, as other people do. One morning before his run I greeted him, "Good morning, sir!"

He replied, "Good morning to you." As he came nearer he extended his hand, and I was surprised when he put something in my hand. It was money—a tip! After shaking hands, he took off running. I ran after him to return the money, but he said, "*Sa iyo na yan*" (that's yours).

Then I saw his keys fall, so I picked up the keys and said, "Sir, your bunch of keys." Again he replied, "*Sa iyo na yan*," thinking I was still trying to return the money. I put both the keys and money in my hand and held them out to him. The chain of keys hanging under my hand was the only thing he took, and off he ran again. I couldn't do anything then about the money, so I just shouted, "Thank you, sir!"

A few mornings later we saw each other again. I again thanked him for his kindness. He cheered me and gave me encouraging words. He told me to keep up the good work and to be patient and faithful in everything I did. "You know, you're a very industrious woman. Keep that attitude. Study well until you graduate. And, most of all, trust God always and He will be with you, guide you, and help you in all you do." He added, "I hope we will meet again,"

"Hopefully, sir, we will meet again." I answered. "Thank you very much for your words of encouragement; they will inspire me as I continue my studies. Thank you for touching my life!"

As we meet people, especially those who serve us from day to day, what an influence we can have on them. A tip for service rendered is good, of course. But kind words and encouragement can go a long way as well. Our words can make a difference!

**Michelle Engcoy Golle**

# The Palmer Method

*Whatsoever thy hand findeth to do, do it with thy might. Eccl. 9:10.*

IN ELEMENTARY SCHOOL we learned to write using the Palmer method. I can still remember George Race, who made his rounds to the public schools to teach us the special method made famous by Austin Norman Palmer (1859-1927). Palmer invented "muscular movement writing," which stressed the importance of physical training, correct posture, relaxing exercises, movement practice, and pen holding. A person could write for hours without his arm or fingers becoming weary or cramped. I remember Mr. Race putting a penny on the back of my writing hand to be sure I was taking his teaching seriously. The penny didn't fall off, so I must have been writing correctly enough to suit him.

Early in United States history few Americans knew how to read, let alone write. Those who could write made their own pens from quills, their own ink from oak tree galls, and their own "pounce" from fine powder to prevent ink from spreading. But what beautiful writing they produced! The American calligrapher Platt Rogers Spencer (1800-1864) was responsible for the elegant age of ornamental penmanship known as Spencerian script. The golden age of beautiful penmanship ran along with a sentimental part of the Victorian era. But gradually the artistic script, with its lavish flourishes and shadings and scrolls, was to be replaced with a rapid and easier writing style that was more businesslike.

And that is where the Palmer method took over. By 1900 the Palmer method had been accepted in public schools, and I learned to write with arm movement which was more relaxing, with a correct posture, and the correct way to hold a pen—all of which I promptly forgot over the years. I'm glad George Race is not around to see my penmanship as it is today! We now live in a world in which people aren't concerned about their handwriting. Some of it is hard to decipher. I don't know when the Palmer method was no longer available in elementary schools, but perhaps it should be brought back for the sake of proper handwriting by the masses.

One of my daughters has mastered the art of calligraphy (script, if you will). It is a talent she uses to reach lives and to share the love of her Creator. God blesses each one of us with talents of one kind or another. There is always some gift that can be used for the Master.

**Laurie Dixon-McClanahan**

# My God Is Incredible

*Before they call I will answer; while they are still speaking
I will hear. Isa. 65:24, NIV.*

BECAUSE OF A DISABILITY, my husband retired at 30 years of
age. We decided to live near Northeast Brazil College, where he
could study theology and our school-aged children could benefit
from the environment.

My husband's disability became more serious, and his difficulties in
getting around became greater. So we felt the need to acquire a vehicle.
He had limitations, so I was the only one who would be able to drive—
and I had to learn how.

I faced the challenge, and we bought a car. I was teaching two shifts and
working on my master's degree in the city. I needed to take the driving theory and practice classes before taking the driving test. Everything had to be
done within six months, before we moved to our hometown. I had many
things to do and little time to practice driving, even though I was very nervous about taking the driving test.

I failed the test twice and was discouraged. The third test was scheduled—time was running out. At the testing location I felt better to see
friends there. When I was directed to the room to get my registration card,
the employee expressed surprise at seeing me. She said, "Why are you here
if you already passed?" I explained that there must have been some mistake,
because I hadn't passed on my second test and had rescheduled the test.
She was upset and said in a low voice, "Go take the test, but you have
already passed. The request for your driver's license has already been sent
to the capital city and will be arriving with the next lot of mail. And do not
tell anyone about this."

I left the registration area almost skipping with joy and assurance, because I knew that this could only have been the work of God so that I could
gain confidence. However, I didn't follow orders, and soon told my friends.
My minister friend encouraged my confidence, stating, "If God has already
passed you on the test, there is no man who will fail you today."

I left, filled with joy and gratitude to God. He is good, and He answers
us while we are still asking. May God increase our confidence and faith so
that we can be living witnesses in little and big things that the Lord has
done for us.

**Marilene Araujo Rangel Cunha**

# Hospital Drama

*For I will restore health unto thee, and I will heal thee of thy wounds, saith the Lord. Jer. 30:17.*

I FELT LIKE ONE OF THE DOCTORS OR NURSES. The long hospital corridors had become all too familiar: stretchers, wheelchairs, moans and groans everywhere. Bloodstains were no longer repulsive. Another sick student was rushed to the hospital. The porters responded quickly, and I hastened to keep up with the stretcher as they wheeled her down the long corridors. The swift hands of the nurses moved with urgency, and the patient soon had life-giving liquid flowing through her veins.

When I worked as a residence hall dean, some students in my care were determined to fight the odds and press their way through the education barriers, which were more difficult because of their disabilities. Their illnesses were many and varied and sometimes required leaving in the dead of night to seek help at the hospital wards. There were often long hours of waiting, holding hands to comfort and cheer the sick ones.

People go to the hospital for different reasons, some because of illness, others to visit the sick and ailing, and still others to pray for and comfort the ill. Going to the hospital can leave one with feelings of sadness and bring on a certain amount of burden. Not everyone likes to visit the hospital nor even take care of those who are sick. But someone has to care.

The parents were not left out when it came to the well-being of the students, but the immediate responsibility was ours. We cared with God's guiding hands, sometimes forgetting our needs and desires. Jesus served communities and individuals, often with much drama, as in the case of the sick man being lowered through the roof (Luke 5:17-26). As God's children, we may have different needs and they may take on an earthly flavor, but we have to be mindful of our needs and desires and take care not to neglect them. As we serve others we can do so with gladness of heart because our needs are met while we extend the hand of love and care.

Hospital dramas are real; the well-being of others and their lives are at stake. The drama was over when the sick student had been attended to and when Jesus touched the sick man lying on his bed. Our heavenly Father has a plan for each of us. Why don't we trust Him with our hopes, dreams, desires, and well-being today?

**Elizabeth Ida Cain**

# Take Heed

*Take heed, watch and pray; for you do not know when the time is. Mark 13:33, NKJV.*

THE DAY'S TEMPERATURE had soared beyond 90° F (32° C)—a perfect day for an ice-cream cone. But because of my desire to improve my health through diet and exercise, storing ice cream in my refrigerator was not an option. I decided to go to the store and purchase some. Everything worked well until it was time to return home. I got into my car, turned the ignition, and, to my utter surprise and horror, the battery was dead. *This cannot be happening,* I thought. *My car is fairly new, and the battery should have a longer life.* I tried again, and the same thing happened.  I had a problem!

Suddenly I had a priority shift. No longer was the ice cream my focus. Within a couple of minutes, getting my car to work had become my main priority. I enlisted the help of a young man in a new pickup truck to give me a jump start, and he willingly assisted a damsel in distress. "I wanted some ice cream but didn't want a supply in my refrigerator, so I came on a quick errand to get some," I explained to him.  We both laughed at my predicament.

In telling my brother about the incident, he informed me that the battery had indeed given me subtle warnings that it was going bad, but I hadn't been tuned in, and so I had missed the warning signs.

*Wow!* I thought of the text for today and wondered about my spiritual life. Are there times in my life that I'm actually disconnected from the Source and not even aware of it? Am I so busy that I have unconsciously tuned out the Holy Spirit's promptings to get my life in order? Am I ignoring the signs of Christ's coming? Am I so busy with living that witnessing about the Second Coming has not been given priority? Am I going to be caught unaware because I have once again missed the warning signs?

*Father, I know there are times I become so preoccupied with life that preparing for Your coming is not given first priority. From outward appearances everything may seem fine, but my spiritual life needs recharging. Help me to be so tuned in to Your Word that I remain connected to the main Source of power. Please forgive me. From this day forward, help me to take heed so that I will not be caught unaware.*

**Andrea A. Bussue**

# Please Replace the Lamp

*Your word is a lamp to my feet and a light for my path. Ps. 119:105, NIV.*

A GROUP OF US WERE GATHERED at a conference center for a three-day seminar. The setting was beautiful—mountains, surrounded by tall pine trees and clear air to breathe, far from the distractions of the city. We were there not only to learn how we could better serve the people in our communities, but also to share ideas and plans.

We began each morning with an excellent speaker, the retired speaker of Faith for Today, who inspired us with devotionals such as "I Saw the Lord," based on Isaiah 6:1. During the day presenters from different parts of the United States illustrated their talks on the projection screen. But there was always a distraction—the words at the bottom of the screen: "Please replace the lamp." I don't know much about such things, so I wondered if the screen might suddenly go dark. Maybe they would replace the lamp, and the next day would be better. But no, there was that annoying message again the next day. Even the beautiful and uplifting special musical selections by a sister duo didn't entirely cancel out the distraction. For the entire time of the seminar the message was always there. But the screen never went dark. For me, at least, it kept my mind from receiving the total impact of the main messages.

Then I began to think about what message I'm projecting in my relationship with others as I try to let Christ's love shine out. Is there something that is a distraction that is keeping the message from getting through? Maybe I'm really thinking more of myself—my likes and dislikes, my desires, my problems—than the needs of those I'm try to help. Sometimes I should be just a good listener rather than try to solve the problems of those I meet along the way. Even in the best of settings and most beautiful surrounding, I can't reach my goal unless Jesus is the center. Replacing the lamp that focuses on me with one that focuses on God's Word will guide my feet so that I can be a help rather than a distraction to others.

*Dear God, please help me to study Your Word so that it will be a lamp to my feet and light to my path today. May the world see Jesus in me is my prayer.*

**Betty J. Adams**

# The Car

*If you believe, you will receive whatever you ask for in prayer. Matt. 21:22, NIV.*

I NEEDED A CAR. I was tired of dealing with rude cab drivers, and buses were out of the question. So I prayed as I watched the traffic go by. Actually, it was more like a complaint: "God, look at all these nice cars! Why don't You give me one?"

As soon as a national holiday came up and my husband had some free time, I convinced him to help me visit some used-car dealerships to find a vehicle. As we drove around, we noticed that all the lots were closed—after all, it was a holiday. But I kept praying and telling him to drive on.

After a while my husband stopped the car across the street from a huge lot. He tried to restart the engine, but the car refused to budge. Maybe it had run out of gas—but the needle wasn't on empty. So he decided to walk to the nearest gas station while I sat in the car and waited—and prayed. From where I was seated I could get a good look at the cars on the lot. They looked nice, and the prices I could make out were reasonable. Now, if only the place were open!

Suddenly a car drove up, and two men and a woman jumped out. They seemed very interested in a sedan, so one of them pulled out his cell phone, looked up at the sign, and apparently called the sedan's owner, who drove up about five minutes later. He let them in so that they could take a closer look at the cars.

Well, now I was praying harder. I wanted my husband to get back before they closed again. Eventually he showed up with the gasoline, and I told him what was happening across the street. He decided to drive around the block to make sure his car was working again. When we got back, the lot was still open. We walked in and bought a car. The people who had made the call didn't buy a car—God had simply put them in the right place at the right time to participate in a miracle He had designed just for me.

Great things happen when we pray. As it says in John 16:24: "Ask and you will receive, and your joy will be complete" (NIV): I encourage you today to place all your needs in God's hands. He'll work things out for your good.

**Dinorah Blackman-Williams**

# Answered Prayer

*And we know that all things work together for good to them that love God,*
*to them who are the called according to his purpose. Rom. 8:28.*

MY GREAT-NIECE, Leah, had come for a visit. She hadn't been back to
Michigan for 16 years. We were so excited to have her come, and had
planned to do a lot of things. Of course, the time was short—she came on
Wednesday and was to leave the next Tuesday.

My children, Nancy and Terry (her cousins), wanted us to come to East
Jordan to see them and their families We were planning to drive to the
Mackinac Bridge, which is about an hour from their house, then on over to
Mackinac Island. Leah and I decided to drive up Thursday afternoon, and
then the next day all of us would drive on up to the bridge. After we arrived, they told us that the weather report wasn't very good—there was
supposed to be a big storm and lots of rain the next day.

When I went to bed, I prayed, "Lord, please have the rain hold off
and have it be a nice day. This is the only day that Leah can do this."
Well, God is good—all the time. The next morning the sun was shining,
and we all took off for the bridge and the island. Terry and Nancy and
their children, Tiffany and Bethany, and Leah and I went across the
bridge, and found our way to the boat that went over to the island. We
had a great day with beautiful weather. Lots of fun! We all took the famous carriage ride and shopped.

That night it rained, and Sabbath was a little rainy, but Leah got to go
to church to hear her cousin, Pastor Terry, preach. We enjoyed a wonderful
fellowship meal afterward, too.

Sunday we visited my daughter Kathy's horse show. Monday we went
to Frankenmuth to see that little German village. We had a great time that
ended all too soon, and the weather was great all the time.

On Tuesday Leah was back on the plane to Washington State. Times
like these are always too short. I'm homesick for heaven, where we won't
have to cut our visits short and we can see our loved ones anytime, and we
won't have to say goodbye. We must be ready for the Lord to come and
take us home. There we can have our loved ones near to spend eternity
with Jesus!

*Lord, make us want to be ready for Your soon appearing.*

**Anne Elaine Nelson**

# It Is More Blessed

*There is one who scatters, yet increases more; and there is one who withholds more than is right, but it leads to poverty. Prov. 11:24, NKJV.*

IN MY HOME CHURCH IN GERMANY there was a young couple from Bulgaria who came to my hometown to study at the local university. Moving from a comparatively poor country in Eastern Europe to a rather rich one in the western part of the continent, they had to live on a very tight budget. When their first child was born, I often wondered how they managed to make ends meet. Without the regular support of the church family it probably wouldn't have been possible for them to survive.

I once visited their home, and their daughter, now 4 years old, wanted so much to give me something—soap from Bulgaria, a small decorative item from their country, and some other things. It was hard for me to refuse. So in order for me to take the gifts home more easily, she decided to put everything into a plastic bag for me—in which she also put a $20 bill! At this moment I became very firm and tried to make it clear to her that I was not going to accept this money. Eventually I had to take it out of the bag and give it back to her mother.

This small incident made a great impression on me. This couple really struggled with their finances, yet they found that "it is more blessed to give than to receive" (Acts 20:35). Who else could have taught their daughter such kind behavior?

Have you ever felt as though you've earned more money than you actually need to pay your bills and meet your daily needs? I have, and I can clearly state that it never made me happy. In fact, I came to find out that I had gotten very much focused on my wealth. I didn't change my lifestyle, and thus I didn't need the extra money, but I realized that it had become more and more important to me. My money increased, but my happiness didn't. How much more rewarding and satisfying it is to share our wealth with less-fortunate people and spend it for the advancement of the gospel! I would not say that it is wrong to have some savings, if possible, but it can become a stumbling block if we focus too much on our possessions. Let's ask the Lord today how, and what, He wants us to invest for His kingdom.

**Daniela Weichhold**

# Frustration to Joy

*Even when you are old I will be the same. And even when your hair turns white, I will help you. I will take care of what I have made. I will carry you, and will save you. Isa. 46:4, NLV.*

*WHY DID I CHOOSE THIS BOOK to provide my musical selections for the evening?* I wondered. It was my monthly opportunity to provide dinner music for my local Christian women's club, but I was encountering many obstacles. My nearly four-score, cataract-shadowed eyes made the pages a blur. Even though I'd asked the Lord to lead me, the book I was using was technically more difficult and of finer print than normal. The somewhat dim light of the restaurant wasn't helping either. Since the last meeting a major low note on the piano had dipped about a quarter tone in pitch, which jarred my mind every time I accidentally used it.

During my first selection a woman I didn't recognize stood beside me, singing softly. Three times I missed a melody note. On the last time around I laughed and said, "I finally made it." I was truly pleading with my friend Jesus to help me get through the evening without disappointing Him.

At the conclusion of the program I greeted the speaker, who was the sweet woman who'd stood by me earlier. As I was apologizing for my less-than-best performance, another woman, who had sat across the table from me, came up to tell me how much she had appreciated my music, especially "Climb Every Mountain." Her daughter had come into her room that morning, and they had shared a special time together listening to that very inspiring song.

As she was telling her story the vocal soloist for the evening moved close to share another incident with me. While she and her mother were together that very morning her mother kept humming a tune, but she couldn't remember the words for it. The daughter was delighted to tell me that "Wouldn't It Be Lovely," another tune from the fine-print book, was the tune she and her mother had relished singing together that morning.

I knew now why I'd chosen the very book that was most difficult for me but ministered most deeply to these two people. Even though my hairs are gray and my eyes dim, I learned that God can still carry me, help me, and rescue me. "Even when I am old and gray, do not forsake me, O God, till I declare your power to the next generation" (Ps. 71:18, NIV).

**Donna Lee Sharp**

# The Bitter Cup

*He went a little farther and fell on His face, and prayed, saying, "O My Father, if it is possible, let this cup pass from Me; nevertheless, not as I will, but as You will." Matt. 26:39, NKJV.*

I WAS ABOUT 10 OR 11, and was convinced that I had cancer. Puberty had started changing my body, and as I was investigating some of these changes I noticed lumps in my breasts. Immediately fearful of the worst, I told no one of my discovery. As I tried to figure out what to do, I thought of the "bush tea" that my mother used to brew for her asthma. I had heard her say that it was good for a lot of ailments. *Would it cure cancer, too?* She usually kept some stored in the freezer. I retrieved the frozen tea and thawed it out. I was certain it wouldn't work if I put anything else in it, so I didn't sweeten it. The first sip was absolutely awful! It was *bitter*. But I had to drink it. In my mind the alternative was very bleak. I set my mind to it and gulped down the entire cupful of bitter tea.

More than 20 years later I look back on that experience with a bemused smile. At the time, however, I was convinced that having the undesirable brew was the only way to remain healthy. It was worth the price to me.

As Jesus' death on the cross loomed before Him, it was something very undesirable to Him. One author describes Jesus' impending fate as a "bitter cup." He saw His own separation from God as a result of paying for our sins. The Bible records that He asked that it be removed from Him, if possible. But Jesus was able to look beyond the horror of the moment and focus on the benefits. My life. Your life.

The Bible tells us that Jesus made His mind up to fulfill His purpose for coming to this earth. "He . . . prayed, saying, 'O My Father, if this cup cannot pass away from Me unless I drink it, Your will be done' " (Matt. 26:42, NKJV). For Him the benefits far outweighed the horror of the most self-sacrificing act ever recorded.

As cute as it may seem in hindsight, my experience with the "cancer-curing" tea has made me more appreciative of what Christ did for me. I was looking after my own interests, yet it was difficult to swallow what I thought was going to cure me. Jesus had never sinned, yet He shouldered the sins of the world when He went to the cross. What selflessness! What love!

**Abigail Blake Parchment**

# An Angel Neighbor

*Before they call, I will answer; and while they are still speaking,*
*I will hear. Isa. 65:24, NKJV.*

I KNOW THAT even before I call, God promises to answer. God has the foreknowledge of my past, present, and future needs, and He puts me in places and situations in which He can manifest His tender care toward me. And so it was, a few years ago, when I moved to Florida, and God gave me a home beside an angel neighbor.

Florida lawns can be pretty, but they require a lot of hard, backbreaking work to maintain. Year after year I dreamed of a beautiful green lawn with a rose garden—to no avail. I spent many dollars and much time and energy plugging the bare spots, putting down sod, weeding and watering, just to repeat it the next year and be rewarded with bare spots or dried-up grass. I was told that I needed to start the grooming process all over again—plugging, sodding, weeding, and watering. The dream of a well-manicured garden seemed to elude me.

It was at one of these times that my angel neighbor appeared. I had gone out once again to purchase sod, hoping to increase my chance of realizing the dream for a lush green lawn. This time, however, I had a back problem. I discovered that the easy part was purchasing the sod and having it loaded into my car. The problem was unloading it. There was no one there to help, and my aching back wouldn't let me. *How will I manage?* I asked myself as I was driving home.

My concern deepened as I turned onto my street that Friday afternoon. I cried out to my heavenly Father. "Please, Lord. Send someone to assist me in unloading the sod." I had no idea from whence this help would come.

I drove into my driveway with a burdened heart. I had expected my heavenly Father to empower me with supernatural strength or to send an unseen angel to help. But nothing like that happened. Instead, my neighbor Dora turned up with a simple question. "Madge, would you like some help unloading that sod?" My fervent "Yes" put her to work immediately.

My angel neighbor helped me unload the sod. Then she not only cleaned the trunk of my car but also swept the driveway messed up by moving the sod. Talk about a God who takes care of the little details of our lives and responds to our needs before we even call!

*Father, I love You. Give me strength to trust You totally. I will call*
*on You.*

**Madge S. May**

# Security in Him

*And thou shalt be secure, because there is hope. Job 11:18.*

THINGS WERE GOING PRETTY WELL in the family. I had gone through the grieving process after the loss of my mother. My oldest daughter had decided to move down South onto our land. Now we would have the privilege of watching some of our grandchildren mature. My husband, who is legally sightless, would have that extra "muscle" as well as some extra sets of eyes.

However, we know Satan, that old serpent, is very busy trying to destroy the family. One beautiful spring day as my husband and I went into town, we stopped to pick up the mail. To our surprise, there was a letter from Social Security saying we owed them thousands of dollars—and they wanted it now. I chuckled and said, "These people must have the wrong Johnsons; there's got to be a mistake." But a couple weeks later we received another letter, demanding we send the money inside their self-addressed envelope, or call and request a waiver. I quickly got on the phone and started making calls. Social Security claimed they had overpaid my husband, giving me the dates and amounts. I asked them to send me the forms for a waiver. There was so much paperwork! We filled out all the details and sent it back; then we had to redo it all three weeks later, along with additional information. Two weeks later we received a letter saying my husband's Social Security would not resume for two and a half years. So, for two and a half years we had very little income—with the same bills, living expenses, and medical bills.

At first we were devastated. I cried and prayed! My answer came quickly. I heard, "I took care of you thus far; I will continue!" Then I remembered the words to a song: "I have never seen the righteous forsaken or His seed begging for bread"(see Ps. 37:25). I continued to work part-time and to pay my tithe faithfully. We kept up with our bills, cut back on wants, and concentrated on needs. Amazingly, it seemed as if we had much more than we'd ever had!

The Lord has truly blessed, and now we know what is meant in Malachi 3:10: "[See] if I will not open you the windows of heaven, and pour you out a blessing, that there shall not be room enough to receive it."

You too can find security in Him.

Elaine J. Johnson

# The Best Bargain

*Come ye, buy, and eat. Isa. 55:1.*

DO YOU LIKE BARGAINS? I do! At one time they were a necessity for us, as I was a stay-at-home mom, and my husband's ministerial salary was modest, to say the least. Finding a bargain was ingrained in our children from an early age. When Tim was still a preschooler and we were spending the summer at the camp of which my husband, Ted, was the director, there was an item Tim had his heart set on. He asked, "When we get home, if it's on sale, can I get it?" I don't remember what it was that he wanted or whether or not he got it, but even at that age he had learned to look for a sale.

Such habits have stayed with us, even in our retirement years. Each week I go over the flyers from the supermarkets, taking note of the things we need, the coupons we might have that we could use, and the place to get the best prices before we go on our weekly shopping trip. I am still looking for bargains.

Earlier this year I was trying to find a suitable dress for our granddaughter's wedding. Yes, our boys grew up, and Tim was now to be a father-in-law. One pretty outfit was not my size, so the department store helpfully ordered it from another of their stores. Unfortunately, it did not fit well, and had to be returned. Having unsuccessfully looked in the likely stores in our town, we drove to a town some distance away. This time, success! I found a lovely dress and jacket—on sale for half price. The one I had returned cost about twice as much. A few days later I found another outfit that was suitable for church, also half price. It was almost the same as the buy-one-get-one-free deals at the grocery stores. I was truly blessed!

As I think about bargains, it occurs to me that there is an incredible offer that far surpasses the double or triple coupons redeemed at the supermarket, or even the "freebies" that we might occasionally run across. We read about it in Isaiah 55:1: "Ho, every one that thirsteth, come ye to the waters, and he that hath no money; come ye, buy, and eat; yea, come, buy wine and milk without money and without price."

Yes, God has given us the best—and it costs us nothing. He not only cares for us each day, but He has given us His grace. As a gift. Now, that's what I call a real bargain!

**Mary Jane Graves**

# Basket of Blessings

*I was young and now I am old, yet I have never seen the righteous forsaken or their children begging bread. Ps. 37:25, NIV.*

RIGHT AFTER WE WERE MARRIED, my husband and I worked in a rural mission school in the south of Brazil. During the two years we were there, we learned much and worked together with wonderful people who helped us immensely. Our small apartment was near the social room, the church, and the local cemetery. In this cemetery rested great men who had taken the gospel message of Jesus' return to this region.

My husband took college classes at night and taught classes in the school during the day. Many nights I stayed alone with our little son and prayed until my husband returned, because he had to walk five miles (eight kilometers) to our apartment from the place he got off the bus. Sometimes when it had rained he couldn't get home at all because the river overflowed and no one was able to cross. At these times he would have to spend the night on the other side of the river in the home of friends who kindly took him in.

God never abandoned us. We many times experienced the fulfillment of His promise, "The angel of the Lord encamps around those who fear him, and he delivers them" (Ps. 34:7, NIV).

When the end of the month arrived, we often experienced difficulties, because by that time our salary had been totally used. These were days of doing without; we prayed a lot for God's help and His protection.

One day one of the individuals who lived in the neighborhood visited us and promised to give us a basket containing enough food to last us the rest of the month. The only condition was that we weren't to tell anyone about his donation. Faithfully we fulfilled this promise. After all, he was the "angel" God had sent to help us. On the set date he came very early with a lovely basket filled with food. Among the things he brought was even a package of cookies for our son.

I praise God, because at the times of greatest need He used His children to help us and to make us strong workers in His cause. You also can always trust in God; He will never abandon His children who are faithful to Him.

**Marlene Esteves Garcia**

# Miracle Photographs

*And whatsoever we ask, we receive of him, because we keep his*
*commandments, and do those things that are pleasing in his sight.*
*1 John 3:22.*

It is fun to go through old photo albums and stroll down memory lane. My oldest daughter was married in 1983, and whenever I look at those wedding pictures I thank my heavenly Father for His miracles.

My youngest daughter and the youngest brother of my son-in-law attended the same college. They were best man and maid of honor at the wedding. We needed more room than our small church could provide for the reception, so it was held at a larger church, at which I worked as a nursery attendant. Many pictures were taken to capture the wedding and reception highlights, to give us wonderful memories of the occasion.

After the honeymoon the bride and groom took up residence in a small apartment near a high school in his home state. My daughter mailed the album of wedding proofs to me so that I could choose the ones I would like to have for my own album. I selected several beautiful pictures and mailed the album back as soon as possible by parcel post. Several days passed, and my daughter still hadn't received the proofs. Many prayers ascended to God for those precious wedding pictures.

One day my daughter's mother-in-law received a phone call from the police. They asked her if she had lost some pictures. Someone had turned in a picture album. The police found one picture of a car in the album in which the license plate was in full view. They tracked the license plate number and the car, which belonged to the best man. Further investigation led them to my son-in-law's parents. God is amazing! Miracles still happen!

Apparently someone, perhaps kids from the high school, found, opened, and then threw away the album when they found nothing of value to them. Someone else found the discarded album and gave it to the police, who followed through with the investigation. The miracle pictures were handled by the perpetrators, the person who found them, and the police. The Lord used many hands to answer our prayers of faith. No concerns are too small for the Lord when you pray in earnest.

**Retha McCarty**

# Homecoming

*And you will receive a rich welcome into the eternal kingdom*
*of our Lord and Savior Jesus Christ. 2 Peter 1:11, NIV.*

THE VOICE OF THE COPILOT on Philippine Airlines Flight 227 woke me from my reverie. He announced the approach of the aircraft to the airport; we would be landing in 15 minutes. My husband smiled at me as he sensed my excitement.

My mind tried to re-create familiar scenes, but all seemed to have been blurred by my 25-year absence. It had been a long time—and I realized that many things had changed as we drove the 31-mile (50-kilometer) stretch of road to my birthplace. Names of towns were the same, although a few new towns had sprung up in between old ones. There were more schools than I had remembered; some rice farmlands had been converted into mango and banana plantations. New landscapes and structures brought a sense of surprise, while old ones created a feeling of nostalgia. The fragrant smell of blossoming rice fields evoked memories of our late father, who loved the farm.

My mother, who had traveled all the way from the United States, welcomed us. She knew that we needed to have someone familiar to make our homecoming more enjoyable and comfortable. What would have I done without her whispering the names of the various relatives?

The site of our once-sturdy home brought tears to my eyes. This was where I had spent happy childhood days, and had endless memories of a carefree youth. But it was not as it used to be. The wooden floors and walls of the upper level were weather-beaten and fragile; wood panels and trusses had been eaten by termites. Evidence of years of neglect was seen everywhere.

All things considered, coming home was a wonderful experience— meeting relatives again; getting reacquainted with neighbors who had stories to tell about my childhood; feasting on fruits and vegetables I hadn't tasted for many years; and sharing the great things the Lord had done with our lives through serving Him. Even the pesky mosquitoes, moths, and other creepy insects of the night could not stifle the happiness and satisfaction within me.

I'm looking forward to another homecoming in which my heavenly Father awaits at the gate to usher me in. Then I'll hear Him say, "Welcome home, child. Welcome home."

**Mercy M. Ferrer**

# I Did It; I Am Sorry

*If you forgive those who sin against you, your heavenly Father will forgive you. Matt. 6:14, NLT.*

I DON'T HAVE ANY FORMAL EDUCATION in psychology, but during my long life's ups and downs I've picked up a few tips, one of which I pass on to you: If you've done wrong, don't let pride stop you from admitting it and saying you're sorry.

I stumbled across this truth when my primary school teacher reprimanded me for talking in class. I felt mortified, but when all the other kids went out to recess, I lingered behind to apologize. Not only did it make me feel better, but from then on our teacher-student relationship was exceptionally cordial.

A woman in an unhappy marriage once confided, "If only he'd say 'I'm sorry' when he tramps mud on my newly washed floor, or spills soy sauce on our best tablecloth. But he doesn't." Foolish man! If he'd only realize that an apology triggers an opposite reaction. Almost always the person wronged hastens to make the apologizer feel at ease by saying "Oh, it doesn't really matter; I'll wait till the mud dries and then sweep it up," or "Don't worry; bleach will take the stain out of the tablecloth."

On one occasion my friend Gloria conducted a Bible lesson in a small church. An attention-seeker kept interrupting to air his own views—at great length. At first she acknowledged his many contributions, then she ignored him. When that didn't work, she huffily told him to take over, and she sat down. By the time she reached home she realized that what she'd done was a childish display of pique. She felt thoroughly ashamed of herself and decided she must apologize. The problem was that she wouldn't be attending that particular church for a month. She had four long weeks in which to stew over that apology, to dread losing face, and to persuade herself that she really didn't need to say anything.

I suggested she pray about it, and she did. She stood up in front of that congregation, admitted her nastiness, and asked for forgiveness. "Not only did my burden vanish, but members came up to me later expressing their understanding and support," she marveled.

It's better not to make mistakes, sisters, but if you do, don't be afraid to apologize.

**Goldie Down**

# Is Mine Good Enough?

*What matters is something far more interior:*
*faith expressed in love. Gal. 5:6, Message.*

HIS LITTLE FINGERS worked diligently as he sat drawing and coloring the best picture ever. It was almost finished, almost perfect.

"Mommy, I need your help to make this just right. Help me write my name. I want to sign this and give it to Daddy," he said.

"Oh, sweetheart, that is beautiful. Your father is going to love it," I said as I stopped my work to write "Love, Richard" for him on another piece of paper for him to copy.

"No, Mommy, I want it to be perfect. You write it." It took a bit to explain to Richard that it would be much more special if he wrote it himself. Even if it wasn't perfect, it would make it more special to Daddy if he had done it himself. "You made the picture because you love Daddy, and that is what makes it so special. Daddy is going to love it because it comes from your heart." The joy in his little face as he gave it to his father that evening was reflected in his daddy's face.

The next day, in my quiet time, I was thinking about the program I was helping with for church. There were so many details to see to. I wanted everything to be just right. There didn't seem to be enough time or help to get everything just the way I wanted it. I was worried. Then in my mind God whispered to me in the quietness of that early morning. "Nancy, it's OK. I love you. I know you love Me. Give Me your best from a heart of love; that's what makes it special. It's the heart I care about."

Have you ever said no to God for fear that your effort might not be good enough? that it might not measure up to someone else's standard? that someone else might be able to do it better? God calls each of us to share our talent with Him each day. How freeing to know that God considers the heart, not the perfection of the work. He has already provided the perfection in His Son, Jesus Christ. And even beyond that, He promises to help us: "Not that we are competent in ourselves to claim anything for ourselves, but our competence comes from God" (2 Cor. 3:5, NIV). That means we can do anything He asks us to do. Furthermore, He says we can do all things through Christ, who strengthens us. Let go of your fear and do something for Jesus today. You know He will be pleased, and it will bring you happiness too!

**Nancy Camara**

# Hurricane Wilma's Blessing

*For great is his love toward us, and the faithfulness of the Lord
endures forever. Praise the Lord. Ps. 117:2, NIV.*

THE BUYERS OF MY HOUSE HAD set the closing date for November 15. I
knew I wouldn't be ready to move out by that date—I needed more time.
My real estate agent suggested renting back my house for another two to
four weeks. We negotiated back and forth, but the buyers wouldn't budge
on the amount they would charge me for rent. Two thousand dollars was
just more than I wanted to spend. I also knew I had to be in Tennessee by
the end of November to take care of business concerning my condo. So I
reluctantly I agreed to pay them $1,000 for two extra weeks.

Then during late October our area of southwest Florida was hit by
Hurricane Wilma. I'd been in Michigan the year before when Hurricane
Charley and a couple of others beat down on our area. So Wilma would be
my first major hurricane in the 20 years I'd lived in Florida. Before a hurricane you make all the necessary preparations, but you can never be really
prepared for the fierce wind and rain that hits you with all its force. Even at
that, I didn't suffer as much damage as many others did. Our electricity
went out and stayed out for two and a half days. There were two or three
loose tiles on my roof, some loose vents in the overhang of the roof. Part of
my mango tree snapped off, as well as small pine branches; and palmetto
branches cluttered the yard. The two tall palm trees in front of the house
were intact. The minor damage to the roof and soffits was easily fixed.

But the financial group buying my house was from Miami, and that
area had been hit by two storms. They were without power of any kind for
nearly two weeks—which effectively delayed the closing on my house. I
didn't have to pay the $1,000 rent for the two extra weeks I stayed in my
house, because now the closing was delayed until the end of November.

Not only did I offer the Lord prayers of thanksgiving, but I also shared
a good bit of the saved rent money with the Lord and His work.

"For the Lord is good and his love endures forever; his faithfulness
continues through all generations" (Ps. 100:5, NIV).

**Patricia Mulraney Kovalski**

# An Urgent Call

*But when he saw the wind boisterous, he was afraid; and beginning to sink, he cried, saying, Lord, save me. And immediately Jesus stretched forth his hand, and caught him, and said unto him, O thou of little faith, wherefore didst thou doubt? And when they were come into the ship, the wind ceased. Matt. 14:30-32.*

IT WAS PAST MIDNIGHT, and I was still awake but extremely tired. After a busy late evening in the office and on the residence hall floors, I finally managed to curl up in bed. The nights seemed so short, so I willed myself to sleep. It wasn't long before the telephone rang. It was one of our faithful residence hall advisors. "Dean, a young woman is not well; can you come quickly, please? We've tried home remedies and over-the-counter medications, but they aren't working." I was groggy, but with an "I'll be there" I hung up the telephone.

We spent about an hour ministering to the young woman with the advice and careful supervision of the campus nurse. Soon all was calm, and she was resting. I had forgotten that I was very tired, as the well-being of another drew my attention. With thankfulness in my heart I made my way back to the apartment to see if I could somehow get some rest. So many are the times we're in trouble, or so many things are going on around us, that we can't seem to cope. Often a simple cry to the Lord for help provides the answer. My experience as a residence hall dean taught me to depend on God constantly for His help in guiding young people.

That night we needed the Lord's intervention, and He answered our prayers. The burden was lessened by not having to take the sick one to the hospital. That night I also discovered that this was one of the many cases in which a few words of encouragement, a little comfort and cheer, make the difference. This had been an urgent call. "I need help; I am going down" was communicated by the sick one. Like Peter when he cried, "Lord, save me!" let us call unto God and trust Him to take care of us.

*Dear heavenly Father, forgive us in those off moments when we cry urgently and our reasons for calling seem so feeble. Help us to gain the blessings You have in store for us, and open our hearts to Your understanding and our eyes that we may see the way You would have us go.*

**Elizabeth Ida Cain**

# God Loves Me

*This is how God showed his love among us: he sent his one and only Son into the world that we might live through him. 1 John 4:9, NIV.*

I WANTED TO LEARN to become a literature evangelist, selling religious books door to door. I thought it might help me learn how to approach people and develop my self-confidence. So I joined a literature evangelist training program. I was very happy and really enjoyed myself, dedicating all of me to the work of God. I knew He would always guide me and lead me.

I ignored all the hardship, but then I began to feel pain in my left arm, near the wrist. One of my colleagues was very concerned and offered to massage my arm to relieve the pain. Many weeks passed, but the pain in my arm was still there. I decided to go back home.

I found other employment, but for five months I continued to suffer great pain near my left wrist. I didn't know what do, because I had no money. So I prayed to God to please help me—I knew He was the only one who *could* help me. One of my former teachers helped me to get an X-ray and to be checked by an orthopedic doctor. The diagnosis: I had a giant cell tumor on my left wrist, and the bone was affected. I needed to have an immediate operation to prevent the spread of the tumor, because it could be cancerous.

I was so very afraid; I had no money for an operation. So I prayed again with hope and faith. God heard all my prayers. Many people helped me financially, and I had my first operation. The doctors told me that they didn't remove all the tumor because had they done so, only skin would remain. They put steel in my arm near the wrist, grafting bone from my right leg. After they had observed the tumor for four months, the doctor scheduled my second operation. That time the doctors removed the entire tumor. I was so scared because I thought they would amputate my left arm. I thank God that I am once again studying in college.

I believe that God is true—He let me feel His presence. He showed me that sometimes something has to be removed to have healthy growth. Because of the removal of the tumor, I have health. God removes our sin so that we may have salvation.

Cecilia Q. Arevalo

# God Changed Our Plans

*Trust in the Lord with all your heart; do not depend on your own understanding. Seek his will in all you do, and he will direct your paths. Prov. 3:5, 6, NLT.*

FLO'S HEALTH WAS FAILING, and she could no longer manage her spacious home, swimming pool, and large garden. So she decided that it was time that she moved to a retirement village. She asked me to accompany her to look at one that she thought would suit her needs. As we were about to set out, my husband decided that he would join us, as he had friends in the village. We spent the morning looking at two available units, a small one available immediately, and a larger one a couple of months later. We talked with the manager, asking relevant questions about village life. By lunchtime, even after all the information, Flo was still undecided which unit to take.

We had lunch with friends and talked about the advantages and disadvantages of living in a retirement village. I suggested that while I did the dishes my husband would go with Flo and help her decide which unit would best suit her needs. But when they returned, no decision had been made. As we sat around talking, my husband suddenly stood up and announced, "Flo, you have more money than we do; you take the larger unit, and we will take the smaller one!" We were all speechless for a few moments, trying to recover from the shocking announcement. You see, my husband and I had decided we were never going to live in a retirement village, at least not for many years. After some thought Flo agreed to the plan, and so did I. So once again we visited the manager to alert him to our final decision—he would be filling both units.

My husband and I were given a month to sell our home and, if unsuccessful, the unit would go to whoever had the cash. It wasn't a boom time for selling homes, but the Lord arranged for ours to be sold on the last day of the month. Flo auctioned her home, and it sold just as her unit became available.

We have never regretted moving into the retirement village, and have been richly blessed spiritually and socially. We praise the Lord continually for directing our path in a way that we did not plan.

**Joy Dustow**

# Choosing the Best Way

*If it is disagreeable in your sight to serve the Lord, choose for yourselves today whom you will serve: whether the gods which your fathers served which were beyond the River, or the gods of the Amorites in whose land you are living; but as for me and my house, we will serve the Lord. Joshua 24:15, NASB.*

THE MORNING FELT RUSHED from the moment my feet hit the floor. I hurried around doing my usual morning routine, stepped into my shoes in the closet, grabbed a quick breakfast to eat on the run, and dashed out the door. It wasn't until later that I paused long enough to look down at my feet. In my haste to get dressed, I had chosen two different-colored shoes, black and dark navy. The styles were similar, but one toe was more pointed than the other. I should have felt the difference when I put them on, but under pressure I didn't realize the choice I'd made. I was very embarrassed at first, of course, though some of my coworkers found it quite amusing.

Because I lived close by, I was able to go home and get a matching pair. I later thought, *Which pair would I have chosen in the first place?* Certainly not a life-altering question, but sometimes critical choices are just that subtle. "Should I accept that lunch date with a male friend?" "One social drink won't hurt me, will it?" "It's only rated R because of violence." "They deserve to be put in their place." "I can buy this now and pay for it later." Every day we make significant choices—and even seemingly insignificant decisions that can determine the direction we take, and who is master of our life.

Making the decision to follow God in every regard has to be a conscious one, a decision to do right because it is right. We don't have to yield to the moment. Praise God, we are not alone in this process. The Lord promises never to leave us (see Heb. 13:5). The Bible declares, "Trust in the Lord with all your heart and do not lean on your own understanding. In all your ways acknowledge Him, and He will make your paths straight (Prov. 3:5, 6, NASB).

Fortunately for us, the Bible also tells us: "I can do all things through Christ who strengthens me" (Phil. 4:13, NKJV). That is a promise for every one of us. We can claim His promises and take Him at His word. The choice is ours!

**Joan Green**

# What Is in the Number?

*But even the very hairs of your head are all numbered. Fear not therefore: ye are of more value than many sparrows. Luke 12:7.*

IT WAS THE WEEK BEFORE THANKSGIVING, and I was preparing for a trip to San Francisco, California, where my family would meet. My husband would be coming from his overseas itinerary, and my two daughters from their schools. I thought I'd go to a thrift store to see if I could find something for my trip. I asked my friend Ana to go with me.

We were enjoying our shopping spree. Then just before going to the counter, I spotted a Samsonite suitcase. It looked quite new, so I went to investigate. The problem was that it was locked. I asked the salesperson who might know the combination for the lock; she didn't know. The manager said that they had tried all the combinations they could think of, but no luck. He said I could buy the suitcase for $5. I told him I'd take it and try to figure out the combination.

At home I tried, setting it to 111, and 000, and 999, and 921—you name it, I tried it, to no avail. But before giving up, I whispered, "Lord, please; I really need this suitcase for my trip. And look—it's even new! This will be a really great buy, Lord, but only if You help me open the case. Please, Father, when I try a combination, let it be right. Amen."

I put my fingers on the combination lock, turned it, and it popped open. I quickly glanced at the number: 586!

After a good Thanksgiving time in California, I noticed that my mother-in-law, who was staying with us, hadn't opened one of her suitcases. When I asked her why, she said that the case was locked and she couldn't open it. I looked at the case—another combination lock. A person in the Philippines had set the combination and then forgotten it. So we tried hundreds of combinations, and even considered breaking the case. But before giving up, I prayed, "Lord, You opened the case from the thrift store; would you do this for me again? When I put my fingers to the combination lock, please let it be the number. Amen."

This time 560 was the number, and the Lord again showed me that He is interested in every detail of our lives. What is in the numbers 586 and 560? Nothing, really—just a reminder that there is a God who cares.

**Jemima D. Orillosa**

# Retrospective Reflection

*But if any of you causes one of these little ones who trusts in me to lose his faith, it would be better for you to have a rock tied to your neck and be thrown into the sea. Matt. 18:6, TLB.*

IT SEEMED IT WAS ALWAYS at a busy time for me when his little voice would say, "Look, Mama." It would be some childish thing he was doing requiring my attention, but a slight glance didn't satisfy. "Look, Mama!" he said not once but many times when I was too busy—or so I thought.

Soon he didn't bother to ask anymore, and day by day, year by year, the fading away lengthened into distances of space and emotion. Too late my heart reaches out to an empty space. Would that I could relive those precious, fleeting moments again!

Caught up in my own emotional hurts from a verbally abusive marriage, I didn't realize then that I was also hurting an even more innocent and helpless child of God, my own little son. Just by momentarily ignoring a seemingly insignificant childish request, I had begun a pattern of dim-sightedness of a highly important motherly task—that of paying attention to the little wants of the "least of these."

Yes, I still hear occasionally from that now-grown son, far away in a godless life, but only on special holidays such as Mother's Day, my birthday, or Christmas—he's probably reminded by his wife. But there is hope that someday that verse in Proverbs 22 will be fulfilled: "Train up a child in the way he should go: and when he is old, he will not depart from it" (verse 6). It is my prayer that someday he will remember that early guidance in the "way he should go" and "not depart from it."

Like those neglectful times of long ago, I think of my neglect of quality time in daily prayer and Bible study, and I wonder if I will hear the Savior say "I do not know you" when He comes to claim His bride, the waiting saints of His church. I've decided to spend more time with those more important things in these precious moments that fly by so quickly and never return again.

*Dear Lord, I want to know You better each day that I, too, may hear Your words, "Come, ye blessed of my Father, inherit the kingdom prepared for you" (Matt. 25:34).*

**Bessie Siemens Lobsien**

# Trust and Believe

*In the day of prosperity be joyful, but in the day of adversity consider: God also hath set the one over against the other, to the end that man should find nothing after him. Eccl. 7:14.*

WE PRAY FOR FINANCIAL BLESSINGS again and again. But if we remember Isaiah 65:24, "And it shall come to pass, that before they call, I will answer; and while they are yet speaking, I will hear," we will know that God supplies all our needs. It may not be to our satisfaction or within our time frame, but He does.

We usually want to blame God, or someone other than ourselves, when we don't succeed or our finances are in disarray. We tend to ask, It's *whose* fault? And we have to answer, *Mine!* That's a hard statement, but we must take ownership.

We want to be joyful when we prosper, but when there is adversity—that's another story. But if you only take the time and effort to make a few changes in your life and lifestyle, the Lord will give you more than just a financial blessing: "A faithful man shall abound with blessings: but he that maketh haste to be rich shall not be innocent" (Prov. 28:20).

Make whatever change is necessary so that your blessings will come. As it says in Proverbs 10:22: "The blessing of the Lord, it maketh rich, and he addeth no sorrow with it." Just trust and believe His Word and thank Him for His goodness.

There is a lesson we can learn from the life of Jesus. He didn't waste anything. I'm grateful for that. He didn't waste even such simple material things as bread and fish; and even more remarkably, He didn't waste the fragments of a life that had been broken.

*"Hear me when I call, O God of my righteousness! You have relieved me in my distress. Have mercy on me, and hear my prayer"(Ps. 4:1, NKJV).*

I think about the creation of this world. God made everything out of nothing. I have nothing to offer Him, but He can make something of me. He can bless financially, socially, emotionally, and, of course, spiritually. I want that kind of prosperity, don't you?

*Even though my life may at times appear to be poor and contain so many broken pieces, help me to remember that in You nothing is lost. "But thou, O Lord, art a shield for me; my glory, and the lifter up of mine head"(Ps. 3:3). You are the Restorer. In Jesus' name, amen.*

**Hattie R. Logan**

334

# The Payroll

*The Lord was with Joseph and he prospered, and he lived in the house
of his Egyptian master. Gen. 39:2, NIV.*

THE STORY OF JOSEPH IN EGYPT fascinates me. His experiences weren't
all pleasant, but God performed miracles, making him prosper even in
prison. I've had some challenges and witnessed God working in my favor,
too. Once God worked in a really spectacular way.

For a short time I'd been working in the hospital as a secretary to the
administrator. God was with me, because everything seemed familiar in the
new job. Everything that my boss requested I was able to carry out skillfully. After one month at the new job the head of the personnel department
contracted tuberculosis and needed to take an immediate leave of absence.
Since the illness was sudden, no one was prepared to substitute for her, and
the hospital administrator appointed me to take her place. At that time the
hospital had 200 employees—physicians, employees in various sectors, and
administrators.

Someone informed my boss that I didn't have enough experience for
this new position, even suggesting that I wouldn't be able to close the books
and prepare the payroll, thus causing a delay in paying the employees. My
boss replied, "I guarantee that Noemi is going to take care of everything,
and the payroll will be ready by the first of the month."

I returned home pleased with my new position but apprehensive of a
task I had not been prepared for. The truth was that I had no idea of how
to go about preparing payroll. That night I sought God in prayer and asked
for wisdom, and in a dream I received the knowledge necessary to do the
payroll. Early the next morning at work I wrote down everything from the
dream, step by step. On the thirtieth the payroll was ready. I verified the information with my boss on the first day of the month and reported that the
payroll was ready. He authorized me to issue paychecks on the same day.
The employees were pleased because their paychecks were received on
time. My job continues to prosper: and my salary quadrupled in one
month. Depending on God is worthwhile, even when challenges are great
and people doubt you. God is greater than every challenge. Like Joseph in
Egypt, we need to be faithful and see how God works great things in our
lives.

**Noemi Iamamoto Madalena**

# Blessings

*My heart trusted in him, and I am helped: therefore my heart greatly rejoiceth; and with my song will I praise him. Ps. 28:7.*

ON THIS FRIDAY I was trying to catch up on all those things that I had planned to do the past week and hadn't done. Then I remembered I had told Rose I'd go to visit her. When I had recently attended her ninetieth birthday party, it had been announced that she would be moving to Atria, an assisted living home. This brought sadness to the occasion, as she loved her big two-story house filled with all the mementos of her long life.

I quickly grabbed a couple of French books and dashed out, remembering she said she'd meet me at 2:00. She was there, waiting with her dog, Bonnie, a 12-year-old German shepherd. Rose told me Bonnie was more adjusted than she was, as all the other people in the home were very fond of the dog. We slowly walked to her room, as Rose now used a cane. I was pleased with the size of her apartment and happy to see her piano in one corner of the big room. She brightened up and said she was taking piano lessons. She quickly sat down and played a couple pieces for me. I, too, was working on my piano and was impressed with her ability.

Our big bond, however, was our interest in the French language. We had met in a French class several years before. She had studied French in college and somehow had kept it up. Her big desire had been to see Paris. But no matter—she was still enjoying the language. We read together, taking turns and translating as we read. She is superb at pronunciation, like a native French person. This was my weak point, so we worked together having fun.

We talked of how we were both interested in art and trying to find our own expressions in it. "You must come over, and we can sketch in the garden," she said. I agreed. But it was now time to leave. "Oh," she said, "I must show you my knitting. I'm left-handed, but I'm learning to knit right-handed." She showed me a green scarf she was making, about 10 rows perfectly done. "I have a good teacher, and she makes me do it over when I make a mistake," she added.

She hugged me and said, "You have made my day." However, I was the one inspired. Let us not forget to thank God for the desires and abilities to enjoy the everyday blessings—He has given us each one.

**Dessa Weisz Hardin**

# My Comfort Zone

*I beseech you therefore, brethren, by the mercies of God, that ye present your bodies a living sacrifice, holy, acceptable unto God, which is your reasonable service. Rom. 12:1.*

"LORD, USE ME" was my constant prayer. I raced out to work each morning, raced up and down on the job, raced to the bank, to the store, to church, and— The list went on. Even when I went on vacation, I found myself still racing to complete last-minute chores, run for a taxi, to the airport, train station, bus terminal, or to a cruise ship. I waited anxiously for retirement. It seemed as if the hustle and bustle would never cease.

The first year of retirement was beautiful. I traveled to several continents. Although I was moving at a slower pace and doing many of the things I wanted to do, my mind was still running like a computer. As time passed, my mind and body began to compromise. But each day I continued to pray, "Lord, use me."

It was the day before Thanksgiving three years later. I was in a deep sleep when the phone rang. "Sister Cora, will you please come over to the church?" It was our community service department seeking someone with a car to run errands. My immediate thoughts were *Why call me? Where are the committee members? I retired so I could sleep late in the mornings if I wanted to, and not be disturbed.* And I was exhausted.

Then a sudden change of mind enveloped me, a transition. This was indeed a wake-up call. *You asked the Lord to use you. Why are you complaining? Are you really willing to be used by Him?* A terrible feeling of guilt swept over me. I didn't want to leave my comfort zone, and I thought of many times that I've been hesitant about doing so. Where would I be had Jesus not left His comfort zone? He left His heavenly comfort zone to come to this sin-sick earth to offer me salvation. He was away from His comfort zone as He hung on the cross, yet Jesus never complained. He endured excruciating pain, He sweated, He bled, and He died thirsty—all out of love just for you and me.

My prayer today is *Lord, help me to forget about leaving my comfort zone when You ask me to help others. Help me to remember how You left Your comfort zone in love as You continue to use me.*

**Cora A. Walker**

# Giving Thanks

*For your Maker is your husband. Isa. 54:5, NKJV.*

LOOKING BACK OVER THE YEARS (as we do when we reach a certain age), I'm encouraged. Giving to the Lord's work became a lifestyle habit. My husband, also a believer, said we were investing in the bank of heaven. Life wasn't easy; times were tough, and we had two children in Christian schools. We had debts, but somehow these were always paid. The Lord led us to Canada, to Inuvik, Northwest Territories, then to Whitehorse, Yukon, to work. As our children's education expenses escalated, the money we earned as government employees paid the bills.

Another transition hit when my husband was only 54, and long-term disability was his lot as a result of a second open-heart surgery and a disabling whiplash injury. The years rolled by, and finally my husband's heart couldn't handle the cold winters anymore. He was 59, and I was 57. Where could I find work in southern British Columbia? But God was still leading us. God placed the right people in the right place at the right time to enable me to get a transfer to another government department, where I worked until retirement. After our move, my wonderful husband was given five more years of life, enabling him to assist in raising up a little church in our small community. It was his baby.

But the best is yet to come, as the saying goes. Yes, I'm a widow, living alone and lonely at times, but it must be that way. I am daily claiming Isaiah 54:5: "For your Maker is your husband." That truly has come to pass for me. My greatest joy has come from beginning a monthly blessings calendar. I begin each day in January documenting things I have been thankful for. What joy it has given me! I read them over often, usually as part of my morning devotions. God is so good. I had set aside money to be used in ministry for others, to give as He directs. But sometimes He impresses me to take back some of the money as a gift from Him just to enjoy. And I do, praising Him again.

I am now 72 and still amazed at God's blessings. I can assure you that never a month goes by that I don't have something to be thankful for. I continue to document these on my blessings calendar. Please try it—it will overwhelm you what God does as we praise Him for His goodness.

**Dorothy Cannon**

# Flu Shot

*There's no need to fear for I'm your God. I'll give you strength. I'll help you. I'll hold you steady, keep a firm grip on you. Isa. 41:10, Message.*

IT WAS THAT TIME OF THE YEAR AGAIN. The news reports predicting a "hard flu season ahead" abounded. Because Jonathan had had several bouts with bad bronchial episodes, his doctor strongly encouraged me to allow him to get the flu shot. On the set day Jonathan wanted to know where we were going. "To the doctor," I answered nonchalantly.

"But I'm not sick," he countered.

"I bet you're going to get a shot," big brother Brandon correctly surmised all too quickly.

The hubbub at the doctor's office kept the children both occupied. After the regular prep we found ourselves sitting in the little examining room. "Am I going to get a shot?" Jonathan asked. Before I could answer, in walked the nurse with needle at the ready. The protesting began, followed by the pleading not to get the shot. "It will help you," I tried to explain, "so that you won't end up in the hospital like before." With tears streaming down his face he made one last request: "Can I hold on to you, Mom?" He quickly sat on my lap. The nurse took his arm, and he turned into my shoulder, his other arm around my neck nearly choking me.

"There, there," the nurse said when it was all done. "It wasn't all that bad, was it?"

"Not if I'm holding on to Mom," he said. "When I hug her, it doesn't hurt as much." As we exited to the main waiting area to pick up Brandon, he repeated the same conclusion to his brother. "When I hugged Mom, it didn't hurt as much." He hadn't said that it didn't hurt, just that the pain wasn't as bad. Simple yet profound, and filled with spiritual meaning.

I wish I could remember this lesson when I feel overwhelmed by the sheer pace of life and all that I must get done. I want to remember to hang on to Jesus for dear life. When others let me down, when deeds are thankless, when I feel hurt and misunderstood, when I'm lonely in a crowd, when life throws me a curve that just isn't what I had expected or hoped for—it's time to hang on to my Savior. It won't hurt as much.

*Lord, help me to remember as I begin today—with its unknown challenges—that You are there. Help me to hug You close, and may I feel in return the warmth of Your love.*

**Maxine Williams Allen**

# My Three Princesses

*Charm is deceptive, and beauty is fleeting; but a woman who fears the Lord is to be praised. Prov. 31:30, NIV.*

I HAVE THREE adorable little granddaughters—Bianca, Kali, and Ariyah—and I have enjoyed watching them grow into three distinct personalities. Spending time with them, whether mealtime, churchtime, or playtime, has been wonderful. It has taken me back to when I played with dolls (and trucks), played hopscotch or double Dutch, rode bicycles, played dress-up with girlfriends, went to Sabbath school and church with my grandma, and enjoyed the carefree life of a child.

One of the favorite things my granddaughters like to do is to play dress-up. They have lots of darling little dresses, princess shoes in a variety of colors, and many crowns and tiaras. Even without seeing themselves in a mirror, they know they are beautiful. The special attire makes them feel that they are beautiful princesses, and they are eager for me or Poppa, their grandpa, to tell them so. And of course we do! When they have to put their regular clothes back on, they're usually quite sad, pleading for more time to be princesses and to talk about princes, queens, kings, and kingdoms. But even as the girls have donned their pretty garments and are glowing outwardly, their natural inclinations to fuss and fight kick in, and attitudes get ugly. After all, two preschoolers and one kindergartner are bound to eventually have tears and unpleasant episodes when playing together for hours, and all claiming to be *the* princess!

Aren't we just like Bianca, Kali, and Ariyah—eager to dress up in our favorite Christian "attire" and parade around for others to see and admire our Christian beauty? We revel in knowing that one day we will meet our King; but in the meantime arrogant, harsh, or mean-spirited dispositions rob us of the Christian beauty we should have as princesses, as daughters of the King. Unpleasant episodes with friends, family, church members, and coworkers happen; then our influence is lost.

*Lord, we want to love and praise You above all else. Help us to be beautiful inside and out—testimony of Your goodness. May Your Holy Spirit take control so that our knowledge, possessions, gifts, talents, and beauty don't hinder us from seeing You, our king, one day.*

Iris L. Kitching

# Waiting Time

*In the morning, O Lord, you hear my voice; in the morning I lay my requests before you and wait in expectation. Ps. 5:3, NIV.*

I DON'T KNOW IF YOU'RE A MORNING PERSON, but I am. I think it's because I like quietness.

The world seems to grow louder day by day, and our senses seem to be invaded at every turn. Our task is to find moments of silence in a world filled with noise. It's in the morning that I feel more relaxed, and my mind is more organized to start the day. It's in the morning that I find silence in my favorite spot, my private world, while the world still sleeps. On the other hand, when you finish a day there are moments you think you have no more energy. You're tired, exhausted, and looking for a good night of sleep; no time for anything else.

The psalmist's advice for us today is that in the morning we should pray and give all our cares to Jesus. Why in the morning? I think our mind is rested, calm, and free of worries. So if we pray, we not only will have a quiet time with God but also will be able to listen to His voice. Also, we are reminded of God's love and protection for the day.

But there is one more element in this text of David's: wait in expectation. Waiting is one of the hardest things to do, especially when years go by and our dreams and plans haven't been fulfilled. In fact, we spend much of our lives waiting for direction. The *American Heritage Dictionary* offers these definitions of *wait:* "To remain inactive or stay in one spot until something anticipated occurs; "to be in a state of readiness." David is saying, "Do not rush; do not despair. Be still. God knows what is best. Trust in Him." "Wait in expectation" in Hebrew means literally "look up." Wait with patience for an answer from above even if God shows you a different plan.

Waiting is hard because nobody likes waiting *patiently.* Pressure is everywhere, and there is often no time to wait. But in terms of spiritual growth, waiting patiently helps us to grow in our faith. If you're praying and waiting in expectation for an answer from God, don't give up. Listen to the One who says everything will be all right, and keep praying and waiting. God is not sleeping. He is with you as you face all your challenges. That's why, before you go out, say, *In the morning, O Lord, You hear my voice; in the morning I lay my requests before You, and I wait in expectation.*

**Raquel Costa Arrais**

# Let Them Come

*Whoever humbles himself like this child is the greatest in the kingdom of heaven. Matt. 18:4, NIV.*

MY ELEMENTARY SCHOOL TEACHER invited my cousin and me to visit the church building belonging to the congregation that had supervision of the school. I was elated and excited to be in such a beautiful building. The atmosphere was awesome. As I entered the building my thoughts centered on the invitation of Jesus: "Suffer the little children to come" (Mark 10:14).

I believe church is supposed to be a place of fun and learning, where children should feel comfortable, but after a few minutes I was shocked by remarks from my teacher. "Look around," he said with a prideful roll of his eyes. "Do you have anything like this in *your* church?" (He indicated the expensive padded pews, the gilded icons, the glittering chandeliers, and the glistening candles.) To my childish, uneducated, unsophisticated mind, this was a direct put-down. My teacher knew my church was a simple roadside structure, built of stone and mortar by the humble hands of members of the community. It was furnished with home-crafted wooden benches, and had no chiming bells. The platform, raised just one foot above the floor, accommodated a simple choir that produced heavenly music, a paean of praise and adoration to the Creator. And I will forever cherish the remarkable sermons that issued from that platform.

I felt greatly humiliated. Excitement gave way to fear. Someone says that when we try to solve our problems by ourselves, the problems became giants and we become grasshoppers. Well, this grasshopper took flight, and without a word to my teacher or my cousin, I ran. Overcome by fear and resentment, I ran as fast as my little feet could take me to the security of home and mother. Now I feel that I denied my Lord. I didn't curse or swear; I just ran. I was thinking only of myself. Now I know that the giants are agents of the devil, whose purpose is to scare and discourage.

Even now the echo of my teacher's words awaken an unpleasant reaction; but it also kindles a feeling of pride for my humble church—not based on tradition or elegant decor, or costly adornments, but energized by love and obedience. It encourages children to come to the Father.

**Quilvie Mills**

# Divine Care

*God is our refuge and strength, a very present help in trouble. Ps. 46:1.*

IN 1974 I worked for a mine consortium in Nova Lisboa, Angola, Africa; I was responsible for the research laboratory. One afternoon my friend, the director of the primary school near the governor's palace, called to tell me that there had been gunfire near the school area and that we should, without panic, go pick up our children. I also needed to advise some of my colleagues who had children in the kindergarten about what was taking place. As calmly as I could, I explained the situation to them and told them to go, one by one, with an interval between each one. I waited until last.

Near the governor's palace soldiers stood behind the columns of the buildings that encircled the central plaza. Noticing that the school parking area was full, I parked outside the schoolyard, near the president's home. As I walked toward the school, I passed near the president's car and heard a strange humming noise by my side. I stepped into a nearby garden just as someone shouted, "Sales, hit the ground!"

I obeyed immediately. Lying down in the grass, between the bushes and flowers, I could see a group of youth who were also protecting themselves. Behind the gate of the president's home I saw some soldiers with guns in their hands. Then I knew that the humming I had heard came from the bullets that flew above our heads. I don't know how long I remained there before I heard a rustling and footsteps coming my way. It was the high school students and one of their teachers taking advantage of the calm and running for home.

I got up, ran to my car, drove into the schoolyard, and picked up my children. I asked them to lie down between the seats in the car so that no one could see them, and drove home, taking a longer and less-familiar route.

Although the school was between the headquarters of the two groups in conflict, God protected us, as well as each child, youth teacher, and employee who worked in the school. I shall never forget how compassionate and merciful the Lord was and how He cared for us on that occasion. He is faithful.

**Maria Sales**

# Cellular Memory

*To the third and fourth generation. Ex. 20:5, NIV.*

MELISSA SKIPPED THROUGH THE KITCHEN, ponytail waving from the back of her cap. "I just love baseball!" *Skip. Skip.* "My children will love the game as much as I do, right?"

"There's no guarantee," I replied, "but if you keep on practicing, you may pass on some cellular memory."

"I'm having nine children—we can have our own team—" She stopped abruptly. "Cellular memory?" That triggered a discussion about current research and that we each start life with two live cells that already contain cellular memory from the behaviors and habits of each parent. By way of personal example, I mentioned that my mother had been a tap dancer and—

"You never told me that!" Melissa interrupted.

"I didn't know myself until shortly before she died," I replied. "It was a family secret." Melissa's slender body curved into a question mark. "From my earliest memories," I continued, "whenever I saw someone tap dancing, every cell in my body wanted to move with the rhythm. I couldn't understand that urge—dancing was unthinkable in our family." I paused, remembering. Shortly before my mother's death she had responded to one of my comments by saying, "Well, I used to be a tap dancer, you know." No, I hadn't known! "In fact, I danced around the house for exercise, off and on, during at least seven of the months I was pregnant with you."

"With that information," I explained to Melissa, "everything made sense. My brain-body cells had stored kinesthetic memories of her tap dancing. Consequently, I experienced unexplained urges to do the same."

*Silence.* Then Melissa said slowly: "Wow! I better choose my behaviors carefully for my children's sake!"

*Bingo!* I thought. Aloud I said, "Good thinking, girl. Better start right now, since you already have all the eggs you're ever going to have, and they're building cellular memory with your every thought, word, and action." But Melissa was moving toward the phone to ask her mother what she had done while she was pregnant with her. I chuckled. *Nine children. She just might do it!*

**Arlene Taylor**

# Tell Everyone!

*I will be glad and rejoice in your love, for you saw my affliction and knew the anguish of my soul. Ps. 31:7, NIV.*

I TEND TO BE STRONGLY INFLUENCED by my emotions. Certain situations can cause me sleepless nights and make me rack my brain for hours. It was one of those times my emotional balance was quite low. For weeks even little things had been worrying me through the night and causing me to have panic attacks. I'm a Christian and do know the "emergency call number," and I had dialed it, but somehow the connection didn't work too well.

At the same time our church was having a Week of Prayer. Just the thought of attending every day was causing me problems. No, I wouldn't go there every day; I simply couldn't at the moment! When evening came and my watch indicated that soon the prayer meeting would start, an inner voice urged me to go to church. This repeated itself every day of the week. So, through the Holy Spirit, God was offering anew the connection that had been disturbed from my side.

Finally, on Sabbath, the last day of the Week of Prayer, God offered me a wonderful experience. In the afternoon I opened our worship book for women to find strength and encouragement from the many experiences shared. I had read a number of devotions when a title caught my special attention: "Lord, Teach Me to Trust You." Yes, trust—that's what I needed right then, and I decided to go on reading this one meditation. After the first few lines I realized I was reading something I had written, an experience I'd had several years before that had strongly influenced my faith then. And now I could draw strength from there. I remembered the close partnership with God and how I clung to Him in that particular situation, trusting in His promises that became true, just as He had said.

*I thank You, dear heavenly Father, for having taken me by the hand again, and that You carried me across the deep river. You always know what I need! I also thank all the women who write for the devotional books for sharing their experiences that have helped not only me but others to get through our lows!*

Yes, tell everyone what the Lord has done for you!

**Anita Eitzenberger**

# Pipes of Praise

*Who is this King of glory? The Lord of hosts, He is the King of glory. Ps. 24:10, NASB.*

MUSIC HAS ALWAYS been a part of my life. I learned the piano as a child, then progressed to the electronic organ. I became a church musician, playing wherever there was a need. I studied the pipe organ, which resulted in a full-time position that I've held for many years, providing music for weekly services, weddings, funerals, baptisms, and other functions.

Playing the "king" of instruments has been a challenge, but also a joyful experience; however, the sounds produced are only as good as the one who creates them—the organist. It can be loud and majestic, or soft as a whisper—all changed by pulling out the various stops.

The blower provides continuous wind supply to the bellows, which gives the pipes sound. Sometimes this is affected by extreme temperature change—stops don't respond, sound fails, or notes go out of tune. On a warm night recently the organ blew the fuse, a strong reminder of how useless this grand instrument becomes without the power of electricity. Great as they may be, all human inventions are prone to failure. Fortunately, these are not common occurrences, and can be excused when taking into consideration that this organ was built in 1881. With regular maintenance by the mechanic, it continues to bring forth music of praise. The instrument I play is considered one of Adelaide's richest-sounding organs.

Every year the church presents a Christmas candlelight service, a special event attended by many. It's thrilling having the trumpet and timpani accompany the organ, and words are inadequate to describe the grandeur of the 90-voice choir surrounding me at the console.

Charles Wesley's hymn "O for a Thousand Tongues to Sing My Great Redeemer's Praise" inspired my thoughts about how wonderful it will be to sing with choirs of angels. In heaven there will be no inharmonious notes or blown fuses—God doesn't rely on electricity or mechanics. All will be harmony, with praise and glory to Him who gave us voice.

Unlike the "king" of instruments, God never fails us. He is power and majesty, and yet, as a still small voice, reaffirms His love as Savior and King of kings over all.

*Thank You, Jesus, for the gift of music. May I be reminded to always play in a manner that brings honor and glory to Your name.*

**Lynn Welk-Sandy**

# Going Up the Mountain

*However, as it is written: "No eye has seen, no ear has heard,*
*no mind has conceived what God has prepared for those who love him."*
*1 Cor. 2:9, NIV.*

AFTER MANY YEARS of total dedication to the Lord's work, we reached our much-anticipated retirement. Since my husband's parents were farmers, he consided himself a son of the country, and his dream was to own a small farm. After years of praying and searching, God gave us what we wanted—a small farm in a pleasant little place with a wonderful climate and many fruit trees in Santa Catarina, southern Brazil.

God always is concerned with what is best for us, many times granting us much more than we ask. The land in front of our farm is flat, with a small mountain in the background. One day I said to my husband, "Let's go up the mountain. You'll see that the view from up there is splendid! Certainly the climb up won't be easy, but it will be worth the effort."

So we made preparations and began our upward climb with our faithful dog companions, Moleque and Bonzão. As we climbed we faced several difficulties. At one point a rock was too big to climb over; at another place the ground was very loose and caused us to slide. There were bushes with thorns. Even a small snake surprised us, causing me to jump in fright. The dogs ran, sometimes ahead and sometimes behind us, even, at times, running between our legs, almost causing us to fall.

Finally we reached the mountaintop and sat on a large rock to look around. How wonderful it was to look from high up and see other mountains, the narrow road, lakes, and winding rivers! "The climb was really worthwhile!" we exclaimed. Overcome by joy at that moment, we sang a hymn.

Our preparation for heaven is no different. We come across many obstacles, find ourselves sliding here and there, face thorns. Many times we have to begin again. At times we receive negative influences from outside our home (and sometimes from within), and it may even happen that we stray from the path that leads us to the "top." Thanks to our good heavenly Father, He never abandons us, and the climb upward is completed. And I am certain that it will be worthwhile!

**Jaci da Silva Vôos**

# "Save" or "Save As"

*Wash me throughly from my iniquity, and cleanse me from my sin. . . . Create in me a clean heart, O God; and renew a right spirit within me. . . . Restore unto me the joy of thy salvation. Ps. 51:2-12.*

FOR THOSE OF YOU who use computers on a regular basis, you know about the options of "save" and "save as" under "file" on the toolbar. Although I hate to admit it, because it may seem that my understanding is severely impaired, it took years for me to understand the difference between those two options. My technologically savvy sons still shake their heads when I mention it.

I was working on the weekly newsletter for my class one day when Arlene, another teacher, walked in and saw what I was doing. After asking a few questions, she immediately realized that each week I was changing the newsletter but not saving the previous one. She asked why I hadn't saved my previous newsletters so that at the end of the school year I'd have all of them. I admitted that I just didn't understand how to do that. She then explained how to use those options. It was at that moment the light came on for me regarding "save" and "save as." I felt so good about finally understanding that! And I was so happy to know that I would benefit immediately and in the future by using it.

Christ wants to save all of us—each and every one of us. But He doesn't want to save us as we are—carnal and bent toward sin. He wants to change us so that through His strength we can become more like Him each day. But we have to make a choice. He is "not willing that any should perish, but that all should come to repentance" (2 Peter 3:9), but the "save as" option will not get us into His kingdom. He wants us to choose the "save" option so that we will open the door for Him to come in and transform us into His likeness. These changes can come only through His strength.

*Dear heavenly Father, please draw me closer to You each day so that I can accept Your salvation and experience victories in You. Then there will be joy in heaven over one sinner who is saved (Luke 15:7).*

**Sharon Thomas**

# Cleaning the Heart

*Here I am! I stand at the door and knock. If anyone hears my voice and opens the door, I will come in and eat with him, and he with me. Rev. 3:20, NIV.*

FORTUNATELY, I CAN SAY I live in a beautiful, organized, tree-filled city in the interior of the country. My city is known as the "Dwelling of the Sun."

It was morning, Christmas was coming, and I was at the bus, waiting for the door to open, lost in my thoughts, headed downtown. With the sun shining beautifully, people were happy. City employees busily cleaned the sidewalk and the asphalt near the curb, pulling all the weeds. (How quickly weeds grow, taking away from the beauty of a location, giving a dirty look to things, making them seem badly kept and abandoned.) I greeted the people who were working there, and I observed their difficulty in removing the weeds. Many different approaches were tried—different angles and various tools were employed. Later, when the work was done, what a difference! How could we have passed by so many times without being bothered with that horrible view? The area was now really beautiful and clean!

Seeing the cleaned area, I could understand what God wants to do in my life. So many times I allow the weeds of bad habits and thoughts, thoughtless words and deep-rooted sins, to take over my heart. All of this creeps in, making my heart ugly, dirty, unkempt, and abandoned. At times I realize the situation and try to pull out the weeds with my own effort. But I can remove only what is on top. The roots remain, and soon the weeds grow again, leaving my heart worse than before. Just like the workers, I sometimes use different tools and angles, but the weeds defy my efforts.

Only when I in truth ask for help from the Lord Jesus, a specialist in removing weeds and expelling bad things, am I using the correct tool to really clean my heart. So much effort and time is wasted. Only Jesus wants to clean my heart, and only He can! I need to open my heart to Him so that He can come in and change my entire life. Best of all, He makes me very happy!

*Thank You, Lord, for the lesson learned today! Come, Lord Jesus, remove the weeds that are deep-rooted, and make my heart Your dwelling forever!*

**Marinês Aparecida da Silva Oliveira**

# "Expensive" Gifts Cost Little

*A gift is as a precious stone in the eyes of him that hath it.*
*Prov. 17:8.*

I THINK THAT SHOPPING for someone who has everything money can buy takes the pleasure out of giving a gift with monetary value. Using a bit of ingenuity, though, I have learned there are priceless gifts that money can't buy. I've reached the age that my needs and wants are minimal, but I'm still the recipient of well-chosen gifts that have given me great pleasure.

One Sabbath a former student, now a grown woman, put her arm around me and said, "I was thinking of you yesterday." From behind her back she presented me with six soft, furry mauve crocuses with wet tissue paper wrapped around their stems. "Remember when I used to bring you crocuses every spring when I was in your classroom?" she continued.

This kind gesture sent a warm tingle up my spine. Crocuses weren't wildflowers in the area where I grew up, so these delicate flowers who braved their way through the ground almost before the last drift of snow melted intrigued me.

Another day, when I returned to my car after working in the school's archives all morning, I noticed a bright dandelion clipped under my windshield wiper. It brought a smile to my face. Although dandelions are pesky weeds we try to control in the lawn, this yellow flower gracing my windshield suddenly took on the value of gold. I have yet to find out who did this spontaneous act. It didn't cost a dime, but it continues to make me smile every time I see dandelions.

My sister is good at special food surprises from time to time. When I come home from work, there may be cookies or crispy fried potatoes, like grandma used to make, on my kitchen counter, still warm and waiting for my dinner.

I recall the winter that schools were closed for two days because of a severe blizzard that blocked roads and driveways. As soon as the roads were cleared, my dad drove 35 miles to shovel out my driveway. And to top off this labor of love, Mother had sent along some syrupy cinnamon rolls.

Let's think of some gift of time or labor we can give today that may be treasured by someone forever.

**Edith Fitch**

# Love Is a Choice

*Just as He chose us in Him before the foundation of the world, that we should be holy and without blame before Him in love. Eph. 1:4, NKJV.*

HAVE YOU EVER EXPERIENCED an awesome discussion that seems to penetrate every aspect of life? Recently I was involved in some lively discussions on the subject of whether love is, or is not, a choice. This discussion was a result of a Bible study guide that discussed unity in both personal and spiritual relationships. Those debating ran the gamut from ministers to Bible workers, Bible class teachers, laypersons, and colleagues. And there didn't seem to be a middle ground. We either strongly agreed or strogly disagreed. Personally, I advocate that love is indeed a choice—whether the relationship is with a spouse, family member, church member, friend, or with God.

When a man and woman marry, they stand before God and make a commitment to love each other in spite of any difficulties. God expects us to honor that commitment by keeping the relationship pure and undefiled. This also applies to relationships between family members, church members, and friends. Satan has convoluted this concept of love by using feelings, instead of divine wisdom, as the dominant enforcer. We cannot rely on our feelings, because they can be deceiving, but a choice can stand like a "tree planted by the rivers of water" (Ps. 1:3).

The same concept extends to our relationship with God. When we become Christians, we are accepting that we are sinners in need of our heavenly Father. We are making a choice to love Him. Luke 16:13 states that we cannot serve two masters. We can honor and respect Him by everything we say and do, or we can reject Him. However, the beauty of God's love is that He allows us to make that choice, and He has set the best example through His only-begotten Son.

Jesus chose to leave His heavenly domain and become our Redeemer. He chose to become the sacrificial lamb. He chose to be rejected and scorned. When He agonized in Gethsemane, He chose the will of the Father over His own feelings. He chose to take upon His shoulders the sins of every human being so that we might have eternal life. He chose to be beaten and crucified on the cross. He chose to die for us and become our heavenly advocate. Yes, love is a choice—a profound opportunity to love the One who first loved us. So the question is What choice will you make?

**Evelyn Greenwade Boltwood**

351

# Stumbling Boards

*And it will be said: "Build up, build up, prepare the road!*
*Remove the obstacles out of the way of my people."*
Isa. 57:14, NIV.

WHEN MY GRANDSON, Gabriel, was about 2 years old, he said something that greatly impressed me. One day he wanted to see a Bible story video he enjoyed. As we headed for the living room, he ran as fast as his little legs would carry him. As he went up the step from the kitchen to the living room, he tripped on the wooden floor and fell. When I heard the sound of his fall, I ran to help him and put him on my lap, comforting him as best I could to lighten the pain and his fright. "Ah, Grandma," he whimpered, "I want to go to heaven." When I asked him why he wanted to go to heaven, he said, "In heaven there are no boards for me to trip on and fall."

I couldn't help myself—I chuckled. Even so, I thought about his words, and I was joyful to learn his positive thoughts about heaven. He wanted to go there because nothing would make him trip and fall.

How many times have we stumbled and fallen? We lie on the ground, hurt, filled with pain, humiliated, unable to get up by ourselves. Many times we use only our own strength and can't get up. We stay there, lamenting our situation. We forget about Jesus. He cannot only lift us up— He can remove the "boards" that made us stumble and fall.

In our daily struggles many things make us stumble; however, if we're holding firmly onto Jesus' hand, we won't fall. He is our strength, our faithful guide during difficult times. Jesus smooths out our paths, removes obstacles, cools the hot days, warms the cold nights, and removes the dark clouds. He is the light at the end of the tunnel. He is the solution to everything in our life. By His side, we have nothing to fear.

He will not abandon us. Certainly He will come to our rescue to heal our wounds. Jesus loves us very much. He wants to see all of us in His eternal home, where there are no boards to make us fall. There we will remain standing forever before our beloved Jesus.

*Dear Jesus, take us today in Your hands—do not let us fall. Strengthen us in our weakness. Take us to heaven, where there will be nothing in our lives to cause us to stumble. Amen!*

**Aparecida Bomfim Dornelles**

# Nice Girl or Good Woman?

*I press on to take hold of that for which Christ Jesus took hold of me. Phil. 3:12, NIV.*

I RECENTLY READ A BOOK by Lynne Hybels titled *Nice Girls Don't Change the World*. Lynne defines a nice girl as one who doesn't make waves, someone who does what is expected of her. A nice girl loves the Lord and wants to follow Him. She tries to be good enough to please God, but at the same time is afraid to allow God to use her as He wants to, fearful of listening to Him instead of other people.

That describes me when I was a teenager and young adult. I was very compliant, always trying to do whatever people in the church said I was supposed to do to please God and be saved. I lived in fear that God might try to push me outside my comfort zone.

In my mid-20s I discovered the beautiful truth of righteousness by faith, that I can never be good enough to save myself but that Jesus has already paid for my salvation and offers it to me for free. As I cultivated an active prayer and Bible study life I realized that what God wants of me is to listen to *Him* and to please *Him*, not people. With my nice girl mind-set, it took years for me to learn to distinguish God's voice from all the other well-meaning but insistent voices.

Later I discovered the companion truth of righteousness by faith, which is grace, and how God's grace covers me daily, and that I'm to extend that grace to others. These two truths helped move me from being a nice girl to what Hybels says is the opposite—a good woman.

A good woman knows her value in Christ, not just in theory but experientially. And she is willing to follow wherever God leads. For someone who had always clung tenaciously to a comfort zone, that was a scary thought. However, as I have practiced listening to God's voice and following Him outside my comfort zone, even when I'm afraid, those are the times I've grown, not just in faith, but also as a person. God led me into women's ministries against my will—I was so fearful of public speaking. But by following Him, at times trembling (literally), I have lost that fear, and many other fears, that controlled and limited me. I've been astounded by the ways God has used me—when I was willing to leave my comfort zone.

Now I can say in all honesty that being a nice girl is overrated—and downright dull. When you're a good woman, God offers adventures you've never dreamed of.

**Carla Baker**

# Life's Turbulences

*Even though the fig trees are all destroyed, and there is neither blossom left nor fruit, and though the olive crops all fail, and the fields lie barren; even if the flocks die in the fields and the cattle barns are empty, yet I will rejoice in the Lord; I will be happy in the God of my salvation. The Lord God is my Strength, and he will give me the speed of a deer and bring me safely over the mountains. Hab. 3:17-19, TLB.*

LIFE IS LIKE TAKING A FLIGHT from one point to another. On some flights you fly without experiencing any turbulence, and you feel very good and are happy. Other flights encounter turbulence that causes you to worry about your own life. Recently I flew from Johannesburg to Washington, D.C., an 18-hour flight with only one stop. We had about 10 hours of smooth flight; the other eight hours were really bad and caused me to worry. I was praying for one thing: that God would hold the aircraft and bring it safely to Washington. He did just that, even though He allowed the severe turbulence. I've been talking about turbulence in the air, but what about turbulence in life?

On this very journey from Johannesburg to Washington, I was coming from Zambia, my home country. During my two-week stay in Zambia I had nursed my sick sister. It was painful to see her condition deteriorate daily. When I asked my mother to come be with us, she came immediately. Upon seeing the condition of my sister, who is her third-born child, her blood pressure shot up. The following day she wasn't able to move her left leg at all. When we rushed her to the hospital, they told us that she had suffered a stroke. *Now, Lord*, I said to myself, *this is too much for me. My sister is sick, and now my mother has had a stroke. How do You expect me to manage this?* Four days later my sister died. My mother was so sick that she couldn't even attend the burial service for her daughter. These were my turbulences in life.

In reviewing all these, I sought Scripture verses that could cheer me up and give me strength to continue life. That's when I stumbled on Habakkuk 3:17-19.

Whatever turbulence you're experiencing in your life today, just hold on and know that joy will come in the morning and that God is with you. He will help you safely over the mountains until the day we behold our heavenly home.

**Judith Mwansa**

# So Much to Do

*Know therefore that the Lord thy God, he is God, the faithful God,*
*which keepeth covenant and mercy with them that love him. Deut. 7:9.*

KELEEN WAS A HAPPY CHILD, growing up, who was consumed with having fun and planning weddings. Whenever her father conducted a wedding ceremony in our home, she took it upon herself to give instructions to the bridal party. She gathered fresh flowers from our garden to make an impromptu bridal bouquet. Sometimes she and her playmate, Omar, would dress as the bride and groom and conduct their own ceremony. She was obsessed with weddings.

One day when my husband was trying to teach Keleen to tell time, she obviously had something else on her mind. Finally she turned to her dad and said, "Daddy, just look at me; I'm just full of life. I don't want Jesus to come now. I want enough time to live. If He comes now, I won't finish college, get married, and learn to play the drum." Keleen wanted few restrictions and didn't want to be bothered with rules and regulations. If Jesus came before she was ready, there would be too many things left undone.

We are amused by a child's simple philosophy of life, but think about it: are we really any different? When we're asked, If Jesus would come now, would you be ready? our response too often is "I'm trying to be ready." But are other things really the priority in our lives?

We treat His return with scant regard, as though we don't want Him to come yet. We haven't married, or we haven't completed the degree. We haven't bought the house, we haven't made peace with the neighbor . . .

Keleen exhibited childlike honesty. What about us? What do we want to do before He comes? What are our priorities? Are we so busy with earthly matters that we can't concentrate or focus on spiritual matters?

*Dear Lord, please forgive us when we become preoccupied with the mundane things of life. Help us to remain focused on You, our heavenly Father, who is never too busy or preoccupied to remember us, because we are precious in Your sight.*

**Gloria Gregory**

# Blessed— That's Who We Are

*But blessed are those who trust in the Lord and have made the Lord their hope and confidence Jer. 17:7, NLT.*

I WAS THE FIRSTBORN in a family of eight children. My dad and mom named me Charity, which of course means love. I call myself blessed, too, for God knows me by name, He knew me before I was born, and He has been with me my entire life. So I rejoice and praise His name.

I'm a wife and a stay-at-home mother of three boys. A high school teacher by profession, I currently have my own business as an independent beauty consultant. Last year, when I decided to be a stay-at-home mom, I had some time to sit back, think, and study who I really am. The question in my mind was Who am I, really? or Who are *we*, really? Are we who we are because of our names? Many people in the Bible were named for their character. When Naomi faced so much grief, she said not to call her Naomi (pleasant), but Mara (bitter).

Many times others tell us who we are or who they think we are. They label us. Does that make us who we are? Our experiences contribute a lot to who we are as well. Through these life experiences I've realized one thing: I am—we are—blessed. God calls us blessed and wants us to be blessed. When we make God our hope and our confidence, we are blessed.

God has been with us since birth; we're told that from our mother's womb He has cared for us. As I grew up I was taught the love of God and the fear of the Lord. I trusted in God then, and I trust Him even more now—and that entitles me to be blessed. We are blessed if we have faith in Him, even though we've never seen Him.

We are blessed with every spiritual blessing because we belong to Christ. We are blessed when things are tough, for we have believed He will do what He has promised. We see many examples of this in the Beatitudes (Matthew 5 and 6): blessed are the poor in spirit, those who mourn, the meek, those who hunger and thirst for righteousness, those who are merciful, the pure in heart, the peacemakers, and yes, the persecuted. David tells us God prepares a feast for us in the presence of our enemies. What a blessing! God has so many more blessings in store that we can't even count them one by one. He never tires of blessing us!

That's who we are—blessed.

**Charity Mwende Nzyoka**

# Exceedingly Abundantly

*Now unto him that is able to do exceeding abundantly above all that we ask or think, according to the power that worketh in us, unto him be glory in the church by Christ Jesus throughout all ages, world without end. Amen. Eph. 3:20, 21.*

MY DECISION to pursue doctoral studies was placed in God's hands. When the acceptance letter arrived, I knew that accepting it required a financial obligation. My question was "How can I do this?" With each passing day I was no closer to acquiring the finances for the first year. While at work one day, I called out to God in my frustration and told Him that I had reached the end. I was approaching my deadline, and I still didn't have the needed money. At that point I was reminded that the battle (for finances) was not mine—that it belonged to the Lord. I was impressed to make a call to a financial consultant. I decided to request a loan or grant for a portion of the amount I needed. Later I would figure out how to get the rest. However, later was just a matter of days.

I made my request and was questioned about where and how I would acquire the balance. Since I didn't know, I couldn't say. The officer thought about it, then made the strangest proposal. "This is your education we are talking about. Let me see how I can work this out."

"How soon will I know if I could get it?" I asked.

"Don't you see the signatures at the bottom?" she responded. "This is already approved. How soon do you want it?"

"Yesterday!" I wanted to scream. I praised God and thanked her simultaneously. That's when I found out she was a Christian. As I recounted the chain of events that led me to her office, we agreed that God was leading me while testing my faith in Him.

The story doesn't end there. The next year I was in a worse position, but I knew where to go. I asked God for His miracle and believed He would give it to me again. Once again God proved His faithfulness to me. When a new officer informed me that the lending institution had decided to finance not only the next year but my entire studies, I was stunned. I hadn't thought or asked for such a great miracle, but the power of God, who works in us, had bestowed it to me. Without God, we can accomplish nothing. With God, indeed all things are possible.

**Brenda D. Ottley**

# A Woman of Faith

*The Mighty One has done great things for me, and holy is his name. His mercy is for those who fear him from generation to generation. Luke 1:49, 50, NRSV.*

THROUGHOUT THE GENERATIONS there have been innumerable examples of women of faith, women who have clung to God during their personal challenges, and women who exercised faith for the benefit of their family, community, and nation. Our world would be so much poorer without the faith of these women. I've had the privilege of meeting such women around the world, but I would love to have been able to meet some of the amazing women of faith in the Bible. We can look forward to having this opportunity in heaven.

At this season of the year it's inspiring to look at the example of Jesus' own mother, Mary. We don't know how old she was—we can guess that she was a young teenager when the angel appeared to her, but she had already built a life of faith. Every young Jewish woman must have dreamed of being the mother of the Messiah, but I don't think any of them dreamed of being an unwed mother. But even after having time to think about this, she could say, "With all my heart I praise the Lord, and I am glad because of God my Savior" (Luke 1:46, 47, CEV).

Many people have noted that Mary's song, known as the Magnificat, has parallels to Hannah's song in 1 Samuel 2. This means that in a day when most women could not read and did not receive an education, Mary was well acquainted with Scripture, the foundation of faith. She was strong, too. She challenged the abuses of the society of her day: "He has performed mighty deeds with his arm; he has scattered those who are proud in their inmost thoughts. He has brought down rulers from their thrones but has lifted up the humble. He has filled the hungry with good things but has sent the rich away empty" (verses 51-53, NIV).

Although Zechariah doubted when the angel appeared to him and announced the birth of John the Baptist, Mary seems to have accepted what she was told, although she did ask how this could be—she knew how babies were conceived. Her response once again was that of faith: "I am the Lord's servant. May it be to me as you have said" (see verse 38, NIV). She was a living example of the truth that "nothing is impossible with God" (verse 37, NIV). We can all believe as Mary did—then we can all be women of faith.

**Ardis Dick Stenbakken**

# Faith by the Gallon

*I have said this to you, that in me you may have peace. In the world you have tribulation; but be of good cheer, I have overcome the world. John 16:33, RSV.*

I WAS TRYING TO ORGANIZE my busy schedule in my mind as I drove down the highway. I had heard the sadness in the voice of the detective as he called to schedule my young patient. As the coordinator of the Sexual Abuse and Assault Center, I see victims of all ages. Today I was scheduled to meet with Jessica, a 12-year-old Hispanic girl who had reported extensive sexual abuse by her biological father, beginning when she was 4 years old. What would she be like? Quiet and withdrawn from the pain she'd lived through, or appearing to be unshaken, believing that if she pretended everything was all right, then somehow it would be? I didn't know what I'd find, but somehow the dread of what I might hear made me wish I could turn my car around and head for home. If I didn't meet her, maybe her experiences wouldn't be real.

I soon found myself face to face with an amazing person who would change my life. As Jessica entered my office I was struck by her beauty. She had long, dark, curly hair; big, dark eyes; and the most incredible smile. She took her seat and looked deep into my eyes, searching to see if I was someone she could trust. After we talked for a while, I asked her about what had happened to her. She began by saying, "It's a very sad thing that's happened, and I'm afraid it is going to tear my family apart. But I know I can't live the way I have been. I have to make it stop. I just feel so confused, because I love him—he's my father. But why does loving my daddy have to hurt so much?" As we continued to talk I found myself wondering, *How does someone like Jessica continue to believe that God loves her?* Then I thought about faith, and I am reminded of God's words in 1 Peter 3:12: "For the eyes of the Lord are upon the righteous, and his ears are open to their prayer. But the face of the Lord is against those that do evil" (RSV).

Jessica knows that God is watching over her, even in her darkest hour. My prayer from that day forward has been for God to grant me the strength of Jessica; she has suffered greatly, yet her faith remains strong. I pray that God helps me know what to say to bring comfort and peace to His children. I also ask for faith by the gallon. After what I've seen, my faith is what keeps me strong and heading down the highway to meet my next little Jessica.

**Heidi Bresee**

# My Father Gives the Best Gift

*Every good gift and every perfect gift is from above, and cometh down from the Father of lights, with whom is no variableness, neither shadow of turning. James 1:17.*

IT WAS LATE AT NIGHT when I was once more in agony, and turned to God for relief for my pain. As I put my thoughts on my Lord and His saving grace, I received peace and renewed strength. An overwhelming desire to see Jesus overcame me. I knew there was a Picture Roll in my room, but I couldn't get there. My legs were too heavy and numb. The only good picture we had of Jesus had been given to the prisoners at the juvenile unit during our last visit.

I prayed a simple prayer: "Please, Lord, influence my friend Loretta to call me. She can arrange for my brother Bob to take me down to the Christian bookstore so I can buy a picture of Jesus to hang in my living room. I really do need a reminder of His wonderful love each day."

That whole painful night I spent with the Lord, and He gave me peace and joy. He took the pain, and I was able to go for my morning prayer walk at 4:00 a.m. Later that morning I went to the clinic to have the university nurse, Tolonga, take my blood pressure and weight. After examining me, she asked if she and her family could come and visit me Friday night and have worship with me. I was happy they would come and visit with me that way. Then she added that they wanted to give me a gift.

She said, "We just want to come and give you a little gift. It's a picture of Jesus. You may wish to hang it up in your living room." Tears of joy rolled down my cheeks as I related to her my prayer to find a picture of Jesus.

Friday came at last. They arrived and presented a large box to me. With great care I solemnly opened the gift and stood back in amazement. The golden-framed picture, showing the loving face of Jesus, follows you wherever you move within the room. I was overjoyed, and we praised God for using my sister Tolonga to minister to me in a very special way. God the Father knows our needs. Through Tolonga my Father gave me more than I expected. What a Father!

Our Father has given the universe's best gift, Jesus, who redeemed us by His blood. That truly is the best gift—something important to think about as Christmas approaches.

**Fulori Bola**

# A Gift for You

*Ask, and it will be given to you; seek, and you will find; knock, and it will be opened to you." Matt. 7:7, NKJV.*

THE CHRISTMAS AND NEW YEAR'S SEASONS are generally opportunities for parents and friends to offer and receive gifts. I observed this one December 19 as my husband and I were returning home after a very hot and tiring day. Harmattan, the season for the dry, parching wind with dust, had just begun here in West Africa. I suddenly remembered that we didn't have bread, so my husband pulled into the parking lot of a supermarket.

While he was gone to get the bread, I seized the opportunity to read a few pages of a book telling about the wonders that God can perform in the lives of those who stand on His promises. But my reading was interrupted by the going and coming of the many shoppers, their shopping carts full of gifts wrapped with bright-colored wrapping paper. I observed that most of them were parents; I assumed they were shopping for gifts for their children for the upcoming holiday season. There were gifts of all kinds, colors, and shapes. Everybody had only one goal at that moment: to give the best gift.

While I watched, my thoughts went heavenward to our heavenly Father; He Himself wants to give us, His children, the best gifts. I thought, *Surely God, our gracious Father, has also put aside more than 6 billion gifts for us. Because He loves us, He knows us and knows best the gift that suits each of us.* In addition, He will never give us a serpent when we ask for bread. If we ask Him for bread, He will give us not only bread but something to go along with it—maybe a cake! What a wonderful Father!

This is what Jesus promised us in Matthew 7:11: "If ye then, being evil, know how to give good gifts unto your children, how much more shall your Father which is in heaven give good things to them that ask him?" He even said to King Solomon, "Ask what I shall give thee. . . . I have also given thee that which thou hast not asked, both riches, and honour" (1 Kings 3:5-13). What a gift!

*Loving heavenly Father, I am looking forward to receiving and unwrapping the gift You have already in store for me for the coming year—for the glory of Your holy name.*

**Angèle Rachel Nlo Nlo**

# First Snowfall

*Unless you . . . become as little children, you will by no means enter the kingdom of heaven. Matt. 18:3, NKJV.*

"GRANDMA, GET UP!" Bethany's excited voice woke me. She switched on the light, and I squinted my eyes against the sudden brightness. *Whatever could make my 11-year-old granddaughter so full of joy?* I wondered.

"It's snowing!" she exclaimed. "Come and see!"

Now, the first snow of the season was indeed worth waking up to see. Since Ron and I had been serving in India, this was my first look at snow in nine years. I threw back the covers, put on my slippers, and joined Bethany at the window in the bedroom across the hall.

It was truly a beautiful sight to see the snow falling in the light from the front porch. The whole world outside took on the look of a winter wonderland. Bare branches were now lined in white. Brown grass was covered in a blanket of snow. I remembered days from my childhood that I would stand at the window and watch the snow work its magic.

The next morning I smiled as a streak of red went by the window and landed on a pine branch, causing bits of snow to fall to the ground. *I wonder if God knew, when He created it, how beautiful a cardinal would look against white snow on green branches.*

Later I watched my two granddaughters, Rachel and Bethany, outfitted in boots, gloves, and scarves, sliding down the hill on snowboards. Oh, to be young again and sliding down the hill near our house. How I loved coming in after a couple hours of play in the snow to the warm kitchen and the smell of vegetable soup simmering on the stove and bread just out of the oven.

I wonder if we don't need to have the eyes of a child again to experience the wonder of snow on bare branches or the beauty of a cardinal on a pine branch. I wonder if the admonition of Jesus to become as children again had anything to do with the innocence of childhood that finds joy in new fallen snow, that doesn't see the problems that snow will bring to drivers and pedestrians, but only the fun that can be had playing in it and making the most of the moment.

*Lord, help me today to be more childlike in my view of the world and my willingness to find joy in the moment and beauty in all You have made.*

**Dorothy Eaton Watts**

# It Wasn't My Jacket

*See, I have engraved you on the palms of my hands. Isa. 49:16, NIV.*

I WAS MAKING THE MOVE from one state to another, from one climate to another. My retirement move from Michigan to Florida could have been drastic had not my mother and I been going to build our dream house together, and that made all the difference.

Knowing that my possessions would have to be in storage for almost a year as our new abode was under construction, I sent my jackets to the dry cleaners before I packed them up. When we finally moved into our new house, it was stifling hot. I needed no winter clothing then. By Christmastime, however, a welcome chill enveloped us.

Dressing for church one Sabbath morning, I reached under a dry cleaning bag for my winter white wool jacket. I knew it would be the perfect accessory for my blue sheath. It felt strange. I looked at it. Yes, it was the double-breasted jacket with the gold buttons. Yes, it was the right size. But no, it was not mine. It was a linen look-alike.

I realized that the dry cleaners had made a mistake. Somebody else had my jacket! And now it was too late—and too far away—to register any complaint. *How could the dry cleaners have been so careless?* I moaned. *Why hadn't they checked the tags?*

Almost immediately another question came to mind: *How could I have been so careless? Why hadn't I checked the tags myself?* I knew I couldn't berate the dry cleaners for their negligence—I could have checked it myself. Ultimately, I was responsible for the disaster.

That incident was not worth the tears I shed, but it did cause me to wonder about my spiritual life. Had I become too busy to pay attention to significant details in my Jesus garb? Had I stored away something as a precious treasure when it was actually a worthless look-alike?

I asked myself another question: If God loves me enough to carve my name in His hands, without even using detachable tags, what was I doing to show my love for Him? In her book *Thoughts From the Mount of Blessing*, Ellen White answers the question: "He does not ask if we are worthy of His love, but He pours upon us the riches of His love, to make us worthy" (p. 22).

Much more important than a well-coordinated, climate-appropriate outfit is the heart it encases. Praise God, He will help me to work on that!

**Glenda-mae Greene**

# Benton's Christmas Bible

*And because you answer prayer, all mankind will come to you
with their requests. Ps. 65:2, TLB.*

"MOM, COME LOOK AT THIS BIBLE!" my son, Benton, yelled
from the far end of the store. I set the dust mop against the wall and
walked back to the book area of the store that we were cleaning.
There my son showed me a Bible that was for sale.

"Have you ever seen such a Bible?" he asked. "This has such interesting material in it. It has a large dictionary, it has Bible studies in it,
and, most interesting of all, it has our church hymnal in it." I agreed that
it seemed to be a special Bible. It even had a zipper to keep it from becoming dog-eared. "I'd like to buy this Bible," he said. "I think I'll start saving
my money to get it." It had a price tag of $90.

"You'd better start saving," I agreed. "It will take you a while to save
that amount."

Two weeks later, when we were cleaning the store, my son found himself once again looking for "his" Bible. Much to his chagrin, the Bible was
gone. Sold.

I thought about how a Bible is not what most 16-year-olds want. *If I
can get it,* I thought, *I'll purchase it for him for Christmas.* After talking with
Lois, the store owner, about it, she said she didn't know if she could get another Bible like that—it had been a special purchase.

So I called another bookstore and asked about purchasing that Bible for
Benton. "You know, I've tried to get that Bible for a woman here in town,"
the manager said. "She's wanted it for more than three months. I've not
been able to get it. If you want to get this for a Christmas present, I'd not
want you to get your hopes up. I doubt it can come in by then, if it comes
in at all." I told her that was fine, then added, "If I am ordering one, why
not two? I have a nephew who doesn't have a Bible, and I'll get him one
too!" She laughed at my persistence.

It wasn't 10 days later that a UPS truck pulled into my yard and thrust
a small package into my hands. It had the bookstore for the return address.
On opening the package, I found not only two Bibles but a bill that stated
that I'd received a 30 percent discount. Benton not only received his Bible
for Christmas, but received it for approximately $65. Doesn't God Bless!

**Charlotte Robinson**

# God's Christmas Gift

*For it is by his grace you are saved, through trusting him; it is not your own doing. It is God's gift, not a reward for work done. Eph. 2:8, NEB.*

NEITHER MY HUSBAND NOR I grew up in families in which gift giving was emphasized. In our own home gifts are not major expressions of love—rather, they are expressions of thoughtfulness. As our extended families are self-sufficient, our Christmas gift to them usually means visiting them, since they all live a long way from us. Part of our Christmas blessing comes from giving gifts to unsuspecting strangers, donations here and there.

One Christmas we were returning home from visiting our family north of Sydney, Australia. After driving for several hours, we reached the southern outskirts of Sydney, where we refueled. Andrew attended to the car while I changed diapers and fixed baby bottles. He went to pay for the gas as I settled the boys back into their seats. I wondered what was taking him so long when I saw him standing at the door to the kiosk, beckoning to me.

The cashier had said that his credit card transaction had been declined! I tried my card. No luck. We were new to credit cards and had kept careful tabs on our spending. We'd chosen a small credit limit, and kept our savings 375 miles (600 kilometers) away. That money wasn't available to us now, and neither of us had cash on hand. We were stuck! Leaving without paying is stealing. Siphoning the petrol out of the tank was pointless—and illegal.

We stepped out of the queue. After brainstorming back and forth we recognized that we had no one to call on to lend us some money. The line was getting longer by the moment, but it wasn't buying us time. A woman who had just joined the back of the queue turned and asked us to explain the problem. Suddenly she was at the front of the queue, telling the cashier that she would pay for our gas also. "After all, it's Christmas!" she said. She gave us her address, and we returned the money, and more, when we got home. Reflecting later, we discovered our reluctance to accept favors and free gifts. We thought about Jesus' free gift and our urge to "buy" the gift when He wants us just to accept it. Receiving gifts from strangers is a humbling experience. "Buying" the gift of salvation is a proud approach to God's grace—undeserved favors. We diminish the gift if we try to "deserve" it.

**Bridgid Kilgour**

# The Gift of Love

*Let your light so shine before men, that they may see your good works, and glorify your Father which is in heaven. Matt. 5:16.*

IT WAS SABBATH MORNING, December 25. The temperature was below freezing, and branches on the trees indicated that the movement of the air was all but calm. Oh, how I had waited for this weather.

"Mom, what church am I taking you to this morning?" my son asked as I got dressed.

"Dupont," I replied optimistically, realizing that winter is not his favorite season of the year. He had informed me the night before that he could not stay for the service.

As he dropped me off he said he would pick me up again as soon as I called. My spiritual high lifted me to another level as I listened to the organist grace us with variations on Handel's *Messiah.* The conductor invited the congregation to sing the "Hallelujah Chorus" with the choir. I was filled to the brim. I sang with all my heart and enjoyed every minute of it.

After services I telephoned to tell my son that church was over. I learned he couldn't pick me up right away. As I waited I noticed one of the deacons locking the doors. When he reached the vestibule he introduced himself as Brother Miller and asked if I were waiting for someone. I explained my situation and expected him to ask me to wait outside. Instead, he said his wife was waiting for him in the car, and they'd be delighted to take me home, even though I explained that it was a least a half-hour's drive to my house from the church.

En route I learned that the Millers had an invitation to dinner in about a half hour—in the opposite direction. I was glad for the ride but felt guilty for taking them so far out of their way. I thought I could pay them, but they refused my offer.

I asked myself, *Am I letting my light shine so that those I come in contact with might see my good works and glorify my Father who is in heaven?* God used Brother and Sister Miller to perform this act of kindness, and as a result, Dupont will always be my church away from home. I thanked the Millers for their good deed, but I give God all the glory and all the praise.

*Father, please help me to extend Your gift of love to others.*

**Cora A. Walker**

# Goodwill 24/7

*Glory to God in the highest, and on earth peace, good will toward men. Luke 2:14.*

"DO YOU CELEBRATE CHRISTMAS?" my friend Wendy asked. That reminded me of my grandma Kate. Grandma used to send me to take gifts of all sorts to her friends, neighbors, and relatives. As a girl of 6, I hated running those errands, so I once asked her why she couldn't wait until Christmas to give to people as others did. But she said she believed that every day should be Christmas, because Christ's message of peace and goodwill should be 24/7, not a one-day or seasonal affair. Further, Grandma said that waiting for Christmas in order to give to others is not enough. How will the needy survive through the whole year? And who knows who will be alive by next Christmas? Why don't we do what we can for others now instead of waiting for a particular day or season? I continued to help Grandma until she died. So it all came back when Wendy asked me whether I believed in Christmas. I told her what Grandma had said.

Often people give their best gifts to friends and relatives; even the poor try to share the little they have at Christmas. I've even read about soldiers in battle putting down their arms for Christmas, only to continue the war after it's over. Can you believe this? If we would accept what Grandma said, if the goodwill message were 24/7, there would be no war. People would give gifts, help, and kindness to others around the clock. Can you imagine how the world would be if everyone were to wake up and think about what they could do to make others happy? How great it would be if all weapons were put down forever!

"By this everyone will know that you are my disciples," Christ said, "if you have love for one another" (John 13:35, NRSV). Grandma got it right: Christmas should be 24/7, not only on December 25. Moses reminded God's people of this when he said, "If there is among you anyone in need, a member of your community in any of your towns within the land that the Lord your God is giving you, do not be hard-hearted or tight-fisted toward your needy neighbor" (Deut. 15:7, NRSV).

*My Jesus, I thank You for this wonderful message of love. Please help me to do the little I can to spread its real meaning to those I come across in the remaining days of my life.*

**Mabel Kwei**

# Are You Ready?

*And you will hear of wars and rumors of wars. See that you are not troubled; for all these things must come to pass, but the end is not yet. . . . And there will be famines, pestilences, and earthquakes in various places." Matt. 24:6, 7, NKJV.*

DECEMBER 26, 2004, will certainly go down in history. Christmas had just passed. Most of the people who were left at the college campus seemed unaware of what was going on in several South Asian countries. My husband and I had our eyes glued to the TV screen because of the devastating news about the 9.0 earthquake that had hit southern Asia. Topping the earthquake news was the catastrophic tsunami, devastating so many countries around the Indian Ocean: India, Sri Lanka, Seychelles, Somalia, Maldives, Australia, Malaysia, and even the most popular island beach resorts of Phuket, Thailand.

Just before this massive destruction occurred, I told my husband that the world just couldn't go on with all the wars, violence, and famines. How much more could this planet take? But we have been forewarned through the Scriptures that these disasters will come prior to the end-time. And now this deadly earthquake had been followed by powerful tsunamis. As we listened to the newscast that morning and viewed the devastation on hundreds of thousands of people and property, we thought of the people who had survived but their loved ones had been swept away by the tidal waves. What a tragedy! Homeless. Alone. Not knowing what the future would bring. Just like that. The tragic events came so suddenly, without any warning. Vacationers went to beach resorts to enjoy themselves, perhaps to spend a well-earned vacation—then tragedy struck. The victims didn't realize that this was the end of their time on earth. Parents lost their children, and children their parents. Many lost their spouses; hundreds of thousands lost their homes and everything in them. What a sobering thought!

The Bible speaks of the impending end of the world. Our God has given us the message of the coming crisis time and time again. And who will be ready when His Son comes again? Am I ready for that great event? It will be most spectacular; every eye will witness it, and every ear will hear it. I want to be in the group that will say, "Lo, this is our God; . . . he will save us" (Isa. 25:9).

**Ofelia A. Pangan**

# The Ultimate Gift

*For God so loved the world, that he gave his only begotten Son, that whosoever believeth in him shall not perish, but have everlasting life. John 3:16.*

LAST CHRISTMAS my boys were given $50 gift certificates for a local store that they don't normally frequent. I treated the certificates with total disregard, not considering their worth.

One day when I was going to the mall, I asked my youngest son for his certificate so that I could find something for him. As he was about to hand it to me, my older son reached for it, but I grabbed it and pushed it into my jacket pocket.

I did a few errands, then decided to head to West Edmonton Mall. I reached into my jacket pocket, and, to my dismay, the gift certificate was not there. Until that point it was just a gift certificate, but now I panicked—I had lost $50! I retraced my steps, but no one had seen the missing "money." I became desperate and rushed home to comb the house and the garage, hopeful that it fell out of my pocket there. No luck. It was nowhere to be found. Now I owed my son $50.

God taught me a valuable lesson that day. I had totally missed the fact that someone cared enough about my sons to give them a gift. I criticized it and thought it worthless—until it was gone.

God cares so much for us that He gave us a special gift, one whose value many don't appreciate. God sent His only-begotten Son to die for us so that we wouldn't have to taste death a second time. What that means is that God recognized the magnitude of sin, that the wages of sin is death. That is what we deserve, as we are all born in sin and shaped in iniquity. Our heavenly Father devised a plan of redemption that is foolproof, and now we are sinners saved by grace, God's grace.

Divinity put on humanity and came to earth as a baby so that He could be tempted as we are, yet sin not. He was mocked and beaten for you and me. He carried that old rugged cross and took the nails in His hands and feet. He became the lamb that was slain. His blood paid the ransom, paid it all for us. We cannot put a price tag on what He did to redeem us. That gift is priceless.

**Sharon Long (Brown)**

# The Skill to Survive

*The Lord will keep you from all harm—he will watch over your life; the Lord will watch over your coming and going both now and forevermore. Ps. 121:7, 8, NIV.*

MY HUSBAND, LUKA, is a keen gardener. He has several varieties of bananas growing around our compound that he tenderly cares for. He waters them during the dry season and covers up the bunches of bananas to keep the fruit away from the flying fox and crows. Birds around our area love to eat green bananas.

There is a particular variety of banana that gives us a long bunch—it normally grows to be more than two feet long—loaded with large bananas. One banana would be enough to keep you satisfied all day. They are usually in season around October and November, the same time the birds on campus have their young. The bowerbird in particular loves to come and nest on the huge bunch of bananas and camouflage itself to be the color of the sack used to wrap the fruit.

One Sunday morning Luka prepared to clean the banana trees by the roadside and to see if the biggest bunch was ready to be harvested. Just as he approached the tree a male bower flew out, circled around him, and landed on the grass close by. It made so much noise! My husband stood still and watched the bird. It then limped along as if it had a broken leg, stretching its left wing fully out, while the other half folded as if it had been ripped apart. Luka watched the bird perform this great drama, and then continued toward the banana tree. The closer he got to the tree, the louder the bird cried and the more dramatic his performance became.

Luka reached the tree and looked closely at the bunch of bananas. There was a nest, and in it two little hairless birds opened their large yellow beaks wide, anticipating food. He immediately realized that the bowerbird was not wounded but had skillfully faked an injury to distract Luka away from the tiny birds. The bower had spared no effort to protect the young birds.

I am content and satisfied to know that God protects us every day, that He watches over our lives. We can put our trust in Him. The enemy may come to threaten our lives, but His promise and presence is ever with us. He made the greatest act of love when He gave His Son to die on Calvary for our eternal destiny. Let's call on Him.

**Maranata Titimanu**

# No Internet Access

*But seek ye first the kingdom of God, and his righteousness. Matt. 6:33.*

SOME TIME AGO while on a trip overseas I found myself without any Internet access for 10 days. Until this happened I never really knew just how much I depended on technology. It was a miserable time for me, and I became quite frustrated. I hadn't realized that the Internet was such an integral part of the way I communicate with others, and I also never realized how helpless I would feel without it. It seemed that I was consumed with thoughts of not being able to stay in touch with family, friends, and my office staff, not to mention the many e-mails that were piling up waiting for my response.

On my return journey home I kept thinking of how happy I would be to connect to these special people again. My feelings of frustration were giving way to feelings of joy and eager anticipation as I came closer and closer to home and Internet access again.

Then my thoughts turned to my relationship with my heavenly Father. I remember times I didn't communicate with Him as often as I should have, and times I let life's events dictate how and when I would spend time with Him. Each time this happened I had a good reason I was unable to communicate with God: went to bed late, not feeling well, busy doing church-related things—all these things were fine, but they were excuses.

As I recall those times, the main feeling I experience is guilt at my neglect, but they were not the same feelings of frustration, loneliness, and misery I felt when I had no Internet access. Why? The answer was obvious, yet not one I wanted to accept. The truth was that my relationship with God was not first priority in my life, for if He were, then my not making time for meaningful, daily contact with Him would have caused me much misery and loneliness.

I've asked God to help me never to forget how important He is in my life. It is a daily struggle to keep God first, but the rewards are worth it. The sense of peace and courage God gives me to face each day, the joy I receive in the midst of my troubles, and, most of all, the knowledge that God walks beside me each day keeps me coming back again and again. Many of you are struggling with the same problem, but don't ever give up. God knows your heart and will give you the strength you need to stay connected to Him.

**Heather-Dawn Small**

# Certain About Tomorrow

*"Do not be afraid of them, for I am with you and will rescue you," declares the Lord. Then the Lord reached out his hand and touched my mouth and said to me, "Now, I have put my words in your mouth." Jer. 1:8, 9, NIV.*

MY DAYS WERE FILLED with great doubts and anxiousness. I couldn't make a decision: should I leave a stable, financially sound job to go after the unknown and the opportunity to grow professionally and spiritually? Motivation and enthusiasm about life escaped me. The year was reaching an end, and I wanted the new year to be different. So I prayed, "Lord, everything is fine, but I feel so empty. I know that You are with me. Why am I not happy with what I have?"

Why do we become so involved in this world? Why are we so concerned with our daily activities—with house, clothing, the supermarket, our children's education? Many times the most important things pass us by, such as playing with the children, or simply chatting with a neighbor or a friend. There were times I've thought that I wasn't going to make it.

"Many times, Lord, I've needed to lean on Your loving arms so that I could believe that I can overcome. By Your side, Father, the struggles of life seem easier, and my heart becomes calmer. Only with You can I see tomorrow. I am not exactly what I want to be. However, I'm certain that whatever I am is because You live in me. All of my good qualities are thanks to You, and the defects that still persist are because I hold back and You cannot transform me.

"I know that You understand me and know that it is difficult to humble my spirit; however, slowly, I'm getting it. You are patient and kind. I know that I still have a chance to be better each day, even if the improvement is small. I'm approaching 50, Lord; I still have many challenges. I'm not able to settle down and retire—I need activity. Please give me a sign as to what I should do. Please."

The next day I opened a drawer in which I had a Bible. When I took it out, it fell open to today's text by the prophet Jeremiah. This was the answer I had asked for. I thanked God, because I now had strength to make my decision.

*I need to change, Lord, and now I know that You are with me. Wherever You shall send me, I will go. I am certain that the new year will be different because You will be with me.*

**Maria de Lourdes Fernandes**

# Encouraging Experiences!

*Have I not commanded you? Be strong and courageous. Do not be terrified; do not be discouraged, for the Lord your God will be with you wherever you go. Joshua 1:9, NIV.*

I LOVE TO LISTEN TO WORSHIPS, but present a worship myself? No! That's not for me. Nevertheless, I've been asked again and again to conduct a worship in our home Bible study circle. After some weary attempts I decided that I'd attend a worship seminar. After two days of theory we were encouraged to create a worship, beginning with a Bible verse from the Psalms. They gave us one day for that. On Friday night each one of us would present our meditation in front of the small group. With my Bible, my concordance, a pencil, and lots of paper, I started my reflection. To my great surprise, I realized how much joy this gave me. I studied until late that night and all through the following day, writing down my thoughts.

Finally we were to present our thoughts from the pulpit. I was quite nervous. I read my text very quickly and scarcely looked up. The instructor took notes throughout the presentations, but didn't make any comments. Only after all of us had presented did he share his comments with us. What would come next? We were told that three of us had been chosen to present our meditations on Sabbath for the sermon—in front of more than 100 people! My heart nearly failed, because I was one of the three. Now I was *really* nervous. I didn't think myself capable of doing the assignment, but the leaders comforted me. We would pray, and God would help. I couldn't sleep for half the night. I was so nervous that even in church I had difficulty breathing. I couldn't understand why God didn't grant me calmness.

The three of us walked to the pulpit and were briefly introduced. I was the last one to speak, and when I walked to the pulpit my knees were trembling. I wondered if I'd be able to utter a single word. Then the miracle happened. As I began speaking, my nervousness vanished. It was as if I'd never done anything else. With a clear voice and rarely looking at my notes at all, I gave my message, closing with my personal testimony.

The fact that God has taken away my nervousness was a really special experience and has strengthened my trust in Him. Since then I have presented several worships and also participated in two preaching seminars. Because of God's help, I wish to start to preach His Word soon.

**Gerti Weck**

# Author Biographies

**Betty J. Adams,** a retired teacher, is a mother, grandmother, and great-grand-mother. She has written for *Guide* magazine and her church newsletter, and is active in community service. She enjoys writing, her grandchildren, scrapbooking, and traveling—especially on mission trips. **Apr. 20, Nov. 1.**

**Priscilla E. Adonis** has been women's ministries coordinator for her local church and chaplain for the federation of women's ministries. She likes to collect poems, articles, quotes, and stories, and share them with women who need uplifting. She loves sharing recipes, some of which have been published. She enjoys reading good books and studying the Bible. **Feb. 26, Jul. 14, Aug. 11.**

**Maxine Williams Allen** resides in central Florida with her husband and two sons, Brandon and Jonathan. She's a licensed real estate professional who enjoys writing, traveling, meeting people, experiencing new cultures, and family ministries. The phrase "just roll with it" has become her personal mantra as she endeavors to discover and live God's plan for her life. **Nov. 27.**

**Judete Soares de Andrade** writes from Brazil. She is a literature evangelist, mother of Jeanne, Jean Carlos, and Jennifer, and grandmother of Jonathan. She enjoys writing, books, and her friends—who she says are presents from God. She lives on a small farm surrounded by flowers. **May 25, Aug. 25.**

**Annabel Petalcorin Aparece** is a senior at Mountain View College, Philippines, where she is majoring in mathematics. She is 23 years old and has two brothers and three sisters. Her hobbies include singing, reading, writing, strolling, and collecting quotations and stories. She is a women's ministries scholarship recipient. **Mar. 16.**

**Cecilia Q. Arevalo** writes from Manila, Philippines. She is a student at Adventist University of the Philippines and is a first-time contributor to this devotional book project. Cecilia has worked as a literature evangelist and dedicates herself, her time, and her talent to the work of God. **Nov. 17.**

**Raquel Costa Arrais** is a minister's wife who has developed her ministry as an educator for 20 years. Currently she works as associate director of the General Conference Women's Ministries Department. She has two sons and one daughter-in-law, Paula. Her greatest pleasure is to be with people, sing, play the piano, and travel. **Apr. 1, May 1, Nov. 29.**

**Lady Dana Austin** writes from the mountains of north Georgia. Her education in nursing led her to a career as a clinical project manager. Her passions are centered on writing, travel, tea, and women's ministries. She is a certified tea consultant, author, and entrepreneur. She plans to open a teahouse to minister to the soul's deepest need of relaxation and reconnection. **Mar. 20, Sep. 29.**

**Rita Back** has been married for 17 years and is the mother of two teenagers, a son and a daughter. She enjoys cooking, cleaning, gardening, sewing, writing, computers, selling magabooks, and taking care of children. She is the leader of the beginners department at church, Adventurers Club, and vespers programs, and is the church school newsletter editor. **Apr. 11.**

**Carla Baker** is women's ministries director for the North American Division of Seventh-day Adventists. Besides her passion for equipping women to serve the Lord, she enjoys walking, reading, traveling, and spending time with her baby granddaughter. **Feb. 1, Dec. 11.**

**Audrey Balderstone** and her husband operate a garden landscaping company in England. Both are heavily involved in church and community activities. Audrey raises thousands of dollars for charity through flower festivals and is president of ASI-Europe, a business and professional association with chapters throughout Europe. **Jan. 26.**

**Jennifer M. Baldwin** writes from Australia, where she works in clinical risk management at Sydney Adventist Hospital. She enjoys church involvement, travel, and writing, and has contributed to a number of church publications. **Jun. 18.**

**Dawna Beausoleil** and her husband, John, live in a cozy cottage in the northern woods of Ontario, Canada. A former teacher, she loves singing, reading, and cats. **Mar. 21.**

**Nelda Bigelow,** a widow who lives on the Eastern Shore of Maryland, has two daughters, six grandchildren, and three spoiled cats. She has attended the same church all her life and has been Sabbath school superintendent for more than 50 years, an office she still holds. She works as a part-time receptionist, and her hobbies are reading and cross-stitching. **Mar. 7**

**Dinorah Blackman-Williams** lives in Panama with her husband and daughter. She has published many articles and one book. One of her greatest passions is encouraging women to trust God in all things. **Nov. 2.**

**Juli Blood** has been happily married to Gary since 1994. They were missionaries in South Korea for a year. Juli now fills her days with raising their two active sons. She enjoys reading and writing, when she can find the time. She has a cat named Sandy, who didn't enjoy South Korea as much as she and her husband did. **Mar. 25.**

**Fulori Bola** writes from Papua New Guinea, where she was director for student services at Pacific Adventist University until 2006, when she became a lecturer in the school of education. A single mother of two teenagers, she loves writing, preparing scripts, and topics related to prayer, and working with women and helping students to find Jesus. **Feb. 6, Jul. 30, Dec. 18.**

**Evelyn Greenwade Boltwood** lives in Rochester, New York, and is a mother of two grown children. She is the Pathfinder and Adventurer coordinator for western New York, and is a member of Akoma, an African-American women's community gospel choir, that raises scholarship money for young women to attend college. She enjoys reading and writing. **Apr. 17, Dec. 9.**

**Loretta Botong** is the women's ministries leader at the Pacific Adventist University Church. She is from Mussau, an island in Papua New Guinea, and worked as a senior clerk at the Pacific Adventist University business office until her retirement in 2006. She and her husband, Bob, have three adult children. She enjoys working with women. **Feb. 21.**

**Althea Y. Boxx,** a graduate nurse from Northern Caribbean University, was the recipient of the Inter-American Division women's ministries scholarship in 1996 and 1997. She is publishing her first book, *Fuel for the Journey*. She enjoys reading, writing, cooking, and traveling. **Apr. 21, Sep. 28.**

**Heidi Bresee** and her husband, Michael, have three teenagers: Ryan, Heather, and Eric. She graduated from the University of Maryland School of Nursing as a pediatric nurse practitioner in 1997. She's the daughter of Bud and Rose Otis, and sister to Todd Otis. Her interests are reading, writing, and spending time with family. **Dec. 17.**

**Darlene Ytredal Burgeson** is a retired sales manager whose hobbies include sending notes and seasonal cards to shut-ins and people living alone. She enjoys writing, gardening, and photography. **Mar. 17, Jul. 13, Sep. 27.**

**Maureen O. Burke** lives in New York, where she is a state-certified counselor and serves her local church as an elder. Among her hobbies are reading, writing, cooking, and conducting seminars for Sabbath school. **Feb. 25, Aug. 24.**

**Andrea A. Bussue** lives on the Caribbean island of Nevis. She holds a master's degree in education, and worked as an administrator in Washington, D.C. In her local church she started the children's choir and has been a Sabbath school superintendent for many years. She is a consultant on disability issues in the school system and hosts a radio program. **Oct. 31.**

**Juliane P. de Oliveira Caetano,** a minister's wife and teacher, likes to embroider, cook, and write. She writes from her home in Brazil. **Feb. 24, Mar. 24, Sep. 25.**

**Elizabeth Ida Cain** served as associate dean of women at Northern Caribbean University in Jamaica. She attends church in Spanish Town, where she serves as a Sabbath school teacher and on the women's ministries committee. At 36, she is majoring in English at the university and developing a writing career. **May 23, Oct. 30, Nov. 16.**

**Nancy Camara** lives with her husband and two sons in Birmingham, Alabama. Family is her priority. She has a master's degree in elementary education, and has taught for 15 years, taking off 11 years to be home with her children when they were small. Her passion is to build up children and show them their value and potential as she teaches. **Nov. 14.**

**Dorothy Cannon** is widowed, retired, and living in Sooke, British Columbia. A mother of two grown children, Dorothy is busy in her local church and with volunteering in her community. She loves gardening and baking bread to share. **Nov. 26.**

**Dorothy Wainwright Carey** is a contented mother and grandmother. Though she must wait until the final trumpet call to see her beloved husband of 48 years again, she knows she can trust her Lord to stay close by her side as she continues to praise Him for His marvelous care and love. **Aug. 23.**

**Evelia R. Cargill** is an early childhood education specialist. As a young girl she had the privilege of serving as a missionary in Central America and Africa with her parents and siblings. **Jan. 25, May 21, Jun. 25.**

**Maria Chèvre,** who writes from Switzerland, is married and has four children and five grandchildren who live in her native Brazil. She is a technician in medial radiology and a science teacher who holds a master's degree in education in public health. Maria works with ADRA and family ministries. Her hobbies include giving Bible studies, traveling, and lecturing on health. **Jan. 27, Apr. 2, Aug. 1.**

**Earlymay Chibende,** who writes from Zambia, Africa, has been married to a church administrator for 19 years. A university lecturer by profession, she enjoys mentoring and supporting pastors' wives, and works as an editor and marketing manager. Her passion is to see women excel socially, emotionally, physically, and spiritually. **Jul. 28, Sep. 18.**

**Marion Newman Chin** lives in Canada, where she is one of the organists at her church. She works with her husband, who has his own financial business. They have three grown children and five grandchildren. She enjoys reading the women's devotional and calls the women writers her friends because she identifies with them so well. **Aug. 28.**

**Birol Charlotte Christo** lives with her husband in Hosur, India. Beginning her church employment career as a schoolteacher, she also worked as office secretary, statistician, and Shepherdess coordinator. She is the mother of five adult children and enjoys gardening, sewing, knitting, and making craft items to finance her projects for homeless children. **Apr. 23, Sep. 17.**

**Sherma Webbe Clarke** is a first-time contributor who is married to Ricardo and writes from Bermuda. She serves as the women's ministries and disabilities leader of her church, and enjoys reading, sewing, traveling, and spending time with her two dogs, Romeo and Julia. **Oct. 2.**

**Muriel Cross,** a first-time contributor from Australia, passed away in October 2006 after a short illness. When she was was 94 years old, Muriel decided to master the computer, and enjoyed writing and receiving e-mails from her family and friends. She was a gracious Christian woman. **Aug. 29.**

**Marilene Araujo Rangel Cunha,** from Brazil, has a master's degree in school supervision and works as a pedagogical coordinator in the public school system. She serves her church in the areas of family ministries, health, intercessory prayer, and youth ministries. She enjoys traveling and talking with her friends. **Oct. 29.**

**Laurie Dixon-McClanahan,** a former Bible Instructor for the Michigan Conference of Seventh-day Adventists, is now retired. Old age prevents many activities, but she enjoys reading and living with family and her cat Benjie. **Oct. 28.**

**Leonie Donald** lives in the beautiful Queen Charlotte Sound, New Zealand. She enjoys long walks with her husband, "devours" books, and admits to spending more time in her garden than doing housework. She attends the Blenheim church. **Oct. 3.**

**Yvonne Donatto,** born in Barbados, currently lives in Huntsville, Alabama, with her husband, Anthony. She's an active member in the King's Daughters' organization, serving as secretary of her local chapter and second vice president at the national level. She enjoys spending time with her granddaughters, Ayana, Maya, and Brianna. **Jul. 18.**

**Aparecida Bomfim Dornelles** is the women's ministries director in the São Gabriel church, Rio Grande do Sul, in Brazil. She is a housewife who likes to cook, exchange recipes, sew, make handicrafts, and observe nature. She has two daughters and two grandchildren. **May 18, Dec. 10.**

**Goldie Down** and her husband, David, did evangelistic work in Australia and New Zealand for 20 years, and served as missionaries in India for another 20 years. Goldie was a prolific writer who had 23 books and numerous articles published. She was the mother of six children, whom she home-schooled. Goldie died in 2003. **Aug. 12, Nov. 13.**

**Joy Dustow** is a retired teacher who enjoys taking an active part in the social and spiritual activities of the retirement village in Australia where she and her husband live. They read the devotional book each day and receive pleasure in knowing that from the sale of the book many have an opportunity to receive an education in a Christian environment. **Nov. 18.**

**Nivischi Ngozi Edwards** writes from Orlando, Florida. She is completing her doctorate in counselor education at the University of Central Florida. In her fulfilling relationship with God, she spends much of her time enjoying the beauty of His creation. This is her first submission to the devotional book. **Feb. 23.**

**Anita Eitzenberger** was baptized in 1999, and her family in 1998. Anita is married and has two sons. She lives in Feldkirchen-Westerham, Bavaria, Germany, and is active in women's ministries and in a successful church planting project in Feldkirchen Westerham. **Dec. 3.**

**Sharon Ellison** is a pastor's wife whose simple faith moves the arm of God. Sharing her testimony with others is something she loves to do. She supports her pastor-husband in ministry, even assisting with preaching for church services and evangelisc programs. One of her hobbies is latch hooking. **Apr. 24.**

**Gloria Stella Felder** lives in Atlanta, Georgia, where she and her retired pastor-husband share a family of four adult children and five grandchildren. Gloria enjoys music, writing, speaking, and spending time with family, especially her grandchildren. She has written articles for several magazines, and is working on a second book. **Apr. 16.**

**Maria de Lourdes Fernandes,** a clinical and organizational psychologist and a specialist in bioethics, has a master's degree in biological sciences. She has two children, a boy and a girl, and likes to collect pens and miniature elephants. She writes from Brazil. **Dec. 30.**

**Mercy M. Ferrer** is mother to Myla (recently married to Robbie) and JR. She and her husband, Sergie, have lived and worked in Egypt, Cyprus, Russia, Canada, Pakistan, and Kenya. After 20 years away, she is thrilled to be back in the Philippines. She loves photography, word games, cooking, and growing an orchid garden. **Jul. 19, Nov. 12.**

**Karen Fettig** is the director of the Wyoming women's ministries. She has a personal health ministry, Window of Hope Ministry, and is a trained lifestyle counselor, support group facilitator, and certified massage technician. Sexual abuse prevention strategies are now a part of her ministry. She is married, with two grown children and four awesome grandchildren. **Apr. 12..**

**Edith Fitch** is a retired teacher living in Lacombe, Alberta, Canada. She volunteers in the archives at Canadian University College, and enjoys doing research for schools and churches, as well as individual histories. Her hobbies include writing, traveling, needlework, Sudokus, and cryptograms. **Jan. 30, Apr. 25, Dec. 8.**

**Lana Fletcher** lives in Chehalis, Washington, with her husband. They have one adult daughter. Her younger daughter was killed in a car accident in 1993. Lana does the bookkeeping for her husband's business and is the church clerk. She enjoys gardening, making Creative Memories albums, writing inspiring Christmas letters, and journaling her prayers. **Jan. 23, Apr. 26, Jul. 20.**

**Edna Maye Gallington** is part of the communication team in the Southeastern California Conference of Seventh-day Adventists, and is a graduate of La Sierra University. She is a member of Toastmasters International, and enjoys writing, playing the piano, entertaining, gourmet cooking with her husband, and their dogs. **May 24.**

**Marlene Esteves Garcia** has a degree in education. She is married to Pastor José Garcia, and has two children: José Newton and Joselene. She enjoys listening to music, taking walks, and cooking. **Nov. 10.**

**Kristi Geraci** calls Bozeman, Montana, home. She specializes in yard sales, making fudge at Christmas, horseback riding, and baking chocolate-chip cookies. **Jun. 28.**

**Meliseanna Gibbons** is a premed student at La Sierra University, in California, where she sings in the church choir. Her hobbies include tennis, piano, travel, and ballet. She has visited 16 countries on three continents. (Three of these were missionary trips.) **Apr. 15.**

**Mystere Gibbons** is a premed student at Atlantic Union College. She is involved as a church leader and choir member. Her hobbies include singing, cooking, and signing. She conducted an evangelistic meeting in her native Cameroon when she was 16, resulting in 11 baptisms. **Apr. 15.**

**Carol Wiggins Gigante** is a former day-care provider who is a teacher at heart. An avid reader, photographer, and flower and bird lover, Carol resides in Beltsville, Maryland, with her husband, Joe, and new puppy, Buddy. They have two grown sons, Jeff and James. Carol volunteers for the March of Dimes each year. **Jul. 12.**

**Michelle Engcoy Golle** writes from Dingalin, Aurora, Philippines. While in college, she was a working student for more than five years, selling religious books and being involved in the Voice of Youth program. She is a women's ministries scholarship recipient. **Jul. 16, Oct. 27.**

**María Susana Mistretta de Golubizky** is a literature teacher and a specialist in literacy. She lives in Tucumán, Argentina, with her husband, and they have four children and a grandchild. She teaches future teachers and works in a UNICEF program that's directed toward children at risk. Maria likes to read and walk, and enjoys nature. **Jan. 22, Jun. 17.**

**Cyntia de Graf** is a minister's wife and the daughter of a minister. She enjoys reading, swimming, playing piano, and singing. She is a basic education and music teacher. She and her husband, Roy, live in Santa Fe, Argentina. **Jun. 16, Sep. 16.**

**Mary Jane Graves** worked at many jobs before retiring with her husband, Ted, in North Carolina. As a part of women's ministries, she started—and maintains—the church library. She also enjoys gardening and sharing the results with friends and neighbors. **Jun. 24, Sep. 15, Nov. 9.**

**Larie S. Gray** is a cosmetologist and freelance contractor currently living in Silver Spring, Maryland. She enjoys reading, singing, writing, playing the piano, and working with computers. **Apr. 5.**

**Joan Green** works as a secretary and receptionist in Boise, Idaho. She has a heart for women's ministries, which is newly established in the Idaho Conference of Seventh-day Adventists. She loves spending time with her two adult daughters and two grandchildren. In her free time she enjoys traveling, short-term mission work, scrapbooking, reading, trying new foods, and building friendships. **Nov. 19.**

**Glenda-mae Greene,** a retired educator, writes from her wheelchair in Palm Bay, Florida, where she is an educational consultant and delightfully dependent on her charming mother. Together they host prayer circles and teach Sabbath school classes. Mentoring women to write their stories gives her great pleasure. Her three nieces and nephew bring her joy as they grow in Christ. **Feb. 27, Sep. 2, Dec. 21.**

**Gloria Gregory** is a minister's wife and the mother to two beautiful adult young women. Gloria works as director of admissions at Northern Caribbean University in Jamaica. She believes that each person is precious in God's sight and was born to fulfill a special mission. She is convinced that her mission is to help others experience their full potential and use their gifts to honor God. **Dec. 13.**

**Diantha Hall-Smith** is a daughter of God. She's married to a devoted Christian husband who serves in the United States Air Force. They have two beautiful children. Born in New York, she has lived in interesting places, domestically and globally. She enjoys writing, traveling, and spending time with her family. **Mar. 2, Jun. 14.**

**Dessa Weisz Hardin** lives in Maine with her husband. She is a mother of three, and grandmother of two charming boys. Dessa enjoys the ocean, traveling, writing, art, music, reading, and working with children. An added dimension is grand parenting. **Jan. 19, Sep. 5, Nov. 24.**

**Peggy Curtice Harris** lives in Maryland, where she is an insurance agent and board chair of WASH (Women and Men Against Sexual Harassment). She is a writer, and an active member of the Beltsville church. She is the proud grandparent of two granddaughters. **May 31.**

**Marian M. Hart**, a retired elementary teacher and nursing home administrator, works with her husband doing property management. A church member for many years, she has served as a volunteer in many different capacities. Six grandchildren make her a proud grandmother. Marian enjoys knitting, reading, growing flowers, and spending winters in Florida. **Feb. 22, Apr. 29.**

**Joana D'arc O. da Silva Hemerly** lives in Rondonia, Brazil. She is married and has a beautiful son, Daniel. She likes to read, travel, and make new friends. **Aug. 22.**

**Ingrid Itzel Hines** is a 20-year-old pastor's daughter from Panama. She graduated from college, obtaining a degree in accounting systems, and is currently a part of the church choir, as well as actively participating in the Adventist Youth Society of the Balboa church in Panama. **Oct. 1.**

**Patricia Hines** is a first-time contributor to the devotional book, and writes from Florida. She is a teacher by profession. Her Christian experience has been a struggle, with many challenges, but she's had many wonderful experiences as a friend of God. She hopes that her devotional writing will touch some heart. **Mar. 23, Aug. 21.**

**Marian Holder** is a retired administrative secretary who lives in Berrien Springs, Michigan, where she is an elder at her church. She has one daughter and two grandchildren, who are the joy of her life. **Feb. 12.**

**Karen Holford** works with her husband in family and children's ministries in southern England. She has authored more than seven books, and she is especially interested in creative approaches to prayer and worship. The Holfords have three teenage children. She is also a family therapist, and enjoys walking in the English countryside and quilting. **Feb. 20, May 20, Jun. 15, Aug. 20.**

**Jacqueline Hope HoShing-Clarke** has served as a school principal, assistant principal, and teacher. She now serves Northern Caribbean University (NCU), Jamaica, as director for the precollege department, and is currently reading for a PhD. She is married to Bylton Clarke; they have two children, Deidre and Deneil, both students at NCU. **May 16, Jun. 29, Jul. 21.**

**Lynn Howell** is a learning support teacher who lives on the Sunshine Coast, Queensland, Australia. Her hobbies include painting, computing, photography, and reading. She enjoys traveling in their van with her husband, Reg, and spending time with their two married daughters and their husbands. **Jan. 16, Sep. 1.**

**Lorraine Hudgins-Hirsch** has recently moved from Loma Linda, California, to Cleveland, Tennessee, to be near her three daughters. She has worked for the media ministries Faith for Today and the Voice of Prophecy, and at the General Conference of Seventh-day Adventists. Her articles and poems appear frequently in various publications. She is the mother of five grown children. **Feb. 19, Jun. 10, Aug. 18.**

**Shirley C. Iheanacho** enjoyed 21 years as the administrative assistant to various presidents of Oakwood College in Alabama, and is currently an administrative assistant to the provost. She enjoys studying the Word, praying, sharing God's love, and encouraging people. She and her husband, Morris, have three adult daughters, Ngozi, Chioma, and Akunna, and two grandsons. **Jan. 15, Sep. 26, Oct. 26.**

**Avis M. Jackson** lives in Pleasantville, New Jersey, and is a mother of five. She works from home as a party planner. Avis has been the women's ministries director in her local church for the past five years. **Jun. 9.**

**Consuelo Roda Jackson** is a nature lover, conservationist, and environmentalist all rolled into one, and is a veteran church greeter. A volunteer at a local hospital, she holds a weekly "singspiration" for the skilled nursing facility residents. Consuelo has a doctorate in wholistic nutrition and has just written her first book, *The Gift of Choice*. **Mar. 19, Sep. 21.**

**Elaine J. Johnson** resides in the southern part of the United States with her husband-best friend, Peter, of 39 years. She is a frequent devotional contributor and enjoys writing and sharing her experiences. She is active in her local church and likes to tinker with all types of electronics, especially her computer. **Aug. 16, Nov. 8.**

**Nicole Reid Johnson,** a first-time contributor, was, at the writing of this devotional, planning her wedding and moving to the state of Maryland. She is a psychiatrist with an emphasis on women's issues. She is a Master Guide and is involved in the youth and women's activities of her church. She loves to cook and travel. **Jul. 4.**

**Barbara Ann Kay** writes from Bryant, Alabama. Once upon a time Barbara used to sew dresses for her girls, and has made all the curtains for her house. One of her favorite pastimes is watching birds come to the feeders that her husband made. She is women's ministries leader at Floral Crest church, and writes "letters of encouragement" for women. **Jun. 1.**

**Bridgid Kilgour** lives in New South Wales, Australia, with her husband and two sons. She is the leader of the family life ministries in her local church. Her hobbies and interests include health sciences, anything to do with books, and everything outdoors. **Apr. 14, Aug. 14, Dec. 23.**

**Iris L. Kitching** is communications leader and newsletter editor/designer for her local church. She is a certified personality trainer, and enjoys giving seminars. She and her husband, Will, delight in quiet walks by the lake, reading and writing projects, and spending time with their adult children and grandchildren. **Apr. 13, Sep. 12, Nov. 28.**

**Becki Knobloch** lives in Mountain Grove, Missouri, where her husband pastors four churches. Having worked as a pastor, she enjoys working with him in ministry. They have two daughters, one in college and one in high school. She works as the wellness director for the local YMCA. Her interests include homemaking, gardening, writing, and music. **Mar. 18, Sep. 30, Oct. 25.**

**Hepzibah Kore** writes from Hosur, India. She enjoys working with and for the women of India. One of the major projects she has been involved with is adult literacy, primarily for the women. It is her desire to make every woman literate, and to open their eyes to see the world and God's Word. **Jan. 13.**

**Patricia Mulraney Kovalski** is a retired teacher and widow who lives in Tennessee. She enjoys traveling, visiting her children and grandchildren, reading, and giving English teas. **Feb. 18, Nov. 15.**

**Annie M. Kujur** is a retiree who comes from northeast India and has settled down in Ranchi, Jharkhand. She has two adult children, a son and a daughter, and two grandsons. She is interested in taking care of poor children, and has run an orphanage. She wrote a school text that was published in India. Her hobbies are writing, sewing, and embroidery. **Mar. 15, Sep. 11.**

**Mabel Kwei** a retired university/college lecturer. She, her pastor-husband, and their three children served in Africa for many years as missionaries. Now living in New Jersey, she reads a lot, loves to paint, write, and spend time with little children. **Mar. 14, Jun. 8, Dec. 25.**

**Nathalie Ladner-Bischoff**, a retired nurse, enjoys homemaking, gardening, volunteering at Gospel Outreach and the local hospital gift shop, reading, writing, knitting, and crocheting. She's published several magazine stories and three books, *An Angel's Touch*, *Touched by a Miracle*, and *Through It All—Then God*. **Jul. 24.**

**Sally Lam-Phoon** serves the Northern Asia-Pacific Division of Seventh-day Adventists as children's, family, and women ministries director, as well as shepherdess coordinator. Her passion is to help children, young people, and women in particular to unleash their potential as they seek to live out God's purpose. She and her husband, Chek-Yat, have two grown daughters. **Mar. 31.**

**Iani Dias Lauer-Leite** writes from Brazil, where she is a college professor and is currently on a leave of absence to finish her doctorate in psychology. She likes to work in the ministry of intercessory prayer, teaching people how to form their own prayer groups. **Apr. 27, Jul. 23, Oct. 24.**

**Gina Lee** published more than 800 stories, articles, and poems. She enjoyed working at the public library and caring for her family of cats. Gina died June 6, 2007, from cancer. Her father, Joseph, and sister Tina also died from cancer. Gina loved writing and books. **Jan. 14, Mar. 13, May 2.**

**Loida Gulaja Lehmann** worked for 10 years as a literature evangelist in the Philippines. She and her husband, Martin, whom she met in Germany, are active members of an English-speaking congregation in Frankfurt. Both are helping to plant churches in the Philippines. Hobbies include traveling, collecting souvenirs, nature walks, and photography. **Jun. 19, Aug. 13.**

**Ruth Lennox** is a wife, the mother of three adult children, and the grandmother of four delightful girls. She has been a family physician, and has worked in women's ministries. She is now retired and still lives in beautiful British Columbia, Canada. **Jan. 12.**

**Olive Lewis** is a caregiver-medical technologist who attends church in Atlanta, Georgia, where she is a youth teacher and an advocate for youth. The works that she has written are with them in mind. She self-published a book in 2004, *Three Shades of Blackness,* and received the crystal award for woman of the year in 2005. She was named poet of the year six times. **May 29.**

**Cordell Liebrandt** lives in Cape Town, South Africa. She serves as an elder at her church and is a paralegal by profession. She enjoys reading, music, traveling, and being out in nature. **Jun. 27.**

**Nelci de Rocco Lima** writes from Brazil. She is a minister's wife and has two children, Theillyson and Thaillys Caroline. She enjoys reading, writing, crocheting, knitting, swimming, playing the piano, and preaching. **Jul. 10, Oct. 18.**

**Olga Corbin de Lindo,** a retired church school teacher and a retiree of the United States Air Force, writes from Panama. Since the death of her husband, she shares experiences of the love and power of God as a means to alleviate her grief. Her hobbies include reading, writing, playing the piano, and visiting her daughter and grandchildren in Orlando, Florida. **Feb. 16, Apr. 18, May 27.**

**Naomi Liptrot** and her husband are retired and now live in Palm Bay, Florida. She was a Bible worker for 26 years. Cooking and fishing are among her favorite pastimes, but she loves to read and study the Word of God most of all. **Oct. 16.**

**Bessie Siemens Lobsien** is a retired librarian and the author of a few published articles, stories, and poems in church papers. She enjoys time with her grandchildren and great-grandchildren and sewing for mission projects. **Jan. 1, Oct. 15, Nov. 21.**

**Hattie R. Logan,** is an analyst at Ford Motor Company. She holds a master's degree in human resources administration. Her interests include singing, traveling, reading, and visiting the sick and shut-ins. She has two sons, David P. Logan II and Darnell L. Logan. **Oct. 14, Nov. 22.**

**Sharon Long (Brown)** is from Trinidad, West Indies. She is a social worker who lives in Edmonton, Alberta, Canada, with her husband, Miguel. She is the senior manager with Alberta Children's Services, and has four adult children and two teenage granddaughters. Sharon is active in her church and enjoys writing, singing, and entertaining. **Jul. 9, Oct. 23, Dec. 27.**

**Rhodi Alers de Lopez** is a bilingual writer who loves to inspire others in their relationship with the Lord. Her bilingual Web site, www.expressionpublishingministries.com, ministers to visitors in varied ways. She is the author of *Suspiros del Alma,* a book of poetry and reflections. Her CD includes 12 of her original songs. **Mar. 12, Jul. 17.**

**Noemi Iamamoto Madalena** lives with her husband in Ourinhos, Brazil. She is a teacher in the beginners class and director of her church choir. **Nov. 23.**

**Amy Smith Mapp**, B.S., M.Ed., is an adjunct instructor at Alabama State University, and an inspirational speaker, mentor, and writer. She volunteers as an aerobic instructor and wellness advisor. Her hobbies include giving Bible studies, doing crossword puzzles, enjoying nature excursions, and gardening. She is married to C. Bernell Mapp; they have three adult children and six granddaughters. **Aug. 15.**

**Tamara Marquez de Smith**, a former New Yorker, writes from Ocala, Florida, where she lives with her husband, Steven, and their two daughters, Lillian and Cassandra. She assists with the Adventist youth program, as well as the nursing home sunshine program. **May 9.**

**Priscila Ferri Sarmento Martins** is from Recife, Pernambuco, Brazil, and is enrolled in the fourth year of law at Brazil Adventist University, Engenheiro Coelho campus. She helps with the youth ministry and Sabbath school in her church, and enjoys traveling, writing, reading, and being in contact with nature, where she can feel the touch of the Great Artist. **May 28.**

**Deborah Matshaya** is a teacher at Marian High in Elsies River in Cape Town, South Africa. Previously she taught at Bethel High. She's had several devotionals published, and enjoys gym and gospel music. **Jun. 7, Aug. 9.**

**Luciana Ribeiro de Mattos** is a minister's wife and a teacher who lives in Ijui, Rio Grande do Sul, in Brazil. She has two children, Thamires and Lucas, and enjoys handicrafts in general, reading, and playing the piano. **Aug. 19.**

**Madge S. May** is a registered nurse who practiced nursing in Canada—from Quebec to the Northwest Territories—and Saudi Arabia before moving to Florida, where she now works. She is the director of the Emmanuel Gazelle Adventurers Club at her church in Plant City. **Aug. 27, Nov. 7.**

**Retha McCarty** is retired, a mother of two daughters, and a grandmother. She has been privileged to be the local church's treasurer since 1977. Her 2005 project was to write a poem regarding the content of each book of the Bible. Her hobbies are sewing, crocheting, cross-stitching, bird-watching, walking, and writing poetry. **Aug. 8, Sep. 10, Nov. 11.**

**Vidella McClellan** is a homemaker and caregiver for seniors in British Columbia, Canada. A mother of three and grandmother of seven, she likes gardening, crossword puzzles, Scrabble, and writing. She also loves cats, reading, and gospel music. She serves in many capacities in her church and helps with the yearly women's retreat. **Jan. 28, Jul. 7, Sep. 23.**

**Patsy Murdoch Meeker** has lived in Virginia for a number of years. She began writing this devotional before she had to have her cat, Tibby, put to sleep because of fibroid problems, and before her two neighbors moved away. She is still grateful that she can drive to "get out and about." She enjoys reading and listening to instrumental music. **Jan. 29.**

**Eva Maria Rossi Mello** works as the educational counselor at Gravataí Adventist Academy in Rio Grande do Sul, Brazil. She is married to a minister, and is the mother of three grown children. She is currently doing graduate work in educational management. Eva enjoys writing and is pleased to have the opportunity to share stories from her experiences. **Mar. 27.**

**Quilvie Mills** is a retired community college professor. She lives with her husband, Herman A. Mills, in Port St. Lucie, Florida, and is actively involved in her local church, where she serves as minister of music, board member, Sabbath school teacher, and member of the floral committee. She enjoys traveling, reading, music, gardening, and word games. **Nov. 30.**

**Marcia Mollenkopf,** a retired teacher, lives in Klamath Falls, Oregon. She enjoys church involvement and has served in both adult and children's divisions. Her hobbies include reading, writing, music, and bird watching. **May 3, Jun. 6.**

**Françoise Monnier** and her husband, Eric, president of the Bolivia Union of Seventh-day Adventists, are missionaries from Switzerland. They have two teenagers. They have worked 19 years in north Brazil, and 11 years in Bolivia. She is the shepherdess, women's, and children's ministries departmental secretary. Françoise enjoys time with her family, swimming, and telling others about the Lord. **Jul. 26.**

**Esperanza Aquino Mopera** is the mother of four adults and grandmother of five. She enjoys being a traveling nurse and gardening. **Jun. 12, Oct. 13.**

**Lourdes E. Morales-Gudmundsson** chairs the department of modern languages at La Sierra University in California. She is a published author in English and Spanish, and is presenter of the popular seminar "I Forgive You, But . . ." Her book by the same title was released in 2007. **Oct. 22.**

**Frances Morford** spent 30 years in Africa as a missionary, teaching Bible, English, typing, and other classes, as needed. She and her husband, Monroe, who now live in Colorado, have been married for 60 years. They have two married children, three grandchildren, and one great-grandchild. Frances likes to write poetry and stories. **Jul. 15.**

**Barbara Smith Morris** recently retired as executive director of a retirement center after 25 years, during which time she presented a devotional over the speaker system daily. She served seven years as a Tennessee delegate, representing housing and service needs of low-income seniors. Barbara is the mother of four grown children, and grandmother of six. **Jun. 23.**

**Bonnie Moyers** lives with her husband and three cats in Staunton, Virginia. She is a musician for a Methodist church and a Presbyterian church on Sundays, and does music on a volunteer basis for her small church on Sabbaths. She writes freelance, and has been published in many magazines and books. She has two adult children and two granddaughters. **Jan. 10, Mar. 11, Aug. 26.**

**Ethel Doris Msuseni** writes from Umtata, South Africa. She is a single parent, professional nurse and teacher, and member of Ngangelizwe Seventh-day Adventist Church, Mthatha. She loves listening to gospel music, baking, cooking, sewing, and gardening. **Sep. 19.**

**Judith Musvosvi,** a first-time contributor, lives with her pastor-husband in Harare, Zimbabwe. They have three children of college and high school ages. Judith is a development worker, and loves working with people in different circumstances of life. Her hobbies are reading spiritually uplifting books and taking walks. **Apr. 30.**

**Judith Mwansa,** who comes from Zambia, lives with her pastor-husband in Laurel, Maryland. She works in the Women's Ministries Department of the General Conference of Seventh-day Adventists. She is the proud mother of four, two sons and two daughters. She enjoys traveling to new places, gardening, taking walks, reading, and spending time with her family. **May 22, Dec. 12.**

**Renata Panini Nadaline** writes from Brazil, where she is an economist in an international firm in Curitiba, in the southern part of the country. She likes to work in the church. **May 26.**

**Anne Elaine Nelson**, a retired teacher, has written the book *Puzzled Parents*. Anne is a widow who lives in Michigan. Her four children have blessed her with 11 grandchildren and three great-grandchildren. She is active at church as the women's ministries leader. Favorite activities include making tie blankets, music, photography, and creative memories with her grandchildren. **May 30, Aug. 30, Nov. 3.**

**Judith P. Nembhard,** Ph.D., is a former college and university English professor and administrator who, in retirement, lives in Chattanooga, Tennessee. She is a freelance writer and an adjunct English instructor in the humanities department at Chattanooga State College. **May 15.**

**Carol Nicks** writes from Canada. She is a librarian at Canadian University College. Her family spent five and a half years as missionaries in Pakistan. She enjoys nature—identifying flowers, hiking, canoeing, and gardening. **Feb. 15, Sep. 24, Oct. 20.**

**Angèle Rachel Nlo Nlo** and her pastor-husband have been missionaries for 17 years. Although she has degrees in family and public law, she supports pastors' wives and works in the publishing department. French is her first language. Her hobbies are reading, traveling, conducting evangelistic campaigns, meeting friends, and cooking. **Dec. 19.**

**Charity Mwende Nzyoka,** originally from Kenya, lives in Maryland. She is married to David, and is the mother of three boys: John, Elijah, and Joshua. Charity is the first-born of eight children; they recently lost their father. She loves the Lord very much and calls herself blessed (*muathime* in her mother's tongue). **Dec. 14.**

**Elizabeth Versteegh Odiyar,** Kelowna, British Columbia, has managed the family chimney sweep business since 1985. She has twin sons and a daughter. Beth enjoys mission trips and road trips across North America, being creative, sewing, cooking vegan, home decorating, organizing, leading Pathfinders and Vacation Bible School, and writing. **Jan. 17.**

**Marinês Aparecida da Silva Oliveira** works as a teacher in Araraquara, São Paulo, Brazil. She is married and the mother of two children. She is an active member of the Central church in that city, serving as church secretary and helping with women's ministries activities. She enjoys reading, writing, and talking with friends. Her favorite word is "perseverance." **Jan. 4, Mar. 9, Dec. 7.**

**Rosinha Gomes Dias de Oliveira** is a science and biology teacher in Esteio and Novo Hamurgo, Rio Grande do Sul, Brazil. She is a minister's wife and has one son. **Mar. 10.**

**Jemima D. Orillosa** works with the Secretariat Department of the General Conference of Seventh-day Adventists. She is active in her local church in Maryland, where she lives with her husband and their two young adult daughters. She finds joy in organizing and joining mission trips. **Jan. 24, Jul. 31, Nov. 20.**

**Rose Otis,** now retired, was director of women's ministries at the General Conference of Seventh-day Adventists and a vice president of the North American Division. The author of two books and numerous articles, Rose is the Sabbath school superintendent in her church. She and her husband, Bud, enjoy fifth-wheeling and their four grandchildren, who live nearby in Maryland. **Feb. 14, Apr. 10.**

**Brenda D. Ottley** was born in Guyana, South America. She is married to Ernest, a Trinidadian, and lives in St. Lucia, where she works as a secondary school teacher and e-tutor in the University of the West Indies distance education program. She and her husband are involved in radio ministry at PrayzFM. **Dec. 15.**

**Hannele Ottschofski** is a pastor's wife who lives in Germany. She has four adult daughters and one grandson. She presents seminars at women's ministries events and evangelistic efforts. She is an elder in her local church. **Feb. 28, Jun. 5, Sep. 9.**

**Ofelia A. Pangan** has been married to Abel, a retired ordained minister, for 47 years. They served as missionaries in Laos and Thailand and served churches in Canada, California, and Hawaii. God has blessed them with three professional married children and nine grandchildren. She loves reading, gardening, visiting her loved ones, and playing Scrabble. **Jan. 11, Jun. 4, Dec. 26.**

**Revel Papaioannou,** from the biblical town of Berea, Greece, works with her retired-but-working pastor-husband of 48 years. They have four sons and 12 grandchildren. She has held almost every local church position, and at present she is Sabbath school superintendent, teaches the adult lesson, cleans the church, and cares for the tiny garden. **Mar. 29, May 11.**

**Abigail Blake Parchment** writes from the Cayman Islands. She says she is, first and foremost, a work of God's creative and transforming power. While waiting for His return, she is sharing her life with her husband, Sean. She is active in her local church in the youth, Sabbath school, and women's ministries departments. **Feb. 3, Nov. 6.**

**Eliana Nunes Peixoto** writes from Brazil. Before her retirement, she was a business administrator, sales manager, and a tour guide. **May 19.**

**Naomi J. Penn,** an accountant, resides in St. Thomas, United States Virgin Islands. She is a single parent of two adult children, Cherise and Shenita. She loves reading, walking on the beach, baking bread, vegetarian cooking, gardening, and keeping a journal. She serves as teacher for the church's earliteens and writes for a church publication. **Aug. 17.**

**Angela Maria Vargas Peres** lives near Brazil Adventist University Campus II, in Engenheiro Coelho, São Paulo, Brazil. She loves her family and is involved in teaching children in her church. She enjoys reading (her favorite author is Ellen G. White). Her favorite pastime is observing nature and taking care of her family. **Sep. 13.**

**Betty G. Perry** now lives in Fayetteville, North Carolina, with her semi-retired pastor-husband. An anesthetist for 34 years, she is now semi-retired. They have two adult children and five grandchildren. Hobbies include playing piano and organ, arts and crafts, trying out new recipes, and, most recently, quilting. She especially enjoys 30-minute water aerobics Monday through Friday. **Sep. 14, Oct. 21.**

**Karen Phillips** works as a human resource generalist. She is a single mother of four children who has a passion for prayer, praying for each contributor to this book as she reads their devotional each day. Her hobbies include singing, playing the guitar, teaching Adventurers, and traveling. She has had previous devotions and articles published. **Jan. 21, May 14, Sep. 6.**

**Birdie Poddar** is a retiree who came from northeast India and settled down in south India. She has two adult children, a daughter and a son, and four grandsons. Her hobbies are gardening, cooking, baking, telling stories, writing articles, and composing poems. To glorify God's name, she is doing handcrafted cards for those who need comfort and encouragement. **Apr. 9.**

**Vicki Redden** loves being a stay-at-home mom to daughter Elaina. She enjoys cooking, photography, and scrapbooking, when she gets the chance. **Jul. 8.**

**Olga Fernandes dos Reis** writes from Brazil, where she has worked in the educational area for more than 20 years. Now retired, she attends the Tiradentes church in Campo Grande and is a minister's wife. She and her husband have two children. She enjoys reading, doing handicrafts, and having fun with her grandson. Her greatest desire is that Christ will return soon. **Apr. 28.**

**Darlenejoan McKibbin Rhine** was born in Nebraska, raised in California, and schooled in Tennessee. She is a widow with one grown son. She holds a bachelor's degree in journalism, and worked in the plant at the Los Angeles *Times* for 21 years. Now retired, she is an author who lives on an island in Puget Sound, Washington, and attends the North Cascade Adventist Church. **Jun. 3, Aug. 7, Oct. 12.**

**Charlotte Robinson** is a third-generation Seventh-day Adventist, on both parents' sides. She lives in Decatur, Arkansas, with her husband and three children. Writing is her therapy and her passion, although she seldom finds time to do so between working and trying to spend time with her college- and high school-aged children Jessica, Benton, and Haley. **Dec. 22.**

**Avis Mae Rodney** is a justice of the peace for the province of Ontario, Canada, where she resides with her husband, Leon. Avis is the mother of two adult children and has five grandchildren. Her interests include community involvement, long walks, and spending time with family and friends. **May 13, Aug. 6, Oct. 19.**

**Nathaly Rose Garcez Rodrigues** is a music school secretary in Guanambi, Bahia, Brazil. Her church activities involve earliteens and reception ministry. She is the youth ministries leader and also helps with Adventurers. She enjoys reading, traveling, and being with friends. **Mar. 8.**

**Zuila Vila Nova Rodrigues** was born in northeast Brazil and was a teacher for 26 years in various schools in São Paulo. Now retired, she has been involved in many Vacation Bible Schools and works with women's ministries. She loves nature and likes to swim. Zuila has three children and four grandchildren. **Jul. 6, Oct. 4.**

**Teri Deangelia Roulhac-Lazaro** is married to Jose and has one daughter, 19-year-old Giana, who is a student at La Sierra University in California. She writes a weekly devotional for women's ministries titled "Women in Christ Overcoming." **Jul. 11.**

**Quetah Sackie-Osborne** is an educator who has taught pre-K through eighth grade. She enjoys reading, singing, writing, and traveling. She also enjoys the adventures of being married to Pastor Charles Ray Osborne III and nurturing their children, Queanna and Charles IV. **Sep. 7.**

**Maria Sales** worked as a missionary in Angola and is currently a secretary in the Seventh-day Adventist Church headquarters in Portugal. She is a widow who has two children and four grandchildren. She enjoys writing poetry, reading, traveling, and walking. **Dec. 1.**

**Deborah Sanders** lives in Alberta, Canada. In 2007 Deborah and her husband, Ron, "with the help of angels," wrote a book, *Our Journey Through Time With Sonny,* who has significant developmental disabilities. The book is a collection of sacred memories shared with the hope that they will be spiritually encouraging to others in the family of God until Jesus comes. **Mar. 22, May 12, Oct. 11.**

**Christiane Morais dos Santos** is the associate director of women's ministries in the Porto Seguro church in Goiânia, Goiás, Brazil. She was born and raised in Brasilia and is preparing to enter public service. She enjoys reading, and dreams of having two children. She is a first-time contributor to this devotional book. **Feb. 11, Jul. 27.**

**Elza C. dos Santos** is a minister's wife in São Paulo, Brazil. She is the mother of three adult children who are preparing for marriage. She likes to organize special church events. She enjoys reading, traveling, crocheting, and helping future mothers. **Jan. 20, May 10, Oct. 5.**

**Marlene Martins dos Santos** never went to school—she learned to read, write, and do math by observing the mothers in the homes in which she worked as they helped their children with homework. She has served her church and her community in many areas. Currently she is in charge of community service and directs the intercessory prayer ministry. **Jun. 26.**

**Sônia Maria Rigoli Santos** is a minister's wife and women's ministries and Shepherdess International leader in the South Parana Conference in Curitiba, Brazil. She has two children, Carlos Eduardo and Carla Beatriz, and really misses her child who lives in another country. She enjoys reading, writing, preparing and presenting radio programs, and taking care of her home. **May 4, Jul. 22, Oct. 10.**

**Sandra Savaris,** a banker, is a first-time contributor who writes from Brazil. She is married and likes to work with children, play the piano, and teach voices in choirs and quartets. **Apr. 8, Aug. 5.**

**Kathy Senessie** is a full-time wife, mother, and specialist midwife who works as an elder at their newly organized church in her hometown. God has blessed her with a wonderful husband, and they have four sons, all of whom are fast approaching adulthood. **Apr. 7, Jul. 5.**

**Donna Lee Sharp** enjoys using her musical talent in her home church, in other churches, and at three care homes, as well as the Christian Women's Club. Her hobbies include gardening, flower arranging, bird-watching, and travel—mainly to visit family members scattered across North America. **Nov. 5.**

**Carrol Johnson Shewmake** and her pastor-husband, although retired, are still active in personal and prayer ministries. She is the author of six books on prayer and has often been a speaker at camp meetings, women's retreats, and churches. She is the mother of four adult children, eight grandchildren, and three great-grandsons. Her special joys are reading, writing, and teaching. **Mar. 30.**

**Sherry Shrestha** is a physician in Gordon, Nebraska. Her husband, Prakash, and daughters, Shanti, Christie, and Jenny, are the light of her life. They still loyally follow along on family adventures she plans, to make sure she doesn't get hurt. They have a wonderful time as a family doing fun things together. **Jun. 22.**

**Rose Neff Sikora** and her husband live in western North Carolina. She is employed at Park Ridge Hospital as a registered nurse. Rose has been a regular contributor to this devotional book series since its inception. Her joy is found in helping and encouraging other people, writing short stories, and further development of her newly acquired computer skills. **Jan. 31, Apr. 6, Jun. 30.**

**Célia de Paulo da Silva** writes from Brazil. She is married and has two children. She is a rural worker and likes to grow vegetable and flower gardens and contemplate the nature that God has made **Feb. 8.**

**Luciana Barbosa Freitas da Silva** is women's ministries director in her church and secretary to the personal ministries department in the Pernambuco Conference in northeast Brazil. She is married to Elias, and enjoys crocheting, embroidery, swimming, and traveling. **Aug. 4.**

**Judy Good Silver,** Jonah and Mary's "Meme," is grateful that the Lord has blessed how she spends her "dash" (1953-?). She and Phil share 32 years of marriage and friendship. She enjoys family, friends, home, writing, gardening, the replenishing gift of the Sabbath, rocking chairs, porches, and her awesome view of the Shenandoah Valley. **Feb. 10, Oct. 9.**

**Heather-Dawn Small** is the director for women's ministries at the General Conference of Seventh-day Adventists. She and her pastor-husband, Joseph, are the parents of daughter Dalonne, 24, and son Jerard, 17. She loves scrapbooking and stamp collecting, and her ministry to women. Her favorite word is "joy," and her favorite saying is "Don't let anyone steal your joy." **May 17, Jul. 25, Dec. 29.**

**Thamer Cassandra Smikle** writes from Jamaica, where she is an auditor in the Jamaica Customs Department. She is attending Northern Caribbean University, where she is pursuing a master's degree in business administration (specializing in financing). She is an active church member who enjoys reading, singing, relaxing, and laughing. **Jan. 9.**

**Eline dos Reis Souza** is a student who lives in Manaus, Brazil. She enjoys reading, writing, talking to her friends, and taking care of her younger siblings. **Feb. 7.**

**Candace Sprauve** is a retired educator. She has three sons, one daughter, and three grandchildren. She presently serves her church as an elder and personal ministries leader. Her hobbies include reading, gardening, and sewing. **Feb. 9, Oct. 8.**

**Ardis Dick Stenbakken** and her husband, Dick, live in Loveland, Colorado. She is proud of her adult children and crazy about her grandchildren, with whom she spends as much time as possible. Though retired, Ardis is still active in women's ministries, speaking, writing, and mentoring as time allows. She is also trying to find time to quilt, read, and do some oil painting. **Jan. 18, Jun. 20, Dec. 16.**

**Saramma Stephenson** writes from Kerala, India. She and her husband have two children, and her hobbies are leading sewing and embroidery classes. She has worked as a teacher for 19 years, but is now directing women's, children's, and family ministries, and coordinating support for pastors' wives. **Apr. 19.**

**Rubye Sue** and her husband live at Laurelbrook Academy in Dayton, Tennessee, where she still enjoys being the retired secretary to the retired president. In the winter they head for Florida, home base for the SOULS group who trains young people for literature evangelism and as Bible workers. Rubye and Bill enjoy traveling, seeing old friends, and meeting new ones. **Feb. 17, Jul. 29, Sep. 20.**

**Carolyn Rathbun Sutton** lives with her husband, Jim, on a small farm in Tennessee. They are field representatives for Adventist World Radio, as well as being involved in their local church, prison ministry, and community events. In her spare time Carolyn hosts a weekly television program for KBLN Better Life TV (Oregon), and writes and speaks at women's events. **Jan. 3, Aug. 2.**

**Loraine F. Sweetland** is retired in Tennessee. She has begun an Adventist food buying club for her church and community. A recent widow, she enjoys writing, machine knitting, her three dogs, computer surfing, gardening, and reading. **Apr. 4, Jun. 21, Sep. 8.**

**Arlene Taylor** is a risk manager for three Adventist Health hospitals in California. An internationally known author and seminar presenter and a member of the National Speaker's Association, she is founder and president of her own nonprofit corporation. Brain-function educational resources are available at www.arlenetaylor.org. **Feb. 4, Apr. 3, Aug. 31, Dec. 2.**

**G. G. (Geneva Gwendolyn) Taylor** is a very active member of the Palm Bay Seventh-day Adventist Church. Though now officially retired, she often spends her nights at the hospital, sitting with Baker Act patients. **Feb. 13.**

**Rose Joseph Thomas** is a passionate first-grade teacher. She recently began teaching at Forest Lake Education Center, her first-time church school teaching opportunity. Rose enjoys cooking, reading, and writing. She lives with her best-friend-husband and their two children, Samuel Joseph and Crystal Rose. She has a passion for young children and is a very grateful mother. **Mar. 6, Jun. 2, Aug. 3.**

**Sharon Thomas** and her husband, Don, are now retirees. Sharon enjoys reading, biking, walking, shopping, and learning how to quilt. They both like traveling and meeting new people. **Dec. 6.**

**Emily Thomsen** runs her own wellness coaching business in Collegedale, Tennessee. She helps people lose weight, lower blood pressure, reduce cholesterol, and improve their physical fitness. Emily enjoys walking and running, reading, music, backpacking and camping, cooking and experimenting to make recipes healthier, entertaining, and spending time with her boyfriend. **Jun. 11.**

**Janet Thornton** lives in Jefferson, Texas. She is a mother of four boys and one girl. Retired and as busy as she wants to be, she volunteers at the community center on a weekly basis, and for Jefferson Christian Academy cafeteria as needed. She loves being retired. **Jan. 8, May 5.**

**Ena Thorpe** is a retired nurse. She is married with three grown children and four grandchildren. She is active in church and enjoys reading, playing Scrabble, and working crossword and Sudoku puzzles. **Feb. 2.**

**Maranata Titimanu** writes from Papua New Guinea. She is principal of the International Elementary School at Pacific Adventist University. Maranata is married to Luka Titimanu; they have three adult children, Fale, Torise, and Matthew. She is completing a master's degree and loves working with her children at the "I" school, and planning activities for women. **Dec. 28.**

**Iralyn Haig Trott**, a retired schoolteacher who spent most of her teaching career in Bermuda, now writes from Palm Bay, Florida. Recently widowed, this mother of two adult children delights in her five granddaughters. She spends much of her spare time communing with God in her garden and with the singing birds in her backyard, and working with prison ministries. **Oct. 7.**

**Nancy Van Pelt** is a certified family life educator, speaker, and best-selling author of more than 20 books. For 20 years Nancy has traversed the globe, teaching families how to really love each other. Her hobbies include getting organized, entertaining, having fun, and quilting. She and her husband live in California and are the parents of three adult children. **Feb. 5, Jul. 3.**

**Carmem Virgínia** is a community health agent who is getting a degree in literature. She writes poems and likes to sing in church. **Jan. 7, Mar. 5, Aug. 10.**

**Jaci da Silva Vôos** and her husband, a retired minister, live in Santa Catarina, Brazil. Although she's retired, her great passion is Christian education. She dedicates her time to evangelizing children. Her dream is to build a church just for children in which they can lead out. She has three adult children and six grandchildren. She enjoys studying music, traveling, and gardening. **Mar. 28, Sep. 4, Dec. 5.**

**Mary M. J. Wagoner-Angelin** lives in Ooltewah, Tennessee, with her husband, Randy, and daughters, Barbara and Rachel. Mary is a stay-at-home mom and a social worker at a psychiatric hospital. She volunteers with the Make-A-Wish Foundation, at her local library, and with Kids in Discipleship. She enjoys her Mothers of Preschoolers group, and humor therapy. **Mar. 26, Sep. 3.**

**Cora A. Walker** is a retired nurse, editor, and freelance writer who lives in Fort Washington, Maryland. She is an active member of the church she attends in Charles County, Maryland. She enjoys reading, writing, swimming, classical music, singing, and traveling. She has one son, Andre V. Walker. **Jul. 2, Nov. 25, Dec. 24.**

**Anna May Radke Waters** is a retired administrative secretary. She has served as an ordained elder and a greeter at church. She has too many hobbies to list, but at the top of the list are her eight grandchildren and her husband, with whom she likes to travel and make memories. She also enjoys doing Bible studies on the Internet and answering prayer requests for Bibleinfo.com. **Jan. 6, May 8, Jun. 13.**

**Dorothy Eaton Watts** is an administrator for her church headquarters in India. Dorothy is a freelance writer, editor, and speaker. She has been a missionary in India for 28 years, founded an orphanage, taught elementary school, and has written more than 26 books. Her hobbies include gardening, hiking, and birding (with more than 1,600 in her world total). **Jul. 1, Dec. 20.**

**Gerti Weck** writes from Germany, where she works for human resources in a large Nuremberg, firm. She serves as a women's ministries leader in the North Bavarian Conference of Seventh-day Adventists. **Dec. 31.**

**Daniela Weichhold** is an administrative secretary at the European Commission headquarters in Brussels, Belgium. At present she is on leave from her job to learn more about medical missionary work. She enjoys cooking, the outdoors, playing the piano, and singing. She also likes discovering cultures and learning foreign languages in order to effectively share the gospel. **Sep. 22, Nov. 4.**

**Lyn Welk-Sandy** lives in Adelaide, Australia. She works with bereaved children and young offenders attending court. Lyn has spent many years as a pipe organist and loves church music, choir work, and helping Sudanese refugees. She enjoys photography and caravanning around outback Australia with her husband, Keith. Lyn is a mother of four and has 12 grandchildren. **Mar. 4, Oct. 17, Dec. 4.**

**Sandra Widulle** lives in Windsbach, northern Bavaria, Germany. She is married and has two children. In her church she designs the bulletin board, sings in the choir, and is active in children's ministry. She enjoys writing and bicycling, and likes to make handicrafts. She also loves to take care of her garden and their rabbits and guinea pigs. **Jan. 5, May 7.**

**Mildred C. Williams** is a widow and a retired physical therapist living in southern California. She enjoys studying and teaching the Bible, writing, gardening, public speaking, sewing, and spending time with her grown children and granddaughter. She likes writing for this devotional book, as it gives her a chance to share God's love with others. **Mar. 3, Apr. 22, May 6.**

**Shelly-Ann Patricia Zabala,** who writes from Puerto Rico, is a registered nurse who is presently a stay-at-home mom with her son, Elias. She is a minister's wife who enjoys children's and women's ministries. Her hobbies include singing, gardening, and entertaining. Together with her husband, Florencio, she serves in the East Puerto Rico Conference. **Jan. 2, Mar. 1.**

**Kathy Sonio Zausa** writes from the Philippines. She is a third-year history and political science student at Adventist University of the Philippines. She is 21 years old and at the time of this writing was looking forward to graduation. **Oct. 6.**

# Prayer Requests

_____

_____

_____

_____

_____

_____

_____

_____

_____

**Through Jesus we may open our hearts to God
as to one who knows and loves us.**

—*Thoughts From the Mount of Blessing*, p. 84.

# Prayer Requests

_____

_____

_____

_____

_____

_____

_____

_____

_____

**In the name of Jesus we may come into God's presence
with the confidence of a child.**

—*Thoughts From the Mount of Blessing*, p. 84.

# Prayer Requests

_____

_____

_____

_____

_____

_____

_____

_____

_____

_____

**Never has one been disappointed who came unto Him.**
—*Thoughts From the Mount of Blessing,* p. 85.